T0260806

Ontology-Based Information Retrieval for Healthcare Systems

Scrivener Publishing
100 Cummings Center, Suite 541J
Beverly, MA 01915-6106

Machine Learning in Biomedical Science and Healthcare Informatics

Series Editors: Vishal Jain and Jyotir Moy Chatterjee

In this series, the focus centers on the various applications of machine learning in the biomedical engineering and healthcare fields, with a special emphasis on the most representative machine learning techniques, namely deep learning-based approaches. Machine learning tasks are typically classified into two broad categories depending on whether there is a learning "label" or "feedback" available to a learning system: supervised learning and unsupervised learning. This series also introduces various types of machine learning tasks in the biomedical engineering field from classification (supervised learning) to clustering (unsupervised learning). The objective of the series is to compile all aspects of biomedical science and healthcare informatics, from fundamental principles to current advanced concepts.

Submission to the series: Please send book proposals to **drvishaljain83@gmail.com** and/or **jyotirchatterjee@gmail.com**

Publishers at Scrivener
Martin Scrivener (martin@scrivenerpublishing.com)
Phillip Carmical (pcarmical@scrivenerpublishing.com)

Ontology-Based Information Retrieval for Healthcare Systems

Edited by
Vishal Jain
Bharati Vidyapeeth's Institute of Computer Applications and Management (BVICAM), New Delhi, India
Ritika Wason
Bharati Vidyapeeth's Institute of Computer Applications and Management (BVICAM), New Delhi, India
Jyotir Moy Chatterjee
Lord Buddha Education Foundation, Kathmandu, Nepal

and

Dac-Nhuong Le
Faculty of Information Technology, Haiphong University, Haiphong, Vietnam

Scrivener
Publishing

This edition first published 2020 by John Wiley & Sons, Inc., 111 River Street, Hoboken, NJ 07030, USA
and Scrivener Publishing LLC, 100 Cummings Center, Suite 541J, Beverly, MA 01915, USA
© 2020 Scrivener Publishing LLC
For more information about Scrivener publications please visit www.scrivenerpublishing.com.

Wiley Global Headquarters
111 River Street, Hoboken, NJ 07030, USA

For details of our global editorial offices, customer services, and more information about Wiley products visit us at www.wiley.com.

Limit of Liability/Disclaimer of Warranty
While the publisher and authors have used their best efforts in preparing this work, they make no representations or warranties with respect to the accuracy or completeness of the contents of this work and
specifically disclaim all warranties, including without limitation any implied warranties of merchant-
ability or fitness for a particular purpose. No warranty may be created or extended by sales representa-
tives, written sales materials, or promotional statements for this work. The fact that an organization,
website, or product is referred to in this work as a citation and/or potential source of further information does not mean that the publisher and authors endorse the information or services the organization, website, or product may provide or recommendations it may make. This work is sold with the
understanding that the publisher is not engaged in rendering professional services. The advice and
strategies contained herein may not be suitable for your situation. You should consult with a specialist
where appropriate. Neither the publisher nor authors shall be liable for any loss of profit or any other
commercial damages, including but not limited to special, incidental, consequential, or other damages.
Further, readers should be aware that websites listed in this work may have changed or disappeared
between when this work was written and when it is read.

Library of Congress Cataloging-in-Publication Data

ISBN 978-1-119-64048-6

Cover image: Pixabay.Com
Cover design by Russel Richardson

Set in size of 11pt and Minion Pro by Manila Typesetting Company, Makati, Philippines

10 9 8 7 6 5 4 3 2 1

To our Parents & Well Wishers

Contents

Preface

With the advancements of semantic web, ontology has become the crucial mechanism for representing concepts in varied domains. For research and dispersal of customized healthcare services, a major challenge is to efficiently retrieve and analyze individual patient data from a large volume of heterogeneous data over a long-time span. This demands effective ontology-based information retrieval approaches for clinical information systems. Further, Information Retrieval (IR) since its inception has matured into an established mechanism for facilitating fast and relevant information retrieval. However, mining relevant information from large amount of distributed data demands understanding the semantics of the desired information using ontology.

Further, with the growth in digital literature, effective search and retrieval of desired documents in the healthcare domain has become challenging. The pages displayed by search engines may not always be relevant. The medical field offers restricted vocabularies that encapsulate semantic information about various biomedical models, their semantic types, and the relationships among them. The current web standard does not support Semantic Web technology. Information retrieval is fundamentally based on keyword-matching approaches. The fact that individuals use diverse terms to denote the same object presents a significant challenge in the healthcare industry.

Healthcare is one of the finest represented subject areas on the Semantic Web currently. Textual query is transformed into a set of representative concepts matched to the indexed documents. End users still have to search for apt documents manually. Hence, the detection of pertinent information becomes a critical task.

This book is an attempt to highlight the key advances in ontology-based information retrieval techniques especially being applied in the healthcare domain. The varied chapters attempt to uncover the current challenges in the application of ontology-based information retrieval techniques to the healthcare systems. The book shall be a first of its kind that shall highlight only the ontology-driven information retrieval mechanisms and techniques being applied to healthcare as well as clinical information systems.

The book can serve as a potential textbook for courses in healthcare systems as well as technologies. It can also serve as a reference book to medical practitioners as well as researchers involved in implementing as well as providing customized health care solutions to patients.

Chapter 1 discusses in details about the roles and responsibilities ontology is playing in terms of healthcare sector.

Chapter 2 provides the relation between neurodegenerative diseases and basal ganglia; the present basal ganglia models stimulate research interest in understanding its functioning to provide different neurosurgical interventions.

Chapter 3 tried an attempt that is made to combine the PSO and PAW-based techniques without sacrificing the usefulness factor.

Chapter 4 discusses about the role of medical oncology as a database management system.

Chapter 5 presents the role of IoT and SWT and usage in addressing the concerns of health and medical sector along with their challenges, various applications, and the future research scope they offer.

Chapter 6 discusses on a Formal Contextual Security Privacy model for healthcare application with aim to provide services in the secure manner.

Chapter 7 presents in details about the ontology-based query retrieval system for E-healthcare.

Chapter 8 discusses an ontology system for a case-based reasoning system that aims at supporting people facing autism spectrum disorders (ASD).

Chapter 9 presents the notion of ontology engineering that involves the major ontology developmentvt methodologies, ontology languages, and ontology tools.

Chapter 10 discusses the content-oriented view and functional view perspectives and presents the major biomedical ontologies and the biomedical Ontology-based systems.

Chapter 11 explains machine learning prediction techniques that are the most effective tools for predicting massive cancer data prediction.

Chapter 12 discusses about the need of ontology-based system in healthcare systems.

Chapter 13 examines and investigates the difficulties related with this new pattern of information retrieval utilizing psychological insightful techniques with focus on medical sectors.

Chapter 14 reviews future IoT-based medicinal service frameworks to gather medical ontologies, which can be applied to generic frameworks.

Chapter 15 after a survey, the available techniques are categorized into traditional streaming data techniques, data mining streaming techniques, and big data techniques for streaming data, and these techniques are discussed in detail with a special emphasis to recent big data based streaming architectures.

Chapter 16 ontology-based information retrieval model is presented for health-related data; ontology is engendered using a kind of basic description logic, which is an appropriate tradeoff between expressivity of knowledge and complexity of cognitive problems.

We like to thank all the authors for their valuable contribution which make this book possible. Among those who have influenced this project are our family and friends, who have sacrificed a lot of their time and attention to ensure that we remained motivated throughout the time devoted to the completion of this crucial book.

The Editors
May 2020

Acknowledgment

I would like to acknowledge the most important people in my lives, my father Aloke Moy Chatterjee, my uncle Mr. Moni Moy Chatterjee, and my late mother, Nomita Chatterjee. The book has been my long-cherished dream which would not have been turned into reality without the support and love of these amazing people. They have continuously encouraged me despite my failing to give them the proper time and attention. I am also grateful to my friends, who have encouraged and blessed this work with their unconditional love and patient.

Jyotir Moy Chatterjee
Department of IT
Lord Buddha Education Foundation (APUTI)
Kathmandu
Nepal-44600

Role of Ontology in Health Care

Sonia Singla

*Independent Researcher, Birmingham, U.K., East West College,
Bangalore University, Rajajinagar, India*

Abstract

As far back as the beginning of Artificial Intelligence and the advancement of the first information-based frameworks during the 70s, individuals have longed for self-learning machines. At the point when information-based frameworks became bigger and the business enthusiasm for these innovations expanded, individuals ended up mindful of the learning procurement bottleneck and the need to (incompletely) automatize the creation and upkeep of information bases.

Medicinal services establishments are intended to focus on the patients to convey legitimate administrations. There is an abundance of information accessible inside the medicinal services frameworks; however, they need powerful investigation instruments to find shrouded connections and patterns in information. Ontologies empower high versatility in looking, extricating, keeping up, and creating data.

E-human services choice emotionally supportive network is created for the reason for improving the medicinal services administrations and power over patient's well-being. The framework encourages speedy got to and specific social insurance administrations, obviously, contingent on the patient's or case history by lessening the visit time to restorative establishments. It gives the human services master quick and cutting-edge understanding well-being information, along these lines lessening the documentation and conventions and expanding the ease of use of the data more successfully and dependably by the therapeutic foundations.

Keywords: Ontology, non-communicable disease, Parkinson, diabetes, cardiovascular disease

Email: ssoniyaster@gmail.com

Vishal Jain, Ritika Wason, Jyotir Moy Chatterjee and Dac-Nhuong Le (eds.) Ontology-Based Information Retrieval for Healthcare Systems, (1–18) © 2020 Scrivener Publishing LLC

1.1 Introduction

Right now, the creating nations are distressed with the double weight of ailment—non-communicable diseases (NCDs) turning into a noteworthy general well-being challenge (Figure 1.1).

Suitable practices, expanded physical action, weight the executives, and restraint from tobacco use and liquor misuse assumes a significant job in their anticipation and the executives. This account audit features the job of different dietary segments—both supplement and non-supplement, in the avoidance and hazard decrease of NCDs. NCDs are disease that are not transmitted directly. It can prove fatal and can be become number one cause of death. About 5 million were reported due to use of tobacco alone and 2.8 million for just being overweight. According to the report of World Health Organization, there are about five main risk factors linked with NCDs mainly tobacco, increased blood pressure, intake of alcohol, air pollution, and increased level of cholesterol. If NCD is remained untreated and not counted the risky factors linked with the disease, it will leads to major disastrous leading to death of more than around 70 million by 2030. It is necessary to take into account the risk factors involved in which youngsters are not taking it seriously. Air pollution is the major cause of death across the world. India is most polluted and is in seventh position in the world. Biomass and fuel wood are major cause of pollution in India.

Not only during Diwali days but during non-festive season also pollution is high in India.

There are numerous cases of people dying from asthma in India. Due to air pollution alone in India about 1.5 million people died in 2012 according to World Health Organization. Disease cases are expanding at a disturbing rate in India. As indicated by the evaluations of the National

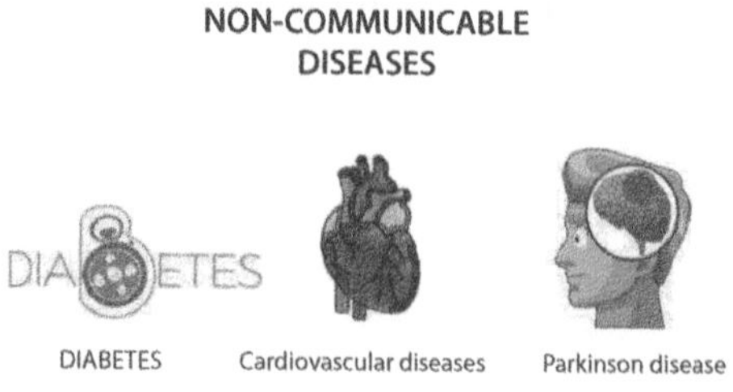

NON-COMMUNICABLE
DISEASES

DIA🕐ETES

DIABETES   Cardiovascular diseases   Parkinson disease

Figure 1.1 Examples of non-communicable diseases [2].

Cancer Control Program (NCCP), by 2026, there will be more than 1.4 million individuals experiencing malignant growth. One of the real purposes behind this would be more noteworthy presentation to natural cancer-causing agents.

Perhaps, the deadliest repercussion of air contamination has been the consumption of the ozone layer in the external climate. The ozone layer goes about as a shield against destructive UBV bright beams emanated by the sun. Be that as it may, because of widespread utilization of chlorofluorocarbons (CFC), a compound substance utilized for refrigeration, the layer has been dispersing consistently.

An Earth-wide temperature boost, otherwise called environmental change, is another symptom of air contamination. It is brought about by changes in the vaporous environmental structure and is perhaps the greatest danger to earth. Corrosive downpour is another consequence of air contamination. Air-borne sulphur dioxide atoms respond with downpour water to shape sulphuric corrosive which at that point tumbles down on earth as corrosive downpour. Corrosive downpour is lethal for sea-going living things. Fish have been believed to die when water bodies turned out to be excessively acidic because of corrosive downpour. Corrosive likewise causes skin maladies in people and decimates woods. An investigation in Hong Kong, China was led to discover relationship of air contamination and asthma affirmation among youngsters, and it presumed that the surrounding levels of PM10 and NO2, however not SO2, were related with asthma in young children. Respiratory maladies in Delhi from 2012 emerged to 5 million [1].

1.2   Ontology in Diabetes

Diabetes is a protected illness, which is a result of having an inactive existence and eating prepared nourishments like rolls, bread, cakes, chocolates, pudding, frozen yogurt, and so on. Case-based reasoning (CBR) has a library of unraveled cases which analyze the unsolved diabetic cases. Each case portrays the issue, arrangement, and result of the equivalent. At whatever point comparable circumstances happen, the significant cases are recovered from the library and used for the analysis of diabetes. Philosophy contains data about diabetes—indications, causes, various sorts of diabetes, and, furthermore, the kind of determination—which helps in successful framework level thinking. In view of the applicable check of the manifestations, cosmology is broke down with sources of info, the significant determination report is recovered from the philosophy and fixed, and existing cases are reconsidered and held for the situation library for some time later. Diabetes Mellitus is linked with insulin secretion defects which could prove fatal and can be responsible for the leading cause of death worldwide by 2030. Some of the symptoms of diabetes includes is feeling suddenly hungry a lot, thirsty, feeling fatigue, and so on. Early detection of diabetes is much better. There are generally two types of diabetes.

Type 1 Diabetes—The body starts attacking its own cell that produces insulin.

Type 2 Diabetes—In these, body doesn't produce enough insulin or it shows no response to insulin. Usually, Type 2 Diabetes is found more common in UK patients about 90% UK patients are found to be suffering from Type 2 Diabetes rather than Type 1 Diabetes. Most important is also eye screening test as it can leads to Diabetic retinopathy that can means loss of sight if not treated [3].

1.2.1   Ontology Process

Stage 1: Specifying Information—The primary target of this stage is to distinguish the need and reason for philosophy development. This stage comprises in setting up a casual archive to portray the diabetes ADE philosophy and gain the information about the diabetes and ADE area to break down the essential prerequisites. It additionally recognizes the scope of the clients and the kind of inquiries which the philosophy should reply. The information for metaphysics can be obtained from, books, inquire about papers, specialists, patients, and reference books.

Stage 2—This stage comprises on sorting out and organizing, the data wellsprings of the space by utilizing a halfway formal portrayal, for example, tables and charts. Toward the end, we acquire a dynamic philosophy (unique model). We present in pursues a case of certain phases of conceptualization of cosmology. Presentation of ideas glossary and its gatherings depicts in common language all the helpful ideas in the field of the diabetes ADEs. Definition of the classes and class pecking order used to distinguish terms; the ideas are demonstrated as classes or sub classes. The connections between the ideas, for each relationship, we determine the source idea, the objective idea, and the cardinality. The properties of classes, it comprises of specifying the properties depicting each idea.

Stage 3—It comprises on formalizing the unique metaphysics got in the past stage to a formal and operational language.

Stage 4—The motivation behind this stage comprises on encoding the formal philosophy on a cosmology usage language to make it operational. It's acknowledged by utilizing an apparatus of ontologies release. The source ontologies were actualized utilizing the Protégé instrument which is a philosophy supervisor that gives a graphical portrayal of the cosmology and creates the code OWL (Ontology Web Language) which can be utilized in ADE aversion on frameworks programming.

Stage 5—This progression comprises on assessing and refreshing of our cosmology. This progression of assessment can be made in parallel with the past three stages. It is made at the dynamic dimension, at the formal and operational dimension. Diabetes ADE cosmology is utilized in drug process to forestall the ADE diabetes. It helps for thinking the cases semantically.

Clinical emotionally supportive network is the data framework that bolsters basic leadership exercises. It is expected to help well-being suppliers assemble valuable data to remind exercises for accomplishing diabetes treatment plan. Since it is important to connect holes between Diabetes master and suppliers, characterizing learning expressly are the significant piece of clinical emotionally supportive network. Metaphysics, a learning systemization, is appropriate to calculated learning since it shares basic comprehension of the structure of data among individuals or programming operators. Also, it is reusable for space learning, ready to make area suppositions express, and to isolate space information from activity information and investigate space learning [40].

Diabetes mellitus is a noteworthy reason for dismalness and mortality in people. Early analysis is the initial move toward the administration of this condition. In any case, an analysis includes a few factors, which makes it hard to touch base at an exact and convenient determination and to develop precise customized treatment plans. An electronic well-being record framework requires an incorporated choice help ability, and ontologies are quickly getting to be vital for the structure of proficient, solid, extendable, reusable, and semantically keen learning bases.

1.2.2 Impediments of the Present Investigation

The rendition of DDO portrayed in this paper has a few constraints. To start with, the philosophy focuses on the determination of diabetes, and no medications have been talked about. Further investigations will include treatment angles, including prescriptions, sustenances, instruction, diet, physical exercise programs, drug– tranquilize communications, and medication and-ailment associations. Furthermore, this examination has just centered around the making of the philosophy. Future research could execute a total CDSS framework associated with the EHR condition. The framework could utilize a standard-based thinking system executed utilizing SWRL rules upheld by the philosophy and use surmising motors, for example, JESS or Pellet. Besides, the cosmology ideas have just been commented on with SCT idea IDs. Future investigations could clarify the ideas with UMLS CUIDs, RxNorm RxCUI, equivalent words, and printed definitions. Numerous aphorisms can be added to the philosophy to demonstrate the connections among medications and fixings, maladies, illnesses and medications, and sicknesses and disarranges. Therefore, future investigations will upgrade the rationale of the metaphysics with such sayings. At last, this investigation just centered around best works on with respect to otology advancement and area information content. Subsequently, our future work will likewise incorporate the structure of assessment concentrates to evaluate how effectively DDO underpins CDSS of diabetes determination.

The reason for this investigation was to build up a hypothetically stable and semantically smart information base for tackling issues identified with the analysis of diabetes. Such learning can empower another class of patient-driven CDSS that can assist doctors with diagnosing diabetics rapidly and precisely. DDO gives a standard cosmology that can bolster the interoperability among CDSS and human services frameworks. Additionally, it very well may be utilized in mix with a standard base to fabricate a standard-based diabetes finding framework. The philosophy is extensive, as it contains all diabetes-related intricacies, research center tests, manifestations, physical tests, socioeconomics, and analyses. DDO is the primary revealed diabetes infection philosophy created to speak to various malady angles in a formal sensible configuration.

1.3   Role of Ontology in Cardiovascular Diseases

Cardiovascular sickness is the most widely recognized reason for mortality in rich nations, and today, it has a similar importance for social insurance as the plagues of past hundreds of years had for drug in before times: half of the populace in these nations pass on of cardiovascular malady. The measure of cardiovascular malady is additionally expanding in the creating nations together with financial development. By 2015, one of every three passing's will all around be because of cardiovascular infections. Coronary illness is an incessant infection that begins in adolescence, regardless of whether the manifestations initially happen in the middle age. The dangers for coronary illness are notable: lipid issue, particularly high serum LDL-cholesterol focus, hypertension, tobacco smoking, weight, diabetes, male sexual orientation, and physical idleness. Heftiness is both a free hazard factor for cardiovascular ailment but at the same time is firmly associated with a few other hazard factors. This audit centers on the association between overweight or stoutness and cardiovascular ailment.

A comprehension of heart advancement is basic in any frameworks science way to deal with cardiovascular infection. The elucidation of information produced from high-throughput advances (for example, microarray and proteomics) is additionally basic to this methodology. Notwithstanding, describing the job of qualities in the procedures fundamental heart improvement and cardiovascular malady includes the non-insignificant undertaking of information examination and mix of past learning. The Gene Ontology (GO) Consortium gives organized controlled natural vocabularies that are utilized to abridge past utilitarian learning for quality items over all species. One part of GO depicts organic procedures, for example, advancement and flagging.

To help high-throughput cardiovascular research, we have started a push to completely depict heart improvement in GO, extending the quantity of GO terms portraying heart advancement from 12 to more than 280. This new philosophy depicts heart morphogenesis, the separation of explicit cardiovascular cell types, and the association of flagging pathways in heart advancement. This work additionally adjusts GO with the ebb and flow perspectives on the heart advancement explore network and its portrayal in the writing. This will empower clients to incorporate heart advancement information crosswise over species, bringing about the extensive recovery of data about this subject. The amended GO structure, joined with quality item explanations, ought to improve the elucidation of information from high-throughput strategies in an assortment of cardiovascular research territories, including heart advancement, intrinsic cardiovascular malady, and heart undeveloped cell investigate [2, 4].

The OBO Foundry is to date a standout among the most critical endeavors to manufacture interoperable ontologies in the biomedical space. It depends on the upper-level pragmatist philosophy Basic Formal Ontology (BFO), which goes for formalizing the broadest classes on which area ontologies ought to be based. In this structure, the Ontology for General Medical Science (OGMS) gives a general model of malady, formalized as an attitude of a creature to experience obsessive procedures, this aura being founded on a basic issue. For instance, epilepsy is formalized as a sickness to experience epileptic emergencies (the obsessive procedures), because of some neuronal irregular structure (the fundamental issue). The OBO Foundry likewise incorporates as a competitor the Human Disease cosmology DOID which records human infections. Although DOID acknowledges OGMS meaning of ailment, DOID classes have not yet been organized by OGMS tripartite model of ailment. The Cardiovascular Disease Ontology (CVDO) goes for redesigning and finishing DOID cardiovascular malady classes on the base of OGMS model of ailment, and to adjust it to anatomical classes removed from the Foundational Model of Anatomy (FMA), so as to assess how OGMS model of sickness can fit in the cardiovascular space. The most recent adaptation of BFO (2.0) was utilized as a top-cosmology, and CVDO was worked in OWL group. CVDO goes for satisfying OBO Foundry's standards; specifically, it concerns a well-defined logical field, cardiovascular infections of the human grown-up. Formulating CVDO demonstrated that a pragmatist cosmology like OGMS empowers to make significant ontological refinements between substances that are not all around recognized in like manner restorative language, to manufacture expound malady orders via programmed thinking, and to determine fascinating surmising's concerning sickness groupings. We recommend that OGMS be enhanced by methodological principles to decide the material premise of a sickness and the end purpose of an ailment course, which may likewise express OGMS formalization with the River-Flow model of ailment.

1.4   Role of Ontology in Parkinson Diseases

Parkinson disease is neurodegenerative disorder that affects nerve cells of the brain and leads to muscle rigidity change in voice as it increases with age. No cure is there yet for this disease and it should be major concern for health issues as it is finding more in developed countries and in older people. Patient suffering from disease suffers depression, congestive, sleeping problems, muscle pains, and loss of balance.

The study done needs to be addressed further whether high estrogen in female was responsible for having less prevalence rate as compared to male and stabilizes at age of more than 80, while in some studies, it increases above age 80.

Study was done on Parkinson disease to know overall impact of disease related age, sex, and geographic location such as Asia, Africa, South America, and Europe/North America/Australia, and the data was collected from 1985 to 2010. Meta -analysis done shows increase in rate of Parkinson disease with age like it was found lower at age of 40–49 years about 41 and with increase in age 107 in 50–59 years and 1903 in age more than 80+ [17].

The study was done in Norway and data was collected from 2007. At age of 60 years, no difference was found in men and women; however, gender differences in incidence of PD appear to differ by ethnicity [18].

The research was done in Egypt in Qena and data was collected from September 2011 to August 2013. Prevalence rate for Parkinson disease was found in 44 patients less in age 50 years and was found more at age of 75 years. The study done also shows that male have higher incidence rate than that of female and is high in Nile valley of Upper Egypt as compared to other Arabian countries [19].

The study was done in Al Kharga district of Egypt to estimate the prevalence of PD in person with age less than 40 years with 62,583 total populations between 2005 and 2009. About 15,482 persons were having age less than 40 years and 49 persons in this population was diagnosed with PD. The prevalence rate was almost found to be same in men and women; it increases with age and were high in rural areas as compared to urban areas [20].

The study was done in Africa with collection of article from 1944 to 2004 which shows that the prevalence is less in Africa then Europe and North America. It is more in male as compared to female [21].

The research was done in India and data was collected from PubMed database till 2014. Parkinson Disease was study from 557 patients from rural and urban areas of North Karnataka, and results show that PD starts at older age and increases with age and is more in men as compared to women and was found more in people with no family history of PD as compared to patients with family history [22].

The study was done in Bombay in 1987 by door-to-door survey on 14,010 people, and among these, 46 people were found to be suffering from PD, results shows that prevalence rate increases with age and is more in men as compared to women [23].

The study was done on 382 patients in-between 2004 and 2015, in South Central India, Telangana State, and results show that onset of disease is 60 years and is more in male as compared to females living in rural areas. With a better health care, life expectancy is also believed to increase and thus chances of increase in PD cases. In India and Asia, PD is low as compared to other developed countries. Due to unknown cause of the disease and different socio economic, presence of genetic and ethnic population across India in many cities more studies and case controls needs to be done [24].

The study was done in Taiwan from 2002 to 2009 by using National Health Insurance database. The results show that the Prevalence and Incidence rate of PD increases with age and is found more in men as compared to women living in rural areas instead of urban area. Increase in PD prevalence is almost double which needs to be further investigated by the studies [25].

The prevalence of PD in some studies shows that it increases with age and some studies shows decrease over 80 years which can be due to small sample size, different survival time, and lower response rate. Future research is required to be done in China as only two studies shows incidence data [26].

The study was done in Northern Jordan in period of 2007 to 2008 where the crude prevalence rate of PD was estimated to be 59/100,000 [27].

The study was done in Australia in Queensland in 2000 and the prevalence of IPD is 146/100,000 [28].

1.4.1   The Spread of Disease With Age and Onset of Disease

In many research studies, the early onset of the disease is 51–60 years in 28.9% patients, whereas in 76.3%, it was 41–70. The study was done in Iran and data was collected from 2000 to 2010. The Prevalence rate in Iran male to female ratio is 2.1:1, as stated in current research is higher, whereas previously, it was 1.46, and in Western, it was 1.58 and in Asia 0.95; however, these studies have many drawbacks which includes not enough patient participants. The mean age of the patients was 12–90 years [29]. The study was done by collecting data from 1985 to 2010 in following Geographical location Asia, Europe, Africa, America, and Australia, and the prevalence was reported at age of about 40 years [17]. The study was done in Australia over 12 month period in 2010 which shows mean age of 55.1 [30]. The study was done in Kuwait in 2015 which shows the mean age onset of 63.24 ± 14 [33]. The study was done in Northern Jordan in period of 2007 to 2008 where the mean onset of the disease is 59.5 [26]. The study was done in Muslim Arab population in Israel in 2010 and the age of onset of the disease in >15 years and 65 [31]. The study was done in Israel in 2002; mean age onset of disease was 66.7 +/− 11 years [32].

The research was done in India and data was collected from PubMed database till 2014. The rate of prevalence and incidence was much higher at age less than 60 and nine studies reports its increases with age; however, in six studies, it shows decline in rate of prevalence and incidence with increase in age. The observed variation can be due to environment and genetic factors and can be due to differences in methodologies for case ascertainment, diagnostic criteria, or age distribution in study population [22].

GO's essential centre isn't ontological in either sense. Positively, it utilizes pecking orders of terms. Be that as it may, its creators have concentrated neither on programming usage nor on the sensible articulation of the hypothesis incorporating these terms, or maybe their endeavors have been coordinated toward giving a for all intents and purposes helpful structure to monitoring the organic explanations that are connected to quality products.

This implies when looked with the exchange off between (1) formal and ontological intelligence, security, and adaptability, and (2) the expedient populace of GO with organic ideas, inclination was given by the GO consortium to the last mentioned. Too little consideration was in this manner paid to the hugeness of those ontological or semi ontological terms—for example, work, part, segment, substance, activity, space, and complex—which were utilized in GO's development [5, 6].

1.4.2   Cost of PD for Health Care, Household

The study was done in Australia for 12 months published in 2017 to know the annual cost of PD. About 87 patients with the help of questionnaire and Medicare data completed the form which shows for health care system, the mean annual cost per person for PD was $32,556 AUD and additional cost for society was $45,000 per annum per person with PD and four times more approx. about $63,569 from the cost of mild patient approx. about $17,537 with people suffering from Parkinson disease from moderate to severe and is further like to grow with increase in disease prevalence [34].

1.4.3   Treatment and Medicines

The study was done in Australia in study published in 2015 which states that there is not yet cure for Parkinson disease but disease management is directed at motor symptoms cure, such as tremors, muscle rigidity, impaired balance, and slowness of movement (bradykinesia). New surgical treatment option Deep Brain Stimulation is found to be less cost effective and safe. Early intervention can prove to be highly beneficial with improve quality of life. Pedunculopontine nucleus is found to be good target for motor symptoms which are less responsive such as freezing of gait, and postural instability. Although most are busy in treatment of motor symptoms, non-motor symptoms can have more impact on quality of life than motor symptoms and there number increases with disease and with treatment such as high dose can get worst [35].

Door-to-door survey was done in some research and some examined by health professional which is mostly different from community-based search as in door-to-door survey less population is covered, and prevalence of PD is high in such cases which can be due to other reasons but it leads to inaccuracy of data mostly in rural areas. Collection of data via door-to-door surveys is an extremely limited approach, and now, devices like mobile phones are being used in India and are increase uses in rural areas in India, but still, it is limited and has many drawbacks [36].

Medline and Embase databases were used mostly in research to collect the data, along with published paper and review paper were excluded only bibliography that was taken into consideration to study the Epidemiology of Parkinson disease worldwide; however, the research paper from that of PubMed and that of Organizations involved were not taken into account.

Some search was focused on caregivers to shows the quality of life they live and improvement needed among them but was not found much information which is of high concern issue.

Research done in Middle East and that in Australia shows high prevalence rate than before and the research done is almost less as compared to other countries; research papers for Middle East found were mostly confined to Arabs and Egypt and were based on door-to-door survey, questionnaire survey, Institut National de Neurologie. Much less information about Organizations and caregivers was taken into consideration, and as a result, more research is required to be done in other parts of Middle East along with Arabs and Egypt and in rural and urban areas to understand the Epidemiology of Parkinson disease in Middle East. Qena and Assuit which form the 4.4% and 4.1% population of Egypt show the prevalence rate almost like European countries.

People living in rural areas have higher risk with use of pesticides and in developed countries uses of industries is risk for Parkinson disease. The disease is more likely to be in developed countries. In Israel, the prevalence rate is increased from 2001 to 2012 in age <65; Egypt and Australia also show the increase in rate of Prevalence. In Australia, PD is increasing and is found more in older patients and about 1% of above 65 years of age and many chances for them are developing other pathologies like dysphagia, constipation in bowl cancer, bladder dysfunction, sleep wake disturbance and represent a difficult management challenge, more care and research needs to be taken to deal with Parkinson disease in older patients [37]. Parkinson disease leads to anxiety disorders which are common and research done on 79 patients in Australia shows about 25% are diagnosed with anxiety [38], Parkinson disease is found in elder age group by the study done in Australia with two phase study one by symptom-based questionnaire and second phase by examination of patient result shows more than 10% high percentage of Parkinsonism then mentioned before in other literature, the authors suggest that the actual reason can be 52 years of age lower cut off point which raise many questions, with less research on older patients and the study method used before in Australia [39].

Some studies shows difference in onset of disease, reasons found to be that of family history concern which needs to be understand more in detail; what environment, genetic, and other key factors have role in onset of disease earlier as the study done in Karnataka from rural and urban areas shows the disease more in patients with no family history.

In almost all studies, it has been found that the disease is found more in areas with industrial region and in rural areas as compared to urban areas, and it is of major concerned issue as it is found more in developed countries which means where the people lives longer, is it due to industrial reason or use of more pesticides or due to ethnicity needs to be addressed.

In some studies, the Prevalence of PD of Beijing and Shanghai was found similar to that of western countries, and Prevalence of PD in North Africa was found similar to European countries, whereas in other studies, Prevalence in China was found less than Western countries and that of Eastern and Western African countries less than that of Western Countries and Prevalence of Australia is more as compared to western countries and china and from research done in 1966, it was based on door-to-door survey and questionnaire which can differ from one country to another which shows that more research is required to be done to know the reason behind difference in detail as peoples from different background is widespread in all countries and can be the major cause of it or the studies were confined to rural areas as compared to urban areas.

Males are found to be more effective than females; however, the ratio is almost equal as it increases with age where further studies are needed to be known about the difference and what are the factors that make males more effective than females and whether the reasons are due to high estrogen presence which is still unknown.

1.5   Role of Ontology in Depression

Depression is a typical psychological well-being issue that makes individuals experience low temperament, loss of intrigue or delight, sentiments of blame or low self-esteem, irritated rest or hunger, low vitality, and poor fixation.

Suicide was one of the significant reasons for death among youngsters matured 15 to 29 years worldwide in 2012 [7], and in South Korea, it was the single biggest reason for youthful passing's. Countless young people (40%–80%) who end it all have a solid connection with discouragement at the season of their demise [8], demonstrating that youthful misery is one of the principle factors adding to self-destructive occasions.

Juvenile wretchedness influences people as well as their families, the network, and the nation in general. Additionally, this effect goes on for quite a while and has wide-extending impacts. Youthful sadness is an unending sickness with a high danger of backsliding. It thwarts the typical advancement and development of young people and adds to increments in network wrongdoings, for example, substance abuse and dangerous sexual practices [9]. Moreover, immature discouragement prompts diminish in profitability [10], which will eventually prompt an expanded weight on the economy [11]. It is accordingly essential to recognize juvenile dejection and give mediations at a beginning period.

Long-range interpersonal communication administrations (SNSs) are currently the most well-known web-based network stages among youths overall [12]. Most South Korean youths (77.1%) have SNS records, and 53% of them associate with in excess of 100 people by means of these records. Over 73% of young people in the European Union matured somewhere in the range of 13 to 16 years have a SNS account [5]. In addition, 51% of young people matured somewhere in the range of 13 to 18 years access their SNS account at any rate once every day [12].

These SNSs contain plenteous data about the sentiments, musings, interests, and examples of conduct of teenagers that can be acquired by breaking down SNS postings. Specifically, subjects, for example, connections with companions and cyber bullying can be analyzed all the more precisely and with less inclination by utilizing SNSs [12], which should along these lines be viewed as a significant wellspring of information for investigating gloom related issues in youths [13].

Content mining, an agent instrument that dissects web-based life information, does not express connections among terms, which is the reason extra data is required to comprehend these connections. To beat these constraints, a methodical structure with an ordered chain of command and connections among terms and phrasing is required. A cosmology that communicates "the mutual ideas and their connections in a particular field" [14, 16] could be utilized as an investigation structure for internet-based life information.

A cosmology can propose powerful methods for improving the nature of information investigation by communicating learning in a space methodically and understanding the information Konovalov *et al.* [14]. Utilized normal language preparing (NLP) to dissect military web-based life postings by utilizing a philosophy applicable to battle presentation as an expository structure. Be that as it may, Konovalov *et al.* did not build up a phrasing including different common language terms, and this made content mining progressively troublesome. A phrasing incorporates equivalent words of ideas and can coordinate different types of common language. Especially, since young people utilize recently authored words or articulations, condensing, and slang words, we need a phrasing where these terms are lined up with philosophy ideas.

1.6   Conclusion

In this paper, we have shown the role of Ontology in various fields of disease used such as CVD, Parkinson disease, depression, etc. Ontology plays a vital role in health care. In the form of xml the information is stored. For different purpose, different ontology has been created. ASP.Net, C#, jQuery, Ajax, CSS is used for implementing the system.

1.7   Future Scope

The future work will concentrate on the improvement of the assembling philosophy by utilizing surely understood existing ontologies, for example, WordNet and MASON. Besides, the creators are keen on the advancement of a multi-specialist framework where self-sufficient operators computerize the entire question process.

References

1. Passi, S.J., Prevention of Non-communicable Diseases by Balanced Nutrition: Population-specific Effective Public Health Approaches in Developing Countries. *Curr. Diabetes Rev.*, 13, 5, 461–476, 2017. https://doi.org/10.217 4/1573399812666160905105951.
2. Rahimi, A., Liaw, S.-T., Ray, P., Taggart, J., Yu, H., Ontological specification of quality of chronic disease data in EHRs to support decision analytics: A realist review. *Decis. Anal.*, 1, 1, 5, 2014. https://doi.org/10.1186/2193-8636-1-5.

3. El-Sappagh, S. and Ali, F., DDO: A diabetes mellitus diagnosis ontology. *Appl. Inf.*, 3, 1, 5, 2016. https://doi.org/10.1186/s40535-016-0021-2.
4. Khodiyar, V.K., Hill, D.P., Howe, D., Berardini, T.Z., Tweedie, S., Talmud, P.J., …Lovering, R.C., The representation of heart development in the gene ontology. *Dev. Biol.*, 354, 1, 9–17, 2011. https://doi.org/10.1016/j.ydbio.2011.03.011.
5. Smith, B., Williams, J., Schulze-Kremer, S., The ontology of the gene ontology. *AMIA Ann. Symp. Proc.*, 609–613, 2003.
6. Foulger, R.E., Denny, P., Hardy, J., Martin, M.J., Sawford, T., Lovering, R.C., Using the gene ontology to annotate key players in parkinson's disease. *Neuroinformatics*, 14, 3, 297–304, 2016. https://doi.org/10.1007/s12021-015-9293-2.
7. http://apps.who.int/iris/bitstream/10665/131056/1/9789241564779_eng.pdf
8. Cash, S.J. and Bridge, J.A., Epidemiology of youth suicide and suicidal behavior. *Curr. Opin. Pediatr.*, 21, 5, 613–619, 2009. https://doi.org/10.1097/MOP.0b013e32833063e1.
9. Anderson, D.M., Cesur, R., Tekin, E., Youth depression and future criminal behavior. *Econ. Inq.*, 53, 1, 294–317, 2015. https://doi.org/10.1111/ecin.12145.
10. Fletcher, J., Adolescent depression and adult labor market outcomes. *Southern Econ. J.*, 80, 1, 26–49, 2013. https://doi.org/10.4284/0038-4038-2011.193.
11. Lynch, F.L. and Clarke, G.N., Estimating the economic burden of depression in children and adolescents. *Am. J. Preventive Med.*, 31, 6 Suppl 1, S143–51, 2006. https://doi.org/10.1016/j.amepre.2006.07.001.
12. Toseeb, U. and Inkster, B., Online social networking sites and mental health research. *Front. Psychiatry*, 6, 36, 2015. https://doi.org/10.3389/fpsyt.2015.00036.
13. Use of social media for research and analysis. GOV.UK." (n.d.). Retrieved May 23, 2019, from https://www.gov.uk/government/publications/use-of-social-media-for-research-and-analysis.
14. Gruber, T.R., Toward principles for the design of ontologies used for knowledge sharing? *Int. J. Hum. Comput. Stud.*, 43, 5-6, 907–928, 1995. https://doi.org/10.1006/ijhc.1995.1081.
15. Konovalov, S., Scotch, M., Post, L., Brandt, C., Biomedical informatics techniques for processing and analyzing web blogs of military service members. *J. Med. Internet Res.*, 12, 4, e45, 2010. https://doi.org/10.2196/jmir.1538.
16. Jung, H., Park, H.-A., Song, T.-M., Ontology-Based Approach to Social Data Sentiment Analysis: Detection of Adolescent Depression Signals. *J. Med. Internet Res.*, 19, 7, e259, 2017. https://doi.org/10.2196/jmir.7452.
17. Pringsheim, T., Jette, N., Frolkis, A., Steeves, T.D.L., The prevalence of Parkinson's disease: A systematic review and meta-analysis. *Mov. Disord.*, 29, 1583–1590, 2014.

18. Das, S.K., Misra, A.K., Ray, B.K., Hazra, A., Ghosal, M.K. *et al.*, Epidemiology of Parkinson disease in the city of Kolkata, India: A community-based study. *Neurology*, 75, 1362–1369, 2010.

19. P. S. Parkinson disease in India: A review. *Ann Indian Acad. Neurol.*, 19, 9–20, 2016.

20. El-Tallawy, H.N., Farghaly, W.M., Shehata, G.A., Rageh, T.A., Hakeem, N.M.A. *et al.*, Prevalence of Parkinson's disease and other types of Parkinsonism in Al Kharga district, Egypt. *Neuropsychiatr. Dis. Treat*, 9, 1821–1826, 2013.

21. Okubadejo, N.U., Bower, J.H., Rocca, W.A., Maraganore, D.M., Parkinson's disease in Africa: A systematic review of epidemiologic and genetic studies. *Mov. Disord.*, 21, 2150–2156, 2006.

22. Kadakol, G.S., Kulkarni, S.S., Kulkarni, B.B., Kulkarni, S.S., Bhaskar, L.V.K.S. *et al.*, Parkinson' s disease in North Karnataka An epidemiological perspective. *Antrocom Online J.Anthropol.*, 8, 1–4, 2012.

23. Yitshak Sade, M., Zlotnik, Y., Kloog, I., Novack, V., Peretz, C., Ifergane, G., Parkinson's disease prevalence and proximity to agricultural cultivated fields. *Parkinsons Dis.*, 2015, 576564, 2015 Aug 18.

24. Jha, P.K. and Chaudhary, N., Epidemiology of Parkinson 's disease in South central India - A longitudinal cohort study. 4, 8–17, 2017.

25. Liu, C.C.1., Li, CY1,2, Lee, P.C.3., Sun, Y.4., Variations in Incidence and Prevalence of Parkinson's Disease in Taiwan: A Population-Based Nationwide Study. *Parkinsons Dis.*, 2016, 8756359, 2016 Jan 19.

26. Zou, Y.-M., Liu, J., Tian, Z.-Y., Lu, D., Zhou, Y.-Y., Systematic review of the prevalence and incidence of Parkinson's disease in the People's Republic of China. *Neuropsychiatr. Dis. Treat*, 11, 1467–1472, 2015.

27. Alrefai, A., Habahbih, M., Alkhawajah, M., Darwish, M., Batayha, W. *et al.*, Prevalence of Parkinson's disease in Northern Jordan. *Clin. Neurol. Neurosurg.*, 111, 812–815, 2009.

28. Chan, D.K., Dunne, M., Wong, A., Hu, E., Hung, W.T. *et al.*, Pilot study of prevalence of Parkinson's disease in Australia. *Neuroepidemiology*, 20, 112–117, 2001.

29. Roohani, M., Ali Shahidi, G., Miri, S., Demographic study of parkinson's disease in Iran: Data on 1656 cases. *Iran J. Neurol.*, 10, 19–21, 2011.

30. K, P.P., Neurological disorders in a rural western Australian population. *Intern Med. J.*, 14, 209–213, 2010.

31. R, M., Prevalence of Parkinson disease in an Arab population, Israel. *Isr. Med. Assoc. J.*, 12, 1, 32–5, 2010.

32. Anca, M., Paleacu, D., Shabtai, H., Giladi, N., Cross-Sectional Study of the Prevalence of Parkinson's Disease in the Kibbutz Movement in Israel. *Neuroepidemiology*, 21, 50–55, 2002.

33. W. Kamel, J. Al Hashel, S. Ahmed. Demographic and Clinical Characters of Parkinson's Disease in Tertiary Hospital in Kuwait [abstract]. Mov Disord. 2017; 32 (suppl 2). https://www.mdsabstracts.org/abstract/

demographic-and-clinical-characters-of-parkinsons-disease-in-tertiary-hospital-in-kuwait/. Accessed April 18, 2020.

34. Bohingamu Mudiyanselage, S., Watts, J.J., Abimanyi-Ochom, J., Lane, L., Murphy, A.T., Morris, M.E., Iansek, R., Cost of Living with Parkinson's Disease over 12 Months in Australia: A Prospective Cohort Study. *Parkinsons Dis.*, 2017, 5932675, 2017 Mar 02.

35. Poortvliet, P.C., Silburn, P.A., Coyne, T.J., Chenery, H.J., Deep brain stimulation for Parkinson disease in Australia: Current scientific and clinical status. *Intern Med. J.*, 45, 2, 134–139, 2015 Feb.

36. Klein, A., Visual parkinson's disease rating scale: A universal iconic questionnaire for epidemiological studies in india. *RIO*, 2, e8834, 2016.

37. Lewis, J. S., Gangadharan, S., Padmakumar, C. P. Parkinson's disease in the older patient. 16, 376–378, 2016.

38. Dissanayaka, N.N.W., Sellbach, A., Matheson, S., O'Sullivan, J.D., Silburn, P.A. *et al.*, Anxiety disorders in Parkinson's disease: Prevalence and risk factors. *Mov. Disord.*, 25, 838–845, 2010.

39. Chan, D.K., Hung, W.T., Wong, A., Hu, E., Beran, R.G., Validating a screening questionnaire for parkinsonism in Australia. *J. Neurol. Neurosurg. Psychiatr.*, 69, 117–120, 2000.

40. G'abor, N., Ontology Development. In: *Semantic Web Services*, R. Studer, S. Grimm, A. Abecker (Eds.), Springer, Berlin, Heidelberg, 2007.

2

A Study on Basal Ganglia Circuit and Its Relation With Movement Disorders

Dinesh Bhatia

Department of Biomedical Engineering, North Eastern Hill University,
Shillong, Meghalaya, India

Abstract

The basal ganglia formed of several synaptically interconnected neurons in the subcortical anatomy plays an important role in controlling different characteristics of psychomotor behaviour. Substantia Nigra containing dopamine neurons helps the ganglia in communicating with striatum to transmit signals to the motor cortex. The basal ganglia are central to the pathophysiology of basic movement disorders controlling various body movements. They are associated with executive functions such as behaviour, motor learning, decision making and emotions. The motor movement in human being is performed through Direct and Indirect Pathway(s). The basal ganglion plays an important role, as it has the property to control the thalamus that performs and controls subsequent motor actions. The study of basal ganglia, its functions, structure, and role in movement disorders has been ongoing since the early 1980s. In this chapter, we will study the relation between neurodegenerative diseases.

Keywords: Basal ganglia, motor cortex, movement disorder, dopamine

2.1 Introduction

In order to learn about basal ganglia, its function, structure, and the role in the undesired condition of movement disorders, the developmental procedure was initiated in the 1980s [3, 11, 16]. The development of testable models for hyperkinetic and hypokinetic movement disorders was planned and executed in a similar scheme [15]. In 1990,

Vishal Jain, Ritika Wason, Jyotir Moy Chatterjee and Dac-Nhuong Le (eds.) Ontology-Based Information Retrieval for Healthcare Systems, (19–36) © 2020 Scrivener Publishing LLC

the research was extended and continued on animal models, and additionally, the recording of neuronal activity during neurosurgery operations in humans was conducted [54]. The presented studies have guided us for the advancement of new surgical and pharmacologic treatments. The basal ganglia and its surrounding nuclei formed several subcortical cell structure occupied initially in movement control, associated with a huge assortment of positions such as executive functions and behavior, motor learning, and emotions. Basal ganglia are the central region of the brain, located as the nuclei between deep in caudate-putamen or striatum and globus pallidus (combined known as brain hemisphere), whereas the related nuclei contains a portion located in the subthalamic nucleus (STN) (diencephalon) and pedunculopontine nucleus (pons). During the 20th century, the basic concept and idea considering the tasks of basal ganglia were largely affected by the clinical inspection. These studies show that any reason which is associated with lesions of the STN or the lenticular nucleus (globus and putamen pallidus) were associated with movement disorders such as Parkinsonian symptoms, hemiballismus, and dystonia [37, 56]. In the past, the pathological basis of movement disorders was referred to as the extra-pyramidal system and extra-pyramidal syndrome. The reason for this distinction is to make a difference between movement disorders and corticofugal neurons which is responsible for the corticospinal projections, where the corticofugal neurons were called a pyramidal system.

The pyramidal system is also known as the corticospinal tract; it is an inverse tract that started from the pyramidal cell of the motor region. It is concerned with discrete, voluntary, and skilled motor operations. So, it is easy to predict intended as well as unintended movements, which are depending upon temporal and spatial structure of the muscle shrinkage. These muscle shrinkages are coordinated and initiated by different patterns in the neural network (NN) and the central nervous system (CNS). The calibration of CNS structure and NN are responsible for motor movement and indispensable for expression of appropriate motor deportment. Many of our complex deportment, as well as practiced movement, have been learned in the growing period and need to be remembered whole life. The basal ganglia, the cerebellum, and the cerebral cortex play an important role in learning the lifelong skilled movement process. The term clumsiness is associated with the problems in learning and performing the movement in childhood; however, the reason for this deficiency is poorly understood [23]. The understanding of the structure and practical association among pathogenesis of diverse movement disorders and the brain structure responsible for motor functions and clumsiness is important for insight into etiology. The implementation of intentional and willed movements frequently needs fine, concerted action of the sensory and motor systems. This can be seen during the eye and hand coordination at the time of fine movements of the fingers or hand. In general, complex movements need to be learned and practiced regularly. The accurate execution of that has been saved as brain functions during motor learning or memory.

Neurorehabilitation shows that one possible consequence therapy, harmonious to DRT, for managing movement disorders as can be seen in the case of Parkinson disease (PD) [10, 18, 22, 27, 48]. Parkinson's disease (PD) is considered a degenerative movement disorder distinguished by cognitive and motor malformation and associated with an active performing and movement expression [36]. When it is compared with the pars compacta of the substantia nigra, the dopaminergic neuronal loss showed as a pathological symptom of PD [30].

2.2 Anatomy and Functioning of Basal Ganglia

The basal ganglia are a variety of synaptically integrated subcortical composition that performs an important role in operating different features of psychomotor conduct as shown in Figure 2.1 [7]. The basal ganglia

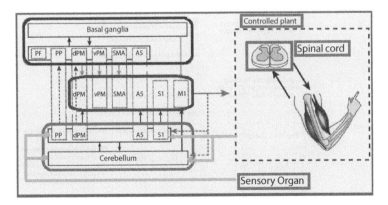

Figure 2.1 Shows controlled muscle movement with basal ganglia [18].

are an intermediate part of the pathophysiology of normal movement disorders such as PD and Hunting Disease (HD). The anatomy has been classified as shown in Figure 2.2.

2.2.1 The Striatum-Major Entrance to Basal Ganglia Circuitry

The Striatum-Major is the largest piece of basal ganglia structure and arranged in two segments: one is ventral and another is dorsal, which can be additionally separated dependent on associations and capacities. The ventral striatum is a blend of the olfactory tubercle and the core accumbens [19, 48]. The core accumbens center and the core accumbens shell amalgamate and made the core accumbens and it is not quite the same as a neural system in cerebrum [48]. The olfactory bulb does not smell odor, although it sends input to olfactory tubercle [48]. The islands of Calleja (located inside ventral striatum, a class of neural granule cells) are present in mammals and also in amphibians, reptiles, and birds [50]. It has been implicated as a basic piece of the circuit of remuneration related property and basic leadership [51]. The dorsal striatum is blended with the putamen and the caudate core. The sections of dorsal striatum, striosomes, and its encompassing network can be seen by recoloring.

The Basal Ganglia	The Striatum-Major Entrance to Circuitary of Basal Ganglia	The Corticostriatal Projection	
		The Thalamostriatal Projection	
		The Nigrostriatal Projection	
		Other Striatal Afferents	
	The Direct and Indirect Striatofugal Projections	Collateralization of Striatofugal Neurons and Co-localization of Dopamine Receptors	
		Multiple Indirect Pathway	
		Pallido-Subthalamo-Pallidal Loops with Parallel pathways	
	Subthalamic Nucleus: Aletrnate entry path to the Basal Ganglia Circuitry	Intrinsic Organization	
		The Corticosubthalamic Projection	
		The Thalamousubthalamic Projection	
	The Basal Ganglia Outflow	Pallidofugal Projections	The Pallidothalamic Projection
			The Pallidotegmental Projection
			The Pallidohabenular Projection
		Nigrofugal Projections	The Nigrothalamic Projection
			The Nigrotegmental Projection
			The Nigrocollicular Projection
			The Nigroreticular Projection
	The Pedunculopontine Nucleus		

Figure 2.2 The anatomy of the basal ganglia.

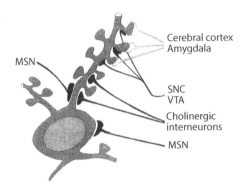

Figure 2.3 Medium spiny neuron schematic representation in the striatum [49].

In the striatum, there are many types of GABAergic interneurons such as cholinergic interneurons, medium spiny neurons (MSNs). Medium spiny neurons are the main part of the striatum section as shown in Figure 2.3 [57]. The categories of these neurons are named as inhibitory neurons. A total of 95% part is contained by MSNs in human striatum [57]. The MSNs are classified as D1-type and D2-type MSNs [19, 40, 57].

The cholinergic interneuron has various important consequences in striatum such as it plays a central role in motor learning and controlling and cholinergic neuron releases acetylcholine. In primates, for example, people and rat, cholinergic interneurons respond to major natural motivator with institutionalized reactions which are in the blink of an eye lined up with reactions of the dopaminergic neurons, and they are present in substantia nigra [21, 38]. The aspiny cholinergic interneurons are large and when they react with D5 dopamine, they generate pretentious dopamine [8].

2.2.2 Direct and Indirect Striatofugal Projections

By utilizing the two pathways available, *viz.*, immediate and rotary [3, 6], the information from the striatum is coordinated by medium spiked projection neurons and relayed to the inner cores of the basal ganglia (GPi and SNr). The immediate pathway coordinate directly with the GPi and SNr with the help of striatal neurons, whereas the unique pathway emerging from these neurons liaison with GPe. As shown in Figure 2.4, the GPe relays information to STN which transfers it further to the inner cores of the basal ganglia, namely, GPi and SNr. These striatal neurons ascent to immediate and rotary pathways which can be recognized as neuroactive

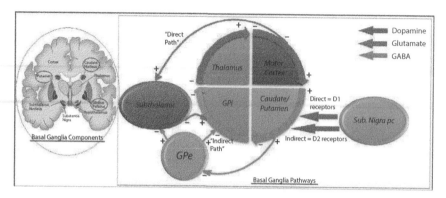

Figure 2.4 The components of basal ganglia components with their related pathways.

peptides and dopamine receptor subtypes. The primary transmitter is GABA; however, the neurons related to GPe contain encephalin and connect with D2 dopamine receptors, while those related to GPi and SNr are connected with advanced substance P and dynorphin or D1 dopamine receptors [20].

As indicated by basal ganglia circuits' functional models, the basal ganglia require a smooth relationship between the action of the immediate and rotary pathways [16]. This uniformity is kept up, to a limited extent, by adjustment of dopamine levels of the striatal neurons. The presence of dopamine allows increased transmission through the immediate pathway but decreases transmission through the rotary pathway. The general impact of striatal dopamine discharge is to diminish the GPi or SNr inhabitation of the thalamus, thereby prompting expanded action of thalamocortical projections by enhancing the speed and direction of developments. Any irregularity of movement of the immediate and rotary pathways can disturb the typical level of GPi/SNr restraint of thalamocortical action leading to hypokinetic or hyperkinetic issue(s) [16]. Different anatomical, biochemical, and sub-atomic investigations have helped in studying the immediate and aberrant pathways, to enhance our knowledge regarding the association of the basal ganglia and its constituents. In the accompanying record, we outline a portion of this information and talk about its importance for basal ganglia pathophysiology.

One of the critical arrangements of information that tested the idea of isolated immediate and circuitous striatonigral pathways is the demonstration regarding the accessibility of the striatofugal neurons. In the presence of single neural cell filling, the general assumption is that the striatofugal neurons are isolated into three sorts in rodents [26]:

1. A first population projection widely related to the GP;
2. A second compose anticipating to both GP and SNr;
3. A third compose anticipating to GP, EP, and SNr.

In 1995, a study showed that similar results as found in rodents were found in monkeys too [43]. Although these results showed the presence of the circuitous pathway, which recommends towards the striatofugal neurons having high level of collateralization but none of them show any undertaking to the GPi (or EPN) or SNr only.

Additionally, the established pathway passing through the GPe and STN has assortment of other circular pathways which transmit data through the basal ganglia. To illustrate, the GPe ascends to the GABAergic pathways in the basal ganglia structures (GPi, SNr) and the reticular thalamic core [42, 45, 47]. Moreover, it has been found that the GPe to the striatum targets the interneurons subpopulations [9]. As STN reflections to the SNe, GPe, PPN, and striatum [9] are additional circuitous pathways which transmit the cortical data to the basal ganglia structures. Even though the correct elements of these associations stay obscure, it is often described that the first model of immediate and roundabout pathways related to basal ganglia hardware is a misrepresentation [45].

2.2.3 The STN: Another Entrance to Basal Ganglia Circuitry

The STN is a lens-shaped and small-sized structure in the brain that forms functional part of the basal ganglia. The STN constitutes a major part of subthalamus located ventral to the thalamus, medial to the internal capsule and dorsal to the substantia nigra. This theory was given by Jules Luys [34]. The STN is specially grown up in humans. It is encapsulated by crucial myelinated fiber bundles, thoroughly vascularized, heavy populated, cerebral peduncle, and zona incerta. There are so many myelinated axons, which transmit information and travel by passing STN [25, 46]. The STN is a member of a population of the cell with pyramidal, spindle shape, and round perikarya [58]. The theoretical terms are the projection neuron, and the length of its dendrites can vary more than 750 micrometer [44]. Every STN increases the stem dendrites connecting the ellipsoidal region similarly to the rostrocaudal base of the nucleus [58].

2.3   Movement Disorders

The primary basal ganglia function in ordinary motor control is still ambiguous, but the changes in its functions clearly show the growth in the movement disorders. These disorders can be classified as: hyperkinetic disorders such as drug-induced dykinesias or hemiballism and hypokinetic disorders like PD. Although, this classification shows limitations for pathophysiologic elucidation of other movement diseases, due to the presence of movement disorders like Huntington Disease (HD) or dystonia. HD shows symptoms that differ from normal movement disorders. During the study of basal ganglia anatomy, results show that network [11] dysfunctions or movement disorders activity related to thalamic neurons, cortical neurons, and basal ganglia neurons.

2.3.1   Parkinson Disease

PD influences growth and development and termed as a degenerative disorder [1]. Early idiopathic PD can be pathologically correlated with the loss of dopaminergic nigrostriatal neurons. Dopaminergic substitution procedures can treat the subsequent PD symptoms, such as tremor, unbending nature, akinesia, and bradykinesia. In the later disease stage, the loss of dopamine can cause additional loss to the basal ganglia structures such as the loss of brainstem [59] and cortical neurons, leading to postural shakiness with autonomic and intellectual brokenness.

The deficiency of dopamine in the early stages of the Parkinson's illness could affect neuronal release in surrounding regions of basal ganglia, which results in the improvement of the cardinal engine irregularities of the ailment. As per the model proposed by neuroscientists [2, 16], the dopamine misfortune results in expanded action along the ambiguous pathway and diminished movement along the immediate pathway. The two impacts together allow prompt cortex excitation, which has been clinically proven to improve the symptoms of the Parkinson's disorder [54]. Deteriorating condition of basal ganglia yield to the partial parenteral nutrition (PPN) may likewise assume a task in the advancement of the pre-eminent system indications of Parkinsonism. A noteworthy contribution in the area is the metabolic overactivity of the PPN site in the Parkinson subjects [37, 41], and it has been demonstrated that inactivation of this site is sufficient to instigate akinesia in test subjects [28, 39]; however, it is still not clear that how it identifies with retarded development in Parkinsonism after PPN inactivation.

PET examinations have examined the movement at the cortex level showing that Parkinsonism is related to a particular movement of the dorsal prefrontal cortex, and frontal related regions which receive subcortical information from the basal ganglia. Further, it seems that there is a compensatory over action of the horizontal premotor and parietal cortex regions that usually encourage engine reactions to visual and sound-related signs [13].

It has been found that expanded basal ganglia might show pathophysiologic signs for improvement in the Parkinsonian symptoms having animated endeavors to decrease this yield precisely by use of pharmacological drugs. As presented in literature, the STN in MPTP-treated primates leads to major indications of Parkinsonism by diminishing GPi movement has stimulated research interests in the area [4, 6]. The Stereotactic injuries of the GPi pallidotomy, reintroduced in human patients, have found to be suitable against the possible symptoms of PD [5, 29]. PET examinations have shown that post pallidotomy, the metabolic movements which were found to be reduced have found to be again active in Parkinson patients [17].

2.3.2   Dyskinetic Disorder

During dyskinesias, the basal ganglia yield is reduced leading to reduced inhibition of thalamocortical frameworks and dyskinesias [3, 16]. This is observed during hemiballism, that pursues discrete injuries of the STN, resulting lower action in GPi in experimental animals and humans [24, 53]. During the Huntington's infection which is found to be similar to hemiballism causing degradation of striatal neurons in the GPe (backhanded pathway) that prompts disinhibition of GPe, trailed by expanded hindrance of the STN and in this way decreased yield from GPi [1, 2]. Hence, in hemiballism, a particular sore in the STN is seen, in early HD the core structure is practically underactive. Medication prompted dyskinesias may lead to a comparative decrease in STN and GPi movements. The legitimacy of these models originates from direct account of neuronal action [7] and digestion considerations in animals, and the quantity of PET examinations exploring cortical and related regions in people with development issues [11, 12]. For example, in creatures with medication instigated dyskinesias, STN and GPi action was enormously diminished, associated with dyskinetic developments.

The pallidal and nigral injuries show that dyskinesias don't result from decreased basal ganglia yield alone. Such sores, when done in people and creatures, don't result in huge dyskinesias, in spite of probably entire suspension of action of the lesioned regions, albeit brief scenes of dyskinsias may be observed instantly after pallidal sores in Parkinsonian patients. During investigations in primates, improvement of dyskinesias was not observed post transient inactivation of little territories of the pallidum with the GABAergic agonist muscimol, due to extensive infused focuses variety and volumes of the medication. These discoveries recommend that unpretentious instead of aggregate decrease of thalamus pallidal yield leading to dyskinesias and that particular adjustments in release designs as opposed to worldwide decrease of pallidal yield might be especially helpful for dyskinetic developments albeit such particular modifications stay slippery. Compensatory systems at the thalamic or cortical level may not allow improvement of dyskinesias after a decrease of pallidal or nigral yield. The significance of these systems is most strikingly clear in creatures and people with hemiballism. As a rule, the dyskinetic developments are transient, regardless of the proceeded with nearness of diminished and unusual neuronal release in GPi. Last, the enlistment of synchronized action over a neuronal population in an uncontrolled manner may assume a job in the advancement of dyskinetic developments.

The important task of the basal ganglia is to create an association path with brainstem system and thalamus and remove the undetermined tasks. Therefore, the PPN and CM/Pf cores of thalamus, specifically, the PPN and the CM/Pf cores of the thalamus, may have critical jobs in the improvement of dyskinesia.

2.3.3   Dystonia

Dystonia is a turmoil described by moderate, managed anomalous developments, and stances with co-constriction of agonist-rival muscle gatherings. Primer pathophysiologic proof shows that it might highlight normal to both hypokinetic and hyperkinetic issues equally. It is certainly not a homogeneous element and might result from hereditary clutters, from central injuries to the basal ganglia or its structures, and disarranges of dopamine digestion. The vast majority of these conditions usually influence the working of the basal ganglia-thalamocortical system, for which no generally acknowledged subject models are accessible.

The accessible creature dystonia models, for example, the hereditarily dystonic hamster, or models of medication prompted dystonia in rodents and monkeys are not found to be attractive as they are either connected with irregular phenotypic highlights or are excessively transient and inconsistent, making it impossible to allow a thorough investigation of the pathological condition. A large portion of the current pathophysiologic proof concerning this condition depends on the after-effects of intraoperative chronicle in a few patients experiencing neurosurgical interventions for the dystonia treatment. This selected patient population presumably does not inform the full scope of dystonic conditions. In light of these accounts, it gives the idea that the movement along both the immediate and backhanded pathways might be expanded in dystonia. The ongoing study in dystonic patients considers experiencing pallidotomy with uncovered low normal release rates in both pallidal sections [14, 31, 33, 52, 53].

The decreased release rates in GPe in these dystonic patients confirm expanded action along the roundabout pathway, which is independent from others, thereby prompting expanded GPi release. The way that release rates in GPi were lessened, contends consequently for extra over action along the immediate pathway.

The GPi yield rates in both dystonia and ballism show lessened elements other than changes in release rates are assuming a critical job in their advancement. These changes signify redesign of the movement of the thalamocortical circuits in dystonia and unpredictable responsive field(s) being portrayed in both the thalamus and pallidum [31, 32, 52]. As per previous recommendations at the cortical level, the debasement of the discrete cortical portrayal of individual body parts exhibited at the different stages in the basal ganglia thalamocortical circuit represents tactile brokenness play a crucial role in the dystonia improvement [33].

2.4   Effect of Basal Ganglia Dysfunctioning on Movement Disorders

Basal ganglia play an important role in motor functioning and it would be important to understand if they have any lesion or any other associated problem affecting the concerned motor functioning associated with it. As explained earlier, relationship exists between movement disorders and basal ganglia. In Figure 2.5, it is shown that during normal and abnormal functioning, substantia nigra pars compacta (SNc), a grey matter of the basal ganglia, plays a major role. Generally, SNc generates the dopamine to transmit through neurons and this communication maintains a balance in the striatal connecting pathway.

The communication between basal ganglia and motor neurons starts deteriorating, which is the cause of motor dysfunctioning. The comprehension of the pathophysiology of development issues and related changes in basal ganglia exercises has advanced since the past few decades [55].

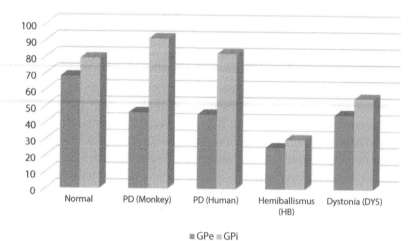

Figure 2.5 The spontaneous neuronal activity mean discharge rates (Hz) in internal (GPi) and external (GPe) segments of globus pallidus, for the normal and Parkinsonian monkeys, respectively, and for human patients with Parkinson, Hemiballismus, and Dystonia.

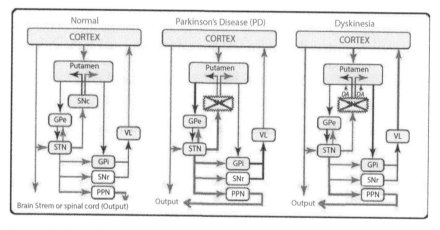

Figure 2.6 The basal ganglia-thalamocortical circuitry under normal and PD conditions. The basal ganglia circuitry includes GPe, GPi, STN, SNr, SNc, and striatum. Output is in the direction of ventral lateral/anterior nucleus of the thalamus (VL/VA) and centromedian (CM), along with pedunculopontine nucleus (PPN). The excitatory connections and inhibitory pathways is represented by red and blue colors, respectively [35].

With availability of detailed anatomical models of the basal ganglia, investigations began in understanding the action designs in creature models of normal development issue and electrophysiological chronicles in development issue of patients experiencing while undergoing neurosurgical methods. These examinations led to the global evaluation of the varying activity changes occurring in the basal ganglia in Parkinsonism and related diseased conditions, with detailed depiction of neurotic action designs, particularly in the burst patterns and oscillatory synchronous release of neurons in these conditions as represented in Figure 2.6.

2.5 Conclusion and Future Scope

Although significant progress has been made to understand the basal ganglia structure and its functional aspects, however, still the nuclei need further investigation. The current available basal ganglia models generate curiosity and interest to explore the field further and provide rationale for carrying out different neurosurgical interventions. However, it is clear that these models have potential shortcomings as they are based on anatomical data and do not take into consideration those patients having reduced pallidal activity. Further, they do not consider the multiple changes occurring in the basal ganglia of patients with movement disorders. Although alternative models have come up with new information, however, they still lack information related to the relationship between the basal ganglia and its related cortex regions which requires further scientific research and knowledge. The new information which would be available from these data recorded will significantly help the scientific community to better understand the functioning of the basal ganglia and the pathophysiology of movement disorders. This, in turn, would improve the existing model(s) and lead to the development of better therapeutic treatment approaches, thereby providing new insights into the research of basal ganglia and its constituents.

References

1. Albin, R.L., The pathophysiology of chorea/ballism and parkinsonism. *Parkinson. Rel. Disord.*, 1, 3–11, 1995.
2. Albin, R.L., Reiner, A., Anderson, K., Penney, J.B., Young, A.B., Striatal and nigral neuron subpopulations in rigid Huntington's disease: Implictions for the functional anatomy of chorea and rigidity- akinesia. *Ann. Neurol.*, 27, 357–365, 1990.
3. Albin, R.L., Young, A., Penny, J., The functional anatomy of basal ganglia disorders. *Tresnds Neurosci.*, 12, 366–375, 1989.
4. Aziz, T.Z., Peggs, D., Georgopoulos, A.P., Lesion of the subthalamic nucleus for the alleviation of 1-methyl-4-phenyl-1,2,3,6-tetrahydropyridine

introduced parkinsonism in the primate. *Movement Disord.*, 6, 288–292, 1981.

5. Baron, M.S., Vitek, J.L., Bakay, R.A., Green, J., Kaneoke, Y., Hashimoto, T., 1 Treatment of advanced Parkinson's Disease by GPi pallidotomy: 1 year pilot study results. *Ann. Neurol.*, 40, 355–366, 1996.

6. Bergman, H., Wichmann, T., DeLong, M.R., Reversal of experiment parkinsonism by lesions of the subthalamic nucleus. *Science*, 249, 1436–1438, 1990.

7. Bergman, H., Wichmann, T., Karmon, B., DeLong, M.R., The primate subthalamic nucleus. II Neuronal activity in the MPTP model of parkinsonism. *J. Neurophysiol.*, 72, 507–520, 1994.

8. Bergson, C., Mrzljak, L., Smiley, J.F., Pappy, M., Levenson, R., Goldman-Rakic, P., Regional, cellular, and subcellular variations in the distribution of D1 and D5 dopamine receptors in primate brain. *J. Neurosci.*, 15, 12, 7821–7836, 1995.

9. Bevan, M.D., Booth, P.A., Eaton, S.A., Bolam, J.P., Selective innervation of neostriatal interneurons by a subclass of neurons in the globus pallidus of the rat. *J. Neurosci.*, 18, 9438–9452, 1998.

10. Bloem, B., Vries, N. d., Ebersbach, G., Nonpharmacological treatments for patients with Parkinson's disease. *Mov. Disord.*, 30, 1504–1520, 2015.

11. Brooks, D., The role of basal ganglia in motor control: Contribution from PET. *J. Neurol. Sci.*, 128, 1–13, 1995.

12. Brooks, D.J., Functional imaging in relation to parkinsonian syndromes. *J. Neurol. Sci.*, 115, 1–17, 1993.

13. Brooks, D.J., Functional imaging of Parkinson's disease: Is it possible to detect brain areas for specific symptoms? *J. Neural. Transm.*, Suppl., 56, 139–153, 1999.

14. Cardoso, F., Jankovic, J., Grossman, R.G., Hamilton, W.J., Outcome after stereotactic thalamotomy for dystonia and hemiballismus. *Neurosurgery*, 36, 501–508, 1995.

15. Chesselet, M. and Delfs, J., Basal Ganglia and Movement Disorders: An update. *Trends Neurosci.*, 19, 417–422, 1996.

16. DeLong, M., Primate models of movement disorders of basal ganglia origin. *Trends Neurosci.*, 13, 281–285, 1990.

17. Dogali, M., Fazzini, E., Kolodny, E., Eidelberg, D., Sterio, D., Devinsky, O., Beric, A., Stereotactic ventral pallidotomy for Perkinson's disease. *Neurology*, 45, 753–761, 1995.

18. Ekker, M., Janssen, S., Nonnekes, J., Bloem, B., Vries, N.D., Neurorehabilitation for Parkinson's disease: Future perspectives for behavioural adaptation. *Parkinsonism Relat. Disord.*, 18, Suppl. 1, S73–S77, 2016.

19. Ferré, S., Lluís, C., Justinova, Z., Quiroz, C., Orru, M., Navarro, G., Goldberg, S., Adenosine-cannabinoid receptor interactions. Implications for striatal function. *Br. J. Pharmacol.*, 160, 3, 443–453, 2010.

20. Gerfen, C.R. and Wilson, C.J., The Basal Ganglia, in: *Handbook of Chemical Neuroanatomy, Integrated Systems of the CNS, part III*, pp. 369–466, Elsevier, Amsterdam, 1996, 369–466.

21. Goldberg, J. and Reynolds, J., Spontaneous firing and evoked pauses in the tonically active cholinergic interneurons of the striatum. *Neuroscience.*, 198, 27–43, 2011.

22. Goodwin, V., Richards, S., Taylor, R., Taylor, A., Campbell, J., The effectiveness of exercise interventions for people with Parkinson's disease: A systematic review and meta-analysis. *Mov. Disord.*, 23, 631–640, 2008.

23. Hadders-Algra, M., Developmental coordination disorder: Is clumsy motor behavior caused by a lesion of the brain at early age. *Neural Plasticity*, 10, 39–50, 2003.

24. Hamada, I. and DeLong, M., Excitotoxic acid lesions of the primates subthalamic nucleus result in reduced pallidal neuronal activity during active holding. *J. Neurophysiol.*, 68, 1859–1866, 1992.

25. Hassler, R., Usunoff, K.G., Romansky, K.V., Christ, J.F., Electron microscopy of the subthalamic nucleus in the baboon. I. Synaptic organization of the subthalamic nucleus in the baboon. *J. Hirnforsch*, 23, 597–611, 1982.

26. Kawaguchi, Y., Wilson, C.J., Emson, P.C., Projection subtypes of rat neostriatal matrix cells revealed by intracellular injection of biocytin. *J. Neurosci.*, 10, 3421–3438, 1990.

27. Keus, S., Munneke, M., Nijkrake, M., Kwakkel, G., Bloem, B., Physical therapy in Parkinson's disease: Evolution and future challenges. *Mov. Disord.*, 24, 1–14, 2009.

28. Kojima, J., Yamaji, Y., Matsumura, M., Nambu, A., Inase, M., Tokuno, H., Excitotoxic lesions of the pedunculopontine tegmental nucleus produce contralateral hemiparkinsonism in the monkey. *Neurosci. Letter*, 226, 111–114, 1997.

29. Laitiner, L.V., Pallidotomy for Parkinson's disease. *Neurosurg. Clin. North Am.*, 6, 105–112, 1995.

30. Lees, A., Hardy, J., Revesz, T., Parkinson's disease. *Lancet*, 373, 2055–2066, 2009.

31. Lenz, F.A. and Byl, N.N., Reorganization in the cutaneous core of the human thalamic principal somatic sensory nucleus (Ventral caudal) in patients with dystonia. *J. Neurophysiol.*, 82, 3204–3212, 1999.

32. Lenz, F.A., Jaeger, C.J., Seike, M.S., Lin, Y.C., Reich, S.G., DeLong, M.R., Vintek, J.L., Thalamic single neuron activity in patients with dystonia: Dystonia-related activity and somatic sensory reorganization. *J. Neurophysiol.*, 82, 2372–2392, 1999.

33. Lenz, F.A., Suarez, J.I., Metman, L.V., Reich, S.G., Karp, B.I., Hallett, M., Pallidal activity during dystonia: Somatosensory reorganisation and changes with severity. *J. Neurol. Neurosurg. Psychiatry*, 65, 767–770, 1998.

34. Luys, J.B., *Recherches sur le système cérébro-spinal, sa structure, ses fonctions et ses maladies*, Baillière: in French, Paris, 1865.

35. Martin, J.P., Hemichorea resulting from a location lesion of the brain (the syndrome of the body of Luys). *Brain*, 50, 637–651, 1927.

36. Mazzoni, P., Shabbott, B., Cortés, J., Motor control abnormalities in Parkinson's disease. *Cold Spring Harb. Perspect. Med.*, 2, 1–17, 2012.

37. Mitchell, I.J., Clarke, C.E., Boyce, S., Robertson, R.G., Peggs, D., Sambrook, M.A., Crossman, A.R., Neural mechanisms underlying parkinsonian symptoms based upon regional uptake of 2-deoxyglucose in monkeys exposed to 1-methyl-4-phenyl-1,2,3,6-tetrahydropyridine. *Neuroscience*, 32, 213–226, 1989.

38. Morris, G., Arkadir, D., Nevet, A., Vaadia, E., Bergman, H., Coincident but distinct messages of midbrain dopamine and striatal tonically active neurons. *Neuron.*, 43, 1, 133–143, 2004.

39. Munro-Davies, L.E., Winter, J., Aziz, T.Z., Stein, J.F., The role of the pedunculipontine region in basal ganglia mechanisms of akinesia. *Exp. Brain Res.*, 129, 511–517, 1999.

40. Nishi, A., Kuroiwa, M., Shuto, T., Mechanisms for the modulation of dopamine d(1) receptor signaling in striatal neurons. *Front. Neuroanat.*, 5, 43, 2011.

41. Palombo, E., Porrino, L.J., Bankiewiez, K.S., Crane, A.M., Sokoloff, L., Kopin, I.J., Local cerebral glucose utilization in monkeys with hemiparkinsonism induced by intracartotid infusion of the neurotoxin MPTP. *J. Neurosci.*, 10, 860–869, 1990.

42. Parent, A. and Hazrati, L.N., Functional anatomy of the basal ganglia. I. The cortico-basal ganglia-thalamocortical loop. *Brain Res. Rev.*, 20, 91–127, 1995.

43. Parent, A., Charara, A., Pinault, D., Single striatofugal axons arborizing in both pallidal segments and in the substantia nigra in primate. *Brain Res.*, 698, 280–284, 1995.

44. Rafols, J.A. and Fox, C.A., The neurons in the primates subthalamic nucleus: A Golgi and electron microscopic study. *J. Comp. Neurol.*, 168, 75–111, 1976.

45. Smith, Y., Bevan, M.D., Shink, E., Bolam, J.P., Microcircuitry of the direct and indirect pathways of the basal ganglia. *Neuroscience*, 86, 353–387, 1998.

46. Smith, Y., Bolam, J., Krosigk, M.V., Topographical and synaptic organization of the GABA containing pallidosubthalamic projection in the rat. *Eur. J. Neurosci.*, 2, 500–511, 1982.

47. Smith, Y., Shink, E., Sidibe, M., Neuronal circuitry and synaptic connectivity of the basal ganglia. *Neurosurgery Clin. North Am. W.B. Saunders.*, 9, 203–222, 1998.

48. Tomlinson, L.C., Patel, S., Meek, C., Clarke, C.E., Stowe, R., Sackley, C.M., Deane, KH., Wheatley K and Ives, N., Physiotherapy versus placebo or no intervention in Parkinson's disease. *Cochrane Database Syst. Rev.*, 9, 9, 1–110, 2012.

49. Ubeda-Bañon, I., Novejarque, A., Mohedano-Moriano, A., Projections from the posterolateral olfactory amygdala to the ventral striatum: neural basis for reinforcing properties of chemical stimuli. *BMC Neurosci.*, 8, 103, 2007.

50. *Ventral striatum – NeuroLex.*, Retrieved from neurolex.org: https://scicrunch.org/scicrunch/interlex/view/ilx_0112346, 2015.

51. *Ventral Striatum Definition – Medical Dictionary*, Retrieved from medical-dictionary.net: http://medicaldictionary.net/ventral-striatum.html, 2015.

52. Vitek, J.L., Chockkan, V., Zhang, J.Y., Kaneoke, Y., Evatt, M., DeLong, M.R., Neuronal activity in the basal ganglia in patients with generalized dystonia and hemiballismus. *Ann. Neurol.*, 46, 22–35, 1999.

53. Vitek, J., Evatt, M., Zhang, J., Hashimoto, T., DeLong, M., Triche, S., Pallidotomy as a treatment for medically intractable dystonia. *Ann. Neurol.*, 42, 409, 1997.

54. Wichmann, T. and DeLong, M., Functional and pathophysiological models of the basal ganglia. *Curr. Opin. Neurobiol.*, 6, 751–758, 1996.

55. Wichmann, T. and Dostrovsky, J.O., Pathological basal ganglia activity in movement disorders. *Neuroscience*, 13, 5, 232–244, 2011.

56. Wilson, S., Disorders of motility and tone. *Lancet Neurol.*, 1, 1–103, 1925.

57. Yager, L., Garcia, A., Wunsch, A., Ferguson, S., The ins and outs of the striatum: Role in drug addiction. *Neuroscience*, 301, 529–541, 2015.

58. Yelnik, J. and Perchron, G., Subthalamic neurons in primates: A quantitative and comparative analysis. *Neuroscience*, 4, 1717–1773, 1979.

59. Zweig, R.M., Cardillo, J.E., Cohen, M., Giere, S., Hedreen, J.C., The locus ceruleus and dementia in Parkinson's disease. *Neurology*, 5, 986–991, 1993.

3

Extraction of Significant Association Rules Using Pre- and Post-Mining Techniques—An Analysis

M. Nandhini[1]* and S. N. Sivanandam[2]

*[1]Department of Computer Science, Government Arts College,
Udumalpet, Tamilnadu, India
[2]Department of CSE, Karpagam College of Engineering, Coimbatore,
Tamilnadu, India*

Abstract

Association rule mining (ARM) is used to discover interesting if-then rules from the dataset. Interesting rules help to discover strong affinities among the attributes of the dataset. One of ARM's key issues is the generation of massive volumes of insignificant rules. The quality of the generated association rules is obviously constrained by the interestingness measures and the quantity of rules [28]. While several pre-mining and post-mining techniques exist, only one technique is used to reduce the rules. The use of either pre- or post-mining techniques does not deliver promising results as expected. In this work, an attempt is made to combine the above two techniques without sacrificing the usefulness factor. Two radically different pre-mining techniques, i.e., PSO-based and PAW-based are independently combined with a post-mining to reduce the quantity of rules. Domain Ontology (DO) is used for sound and interactive post-mining. An experimental analysis is performed using the Adult dataset from the UCI machine learning repository to determine the effects of pre-mining and post-mining on ARM.

Keywords: Association rules, pre-mining, post-mining, PSO, information gain, domain ontology, filters, rule schemas

*Corresponding author: nandumano@yahoo.co.in

Vishal Jain, Ritika Wason, Jyotir Moy Chatterjee and Dac-Nhuong Le (eds.) Ontology-Based Information Retrieval for Healthcare Systems, (37–68) © 2020 Scrivener Publishing LLC

3.1   Introduction

The mining of interesting association rules between large sets of data items is an important task. One of the main problems with association rule mining (ARM) is the production of large volumes of uninteresting rules. The quality and quantity of the association rules are largely determined by the measures of interest. Interestingness measures are used to analyze the user-interest rules. In literature, broadly, there are two types of measures of interest, objective, and subjective. Objective measures depend on the statistical significance and composition of the itemsets. They are data-driven and domain-independent used to measure the efficiency and usefulness of the rules. On the other hand, subjective measures depend on the user and the domain. They depend on the subjectivity of the user who evaluates the rules of association with regard to novelty, actionability, and unexpectedness.

Generally, the removal of duplicate and insignificant rules helps to mine significant rules. This crucial issue of rule mining can be dealt with in two stages of the rules generation process, i.e., either before the discovery of rules or after the discovery of rules. The use of appropriate measures [2], setting optimal threshold values for interestingness measures [19], specifying meta-patterns, and constraints [33] are some of the pre-mining techniques used to generate a small amount of significant rules before or during the rule mining process. Most pre-mining techniques deal with objective measures like support and confidence. Post-mining tasks are carried out by end-users to analyze and interpret the discovered rules. In terms of the requirements and subjectivity of the users, the end-users design and develop filters and operators over a set of rule schemas (RS) to mine the small subset of preferred association rules. Subjective measures such as unexpectedness [21] and actionability [20] are used to design filters and RSs.

This paper's primary objective is to cut down the number of rules by blending pre-mining and a post-mining techniques without sacrificing its computing capacity. In this work, two different pre-mining techniques are combined independently with a post-mining technique to reduce the number of rules. The first pre-mining technique uses the Particle Swarm Optimization (PSO), an optimization algorithm, to calculate the optimal support and confidence threshold values. Optimal threshold values calculated by PSO are taken in the process of generating rules. The second pre-mining technique focuses on mining association rules based on attribute weights, i.e., Weighted Association Rules (WARs). Interesting WARs are mined by pre-assigning weight (PAW) for each attribute. In this work, the significance of the attribute is calculated using Information Gain (IG) measure and it is assigned as the attribute weight. The use of IG value as a weight parameter naturally reduces the size and number of frequent weighted item sets produced during each iteration. This ultimately reduces the amount of rules generated in comparison with the pre-mining technique based on PSO.

DO is utilized to lead sound and interactive post-mining. DO assists with giving a formal and unambiguous representation of a typical conceptualization. Interactively, the end-user can extract and exclude rules using filters and operators defined by a set of RSs. Experiments are conducted using the Adult dataset from the UCI machine learning repository. The results show that the combination of PAW and DO improves the computational efficiency of mining rules without affecting the utility factor.

The remainder of the paper is as follows. Section 3.2 examines the review of literature. Section 3.3 layouts the methodology used in the proposed work. Experiments and results are examined in Sections 3.4 and 3.5 concludes the paper.

3.2 Background

ARM is one of the main tasks of data mining, where rules indicate certain relationships between dataset attributes. It aims at finding relevant connections and similarities from the dataset [41]. The main disadvantages of ARM are that it generates a large number of rules. Extracting useful knowledge from the voluminous rules is challenging because the relevant mining information is concealed within the rules. The choice of the correct interest measures and the setting of optimum threshold values depend on the application. One of the factors for the insignificant rule generation is the lack of user involvement/interaction in the mining of interesting rules based on prior domain knowledge.

3.2.1 Interestingness Measures

Interestingness measures play a vital role in mining significant itemsets/patterns. They are used to rank and select the patterns with respect to the user's preferences. The use of appropriate interesting measures always reduces space and time complexity [14]. In literature, there exist nine criteria to determine and define interestingness measures. According to [27], interestingness measures are categorized into three, namely, objective, subjective, and semantic. Objective measures depend on the structure, statistical strengths, or properties of the patterns discovered, while subjective measures are based on the beliefs and expectations of the user in a particular field. A semantic measure, a particular form of subjective measure [43], relies on the semantics and description of the patterns. It requires the user's domain knowledge.

3.2.2 Pre-Mining Techniques

Pre-mining techniques are nothing but the techniques used before or during the mining process to limit the quantity and size of frequent itemsets and/or the association rules. There are several techniques proposed and discussed below.

Extracting very few important frequent itemsets is a key issue in the process of ARM. The brute force method is generally adopted for the mining of frequent itemsets. Frequent itemsets are itemsets whose support value is greater than or equal to minimum support. It produces all feasible candidate itemsets and discards the infrequent itemsets. Although the task of producing frequent items is simple, it suffers from computational complexity because there are too many comparisons. Several frequent itemset generation strategies are attempted in the literature to cut down the number of candidates, transactions, and comparisons to improve computational efficiency.

3.2.2.1 Candidate Set Reduction Schemes

Apriori [1] is the first rule mining algorithm that uses the anti-monotonic property to reduce candidate numbers. By computing the support, it enumerates all possible candidate sets. This algorithm also produces a large number of itemsets that satisfy the minimum support threshold, particularly when the threshold is set low. This is due to the Apriori property, i.e., if an itemset is frequent/large, each of its sub-itemsets is also frequent. A large itemset can include several smaller sub-itemsets, which are frequent. Closed and maximal itemset mining was established to overcome this problem.

An itemset is closed if none of its immediate supersets has equivalent support with that of the itemset. Attributable to its inherent feature, the amount of closed itemsets generated is extremely less compared to frequent itemsets which mechanically reduces the amount of rules. There have been several algorithms projected to come up with closed sets alternative to frequent itemsets, with equivalent analytical power and a smaller set of rules. A-Close [31] CLOSET [32], CHARM [46], and CLOSET+ [44] are some of the favored algorithms accustomed to generate closed itemsets.

Maximal itemsets are itemsets if none of its immediate supersets is frequent. The number of maximal itemsets generated is still smaller in number compared to closed itemsets and frequent itemsets. Bayardo [5] proposed MaxMiner, an apriori-based algorithm to produce maximal itemsets by performing superset frequency trimming and subset infrequency pruning to decrease search space. MAFIA [8] is projected to create maximal itemsets by using vertical bitmaps to reduce the transaction Id list.

3.2.2.2 Optimal Threshold Computation Schemes

Interesting measures and their set threshold values generally determine the quality and quantity of interesting rules. Support and confidence are the main objective factors that are used to create interesting rules. Setting the ideal threshold values for support and confidence improves algorithm performance [19]. Users employ trial and error methods in classical algorithms to pick certain threshold values. This experimental method generates voluminous rules, in which many of them are not valuable. Hence, it is important to consequently find the ideal, i.e., optimal values for support and confidence measures in large data sets. Finding the ideal threshold values for these measures becomes an NP-complete problem. Setting too low values for these measures will lead to a colossal number of rules with less analytical value. Too high creates common-knowledge rules. The setting of the optimal values for these measures poses problems for the users.

In literature, heuristic algorithms are used to find optimal threshold values as well as to generate significant rules without explicitly specifying the threshold values for the interestingness measures. Genetic Algorithm (GA) is employed to generate rules without considering minimum support [42]. This method does not require user-specified minimum support and confidence; instead, the method is designed to automatically find it. This GA-based rule generation method shows a considerable reduction in computational cost. The GA-based framework provides flexibility for the user to define multi-objective fitness [34]. Optimal threshold values for support and confidence are identified using PSO [3, 19]. PSO looks for particles with an optimum fitness value and selects their respective support and confidence values as "best" threshold values to extract useful rules. Weighted Quantum PSO (WQPSO) [11] algorithm is proposed to find optimal threshold values for support and confidence measures. The support and confidence of the particle with the highest fitness value is taken as the "best" values and is taken to the Apriori algorithm as the minimum threshold values for generating association rules. In a single iteration, significant rules are developed using the Firefly algorithm without using the minimum support and confidence thresholds [29, 36].

3.2.2.3   Weight-Based Mining Schemes

The traditional notion of ARM assumes that all data items have equal importance with respect to support. In contrast, each item has its own importance in the dataset. Therefore, weighted frequent itemset mining has been introduced to provide a concept of importance to each item. In addition to support and confidence, it requires the user to assign weights to each item. Two new algorithms are instructed to search out weighted frequent item sets [9]. The items are assigned with weights to mirror their importance to the user. The primary step of those algorithms is to look for the maximum size of the frequent itemsets. These two algorithms support candidate set generation and pruning techniques. A weighted support measure within the MINWAL algorithmic rule is computed by multiplying the support of the itemset with the average weight of the itemset. The working principle of MINWAL is similar to the Apriori algorithm. In literature, several parameters like cost, density, frequency, etc., are considered for deriving the item weight. Generally, parameters considered for setting up weight assignment is purely application dependent but, compulsorily, all items in the database must be assigned with weights for weighted rule mining. WIS algorithm [35] is proposed to derive the weighted rules. In their work, the cost is taken as a weight parameter. Costs are assigned to both items and transactions. Rules which have weighted support greater than a given threshold are selected as interesting ones. In the process of WAR generation, there exist two methods in assigning weights to each item. In the first method, item weights are assigned before generating the rules, whereas in second, after rule generation, weights are assigned to the items. MINWAL (O) and MINWAL (W) algorithms proposed in [9] generate rules with pre-assigned weights. A framework for weighted rule mining with weighted support and significance is planned in [39]. The rules are generated with pre-assigned weights. Wang et al. [45] suggest a way for mining WARs. It generates frequent itemsets while not considering weights initially. WAR works almost like the Apriori algorithm. Generally, weighted rule mining methodology with pre-assigned weights outperforms the not pre-assigned weights by eliminating several frequent supersets resulting in high rule reduction.

3.2.3   Post-Mining Techniques

The Post-mining often competes with a massive number of discovered association rules, and hence, it is very difficult for the user to identify the interesting rules. A most desirable feature of post-mining is to eliminate insignificant and redundant rules from the discovered rule base. Rule pruning, filtering, and processing are the various schemes performed as post-mining techniques.

3.2.3.1 Rule Pruning Schemes

The Post-mining technique mostly deals with pruning operations that occur after the rule generation process. Since pruning is independent of specified mining algorithms, this method has got much attentions which in turn gave the way for the development of several outstanding pruning methods. A technique for pruning and summarizing is proposed to discover association rules by first eliminating the insignificant associations and then forming direction-setting rules [22]. A novel rule filtering model, called rule schemas (RS), is proposed to increase the quality of association rule selection process [26]. User's expectations in terms of interesting/obvious rules are represented using RSs. As an end result, RS expresses the fact that the user expects certain factors to be related within the extracted association rules. Pruning and filtering operators are defined over RSs for reiterating the filtering procedure. Filters are used to remove and preserve redundancy and interesting rules. In literature, numerous filters are available for choosing interesting rules. Minimum Improvement Constraint Filter (MICF) [6] selects rule with confidence greater than the confidence of any of its simplifications. The Item-Relatedness Filter (IRF) [30] introduces the concept of relatedness among items within the antecedent and consequent with the aid of measuring the semantic distance among them using item taxonomies.

3.2.3.2 Schemes Using Knowledge Base

Knowledge bases like ontology and taxonomy are used to organize knowledge in the domain. The knowledge base plays an important role in all KDD steps. Ontology is a theory that concerns the nature and relationships of human beings. Ontologies [10] have gotten a lot of consideration in various domains, such as information retrieval, multiple agent systems, and database design. Ontologies are content concepts about the classes of individuals, the properties of individuals, and the relationship between individuals in a given field of knowledge, while taxonomies are simple class arrangements without restrictions on any property at any level of the hierarchy. Four types of ontologies are proposed in [15]. Srikant and Agrawal [37] are the first to apply taxonomy for mining generalized association rules (GAR). Taxonomy is used to generalize and prune association rules in every step [12]. A GART algorithm is developed to define taxonomies over attributes in order to maintain the relationship between attributes. Liu *et al.* [22] use taxonomy, i.e., an organization for describing the items.

Classification ontology is used to perform dynamic mining of association rules with non-uniform minimum supports constraint [40]. Ontology is used to enhance the knowledge discovery process especially connected to the task of ARM [38]. An integrated framework for extracting association rules using ontology is proposed in [7]. Domain-specific constraints are allowed in the system to define the interesting rules. It is proved that the quality of the extracted association rules is improved in terms of relevance and understandability. Domain Ontology (DO) is used as an instrument to enhance the mining results of association rules [13]. It is obtained that DO reduces the number of generated association rules. The Ontology-based method for ranking unexpected rules is proposed in [16]. This calculates semantic distance based on prior knowledge of context defined by a DO structured as a hierarchy of DAG (Directed Acyclic Graph). An interactive framework for integrating user knowledge in ARM using ontologies and rules schemes is proposed [26]. This integrated method effectively reduces the quantity of rules without having to trade off the consistency of the rules.

3.3 Methodology

In this proposed method, association rules are generated by means of combining pre-mining and put up-mining strategies. Figure 3.1 illustrates the proposed framework used to interactively mine the interesting rules. It incorporates three major phases: pre-mining, association rule generation, and post-mining. In the first phase, pre-mining tasks are performed using PSO and PAW. The second phase involves the generation of rules using Apriori and Weighted Association Rule Mining (WARM) algorithms. In the final phase, DO is created to map the dataset. Based on the subjectivity of the user, operators defined over a set of RSs and filters are designed to post-mine a small subset of useful rules.

3.3.1 Data Preprocessing

The adult data set also known as the Census Income dataset is taken from the repository of UCI machine learning. Using census data, the person's income exceeds $50K/yr or not can be determined. It consists of 14 attributes and 48,842 tuples (training 32,561 and 16,281 test tuples) with many continuous-valued attributes that cannot be taken directly to processing. Only the training tuples are taken for a significant rule mining process.

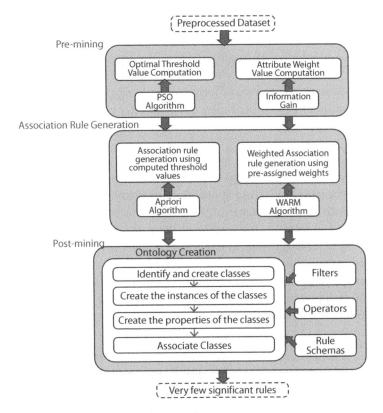

Figure 3.1 Significant rule mining framework.

With Weka 3.7, the continuous-valued attributes of the training tuples (i.e., 32,561) are discretized using discretize filter. As part of data preprocessing, the following are some of the attributes discretized:

- The "Age" attribute which is continuous is discretized into three categorical values, namely, "Young", "Middle-aged", and "Old".
- The "Capital-Gain" and "Capital-Loss" are continuous attributes discretized into three categorical values, namely, High, Low, and Medium.
- The "Hours-Per-Week" attribute is discretized based on the number of hours they work every week into four categorical values, namely, Part-time, Full-time, and Over-time

Even the missing values of the attributes are handled according to the attribute type. The missing values of the categorical attribute are filled with probable value whereas they are filled with the mode/average mean in case of numeric attributes. Continuous attributes such as "Fnlwgt" and "Education number" contain many unique values which can't be discretized. These attributes are removed from the dataset. Redundant tuples generated after discretization are handled properly. Finally, the discretized dataset is converted into binary form for applying pre-mining techniques. Thus, the number of training tuples obtained after preprocessing is 30,675.

3.3.2   Pre-Mining

Data mining is one of the steps used in the KDD process to find patterns. Date preprocessing, selecting appropriate measures, and calculating optimal threshold values are some of the tasks performed before the patterns are extracted to improve the quality of the patterns to be achieved. There are various types of patterns in data mining and the representation of patterns depends on the task of data mining. Each association rule represents a model in the ARM task, whereas classification rule or decision tree is a classification task pattern. Two pre-mining techniques are used independently in conjunction with post-mining to generate interesting rules in this work.

3.3.2.1   Pre-Mining Technique 1: Optimal Support and Confidence Threshold Value Computation Using PSO

PSO is a metaheuristic technique for optimization presented by Kennedy and Eberhart [17]. PSO is motivated by its organizational accomplishment and social behavior. In PSO, a predetermined speed is allocated to every possible solution, called a particle, and the current optimal particles traverse the problem space. PSO is initialized with a collection of particles distributed evenly across the space of the solution. The location of each particle is measured against an objective function. If the particle's current position is better than its previous position than the actual position of the particle is changed. Based on two "best" values, "pbest" and "gbest". Each particle position is modified. "pbest" represents the best solution of a particle achieved so far and "gbest" represents the best solution achieved so far by any particle in the population. Each particle updates its velocity and position using Equations (3.1) and (3.2).

$$V_i^{t+1} = \omega V_i^t + c_1 r_1 \left(pb_i^t - x_i^t \right) + c_2 r_2 \left(gb^t - x_i^t \right) \qquad (3.1)$$

$$x_i^{t+1} = x_i^t + V_i^{t+1} \qquad (3.2)$$

Where,

- V_i^{t+1} the ith particle's velocity at time instance $t+1$.
- V_i^t the ith particle's velocity at time instance t.
- ω is the inertia weight.
- r_2 and r_2 are random numbers, $0 \le r_1 \le 1, 0 \le r_2 \le 1$.
- c_1 and c_2 are learning parameters generally set as $c_1 = c_2 = 2$.
- x_i represents the current solution of the particle.
- pb_i represents the particle-best.
- gb represents the global best solution.

The pre-processed dataset is initially converted into binary form, and then, the partition point is determined for each tuple. Using the method [19], PSO is used as a module that calculates the best fitness value. In the following steps, the process for representing the chromosome, measuring the fitness value, generating the population, and determining the best criterion for particle and its termination is explained.

Binary Transformation and Chromosome Encoding: Each tuple of the data set is converted to a binary form that is 0 or 1. The value of the attribute in the tuple is indicated by 1 and the absence is indicated by 0. Each tuple is taken as a particle and it is encoded by a string encoding approach. Since the dataset considered here, is of non-transactional type, all the tuples are of the same length. In order to calculate the fitness value for each chromosome, i.e., an association rule, the tuples must choose the front and back partition points. According to the definition, if P→Q is an association rule, then the intersection of antecedent (P) and consequent (Q) must be empty, i.e., attributes/items in the antecedent(P) do not appear in the consequent(Q), and vice versa. This property is used to fix the front and back tuple partition points. Front and back partition points are selected in such a way that the attribute intersection before the front partition point (taken as antecedent "P") and the attributes among the front and back partition points (taken as consequent "Q") must be null.

Fitness value calculation: The fitness value computation is performed to determine the particle's optimality. The quality of fitness value is achieved from the fitness function. The fitness value can be intended either to maximize or minimize fitness function. The fitness function (3.3) used in [18] is taken to determine the fitness value of the association rule P→Y.

$$Maximise\ (Fitness_a\ (P{\rightarrow}Y))=Conf_a(P{\rightarrow}Y)^*\quad \log(Supp_a(P{\rightarrow}Y)^*Leng_a\ (P{\rightarrow}Y)+1$$

$$(3.3)$$

Where

- $Conf_a(P \rightarrow Y)$ signifies the confidence of the association rule $P \rightarrow Y$ of type "a".
- $(Supp_a (P \rightarrow Y)$ signifies the support of the association rule $P \rightarrow Y$ of type "a".
- $Leng_a (P \rightarrow Y)$ signifies the length of association rule $P \rightarrow Y$ of type "a".

The binary dataset is arranged into a two-dimensional matrix where the rows represent tuples and the columns represent attribute values.

Population Generation: The initial population consists of particles having greater fitness values. When convergence has to be quicker, the population size should be large.

Particle Updation: First, the highest fitness particle is taken as the "best". The initial position of each particle is taken as "pbest". The initial position of the particle will be updated using the cognitive and social variable values [Equations (3.1) and (3.2)].

Termination Condition: The termination condition is needed to complete the evolution of the particles. The evolution cycle can only be halted if the fitness of all particles in a population is the same and the solution obtained is not enhanced or if it exceeds the maximum number of iterations that is set as a termination limit. The particle with maximum objective function value shall be considered as the best particle after the end condition. Support and confidence values of the best particle are taken as the threshold values for the minimum support and confidence measures.

3.3.2.2   Pre-Mining Technique 2: Attribute Weight Computation Using IG Measure

A new form of ARM using attribute weights is proposed in [9]. Each attribute is given with appropriate weight based on its importance. Some attributes are more profitable and their existence contributes significant knowledge, and hence, rules having these attributes are of greater value for decision-making. ARM with respect to the significance of the attributes may be desirable to generate interesting rules.

In this work, an effort is made to minimize the number of rules, by generating WARs using attribute significance as weight parameter. Since the dataset considered in this work is of binary class multidimensional, non-transactional in nature. Each and every non-class attribute contain information about the classification attribute and they play significant role in classification. Hence, determining the attribute significance is an essential task to mine interesting rules. IG, Gain ratio, and Gini index are some of the attribute selection measures used to determine the attribute significance. IG is one in which it selects a significant attribute by calculating the IG with respect to the class attribute. It is more suited for the binary class datasets containing attributes with few distinct values. IG value of an attribute "A" containing "m" values is computed using Equations (3.4), (3.5), and (3.6).

$$IG(A) = I(p,n)-E(A) \tag{3.4}$$

$$E(A) = -\sum_{i=1}^{m} \frac{p_i + n_i}{p+n} I(p_i, n_i) \tag{3.5}$$

$$I(p,n) = -\frac{p}{p+n} \log_2 \frac{p}{p+n} - \frac{n}{p+n} \log_2 \frac{n}{p+n} \tag{3.6}$$

Where
- $E(A)$ represents attribute entropy of the dataset.
- $I(p,n)$ represents the expected information required to satisfy a given dataset.
- p represents the total positive tuples of the dataset.
- n represents the total negative tuples of the dataset.
- p_i represents the number of positive tuples covered by the ith value of the attribute A, which is to be included in the rule-antecedent.
- n_i represents the number of negative tuples covered by the ith value of the attribute A, which is to be included in the rule-antecedent.
- m represents the number of values of an attribute "A".

In literature, it is found that the Gain ratio measure computes the significance of an attribute without examining other attributes. If the attributes are highly independent, then the Gain ratio will select inappropriate attributes as "best" [25]. At times, the selection of many irrelevant attributes may overrule significant attributes. Presence of many insignificant attributes in the dataset will have a negative influence on the quality of the association rules generated. Though Gini Index is one of the best alternatives of IG used for attribute selection, but it is biased towards multivalued attributes. It selects a large number of attributes and finds it complicated in selecting the attributes when the number of classes is large [23]. Comparing the Gain ratio and Gini index, IG is found to be the best attribute selection measure. The significance of all the attributes with respect to class attribute is calculated using IG measure (4). The calculated IG value is compared with the user-specified significance threshold. Attributes with IG value higher than or equal to the threshold are retained and the rest are ignored. This process of attribute selection naturally reduces the number of attributes in the dataset. This eventually reduces the quantity of weighted frequent itemsets and rules generated as compared to the other classical rule mining techniques.

3.3.3   Association Rule Generation

This section discusses the rule generation using Apriori and WARM algorithms which are applied after pre-mining techniques 1 and 2, respectively.

3.3.3.1   ARM Preliminaries

An association rule can be mathematically represented as follows:

> Definition 1. An association rule is defined as the implication $P{\rightarrow}Q$, where P and Q are two disjoint itemsets, P is known as antecedent/condition of the rule, and Q is known as consequent/conclusion of the rule. The number of items in an itemset represents the length of an itemset. An itemset is of length k and is referred to as k-itemset.
>
> Definition 2. A rule $P{\rightarrow}Q$ is described using two important measures such as support and confidence.

$$Support\left(P \rightarrow Q\right)=\frac{support\left(P\bigcup Q\right)}{T} \tag{3.7}$$

> Where, T is the number of tuples of a dataset and is the ratio of tuples which support antecedent and consequent of the association rule and the total number of tuples within the dataset.

$$Confidence\left(P \rightarrow Q\right) = \frac{Support\left(P \cup Q\right)}{Support\left(P\right)} \qquad (3.8)$$

It is defined as the percentage of tuples that support both the rule antecedent and the consequent out of all tuples that support the rule antecedent.

Definition 3. An itemset (P) whose support is equal to or above the agreed minimum support is said to be frequent/large.

$$Support \ (P) \geq minsupport \qquad (3.9)$$

Definition 4. Any subset of a frequent/large itemset should be frequent/large itemset. This is said to Apriori/Downward closure property.

Definition 5. A rule is said to be an interesting rule if its confidence is equal to or greater than an agreed minimum threshold value referred to as a confidence threshold.

$$Confidence \ (P \rightarrow Q) \geq minconf \qquad (3.10)$$

Apriori algorithm

Apriori algorithm is one of the commonly used algorithms for rule mining [10]. A common strategy of the Apriori algorithm is to break the problem into two main sub-tasks:

- Frequent Itemset Generation: Frequent itemsets are itemsets that satisfy the minimum support threshold are generated.
- Rule Generation: All high confidence rules are derived from the frequent itemsets. These are called strong rules.

Different interestingness measures are used to haul out frequent itemsets and strong rules. In general, support and confidence are the two primary measures that are used to generate interesting rules. Usually, in a multidimensional dataset, Apriori generates a huge number of candidate itemsets on each iteration which in turn generates a huge volume of rules corresponding to a specific attribute. With respect to a particular business objective, utilizing these association rules for extracting interesting affinities among attributes of a dataset is difficult. Moreover, the relevant mining information may be hidden within the rules, which is complex to query. Setting the support and confidence thresholds also plays a crucial role and it influences the number of rules produced by the Apriori algorithm. Hence, setting the optimal threshold values for support and confidence puts the users in the problem. In this work, as an attempt, this problem is resolved using PSO. Before rule generation, the computation of optimal threshold values for support and confidence is done as a pre-mining activity. To generate significant rules, the optimal threshold values obtained using PSO are taken into the Apriori algorithm.

3.3.3.2   WARM Preliminaries

A WAR can be mathematically represented as follows:

> Definition 6. Each and every attribute/item is assigned with attribute/item weight, w, where $0 \leq w \leq 1$. "w" defines the significance of the attributes. 0 and 1 represent the least and most important attributes, respectively.
>
> Definition 7. A WAR is defined as the implication $P \rightarrow Q$, where P and Q are two disjoint itemsets, P is called as antecedent/condition of the weighted rule, and Q is called as consequent/conclusion of the weighted rule. Each attribute/item in P and Q are assigned with weights.
>
> Definition 8. A WAR $P \rightarrow Q$ is described with two important measures such as weighted support (*wsupport*) and weighted confidence (*wconfidence*).

$$wsupport(P \rightarrow Q) = \left(\sum_{i_j \in P \cup Q} w_j \right) \frac{support\left(P \cup Q \right)}{T} \qquad (3.11)$$

Where, $\{w_1, w_2, ..., w_n\}$ are the assigned weights of the attributes $\{i_1, i_2, ..., i_n\}$ present in both P and Q. T is the number of tuples of the dataset and is the ratio of aggregated weights of attributes in the antecedent and consequent of the WAR present in the number of tuples and the total number of tuples of the dataset. It is the adjusting ratio of support.

$$wconfidence\left(P \rightarrow Q\right) = \frac{wsupport\left(P \bigcup Q\right)}{wsupport\left(P\right)} \qquad (3.12)$$

wconfidence is the ratio of the sum of attribute weights in the antecedent and consequent of the WAR present in the number of tuples to the sum of attribute weights present in the antecedent in the number of tuples.

Definition 9. An itemset(P) is said to be frequent/large weighted itemset if its weighted support is equal or greater than an agreed-upon minimal weighted threshold value which is referred as the weighted support threshold.

$$wsupport\ (P) \geq wminsupport \qquad (3.13)$$

Definition 10. Every subset of a weighted frequent/large itemset may not be weighted frequent/large itemset. i.e., the downward closure property does not hold in weighted rule mining.

$$wsupport\ (P) \geq min\ (wsupport\ (P_1), wsupport\ (P_2),..., wsupport\ (P_m)) \qquad (3.14)$$

Where, $\{P_1, P_2,...,P_m\}$ are subsets of P, where P is the weighted frequent/large itemset.

Lemma 1. In order to support downward closure property, the definition for weighted frequent/large itemset is modified as follows:

An itemset P is said to weighted frequent/large itemset, if P must satisfy the following condition

$$supportcount\left(P\right) \geq \frac{wminsupport\ ^*\ T}{\sum_{i_j \in\ P} w_j} \qquad (3.15)$$

Where, P is the j-itemset, i.e., contains j-items $\{i_1, i_2...,i_j\}$, *supportcount* (P) s the correct number of tuples contains P,

T is the number of tuples of the dataset, and $\sum w_j$ is the sum of the weights of "j" items in the itemset P. $_{i_j \in P}$

Definition 11. A WAR $P \rightarrow Q$ is said to be an interesting weighted rule, where its weighted confidence is equal to or greater than the agreed minimum weighted threshold value referred to as the weighted confidence threshold.

$$wconfidence(P \rightarrow Q) \geq wminconfidence \qquad (3.16)$$

WARM Algorithm

Many techniques have been proposed to generate interesting and non-redundant rules by reducing the quantity of insignificant rules. One such technique is to assign weights to dataset attributes. In weighted rule mining, several parameters like cost, density, frequency, etc., are considered for deriving the attribute/item weight. Weight computation based on the item cost, frequency, and density is appropriate for a transactional dataset, whereas it does not suit for a non-transactional dataset. Mostly assigned weights of the attributes are treated as uniformly important. Weights are assigned to the attributes to represent their essentialness to the user [24]. There are a couple of techniques for analyzing datasets with weighted settings. Hence, weight computation using attribute significance is indispensable for a binary class, multidimensional, non-transactional dataset. There exist two methods in assigning weights to each item. In the first method, attribute/items weights are assigned initially, i.e., before generating the rules whereas in second, after rule generation, weights are assigned to the attributes/items.

MINWAL [9] is one of the well-known WARM algorithms analogous to the Apriori algorithm. Similar to Apriori, the strategy adopted by MINWAL algorithm is to decompose the problem into two major sub-tasks:

- Weighted frequent/large itemset generation.
- WAR generation using obtained weighted frequent itemsets.

In this work, the IG value of the attribute is taken as attribute weight. The preprocessed binary form of the dataset with attribute weights is taken as input for the WAR generation process. The steps involved in the generation of WARs are explained as follows:

Candidate Set Generation: Initially, support of the 1-itemset is calculated by scanning the database. The *wsupport* of 1-itemsets is calculated using their supports and attribute weights (3.11). The 1-itemsets whose *wsupport* qualify the *wminsupport* value are taken as weighted frequent/large itemsets (3.13). Because of its inherent nature of weighted rule mining, weighted frequent itemsets does not hold the downward closure property (3.14); hence, all weighted frequent itemsets produced cannot be taken for next level candidate set generation.

k-Support Bound Calculation: In order to bring downward closure property in weighted rule mining, the k-support bound is introduced. It is used to generate a candidate set for higher-level weighted frequent itemsets. It is calculated using (3.17) and (3.18).

Let I be the itemset, containing all attributes/items. Y represents a q-itemset, where $q < k$. In the set of remaining items $(I - Y)$, let the items with the $(k - q)$ greatest weights be $i_{r_1}, i_{r_2}, \ldots, i_{r_{k-q}}$. The maximum possible weight for any k-itemset containing Y is

$$W(Y,k) = \sum_{i_j \in Y} w_j + \sum_{j=1}^{k-q} w_{r_j} \qquad (3.17)$$

Where, $\sum_{i_j \in Y} w_j$ is the sum of the weights for the q-itemset Y, and the $\sum_{j=1}^{k-q} w_{r_j}$ is the sum of the $(k - q)$ maximum remaining weights.

The k-support bound(B) of item set Y is given by:

$$B(Y,k) = \frac{wminsupport * T}{W(Y,k)} \qquad (3.18)$$

Where, *wminsupport* s weighted support threshold, T is the total number of tuples in the dataset and $W(Y, k)$ calculated using (3.17). The inequality given in (3.14) is the lower bound on the minimum count for the weighted frequent itemsets and k-support bound (3.18) is taken as upper bound. The itemsets whose support count qualifies the lower

and upper bound are taken as candidates for the next iteration to generate higher-level weighted frequent itemsets.

WAR Generation: Once the weighted frequent itemset generation process stops, interesting WARs are generated from the
obtained weighted frequent itemsets using *wminconfidence*
(3.16).

3.3.4 Post-Mining

The most desirable feature of post-mining is to eliminate insignificant
and redundant rules from the discovered rule base. Post-mining tasks are
carried out by the end-user to analyze and interpret the discovered rules.
Knowledge-based interactive post-mining of rule framework is proposed
in [26]. DO is designed in this work as an attempt to map the dataset.
Protégé 3.4.1 is open source software that is used for ontology development. The DO is composed of dataset concepts. The ontology defines the
vocabulary of the concepts. Each concept is represented as class and it can
have any number of sub-classes. The sub-classes are used to represent the
properties of classes. Instances are created for each sub-class and dataset values are mapped to the respective sub-classes. Object and data type
properties are provided for the ontology classes. The classes are created
along with their instances.

The post-mining technique mostly deals with filtering and pruning
operations that occur after the rule generation process. With respect to the
users' need and their subjectivity, the end-users use filters and operators
defined over a set of RSs to mine the small subset of preferred association
rules. The filters and operators defined over a set of RSs are used to perform interactive post-mining of rules using user and domain knowledge.

3.3.4.1 Filters

In the literature survey, several filters were used to remove the redundant
rule. Two popular filters used in this work are MICF [6] and IRF [30].

Minimum Improvement Constraint Filter (MICF): MICF chooses the
rules with greater confidence than any of its simplifications. Using the
example below, it is explained:

For example, the following are the three association rules considered:

Age=young,Marital_status=married→ Education=Post_Graduate
(conf: 85%)

Age=young →Education=Post_Graduate   (conf: 90%)

Marital_status=married→Education=Post_Graduate   (conf:83%)

The last two rules are the simplifications of the first one. From the principle in [6], the first rule is only interesting if its confidence is higher than the confidence of all its simplifications. In this case, the first rule does not suit the principle, and therefore, it is considered as an irrelevant rule and can be excluded from the rule set.

Item Relatedness Filter: Semantic distance between attributes/items in the respective taxonomies/ontologies specifies the relatedness of the attributes. There are three ways in measuring the relatedness:

- Between attributes in the antecedent.
- Between attributes in the consequent.
- Attributes between antecedent and consequent of the rule.

Most interesting is the last type of item relatedness (IR) used to find the interaction between item sets that have different functionalities from different domains. A rule is said to be uninteresting if a minimum semantic distance or minimum path exists between the antecedent and the consequent of the rules. Uninteresting rules can be excluded from the discovered rule set. It is explained using the Adult dataset ontology and the association rule R1, given below, a part of ontology is shown in Figure 3.2.

R1:   Age=young,Marital_status=Married→Education=Post_Graduate

IR(R1) = min{d (Young,Post_Graduate),d(Married,Post_Graduate)}
       = min{4,4} = 4

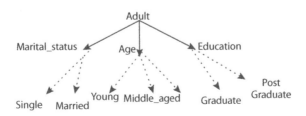

Figure 3.2 Visualization of part of ontology created for adult dataset.

3.3.4.2   Operators

The post-mining depends on the operators that apply over the RSs. In the post-mining process, four operators are employed. These are as follows:

Pruning: When using a pruning operator P over the rule schema RS, P(RS), all association rules that fit the rule schema(RS) are excluded from the rule set that has been found.

Conforming: When using a conforming operator C over rule schema RS, C(RS), the discovered rule set extracts all association rules that fit the rule schema(RS).

Unexpectedness: When using a unexpectedness operator U over rule schema RS, U(RS), all unexpected rules with respect to the consequent, antecedent and to both sides are discovered from the discovered rule set.

Exceptions: When using an exception operator E over implicative rule schema RS(A→B), E(RS), all association rules that match the new implicative rule schema A∩Z→¬ B, are discovered from the discovered rule set, where Z is a set of items.

3.3.4.3   Rule Schemas

The language of specialization in the form of RS is introduced in [22]. A rule schema defines user expectations in terms of rules. Using these rules schemas, the discovered rules are filtered. The types of rule are given below with respect to the RSs:

Conforming rule: A discovered rule $R_i \in R$ is said to be conforming with the user's knowledge/specification $U_j \in U$, if both the antecedent and consequent parts of R_i exactly match those of $U_j \in U$.

Unexpected rule: There are three types of unexpected rules that could be generated after post-mining; these rules are unexpected with respect to the consequent, antecedent, and both sides. They are extracted from the discovered rule set.

- Unexpected consequent rules: A discovered rule $R_i \in R$ is said to be the unexpected consequent rule, where it has an unexpected consequent part with respect to the user's knowledge/specification $U_j \in U$ and antecedent part of R_i exactly matches U_j, but not the consequent part.

- Unexpected antecedent rules: A discovered rule $R_i \in R$ is said to be the unexpected antecedent rule, where it has an unexpected antecedent part with respect to the user's knowledge/specification $U_j \in U$ and consequent part of R_i exactly matches U_j, but not the antecedent part.
- Both-side unexpected rules: A discovered rule $R_i \in R$ is said to be both-side unexpected rule/totally unexpected rule with respect to the user's knowledge/specification $U_j \in U$ where both the antecedent and consequent parts of the rule R_i do not match U_j.

3.4 Experiments and Results

Experiments are carried out using the Adult dataset from the UCI machine learning repository having 32,561 training tuples with 14 attributes. Using Weka 3.7, the data reduction and transformation techniques are applied to preprocess the dataset. After preprocessing, the number of tuples is reduced to 30,674. The preprocessed dataset is then transformed into a binary format consisting of 112 binary attributes. The binary form of the dataset is then taken for pre-mining tasks. After pre-mining, rules are generated from the dataset. Further, the post-mining tasks are carried out to mine the user-defined rules. In this paper, two works (listed in Table 3.1)

Table 3.1 Combination of pre-mining and post-mining carried out in this work.

Work	Pre-mining tasks	Rule generation algorithm	Post-mining tasks
1	Optimal threshold values (i.e., Minimum Support and Confidence) computation using PSO	Apriori algorithm with optimal threshold values	• Creation of Domain Ontology to map the dataset. • Filters and operators defined over rules schemas.
2	Attribute weight computation using Information Gain (IG) measure	MINWAL, an Apriori-based WARM algorithm with attribute weights	• Creation of Domain Ontology to map the dataset. • Filters and operators defined over rules schemas.

are carried out to analyze the impact of pre-mining and post-mining techniques in generating significant rules.

3.4.1   Parameter Settings for PSO-Based Pre-Mining Technique

There are several strategies proposed for inertia weight settings [4]. The basic PSO, presented in [17], has no inertia weight. In this work, basic PSO is applied. r_1 and r_2 are random numbers that take the value 0.5. c_1 and c_2 are learning parameters which is set as $c_1 = c_2 = 2$. The parameters such as the swarm size and minimum threshold fitness value are set as 100 and 0.5. The termination criterion is set as "no improvement observed for 20 iterations (i.e., similar fitness value achieved for 20 consecutive iterations)" or the maximum number of iterations reached. Here, the maximum number of iterations is set as 100. Different types of association rules with respect to the length of antecedent and consequent parts of the rule are generated from the preprocessed dataset using front and back partition points. The position of these points is fixed in each tuple in such a way that intersection of attributes before front partition, i.e., antecedent and attributes between front and back partition, i.e., consequent must be null. Fixing front and back partition points in each tuple generates different types of association rules. The fitness value of each rule/particle is calculated using Equation (3.3). The position of each particle in the population is updated using Equations (3.1) and (3.2). At every iteration, the termination condition is verified.

Table 3.2 presents the optimal threshold values obtained for support and confidence using PSO. The fitness value of the 10 particles obtained in the 20th iteration is shown in Table 3.2. From the results, it is found that similar fitness values obtained for most of the particles. Average fitness values are also converged, and hence, the optimization process stops at 20th iteration. After 20th iteration, the support and confidence of the best particle, i.e., the particle with highest fitness value (0.145482) is taken as optimal threshold values and they are taken into the Apriori algorithm. Apriori algorithm with PSO generated optimal threshold values is applied over the Adult dataset to extract interesting rules. There are 2,936 rules that are generated from the dataset satisfying the optimal threshold values.

3.4.2   Parameter Settings for PAW-Based Pre-Mining Technique

Simultaneously, the second pre-mining task using IG is performed over the binary form of preprocessed datasets. The significance of the attributes with respect to class attribute is calculated using IG measure (3.4). As a

Table 3.2 Optimal threshold values generated by PSO.

Particle	Support	Confidence	Fitness
1	0.033656	0.040038	0.137476
2	**0.077241**	**0.177982**	**0.145482**
3	0.077971	0.192171	0.126918
4	0.078234	0.199823	0.128998
5	0.080123	0.21234	0.136789
6	0.080124	0.21239	0.136788
7	0.080120	0.21234	0.136787
8	0.080125	0.21246	0.136789
9	0.080122	0.21223	0.136786
10	0.080123	0.21223	0.136786

sample, IG values obtained for the attributes are shown in Table 3.3. After applying the IG measure, it found that many attributes have zero as its gain value. Attributes with zero IG values are removed. After the removal of zero significant attributes, only 79 attributes out of 112 are retained. The obtained IG values for these 79 attributes are pre-assigned as their corresponding weights.

MINWAL, a popular Apriori-based WARM algorithm, is applied over 79 binary attributes to generate WARs using attribute weights. If the weighted support threshold and weighted confidence threshold is set with the same threshold values obtained in the pre-mining technique 1, 310 interesting WARs are extracted from the dataset (i.e., S = 0.077241 and C = 0.177982).

From the experiments, it is observed that the WARM algorithm produces the best outcomes in terms of a small set of significant rules generated. WARM generates 310 rules whereas the Apriori algorithm yields 2,936 strong rules for the same dataset. The number of rules generated after pre-mining tasks is still high and is relatively unrealistic for the end-users to acknowledge or authenticate such a huge number of association rules.

In order to encourage the usefulness of the rule mining results, the discovered rules are taken into post-mining tasks individually. DO, filters, and operators defined over RSs are designed to perform knowledge-based interactive post-mining of rules. Two filters such as MICF and IRF are applied over the discovered rules to eliminate the redundant and

Table 3.3 Gain values obtained using IG measure.

S. No.	Attribute	IG value
1	Marital-status=Married-civ-spouse	0.152744
2	Relationship=Husband	0.117468
3	Age=Young	0.065486
4	Capital-gain=High	0.043517
5	Sex=female	0.03745
6	Hours-per-Week=Over-time	0.036201
7	Occupation= Exec-managerial	0.028943
8	Education= Bachelors	0.020925
9	Capital-loss=high	0.012941
10	Work-class= Self-emp-inc	0.011715

uninteresting rules. Table 3.4 shows the number of rules along with the percentage of rules retained after various combinations of filters such as MICF and IRF.

Table 3.4 shows that the combination of MICF and IRF filters at most reduces the 80% of rules in the WARM rule set whereas only 66% of rules are reduced in the Apriori rule set. The four possible combinations of filters are applied to the initial rule set for each RS. From Table 3.4, it is identified that the combination of MICF and IRF filters yields better PAW-DO performance. Based on the domain knowledge and user's subjectivity, nine RSs are designed. The conforming and pruning operators defined over these RSs are given in Table 3.5.

Table 3.4 Number of rules obtained for each filter combination.

Combos	MICF	IRF	No. of rules generated	
			PSO + DO	PAW + DO
1			2936(100%)	310(100%)
2	*		1756(60%)	117(38%)
3		*	2105(72%)	206(66%)
4	*	*	996(34%)	61(20%)

Table 3.5 User-defined rule schemas with operators.

User-defined rule schemas	Operator	Meaning
RS1: <Relationship → Sex>	$U_a(RS1)$	Unexpected antecedent
RS2: <Age, Race → Occupation>	$U_a(RS2)$	Unexpected antecedent
RS3: <Sex, Race→ Class>	$U_a(RS3)$	Unexpected antecedent
RS4: <Hours-per-week, Capital-gain→ Class>	$U_c(RS4)$	Unexpected consequent
RS5: <Work-class,Capital-gain→ Race>	$U_c(RS5)$	Unexpected consequent
RS6: <Occupation, Education → Sex>	P(RS6)	Pruning
RS7: <Sex, Native-Country →Class>	P(RS7)	Pruning
RS8: <Marital-status, Occupation → Class>	C(RS8)	Conforming
RS9: <Hours-per-week→Capital-gain>	C(RS9)	Conforming

DO-based rule mining process has been implemented in this work, which relies on an interactive loop where the user controls and guides the whole post-mining process. This post-mining process helps the user to analyze the task and allows the user to reiterate the filtering process for selecting the relevant rules. The number of rules obtained for each scheme of rules is given in Table 3.6.

3.5   Conclusions

In this work, the basics of the association rule and weighted rule mining techniques have been reviewed. It addresses the issues of significant rule mining. It also gave a walkthrough of the pre-mining and post-mining techniques used to generate significant rules. Two different pre-mining techniques are developed to generate significant rules. In addition, interactive post-mining based on DO was carried out using user-defined RSs with operators. In the pre-mining techniques, objective measures such as support, confidence, and significance were used while post-mining deals with subjective measures such as unexpectedness and actionability. Parameters such as support and confidence and its threshold values are identified and they greatly influence the performance of the Apriori

Table 3.6 Number of rules obtained for user-defined rule schemas over operators.

Combos	U_a(RS1)		U_a(RS2)		U_a(RS3)		U_c(RS4)		U_c(RS5)		P(RS6)		P(RS7)		C(RS8)		C(RS9)	
	PSO -DO	PAW -DO	PSO -DO	PAW -DO	PSO -DO	PAW -DO	PSO -DO	PAW -DO	PSO -DO	PAW -DO	PSO -DO	PAW DO	PSO -DO	PAW DO	PSO -DO	PAW -DO	PSO -DO	PAW -DO
1	2380	276	2215	243	1678	164	1258	146	2156	208	2390	245	2468	260	468	68	256	36
2	1123	58	976	68	882	72	874	45	956	78	1342	52	1432	59	256	32	142	22
3	1454	112	1123	86	1102	124	1003	82	1212	89	1714	132	1856	146	312	41	168	34
4	654	43	651	49	554	33	452	28	250	51	612	47	796	51	104	18	13	12

PSO-DO [PSO and Domain Ontology(DO)] –Combination of PSO in pre-mining task and Domain Ontology (DO) in post-mining task.
PAW-DO [PAW and Domain Ontology(DO)]- Combination of PAW in pre-mining task and Domain Ontology (DO) in post-mining task.

algorithm. PSO, an evolutionary algorithm, has been used to calculate optimal support and confidence threshold values. The results show that the performance of the Apriori algorithm using PSO calculated threshold values has been improved in terms of the rules generated. In addition, this work identifies the limitations of the traditional ARM model. In particular, all items/attributes in the dataset are treated equally by considering the presence and absence of an item in the transaction/tuple. In order to treat all attributes fairly, it was suggested that a new parameter called IG value should be used as attribute weights in WARM. Experimental results have proved legitimate and justify the effectiveness of the strategy of weighted rule mining. For the set of user-defined rules, it is noted that PAW-DO offers better results than PSO-DO. Finally, the combination of pre-mining and post-mining techniques reduces the excessive amount of rules without jeopardizing the utility factor. This work bridges the gap between pre-mining and post-mining techniques and shows the potential for joint application to reduce the amount of rules and increase rule mining computational efficiency. This research can also be applied to boost WARM's efficacy and equate it with other significant metrics such as the Gini index and the Gain ratio. Filters other than MICF and IRF may also be used to improve the post-mining process.

References

1. Agrawal, R., Imieliński, T., Swami, A., Mining association rules between sets of items in large databases. in: *Proc. ACM SIGMOD international conference on Management of data*, vol. 22, pp. 207–216, ACM, 1993.
2. Agrawal, R. and Srikant, R., Fast algorithms for mining association rules, in: *Proc. 20th int. conf. very large data bases*, vol. 1215, VLDB, pp. 487–499, 1994.
3. Asadi, A., Shojaei, A., Saeidi, S., Karimi, S., Karimi, E., A new method for the discovery of the best threshold value for finding positive or negative association rules using Binary Particle Swarm Optimization. *Int. J. Comput. Sci. Issues*, 9, 315–320, 2012.
4. Bansal, J. C., Singh, P. K., Saraswat, M., Verma, A., Jadon, S. S., Abraham, A., Inertia weight strategies in particle swarm optimization. in: *Proc. 3rd world congress on nature and biologically inspired computing*, pp. 633–640, IEEE, 2011.
5. Bayardo, R.J., Jr., Efficiently mining long patterns from databases, in: *Proc. ACM SIGMOD international conference on Management of data*, vol. 27, pp. 85–93, ACM, 1998.
6. Bayardo, R.J., Agrawal, R., Gunopulos, D., Constraint-based rule mining in large, dense databases, in: *Proceedings 15th International Conference on Data Engineering (Cat. No. 99CB36337)*, IEEE, pp. 188–197, 1999.

7. Bellandi, A., Furletti, B., Grossi, V., Romei, A., Ontology-driven association rule extraction: A case study, in: *Proc. workshop on Contexts and Ontologies Representation and Reasoning*, pp. 10–19, 2007.

8. Burdick, D., Calimlim, M., Gehrke, J., Mafia: A maximal frequent itemset algorithm for transactional databases, in: *ICDE*, vol. 1, pp. 443–452, 2001.

9. Cai, C.H., Fu, A.W.C., Cheng, C.H., Kwong, W.W., Mining association rules with weighted items. In *Proc. IDEAS'98. International Database Engineering and Applications Symposium (Cat. No. 98EX156)*, pp. 68–77, IEEE, 1998.

10. Chandrasekaran, B., Josephson, J. R., Benjamins, V. R, What are ontologies, and why do we need them?, *IEEE. Intell. Syst.*, 14, 1, 22–26, 1999.

11. Deepa, S. and Kalimuthu, M., An optimization of association rule mining algorithm using weighted quantum behaved PSO. *Int. J. Power Control Signal Comput.*, 3, 1, 80–85, 2012.

12. Domingues, M.A. and Rezende, S.O., Using taxonomies to facilitate the analysis of the association rules. *arXiv preprint arXiv*, 1112, 1734, 2011.

13. Ferraz, I.N. and Garcia, A.C.B., Ontology In Association Rules Preprocessing And Post-Processing, in: *IADIS European Conf. Data Mining*, pp. 87–91, 2008.

14. Geng, L. and Hamilton, H.J., Interestingness measures for data mining: A survey, in: *ACM Computing Surveys (CSUR)*, vol. 38, p. 9, 2006.

15. Guarino, N., (Ed) Formal ontology in information systems. *Proceedings of the first international conference (FOIS'98)*, Trento, Italy, June 6-8, vol. 46, IOS press, 1998.

16. Hamani, M.S. and Maamri, R., Ontology-Driven Method for Ranking Unexpected Rules, in: *CIIA*, 2009.

17. Kennedy, D.J. and Eberhart, R., Particle swarm optimization, in: *Proceedings of IEEE International Conference on Neural Networks*, pp. 1942–1948, 1995.

18. Kung, S.H., *Applying genetic algorithm and weight item to association rule Doctoral dissertation, Master Thesis*, Department of Industrial Engineering and Management, Yuan Ze University, Taiwan, 2002.

19. Kuo, R.J., Chao, C.M., Chiu, Y.T., Application of particle swarm optimization to association rule mining. *Appl. Soft Comput.*, 11, 1, 326–336, 2011.

20. Ling, C.X., Chen, T., Yang, Q., Cheng, J., Mining optimal actions for profitable CRM, in: *2002 IEEE International Conference on Data Mining*, IEEE, pp. 767–770, Proceedings, 2002.

21. Liu, B., Hsu, W., Chen, S., Using General Impressions to Analyze Discovered Classification Rules, in: *KDD*, pp. 31–36, 1997.

22. Liu, B., Hsu, W., Mun, L.F., Lee, H.Y., Finding interesting patterns using user expectations. *IEEE. T. Knowl. Data. En.*, 11, 6, 817–832, 1999.

23. Liu, T., Liu, S., Chen, Z., Ma, W.Y., An evaluation on feature selection for text clustering, in: *Proceedings of the 20th international conference on machine learning (ICML-03)*, pp. 488–495, 2003.

24. Lu, S., Hu, H., Li, F., Mining weighted association rules. *Intell. Data Anal*, 5, 3, 211–225, 2001.

25. Mahmood, A. M., Kuppa, M. R., Reddi, K. K., A New decision tree induction using composite splitting criterion, *J. Appl. Comput. Sci. Math.*, 9, 4, 67–71, 2010.

26. Marinica, C. and Guillet, F., Knowledge-based interactive postmining of association rules using ontologies. *IEEE. T. Knowl. Data. En.*, 22, 6, 784–797, 2010.

27. McGarry, K., A survey of interestingness measures for knowledge discovery. *Knowl. Eng. Rev.*, 20, 1, 39–61, 2005.

28. Nandhini, M., Janani, M., Sivanandham, S.N., Association rule mining using swarm intelligence and domain ontology, in: *Proc. International Conference on Recent Trends in Information Technology*, pp. 537–541, IEEE, 2012.

29. Nandhini, M., Rajalakshmi, M., Sivanandam, S. N., Experimental and statistical analysis on the performance of firefly based predictive association rule classifier for health care data diagnosis. *Control. Eng. Appl. Inf.*, 19, 2, 101–110, 2017.

30. Natarajan, R. and Shekar, B., A relatedness-based data-driven approach to determination of interestingness of association rules, in: *Proceedings of the 2005 ACM symposium on Applied computing*, pp. 551–552, ACM, 2005.

31. Pasquier, N., Bastide, Y., Taouil, R., Lakhal, L., Discovering frequent closed itemsets for association rules, in: *International Conference on Database Theory*, Springer, Berlin, Heidelberg, pp. 398–416, 1999.

32. Pei, J., Han, J., Mao, R., Closet: An efficient algorithm for mining frequent closed itemsets, in: *ACM SIGMOD workshop on research issues in data mining and knowledge discovery*, vol. 4, pp. 21–30, 2000.

33. Psaila, G., Discovery of association rule meta-patterns, in: *International Conference on Data Warehousing and Knowledge Discovery*, Springer, Berlin, Heidelberg, pp. 219–228, 1999.

34. Qodmanan, H.R., Nasiri, M., Minaei-Bidgoli, B., Multi objective association rule mining with genetic algorithm without specifying minimum support and minimum confidence. *Expert. Syst. Appl*, 38, 1, 288–298, 2011.

35. Ramkumar, G. D., Ranka, S., Tsur, S., Weighted association rules: Model and algorithm, in: *Proc. Fourth International Conference on Knowledge Discovery and Data Mining*, pp. 661–666, ACM, 1998.

36. Sehrawat, P. and Manju, H.R., Association rule mining using Firefly algorithm. *Int. J. Latest Trends Eng. Technol.*, 3, 2, 263–270, 2013.

37. Srikant, R. and Agrawal, R., Mining generalized association rules. *Future. Gener. Comp. Sy.*, 13, 2–3, 161–180, 1997.

38. Svátek, V., Rauch, J., Ralbovský, M., Ontology-enhanced association mining, in: *Semantics, Web and mining*, pp. 163–179, Springer, Berlin, Heidelberg, 2005.

39. Tao, F., Murtagh, F., Farid, M., Weighted association rule mining using weighted support and significance framework, in: *Proceedings of the ninth ACM SIGKDD international conference on Knowledge discovery and data mining*, pp. 661–666, ACM, 2003.

40. Tseng, M.C., Lin, W.Y., Jeng, R., Dynamic mining of multi-supported association rules with classification ontology. *J. Internet Technol,* 7, 4, 399–406, 2006.
41. Vinu, M.R. and Nandhini, M., Interactive postmining of weighted association rules. *Nat. J. Technol.,* 10, 4, 55–61, 2013.
42. Yan, X., Zhang, C., Zhang, S., Genetic algorithm-based strategy for identifying association rules without specifying actual minimum support. *Expert. Syst. Appl,* 36, 2, 3066–3076, 2009.
43. Yao, H. and Hamilton, H.J., Mining itemset utilities from transaction databases. *Data. Knowl. Eng,* 59, 3, 603–626, 2006.
44. Wang, J., Han, J., Pei, J., Closet+: Searching for the best strategies for mining frequent closed itemsets, in: *Proceedings of the ninth ACM SIGKDD international conference on Knowledge discovery and data mining,* ACM, pp. 236–245, 2003.
45. Wang, W., Yang, J., Philip, S. Y., Efficient mining of weighted association rules (WAR), in: *Proceedings of the sixth ACM SIGKDD international conference on Knowledge discovery and data mining,* pp. 270–274, ACM, 2000.
46. Zaki, M.J. and Hsiao, C.J., CHARM: An efficient algorithm for closed itemset mining, in: *Proceedings of the 2002 SIAM international conference on data mining,* Society for Industrial and Applied Mathematics, pp. 457–473, 2002.

4

Ontology in Medicine as a Database Management System

Shobowale K. O.

Department of Mechanical Engineering, Universiti Teknologi PETRONAS,
Persiaran UTP, Seri Iskandar, Perak, Malaysia

Abstract

The advent of the growth of numerous global data in medicine brought data management complexity; this has necessitated the use of improved tools to further enhance the functionality of these data such that it becomes reusable to be able to make useful inference for informed decisions. In today's world, collaboration among different fields of knowledge is inevitable. This has created innovations that have yielded better productivity through automation in medical field management, less mistakes in diagnosis and prescription by medical personnel, enhancement of knowledge for young medical personnel, to mention a few. The rich semantics and knowledge representation techniques of Ontology has been used to further enhance medical domain data such that as the data is used to generate information across platforms, the data is transformed through ontology semantics which has the advantage of closely relating to human semantics to information, which makes information re-useable, consistent, accurate, and reliable for proper storage, retrieval, and updating. Interoperability through the medical field terminologies among systems on different platforms is one of the major concerns. A standardized ontology database or a guideline for developing an ontology database that can be used to provide better medical services in various capacities in medicine. The techniques that make ontology suitable for database as a management system is its ability to make semantic relations that gives it a structure through which informed conclusions can be drawn.

Email: kshobowale@yahoo.com

This chapter discusses the role ontology is playing as a knowledge base system in database management in medical practice and the challenges that are still pertinent that is not making the full potential of ontology to be realized.

Vishal Jain, Ritika Wason, Jyotir Moy Chatterjee and Dac-Nhuong Le (eds.) Ontology-Based Information Retrieval for Healthcare Systems, (69–90) © 2020 Scrivener Publishing LLC

Keywords: Ontology, medicine, interoperability, knowledge base, standards, evaluation

4.1   Introduction

Ontology models data through a domain defined concepts together with the relationships that can exist between the concepts which possess share ability capability [1]. According to [2], ontology can also be used in information retrieval as a thesaurus, in linked data as a model representation in OWL, databases as XML schema, decision support as a knowledge base, and in natural language processing. This helps to differentiate Ontologies with regard to their goal, content, and use. Knowledge management and information integration in Medicine are task that can be easily accomplished with Ontology [3–7], and a core part of the semantic web, Ontology has been reported to mitigate structuring and modeling concerns in Knowledge Management [8]. The classification of the domain concepts categorize the instance and the relationships that can exists with the instance and the knowledge base systems stores data that are part of the ontology instance [1]. The three basic building block of ontology is depicted in Figure 4.1. Features of Ontology language are appropriate definition of concept, adequate representation of instance, sufficient expressiveness, and query ability [1]. Different level of semantic expressiveness can be obtained from different types of data and these data can be integrated with ontology for better inference (Figure 4.2).

Four approaches that have been used to extract concepts in ontology are [10]: formal query languages (through SPARQL, RDF, and OWL syntax), graphics, forms, and natural language. Reuse of clinical data by sharing and integration of data is an important interest for the biomedical community

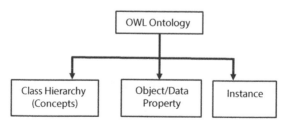

Figure 4.1 The basic building block of ontology (Source: [1]).

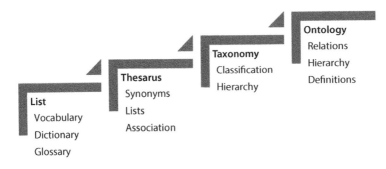

Figure 4.2 Expressivity level from small to high (Adapted from [9]).

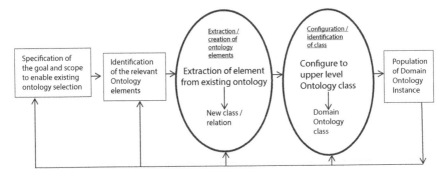

Figure 4.3 Ontology reuse method (Adapted from [4]).

for advancement of medical systems [11], the steps to reuse medical ontology was proposed by [4]. The steps are depicted in Figure 4.3.

Different form of data that is relevant to the domain is connected through external systems to ease the task of management and integration. A reasoner helps infer related concepts that are not previously defined and organize, discover, search, and compare information on the ontology [4].

There are basically two types of ontology:

1. Domain Ontology: they are domain specific Ontologies that define the concept in a domain of interest. Some of these Ontologies typically reside on the local repositories of the developer.
2. Upper level Ontology: they are multi-domain Ontologies that define common concept that are applicable to many domains. Domain Ontologies built on upper level ontology have the advantage of interoperability that will facilitate the

ontology reuse. They can be built on platforms that include: the Descriptive Ontology for Linguistic and Cognitive Engineering (DOLCE) and the Basic Formal Ontology (BFO). Concepts categorized from the UMLS Metathesaurus which are created from UMLS Semantic Network has been considered as biomedical upper level ontology too [12].

4.1.1 Ontology Engineering and Development Methodology

Ontology engineering according to [13] is an intelligent and refined version of conventional knowledge engineering. It has been defined as a research methodology that defines the design basis for a knowledge base, kernel conceptualization of the domain of interest, semantic constraint of domain concept with the right theories, and technologies which makes knowledge accumulation easy. All these are essential in the real world for knowledge processing [2, 13]. Ontology engineering development methods have been proposed by different authors (Table 4.1). Each of the methods has its own merits and demerits. It has been argued by most of the authors that there is no single development methodology for building Ontologies. Fit for purpose ontology can be built by following steps which include: purpose, the knowledge acquisition, knowledge formalization, and evaluation [14]. They suggested that following this guideline and arranging in an organized and systematic way can result into high quality ontology. Methondology has been judged as one of the most matured of the ontology engineering development methodology [13].

4.2 Literature Review on Medical Data Processing

Till date, medical data and ontologies are still reported to lack interoperability, and so, many medical ontologies are springing up [12, 16] but significant improvement has been achieved by BioPortal, OBO Foundry, and other standard medical ontology repository through guidelines and upper level ontological developmental process that should be followed and improved on. The interoperability will enable inference to be made across multiple ontologies which could facilitate patterns, trends, and predictions in the ontology information as reported by [17] that consolidated medical drug ontologies can help predict adverse drug reactions in a patient; this is also applicable in many other applications.

The current advances in the development of medical Ontologies reveals trends that has been used such as resources, types, terminologies,

Table 4.1 Ontology engineering development methodology.

Methodology	Description
Methontology	The steps are: (i) Organization of project phase (includes planning, control, and quality assurance); (ii) Development phase (includes specification, conceptualization, formalization, and implementation); (iii) Support phase (includes knowledge acquisition, evaluation, integration, documentation, and configuration management). ITEMAS [15] is an example of Ontology developed using this method.
Uschold and King Method	The steps are: (i) Identification of the purpose; (ii) Ontology building (includes capturing the ontology, coding, integration with existing ontology); (iii) Evaluation (includes requirement specification, competency questions); (iv) Documentation. Enterprise ontology is an example of Ontology developed using this method.
Grüninger and Fox Method	The steps are: (i) Motivation scenarios capturing; (ii) Preliminary formulation of competency question; (iii) Ontology specification terms in formal language (includes informal terminology acquisition, formal terminology specification); (iv) Formal competency questions formulation with the ontology terminology; (v) Axioms and specification of ontology terms within the formal language; (vi) Completeness of the ontology through characterization using proven conditions. Toronto virtual enterprise (TOVE) ontology is an example of Ontology developed using this method.
Berneras Method	The steps are: (i) Application specification; (ii) Preliminary design upper ontology; (iii) Structure shaping and refining. Electrical network Ontologies are examples of Ontology developed using this method.

knowledge representation, methodologies, and standards that has been adopted to build the ontologies. The medical ontology resources such as Systematized Nomenclature of Medicine–Clinical Terms (SNOMED-CT), The Unified Medical Language System (UMLS), ON9 medical ontology, bio-medical Ontology (MedO), Generalized Architecture for Languages,

Encyclopedias, and Nomenclatures in Medicine (GALEN) and Galen-Core ontology and others enumerated the various effort that have been made and reported by different authors and also collaboration among authors. These medical ontologies are built on various methodologies and serves different purposes in medicine, for instance, the ON9 ontology is built on ONIONS methodology, and these methodologies are discussed and evaluated based on their current usage and success in building efficient and reusable medical Ontologies. The ontology type discusses the different scope of medical Ontologies that has been developed such as ontology at the upper level (formal ontology) and ontology at the domain level. Ontology at the upper level includes: biomedical concept (of human anatomy, diseases, drugs, signs, and symptoms), ontology of diseases and prescriptions, formal ontology for antibiotics prescription, ontology within a medical system; such as in laboratory, pathology, billing, radiology, and others to mention a few together with the terminologies that was used. Medical Ontologies whose semantics has been integrated with other Ontologies through collaboration are also increasing. The knowledge representation has been reported to be a very important aspect to look at in the development and evaluation of Ontologies. Knowledge representation expressivities differ from one variant to another. Knowledge representation types include: Web Ontology Language (OWL), First-Order Logic languages, and others all have different variant that has different level of expressibility. The current state of medical ontology standardization efforts which includes the Gene Ontology (GO) consortium that is built on OBO is judged as one of the most successful medical Ontology [18].

Ontology-based applications in the medical field is discussed in this paper in terms of the tools that have been used and systems and environment that it has been deployed in. The ontological tools and usage of these information technologies enabled medical services such as the cooperative open ontology development environment (CO-ODE), hybrid ontology development for usability (HyOntUse) tools and the impact it has had in the development of medical Ontologies is also discussed in this chapter together with different environments such as Protégé, ontolingua, chimaera, and other development environments with the evaluation that can be used for verifying the ontologies in these environments that can further enhance the productivity of the ontology database management systems for retrieving medical information. The current medical ontology database management is also reviewed to reveal the aspects that require further studies and recommendations are proposed as a contribution to knowledge in this field. Knowledge reuse through integration of medical data, how data is modeled and represented, and to what extent have these systems enhance performance in the medical industry. This chapter can be a source of information on ontology as a database management system in medicine.

Ontology evaluation through the verification and validation process has taken different dimensions over the last decade. Verification has been achieved through different methods as reported in the literature such as through the reasoner and axioms that are part of the ontology development environment or an external package that can be installed in the development environment as a pluggin for more enhancement of the ontology development process. Validation has also been reported based on different approaches and metrics. Some of which has been through expert validation, evaluation using natural language techniques, testing with case studies for content and correctness, ontology matching, measurement of precision, and recall of information retrieval. Approaches such as a task based, a criterion based, a gold standard based, and a corpus based have also been reported and discussed in this chapter. Metrics such as accuracy, adaptability, clarity, consistency, completeness, conciseness, and computational efficiency are usually used for evaluations as reported in the literature.

A lot of work has been put into the development of medical Ontologies; but most of these works are fragmented and loosely coupled. Concise information of Ontologies as a database management system that discusses every crucial aspect of the development of the system that is systematically put together can enhance knowledge for parties interested in developing this system on the latest and key aspects to work on during the construction of medical ontology development. This chapter aims to provide this concise information that can serve as a handy source of information for using ontology as a knowledge management system in various aspects of the medical domain.

4.3   Information on Medical Ontology

In medicine, Ontologies are professed as the solution through its semantics to process important data and information related to biomedical terminologies [4]. Development of Medical Ontology entails some processes which are necessary and determine how useful the ontology can be.

4.3.1   Types of Medical Ontology

Basically, types of Medical Ontology can be: Upper level ontology (through: the DOLCE and BFO), for interoperability and re-usability. BFO is perceived as the most widely used upper level ontology as reported by [12]; that a lot of medical Ontologies has reused OBO (Open Biomedical Ontologies) family and the Bio-Top. Adverse Event (AE) ontology which includes Ontology of Adverse Events (OAEs) and Ontology of Drug Neuropathy Adverse Events (ODNAEs) have also been developed using the BFO [4].

4.3.2   Knowledge Representation

The type of knowledge representations include: First-order logic, Descriptive logic (DL), Web Ontology Language (OWL), Resource Descriptive Framework (RDF), Extensible markup language (XML), Semantic web rule language (SWRL), OBO format, and SKOS (Simple Knowledge Organization System). OWL is reported to have high expressive semantic constructs [8] and a key knowledge representation of the semantic web.

4.3.3   Methodology of Developing Medical Ontology

Basically, the methodology used in developing Medical Ontology includes: Methontology, Enterprise Ontology, TOronto Virtual Enterprise (TOVE).

Tools: Some of the tools that have been developed and used on medical data to generate semantic data are [16]:

> CardioSHARE as a generic framework for heart disease clinical analysis; it is in many formats and reported to work with any data
>
> RDF Data Cube Vocabulary is used to convert World Health Organizations Global Health Observatory datasets to RDF
>
> Bio2RDF is a Semantic Web technology used to provide Linked Data from a different data from different sources (for example, from PubMed and others from the biomedical domain).
>
> HCLS knowledge base is used for changing, circulating, and interlinking biomedical data from 15 different data sources (such as MeSH, PubMed).

Ontology development Editors tools: Protégé (by Stanford University), OBO-Edit (by Berkeley Bioinformatics/Gene Ontology Consortium), OilEd (by the University of Manchester),Web ODE (by OEG, Technical University of Madrid), JAVA Ontology editor (OntoEdit by University of Karlsruhe AIFB Institute), BioPortal web ontology repository system, Ontoanimal, a web-based tools that include: OntoFox, Ontodog, Ontorat, Ontobee, and Ontobeep. Ontologies built with Ontoanimal tools include: OAE, OVAE, and ODNAE [18], which are notable Ontologies in the medical domain.

Ontology Reasoners includes: Pellet, Fact++, Hermit, Jena, and Racer. Reasoners function as an inference system in ontology development.

4.3.4   Medical Ontology Standards

Ontology is a knowledge representation used in extracting knowledge to make intelligent decisions. A lot of intelligent agents use ontology to infer intelligence, and this knowledge can be used in other intelligent agents [8]. The first publication of GO was in year 2000, as at late 2015, its citation in PubMed publications is over 9,000, and in Google Scholar, it's over 110,000 [18]. Representation of life-science and clinical investigations was the reason for creating the Ontology for Biomedical Investigations (OBI) which was jointly developed by over 20 biomedical communities. More than 10 Ontologies have been created from OBI, and it is also used for representing different investigations [18]. Ontology representation of AEs, the processes leading to it and its related genetic interaction networks as a knowledge model has been developed by some authors [4, 18]. AE repositories include [4, 18]: MedDRA (Medical Dictionary for Regulatory Activities); CTCAE (Common terminology criteria for AEs) from the US National Cancer Institute (NCI) for cancer therapy drugs standardization classification of AEs; WHO-ART (The World Health Organization Adverse Reactions Terminology) functions as database of adverse reaction terms dictionary; Onto-EIM, this ontology extends AE entities dictionary; ADEpedia is an AE drug knowledge base comprising of drug Ontologies and data from different sources; International Classification of Disease (ICD); Systematized Nomenclature of Medicine Clinical Terms (SNOMED-CT). He [19] proposed software product line (SPL) as a tool that can be integrated with the development of Ontologies to increase interoperability.

Adhering to specific principles and guidelines is the goal that is set to create a formal ontology. One of the joint collaboration for developing ontologies that are platform independent and can interoperate and be reusable is the OBO Foundry [18]. Some core OBO Foundry principles are: advocacy for open Ontologies, advocacy for collaboration in ontology development, and the use of a generalized unambiguous standard for defining Ontologies relation. Some of the AE Ontologies developed using the OBO Foundry principles are [18]:

- OAEs (Ontology of Adverse Events): AEs are modeled as bodily processes after a medical intervention. The wheel is not reinvented in building OAE, as its core is existing ontology terminology (such as: Ontology of General Medical Science, OGMS and others) which is used in inferring new OAE-specific terms and it is built on the BFO.
- OVAEs (The Ontology of Vaccine Adverse Events): Vaccine AEs Knowledge Base. It's expansion of OAE and VO (Vaccine Ontology)
- ODNAEs (Ontology of Drug Neuropathy Adverse Events) generates knowledge for its knowledge base from clinical practices and biomedical researches. It is machine readable ontology; and it is used for neuropath AE representation of data, integration and exchange.

4.4   Ontologies as a Knowledge-Based System

Ontology can be designed as a domain ontology whose application can be localized for application that is specific to Ontologies with big scope, which can contain integration of several Ontologies whose application is for a wider population. BioPortal, OBO Foundry, and ONIONS (ONtological Integration Of Naive Sources) are regarded as some of the medical Ontology standards. Some referenced terminologies includes: SNOMED-CT; metathesaurus such as the Unified Medical Language System (UMLS); thesaurus such as the Medical Subject Headings (MESH). Medicine domain Ontology can be integrated in ONIONS, which can be used for retrieving information, integrating databases and analyzing Ontologies [20]. Medical Ontology can be built using ONIONs through reuse to extend the domain information depending on the aspect the Ontology seeks to address. Onion tools include: formalisms, tools which implement and support the use of the formalism, generic Ontologies (formal/informal literature resources which is translated/adapted to ONION formalism) [20].

ONIONS products include: Ontology ON9 library; Integrated Medical Ontology (IMO) which comprises of five medical top-levels terminologies integrated together with their mappings.

4.4.1   Domain Ontology in Medicine

Ontologies have been used in Artificial Intelligence and machine learning which has yield fruitful results, judging Ontologies as the means through which timely right information can be retrieved for informed decisions in knowledge management applications [8]. Medical ontology is developed to serve different purposes such as: Disease ontology [21], ICD (International Classification of Diseases) and MeSH that are notable and frequently reported (a comprehensive list can be found in [21]), Human Phenotype Ontology (HPO), SNOMED-CT, and UMLS, National Cancer Institute Thesaurus (NCIt), Online Mendelian Inheritance in Man (OMIM), Digital Anatomist Symbolic Knowledge Base, Clinical Data Interchange Standards Consortium (CDISC)—clinical terminologies; Health Language Seven (HL7)—clinical terminologies Foundational Model of Anatomy (FMA) [22], NCBO BioPortal holds a chunk of information of information and system for development of Ontologies in biomedical [23].

SNOMED-CT is medical health terminology for clinical health records; it represents standard clinical terms for ease of interpretation [22]. OBOs and the OBO Foundry is clinical and molecular biology ontology which was used to develop GO and HPO. UMLS contains biomedical and health vocabulary. NCBI taxonomy (National Center for Biotechnology Information, in the US): it is a collection of health and biomedical vocabularies, Ontologies, and standards with more than 60 sets of biomedical vocabularies [22]. ICD usage is in general medicine and primary health care. MeSH is a vocabulary thesaurus.

UMLS three major components [22] are the Metathesaurus (store house of interconnected concepts in biomedicine encapsulating codes and terms from different data sources), Semantic network (advanced group of concepts in Metathesaurus), and Specialist Lexicon (lexical variants generator of terms in biomedicine). UMLS has resources for several medical domains some of which are depicted in Figure 4.4. Extraction of clinical data (name entities and other data in the medical records of patients) from word text in natural language with the aid of natural language processing tools (GATE), convert the data into knowledge to build a domain Ontology instance to be used as an ontology knowledge base; whose function is to work in other processes as a software agent. The system was evaluated using precision, recall, and F-measure [24].

Medical emergency was the focus of [25], they developed domain ontology for information technology-based healthcare system to tackle efficient handling of problems during emergencies while [26] surveyed the effectiveness of ontology in data quality of routine medical data in chronic

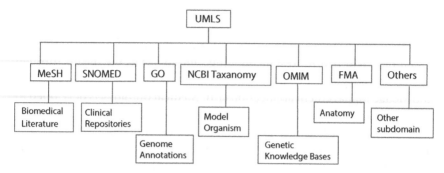

Figure 4.4 Subdomains in UMLS (Adapted from [22]).

disease management. They concluded that using ontology to manage data quality may be more effective in terms of cost, accuracy, validity, and data collection reliability than other information modeling. In [27], the use of medical knowledge base was made possible by Ontology, using UML data to state relationships that semantically link the classes and relations of gastric cancer to establish the domain knowledge terms. Fuzzy-based case base reasoning ontology (CBRDiabOnto—case-base fuzzy OWL2 ontology) was developed by [28] for diabetes mellitus. The source medical concepts of electronic medical records (EMRs) from different sources were developed into ontology by [29]. EMRs that are not standardized are mapped and standardized with the ontology they developed. The system performs knowledge management for EMR of the Erlangen University hospital Germany. The work by [30] focused on developing ontology as a guideline for medical system for supporting information retrieval of hepatitis through query. Some abnormal ailment has not be left out as reported by [11], on the developed ontology of Managing Epilepsy Well (MEW) Network informatics system that has a database for supporting prospective research, queries, and data analysis, which could be applied through the MEW Network sites. Physiology, anatomy, and pathology ontology named OBR-Scolio ontology was developed from FMA referenced ontology to model scoliosis as a pathological state of spine [22].

The processing of documents that has a link with digital images that are semantically annotated using Natural language processing for domain ontology for medical information retrieval was the goal of ontology termed the semantic web for pathology [22]. The reuse of UMLS semantic network Metathesaurus to develop OntoMOVE (Ontologies on the MOVE), also reuse (OBO) to develop Under CHRONIOUS (Chronic Disease Management Platform for Renal Insufficiency) bibliography retrieval search engine of the seventh Framework Program (FP7) [22]. In [31], SciMiner literature mining ontology was developed to deduce Adverse Drug Reaction from labels of drugs in a 2017 Text Analysis Conference, containing more than 53 drug labels in neuropathy inducing drugs (NIDs). It was concluded that ontology network analysis and literature mining can ably spot and study drugs specific group and their related ADRs. Tropical diseases (Dengue, Malaria, Chikungunya, Melioidosis, and Leptospirosis) were the focus of [32] in developing domain Ontology for the South East Asia region using Protégé 4.1 and OWL DL syntax. Ontology is used in data storage, interpretation, integration, and accessing for the Internet of Things (IoT) data for information system in the domain of emergency medical services [33].

4.4.2   Brief Introduction of Some Medical Standards

4.4.2.1   Medical Subject Headings (MeSH)

MeSH, a thesaurus, is developed by the National Library of medicine (NML) in the US [34]. This contains biomedical information of NLM databases that includes: MEDLINE/PUBmed and others; the pharmaceutical RxNorm database; link to UMLS and SnoMed database) in hierarchy to index and catalog its terminologies. MeSH can be generated in resource description format (RDF). From (MeSH), RxNorm (is a drug vocabulary used for keeping information pertaining to drugs); UMLS Metathesaurus (its information is from many medical term sources to derive names and codes in the medicine); NLM Classification (in the field of medicine, it is used for the library materials arrangement); Daily Med (has information on drugs marketed).

4.4.2.2   Medical Dictionary for Regulatory Activities (MedDRA)

This is a medical terminology standard to ease dissemination of international regulatory information for human medical products. MedDRA scope includes: pharmaceuticals, biologics, vaccines, Nutraceuticals, Dietary supplements, and drug-device combination products. Support registration, documentation, and safety monitoring of medical products [35] can interoperate with some repositories such as MeSH, ICD, and SNOMED-CT. The MedDRA ontological framework makes it easy to map MedDRA with other repositories.

4.4.2.3   Medical Entities Dictionary (MED)

The MED standard has been used at some hospitals in the United States for more than two decades. It is a clinical data for radiology, pharmacy, and laboratories. It can be coded uniquely and it is applicable for general medicine and as a decision support tools. It is comparable to UML, which unifies standard medical terminologies [36].

Others include:

> International Classification of Functioning, Disability, and Health (ICF). ICF is World Health Organization framework for measuring health and disability at all levels [37]. ICF Ontology has been developed as an added enhancement to ICF.
> ICD-O (International Classification of Diseases for Oncology)
> IDO (Infectious Disease Ontology)

4.4.3   Reusing Medical Ontology

It will be incomplete to not mention the applications of medical standards that have been designed to aid in the development of various Ontology Medical knowledge based systems. In [38], it was reported that some challenges with developing clinical decision support systems lies in interoperability features and implementation cost, in their work, they affirmed that the use of medical standard terminologies that is based on an established medical databases can be employed to resolve these issues. They used openEHR Archetypes (LOINC terminology) to detect in the intensive care for pediatric the systemic inflammatory response syndrome (SIRS). They developed an automated ontology based SIRS system. They reported that the openEHR enables the system to have interoperable concepts that can make reuse possible. They tested the system with a prototype from an openEHR-based data storehouse of the Hannover Medical School Translational Research Framework (HaMSTR). Sanford Guide to Antimicrobial Therapy terms was used to develop an antibiotic prescription formal Ontology using the BFO to assure interoperability and re-usability by [39], which was implemented in Protégé-OWL. Validation was measured using ontology design rules and review by domain experts. Another approach is myGrid ontology which was adapted by [40] to develop an Ontology representation model in OWL in the domain of SPL for suggesting scientific experiments to scientist in Bioinformatics. The system was named scientific SPL. They justified the reason for choosing myGrid ontology due to its level of details in Bioinformatics domain and its description of the dimensions. They stressed the usefulness of ontology technology for constraints formal representation between the variation points of a SPL. Evaluation was through case studies. SNOMED-CT ontology was used as the domain ontology; develop in OWL2 as a case-based reasoning system by [41]. They evaluated the system with a case study of diabetes diagnosis. Foundational Model of Anatomy (FMA), OBO Foundry, the National Center for Biotechnology Information Organismal Classification (NCBI Taxon) and Infectious Disease Ontology data repositories were used to develop the BCIDO (Bacterial Clinical Infectious Disease ontology) in OWL and Protégé-OWL editor by [42]. Concept unique identifiers of UMLS were used to map the BCIDO classes.

Formal ontology (BFO) for antibiotic prescription was developed in Protégé-OWL using the Stanford Guide to Antimicrobial Therapy data as the main standard for the ontology knowledge management by [39]. They used other medical guideline repositories such as the OBO Foundry, NCBO BioPortal, Systemized SNOMED-CT, MED, GALEN, and data from the New York Presbyterian such as ID guidelines for organism emanating from blood, urine cultures, and respiratory systems direct treatment, guidelines for empiric antibiotic therapy pneumonia acquired in the community and infection of the urinary tract was also used, they stressed the importance of using a formal ontology evaluation methods with emphasis on correctness and usefulness of their developed ontology together with domain expert review. In [27], they employed ontology as a knowledge base system in case-based reasoning clinical decision of gastric cancer. Clinical medical repository is used for the development of the ontology and definition of the semantic relations between the classes and relations was achieved using UML. MedDRA terminology is described in a formal language in OntoADR. SNOMED CT was used to define the properties of the adverse drug reactions (ADRs) [10]. In the work by [7], they developed ontology imaging for ultrasound knowledge base system for obstetrics and gynecology to detect ectopic pregnancy. Ultrasound diagnosis of ectopic pregnancies during early stage was used as a model for ectopic pregnancy as an imaging concept for the types of ultrasound modes, ectopic pregnancy, echographic signs, and echographic views. Ultrasound reports of ectopic pregnancy indexed with the MeSH term for the domain of interest serves as the medical text and ultrasound images was used to develop the ectopic pregnancy ontology. The developed system was a programmed internal system that uses text mining and Ontologies personalized for search (from biomedical repositories of drug discovery and development) and knowledge extraction. The automated system used the ability of ontology of names targeting to identify information of interest in oral and poster presentations in other sources such as a conference and extracts relevant relationships [43, 44].

The OAE was used to build ODNAEs, target Drug Ontology (DrON) with their chemical ingredients defined in ChEBI, drug mechanisms of action from NDF-RT and biological processes represented in Gene Ontology (GO) [45], built on web ontology language (OWL2) and Protégé editor. Subset of different Ontologies related terms were extracted using OntoFox (web-based program). RxNorm and NDF-RT identifiers were assigned to DrON matching annotation Property drug terms using OntoRat. The goal of ODNAE is for users to be able to create and analyze an ontology knowledge base of drug-associated neuropathy adverse effects.

In [3], they developed a Clinical decision support system (CDSS) for aiding physicians in diabetes diagnosis by reusing the diabetes diagnosis ontology (DDO) which is an upper level ontology (on Basic Formal Ontology, BFO 2) was built in OWL2 and available in BioPortal.

Ontologies (such OAE, OVAE, MedDRA, SNOMED CT) are reused by [4] using OntoFox in the development and usage requirements built on the principles of upper ontology (BFO) for AE in chronic kidney disease. The application of the knowledge base was for integration and analysis. Protégé 5.2 was used to develop the DSOAE in CKD. CDSS exists abundantly, but they are usually not widely used or shared which is a drawback that is debarring ontology to achieve its full potential in medicine [38].

Domain ontology was used to enhance the performance of service-oriented architecture application for handling emergency health care system (such as in patient care, patient diagnostics, assisting devices, clinical, and administrative decisions) in Methondology. They affirmed that the use of ontology ensures proper interpretation and sharing of data with the concepts formal specification. Ontology part duty is to remove terms ambiguity together with a reasoner to infer new knowledge discovery [25]. Ontology of genetic factors, clinical features, environmental factors, and treatments of Pre-eclampsia (PEO) was developed in OWL2 by [46] in BFO using terminologies from standard libraries [through NCBO's BioPortal, the Ontologies include: Chemical Entities of Biological Interest Ontology (CHEBI), HPO, Systematized Nomenclature of Medicine Clinical Terms (SNOMED-CT), Alzheimer's Disease Ontology (ADO), Medical Subject Headings (MESH), Medical Dictionary for Regulatory Activities (MEDDRA), Online Mendelian Inheritance in Man (OMIM), Health Level Seven Reference Implementation Model Version 3 (HL7) and Exposure Ontology (ExO)] to retrieve information in the domain.

Genetic Glyco-Diseases Ontology (GGDonto) and RDF/SPARQL-based user interface was developed using Semantic Web technologies. GGDonto was made using RDF, RDFS, SKOS, and OWL, with a SPARQL queries user interface [47].

The organization and description of scientific information into knowledge bases, establishing links among information resources that are related is achievable with Semantic Web technologies and have been the core of biomedical processes and it has continued to grow [6, 47]. The domains where medical Ontologies have been applied include: diseases, anatomy, drugs, and clinical information [6]. The application ontology knowledge base was built for ectopic pregnancy ultrasound image annotation in OWL. Radiology Lexicon (RadLex), EPO (Ectopic Pregnancy Ontology) was reused [5]. In [6], they developed a River Flow Model (RFM) of diseases (based on disease ontology and abnormality ontology), representing what causes diseases, the progression of diseases, and the aftermath of diseases. Hozo (the theory of a role based on XML) ontology editing tool was used.

4.4.4   Ontology Evaluation

Some authors [28, 39] have argued that there is no specific way of evaluating medical Ontologies and Ontologies in general. It will continue to be an ongoing process for most relevant knowledge bases such that as modification is made, the system is re-evaluated to ensure it is serving its intended purpose. Metrics such as: accuracy, clarity, efficiency, consistency, usability, adaptability, functionality, completeness, conciseness to check the ontology's syntax, semantics, structure, and content coverage. Nevertheless, some evaluation methods have been reported which has been used in biomedical Ontologies and they include [23, 42, 48]: conformance to a philosophical principle, task-based, data-driven evaluation, user-based evaluation, and the gold standard (comparison with predefined gold standards). Verification (pertains to content and structure) and validation (pertains to usability in the real world) has also been used to evaluate medical Ontologies [49–52]. Measuring the system through competency questions that defines the system purpose has also been widely adopted.

A total of 200 biomedical Ontologies from the National Center for Biomedical Ontology (NCBO) BioPortal was sampled by [23] with each ontology checked out for publications on PubMed and Google Scholar, about 15 of the Ontologies discussed their evaluation methods. It was argued that not many developed medical ontology management system is properly evaluated.

A bacterial clinical infectious diseases ontology (BCIDO) was proposed and developed by [42, 52] as a standard to evaluate the ontology knowledge base for infectious disease. They used a semi-automatic method with data from different sources (electronic health records, international repositories of infectious disease guidelines, and case scenarios generated by expert's) to create infectious disease knowledge and used the knowledge to evaluate the accuracy and coverage of BCIDO. The international repositories of infectious disease guidelines they used are: Australasian Society for Infectious Diseases (ASID), the Infectious Disease Society of America (IDSA), the European Society of Clinical Microbiology and Infectious Diseases (ESCMID), and the National Institute for Health and Care Excellence, United Kingdom (NICE). BCIDO was built using Infectious Disease Ontology (IDO) as the upper ontology, on ontology development guidelines, OBO Foundry framework was used, terminologies from Cimino's Desiderata, standardization, and data resource integration using Unified Medical Language System for the BCIDO development [42]. The system is linked with SNOMED-CT and ICD. Bacterial terms ware reused from the National Center for Biotechnology Information Organismal Classification (NCBITaxon). Anatomical terms were reused from the Foundational Model of Anatomy (FMA) and were used to define the location of infectious processes. The ontology was represented in OWL 2 EL Web Ontology Language (OWL) as a single hierarchical structure using the Protégé-OWL editor.

4.5 Conclusion

Medical Ontologies have come a long way, what is apparent is that they have made significant contributions to the various aspect of the medical field through enhancing data and information management for an informed decision making process. As compared to other fields where ontologies have been used, it has been established that ontology in knowledge base system has been beneficial in a number of medical domains that have made use of it. Some standards have been established and other Ontologies have reused them, leveraging on their contents, which is a significant step towards a coordinated and collaborated efforts in the medical field. This will mitigate the fragmented systems that exist by challenging efforts towards a unified goal for each domain of interest.

4.6 Future Scope

Further studies will focus on area in medicine that is yet to utilize the advantages of ontology as a knowledge base and the external systems from different sources that aid the development and appropriate usage of the ontology in medicine.

References

1. Shobowale, K.O., *Decision support system for subsea multiphase pump using ontology knowledge base, Unpublished PhD thesis, Universiti Teknologi,* PETRONAS, Malaysia, 2018.
2. Catherine, R., Francois, P., Myoung, A.K., Oscar, C., *An introduction to Ontologies and Ontology Engineering,* Springer-Verlag, Berlin, Germany, 2011.
3. Shoaip, N., El-Sappagh, S., Barakat, S., Elmogy, M., U-Healthcare Monitoring Systems, Ontology enhanced fuzzy clinical decision support systems: A literature review, 1, 61–87, 2019. https://doi.org/10.1016/B978-0-12-815370-3.00007-4.
4. Kang, Y., Fink, J.C., Doerfler, R., Zhou, L., Disease Specific Ontology of Adverse Events: Ontology extension and adaptation for Chronic Kidney Disease. *Comput. Biol. Med.,* 101, 210–217, 2018. https://doi.org/10.1016/j.compbiomed.2018.08.024
5. Dhombres, F., Maurice, P., Friszer, S., Guilbaud, L., Lelong, N., Khoshnood, B., Charlet, J., Perrot, N., Jauniaux, E., Jurkovic, D., Jouannic, J.M., Developing a knowledge base to support the annotation of ultrasound images of ectopic pregnancy. *J. Biomed. Semant.,* 8, 4, 2017.
6. Kozaki, K., Yamagata, Y., Mizoguchi, R., Imai, T., Ohe, K., Disease Compass– a navigation system for disease knowledge based on ontology and linked data techniques. *J. Biomed. Semant.,* 8, 22, 2017.
7. Maurice, P., Dhombres, F., Blondiaux, E., Friszer, S., Guilbaud, L., Lelong, N., Khoshnood, B., Charlet, J., Perrot, N., Jauniaux, E., Jurkovic, D., Jouannic, J.M., Towards ontology-based decision support systems for complex ultrasound diagnosis in obstetrics and gynecology. *J. GynecolObstet Hum. Reprod.,* 46, 423–429, 2017.
8. Nachiya, P.Y., Sekar, K.R., Manikandan, R., Ravichandran, K.S., Investigation of Obsessive Compulsive Disorder through Domain Ontology Construction-Survey. *Int. J. Pure Appl Math.,* 119, 7, 643–651, 2018.
9. Harrow, I., Balakrishnan, R., Jimenez-Ruiz, E., Jupp, S., Lomax, J., Reed, J., Romacker, M., Senger, C., Splendiani, A., Wilson, J., Woollard, P., Ontology mapping for semantically enabled applications. *Drug Discovery Today,* 24, 2068–2075, 2019.
10. Souvignet, J., Declerck, G., Trombert-Paviot, B., Asfari, H., Jaulent, M.C., Bousquet, C., Semantic Queries Expedite MedDRA Terms Selection Thanks to a Dedicated User Interface: A Pilot Study on Five Medical Conditions. *Front. Pharmacol.,* 10, 50, 2019.
11. Sahoo, S.S., Ramesh, P., Welter, E., Bukach, A. *et al.,* An Ontology-based integrated database and analysis platform for epilepsy self management research. *Int. J. Med. Inf.,* 94, 21–30, 2015.
12. Fung, K.W. and Bodenreider, O., Knowledge representation and ontologies. *Clin. Res. Inf.,* 313–339, 2019. Springer.

13. Mizoguchi, R., Introduction to Ontological Engineering, in: *New Generation Computing*, vol. 21, pp. 365–384, Ohmsha Ltd and Springer-Verlag, Berlin, Germany, 2003.

14. Nelson, L., Kim, L.S., Nicole, T., An Ontology development methodology to integrate existing ontologies in an ontology development process. *Commun. ICISA: Int. J.*, 13, 31–61, 2012.

15. Moreno-Conde, A., Parra-Calderón, C.L., Sánchez-Seda, S., Escobar-Rodríguez, G.A., López-Otero, M., Cussó, L., del-Cerro-García, R., Segura-Sánchez, M., Herrero-Urigüen, L., Martí-Ras, N., Albertí-Ibarz, M., Desco, M., ITEMAS ontology for healthcare technology innovation. *Health Res. Policy Syst.*, 17, 47, 2019.

16. Zenuni, X., Raufi, B., Ismaili, F., Ajdari, J., State of the Art of Semantic Web for Healthcare. Procedia -. *Social Behav. Sci.*, 195, 1990– 1998, 2015.

17. Ibrahim, Z., Izhar, T.A.T., Shahibi, M.S., Hariro, A.Z., Kamarulzaman, M.R.S., Noor, M.M., Azman, S., Semantic relationships rules identification for the construction of medicinal herbs domain ontology. *Int. J. Acad. Res. Bus. Social Sci.*, 7, 12, 979–990, 2017.

18. He, Y., Ontology-Based Vaccine and Drug Adverse Event Representation and Theory-Guided Systematic Causal Network Analysis toward Integrative Pharmacovigilance Research. *Curr. Pharmacol. Rep.*, 2, 113–128, 2016.

19. He, Y., Zuoshuang, X., Jie, Z., Yu, L., James, A.O., Edison, O., The eXtensible ontology development (XOD) principles and tool implementation to support ontology interoperability. *J. Biomed. Semant.*, 9, 3, 2018.

20. Pisanelli, D.M., Gangemi, A., Steve, G., A medical Ontology library that integrates the UMLS Metathesaurus, Springer Science and Business media, Berlin, Germany, 1999.

21. Haendel, M.A., McMurry, J.A., Relevo, R., Mungall, C.J., Robinson, P.N., Chute, C.G., A Census of Disease Ontologies. *Annu. Rev. Biomed. Data Sci.*, 1, 305–31, 2018.

22. Komenda, M., Schwarz, D., Švancara, J., Vaitsis, C., Zary, N., Dušek, L., Practical use of medical terminology in curriculum mapping. *Comput. Biol. Med.*, 63, 74–82, 2015.

23. Muhammed, I.T., Manion, F., Liang, C., Harris, M., Wang, D., He, Y., Tao, C., OntoKeeper: Semiotic-driven ontology evaluation tool for biomedical onologists. *IEEE International Conference on Bioinformatics and Biomedicine*, 2018.

24. Cedeno-Moreno, D. and Vargas-Lombardo, M., An Ontology-Based Knowledge Methodology in the Medical Domain in the Latin America: The Study Case of Republic of Panama. *Acta. Inform. Med.*, 26, 2, 98–101, 2018.

25. Zeshan, F. and Mohamad, R., Medical Ontology in the Dynamic Healthcare Environment. *Procedia Comput. Sci.*, 10, 340– 348, 2012.

26. Liaw, S.T., Rahimi, A., Ray, P., Taggart, J., Dennis, S., de Lusignanf, S., Yeo, A.E.T., Talaei-Khoei, A., Towards an ontology for data quality in integrated

chronic disease management: A realist review of the literature. *Int. J. Med. Inf.*, 82, 10–24, 2013.

27. Ying, S., Joël, C., Armelle, J.A., Kai, L., Emerging medical informatics with case-based reasoning for aiding clinical decision in multi-agent system. *J. Biomed. Inf.*, 56, 307–317, 2015.

28. El-Sappagh, S. and Elmogy, M., A fuzzy ontology modeling for case base knowledge in diabetes mellitus domain. *Eng. Sci. Technol. Int. J.*, 20, 1025–1040, 2017.

29. Mate, S., Köpcke, F., Toddenroth, D., Martin, M., Prokosch, H.U., Bürkle, T. *et al.*, Ontology-Based Data Integration between Clinical and Research Systems. *PLoS ONE*, 10, 1, e0116656, 2015.

30. Yunzhi, C., Huijuan, L., Shapiro, L., Travillian, R.S., Lanjuan, L., An approach to semantic query expansion system based on Hepatitis ontology. *Jur. of Biol. Res-Thessaloniki*, 23, Suppl 1, S11, 2016.

31. Hur, J., Özgür, A., He, Y., Ontology-based literature mining and class effect analysis of adverse drug reactions associated with neuropathy-inducing drugs. *J. Biomed. Semant.*, 9, 17, 2018.

32. Satria, H., Priya, R.S., Ismail, L.H., Supriyanto, E., Building and Reusing Medical Ontology for Tropical Diseases Management. *Int. J. Educ. Inf. Technol.*, 1, 6, 2012.

33. Xu, B., Xu, L.D., Cai, H., Xie, C., Hu, J., Bu, F., Ubiquitous Data Accessing Method in IoT-Based Information System for Emergency Medical Services. *IEEE Trans. Ind. Inf.*, 10, 2, 2014.

34. MeSH, https://www.nlm.nih.gov/mesh/meshhome.html, 2019.

35. MedDRA, https://www.meddra.org/, 2019

36. Baorto, D., Li, L., Cimino, J.J., Practical experience with the maintenance and auditing of a large medical ontology. *J. Biomed. Inf.*, 42, 494–503, 2009.

37. ICF, 2019. https://www.who.int/classifications/icf/en/.

38. Wulff, A., Haarbrandt, B., Tute, E., Marschollek, M., Beerbaum, P., Jack, T., An interoperable clinical decision-support system for early detection of SIRS in pediatric intensive care using openEHR. *Artif. Intell. Med.*, 89, 10–23, 2018.

39. Bright, T.J., Furuya, E.Y., Kuperman, G.J., Cimino, J.J., Bakken, S., Development and evaluation of an ontology for guiding appropriate antibiotic prescribing. *J. Biomed. Inf.*, 45, 120–128, 2012.

40. Costa, G.C.B., Braga, R., David, J.M.N., Campos, F., A scientific software product line for the bioinformatics domain. *J. Biomed. Inf.*, 56, 239–264, 2015.

41. El-Sappagh, S. and Elmogy, M., An encoding methodology for medical knowledge using SNOMED CT ontology. *J. King Saud Univ. – Comput. Inf. Sci.s*, 28, 311–329, 2016.

42. Gordon, C.L. and Weng, C., Combining expert knowledge and knowledge automatically acquired from electronic data sources for continued ontology evaluation and improvement. *J. Biomed. Inf.*, 57, 42–52, 2016.

43. Ying, S., Joël, C., Armelle, J.A., Kai, L., Emerging medical informatics with case-based reasoning for aiding clinical decision in multi-agent system. *J. Biomed. Inf.*, 56, 307–317, 2015.

44. McEntire, R., Szalkowski, D., Butler, J., Kuo, M.S., Chang, M., Chang, M., Freeman, D., McQuay, S., Patel, J., McGlashen, M., Cornell, W.D., Xu, J.J., Application of an automated natural language processing (NLP) workflow to enable a federated search of external biomedical content in drug discovery and development. *Drug Discovery Today*, 21, 826–835, 2016.

45. Guo, A., Racz, R., Hur, J., Lin, Y., Xiang, Z., Zhao, L., Rinder, J., Jiang, G., Zhu, Q., He, Y., Ontology-based collection, representation and analysis of drug-associated neuropathy adverse events. *J. Biomed. Semant.*, 7, 29, 2016.

46. Mizuno, S., Ogishima, S., Nishigori, H., Jamieson, D.G., Verspoor, K., Tanaka, H. *et al.*, The Pre-Eclampsia Ontology: A Disease Ontology Representing the Domain Knowledge Specific to Pre-Eclampsia. *PLoS ONE*, 11, 10, e0162828, 2016.

47. Solovieva, E., Shikanai, T., Fujita, N., Narimatsu, H., GGDonto ontology as a knowledge-base for genetic diseases and disorders of glycan metabolism and their causative genes. *J. Biomed. Semant.*, 9, 14, 2018.

48. Raad, J. and Cruz C., A., Survey on Ontology Evaluation Methods, in: *Proceedings of the International Conference on Knowledge Engineering and Ontology Development, part of the 7th International Joint Conference on Knowledge Discovery*, Knowledge Engineering and Knowledge Management, Lisbonne, Portugal, Nov 2015, 10.5220/0005591001790186. hal-01274199.

49. Bilgin, G., Dikmen, I., Birgonul, M.T., Ontology Evaluation: An example of delay Analysis. *Procedia Eng.*, 85, 61– 68, 2014.

50. Amith, M., He, Z., Bian, J., Lossio-Ventura, J.A., Tao, C., Assessing the practice of biomedical ontology evaluation: Gaps and opportunities. *J. Biomed. Inf.*, 80, 1–13, 2018.

51. Ivanović, M. and Budimac, Z., An overview of ontologies and data resources in medical domains. *Expert Syst. Appl.*, 41, 5158–5166, 2014.

52. Gordon, C.L. and Weng, C., Bacterial clinical infectious diseases ontology (BCIDO) dataset. *Data in Brief*, 8, 881–884, 2016.

53. Zaman, S., Sarntivijai, S., Abernethy, D.R., Use of Biomedical Ontologies for Integration of Biological Knowledge for Learning and Prediction of Adverse Drug Reactions. *Gene Regul. Syst. Biol.*, 11, 1–7, 2017.

5

Using IoT and Semantic Web Technologies for Healthcare and Medical Sector

Nikita Malik[1]* and Sanjay Kumar Malik[2]

[1]Department of Computer Applications, Maharaja Surajmal Institute, GGSIP University, C-4, Janakpuri, New Delhi, India
[2]Department of Computer Science and IT, University School of Information, Communication and Technology, GGSIP University, New Delhi, India

Abstract

The computerization of health and medical industry, which includes the employment of information systems and use of technological medical gadgets, produces huge amounts of data in hospitals, clinics, and other medical establishments on a regular basis. This enormous volume of health and medicine associated data from medical records, patient monitoring, etc., continues to grow and thus needs to be managed properly for facilitating better healthcare services and development of enhanced practices and biomedical products. This poses the challenge of finding valuable information, analyzing it, and transforming it to knowledge for enabling better decision making. However, the key challenge of maintaining the interoperability of health-related data which is huge, disparate, and distributed, needs to be addressed. Internet of Things (IoT) and Semantic Web Technologies (SWTs) are two key emerging technologies that present a significant role in overcoming these challenges of handling and presenting data searches. Their role and usage in addressing the concerns of health and medical sector has been explored through this chapter, along with their challenges, various applications, and the future research scope they offer. Further, the integration of data mining and machine learning for healthcare and medical data analytics is also discussed in this chapter.

Keywords: Healthcare and medical sector, IoT, semantic web technologies, ontology, semantic web of things, healthcare data analytics, data mining, machine learning

---

Corresponding author: nikitamalik92@gmail.com

Vishal Jain, Ritika Wason, Jyotir Moy Chatterjee and Dac-Nhuong Le (eds.) Ontology-Based Information Retrieval for Healthcare Systems, (91–116) © 2020 Scrivener Publishing LLC

5.1   Introduction

5.1.1   Significance of Healthcare and Medical Sector and Its Digitization

Among the world's fastest growing business fields is the health and medical sector, which also is a very significant market for several countries and areas [1]. Health has been realized as an essential not just for general human well-being and happiness, but also as a significant contributor towards economic progress, since healthier populations have longer lifespans and are more productive, thus save more [2]. With the development of society, the health and medical model is also evolving from just a "bio-medical model" to a whole "biological-psychological-social medical model". Patients are now participating actively in their own health plans and activities and demand for personalized treatment where they are involved through knowledge and responsibility sharing with the health professionals [3].

A health system generates huge amounts of data from clinical practices, medical services, equipment, research, etc., on a daily basis, which would amount to loads of information to maintain. Also, the traditional health services face shortage of medical resources to be able to fulfill the people's growing demands. This led to the healthcare system to move steadily towards maintaining electronic health records (EHRs) and employing information and communication technologies (ICT).

Healthcare and medical sector essentially requires the digital transformation to be able to provide improved patient care through affordable health solutions, reduced complexity, improved efficiency, and empowered physicians with access to actionable information at the point of care. Digitization in healthcare and medical industry also addresses the need for consolidation of health care data and platform, provides a solution for physician burnout, understands the patient's needs better, and thus can effectively help save lives and improve quality of life significantly[1].

5.1.2   e-Health and m-Health

Electronic health (e-Health) and mobile health (m-Health) are modernizations in the healthcare and medical domain. Both these platforms promise of easy, time-saving, and cost-efficient delivery of personalized healthcare [2].

---

[1] https://www.who.int/hdp/.

The healthcare delivery task which is facilitated by electronic processes is e-Health or electronic health, which offers an easier alternative to people wherein they are no longer required to carry with them all their files of medical records everywhere. Instead, electronically stored data is available about the patient's medical history, which can be tracked easily, anytime and anywhere using computers and electronic networks. Further, mobile health or m-Health forms a subset of e-Health in which healthcare delivery is facilitated through the use of mobile devices such as smartphones, tablets, etc. This way, the devices act as a personal storage of healthcare and medical data, enabling easy interactions among providers and users of healthcare and medicine, that is, patients can themselves monitor their electronic medical records to keep track of their health, and also have physicians access to all health-related data on their mobile phones for consultation and emergency-handling. Figure 5.1 represents e-Health and m-Health concepts and their association.

With the ongoing advancement in the ICT, new applications are developed for the m-Health and e-Health field. In fact, e-Health can be broadly defined as "the use of information and communications technology, especially the Internet, to improve or enable health and healthcare" [4]. Similarly, m-Health can be defined as "medical and public health practice supported by mobile devices, such as mobile phones, patient monitoring devices (like heart rate monitor), personal digital assistants (PDAs), and other wireless devices" [2].

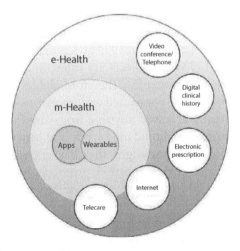

Figure 5.1 e-Health and m-Health.

Some of the technologies encompassed by e-Health are EHR, lab systems, and patient administration systems, which offer scope in the areas of informed decision making, collaborative health information, telemedicine, etc., having opportunities to further extend into health portals, wearable health monitoring devices, computer-assisted surgery, etc. Some of the initiatives in m-Health include emergency toll-free telephone services, health surveillance and awareness raising, decision support systems, mobile telemedicine, etc. [4].

The advantages offered by e-Health and m-Health are numerous, especially in the conduction of health interventions in areas of low reach and isolation. They present an opportunity to reach out to places which are devoid of healthcare infrastructure and have lesser doctors to provide medical care, such as to traditionally underserved groups, people with low socio-economic status, older adults, people with disabilities, and ethnic minorities [2]. Considering the crucial influence e-Health and m-Health have had on plenty of patients and doctors, and the society in general, it can be aptly asserted that they are the most contemporary approaches to a healthy way of life.

5.1.3   Internet of Things and Its Use

In recent years, there's been a massive growth in the number of electronic devices and smartphones, and the physical or wireless connection and communication among these various devices has become essential in our daily lives. This has led to the next generation of the connected world—the Internet of Things or IoT, which connects appliances, sensors, devices, and "things" in general, that are uniquely identifiable smart objects that comprise RFID (radio-frequency identification) tags or actuators or sensors, etc. The term was introduced first in 1999 by Kevin Ashton who envisioned a system in which all physical objects are interconnected via ubiquitous sensors with the help of Internet [5]. Therefore, the concept of IoT reflects the idea that anything can be connected and information or service on any object can be efficiently accessed anytime from anywhere within today's Internet infrastructure, with broadened scope and benefits [6].

As the new computing paradigm that has emerged in today's era, IoT allows a variety of communication protocols like Wi-Fi (Wireless Fidelity), Bluetooth, GSM (Global System for Mobile communications), Zigbee, etc., to interconnect heterogeneous devices, for the purpose of serving as the backbone for enabling ubiquitous computing and allowing smart environments to be able to identify real objects and retrieve information from them, hence establishing its three basic paradigms of sensors, internet-oriented, and knowledge [7]. The technologies of cloud computing and IPv6 (Internet Protocol version 6) further promote the integration of IoT and the Internet, as this development can accomplish assigning a unique address identification to all real world objects connecting to IoT and also provides greater opportunities of data collecting, processing, and other new services [5].

This emerging technology of IoT can affect the entire spectrum of business and aims at extending the Internet's benefits with capabilities of data sharing, remote control ability, constant and advanced connectivity beyond the M2M (Machine-to-Machine) scenarios, etc. [5, 6]. It is nowadays used in a variety of fields of life, with a wide range of applications like healthcare, emergency services, security, smart cities, waste management, traffic congestion, logistics, industrial control, etc. [6]. Figure 5.2 illustrates the architecture of IoT, highlighting its basic layers and technologies [7].

Therefore, it can be realized that using IoT, it is conceivable to introduce automation in nearly every field, and the application of ubiquitous technologies such as wireless sensor networks (WSN) and RFID can rise on addressing the emerging challenges of embedding intelligent ICT within the environment that surrounds us, and bringing the implementation very close to that of the modern society [6, 7].

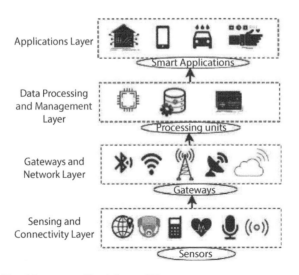

Figure 5.2 IoT architecture and basic layers [7].

5.1.4 Semantic Web and Its Technologies

Information forms the foundation on which the web thrives, and with the growth of the content on the web, and since the arrival of the World Wide Web (WWW), the need to manage information and knowledge has risen. The lack of a common standard and structure of information on the Internet poses a challenge for effective extraction of meaningful information. New tools for effectively managing this vast resource of information are being developed and the web is subsequently being evolved to what is now called as the Semantic Web. The World Wide Web Consortium (W3C) is managing the semantics of web and its standardization. The need for Semantic Web was felt owing to the shortcomings of the present Web version 2.0, which is primarily keyword based. Also, the data on the web is largely present in unstructured form and the search results for user queries display a lot of irrelevant content since the current web does not understand the meaning and context of this information [8].

The Semantic Web is Tim Berners Lee's vision of a web of linked data which overcomes the inadequacies of the existing web technologies by associating meaning with the data such that it can be processed intelligently by the machine, requiring minimum human intervention [9]. It can be seen as a component of "Web 3.0". With the introduction of Semantic Web and its technologies that build beyond the basic HTML (Hyper Text Markup Language) web pages, the data on the web can be understood by the machines such that a better cooperation between humans and machines is developed [8]. The idea of Semantic Web is to create a meaningful web system which provides a better platform for representation of knowledge that is globally processable by machines. The web resources in semantic web are rich in metadata, which describes their meaning, and allows the computer to interpret data and to carry out various activities like extensive searching, integrating disparate information sources using ontologies, scheduling and coordinating tasks, etc. This is the notion of a "highly intelligent web", which can efficiently and precisely carry out tasks and take decisions reducing human involvement. The dream tried to achieve through this smart web is of creating an open and linked Web of Data where a common knowledge is shared among all applications across different domains [9].

Berners-Lee gave a semantic web stack that represents the hierarchy in which every layer represents a technology and exploits the capabilities of the layers beneath it. These Semantic Web Technologies (SWTs) contextualize and give meaning to the data, enabling its linking, sharing, reuse, automation, and integration across various applications. As shown in

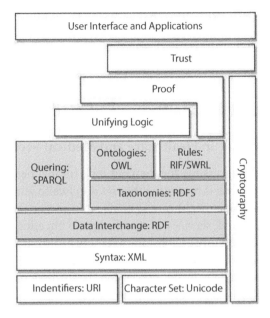

Figure 5.3 Semantic Web Stack[2].

Figure 5.3, they be categorized into hypertext web technologies (at the bottom of the stack), standardized SWTs (the shaded layers), and unrealized SWTs[2].

Of the various layers in the shown layered architecture, the standardized SWTs are of key concern: RDF (Resource Description Format)—it serves as a conceptual model for publishing and linking data, including metadata on the web, where directed acyclic graphs (DLGs) represent the statements in the form of triples of subject-predicate object as nodes and arcs between them;   RDFS (RDF Schema)—it is an ontology development language that provides vocabulary to the RDF and a mechanism to group related resources as classes, with their properties and relationships, in a taxonomical structure; OWL (Web Ontology Language)—it is a language which captures the ontologies (i.e., a domain's concepts and their relationships) and using the expressive and reasoning power of description logic (DL), acts as a representation tool for the understanding and sharing of a common knowledge; SPARQL (SPARQL Protocol and RDF Query Language)—it's a standard language for querying data expressed in RDF form, including graph patterns, and also acts as a protocol for accessing the ontologies

---

2 https://en.wikipedia.org/wiki/Semantic_Web_Stack

and RDFS data; RIF (Rule Interchange Format)—it allows the exchanges among rule systems and SWRL (Semantic Web Rule Language) covers the specification of all kinds of rules, which may be used for reasoning [10].

5.2   Use of IoT in Healthcare and Medical Domain

5.2.1   Scope of IoT in Healthcare and Medical Sector

As the society is progressing, the demand for personal healthcare applications and interventions is becoming the trend in health and medical development. The traditional healthcare system's scale and quality of health and medical resources and services is insufficient in meeting these personal medial needs and therefore establishing a remote health surveillance system based on the Internet is of high significance [11]. Since the IoT technology is evidently advantageous in the perception, transmission of data and the application of ICT, its implementation in the healthcare and medical sector offers tremendous scope for beneficiating patients and physicians both [3].

A new market based on Internet of Health Things (IoHT) is emerging, which can be viewed as IoT innovations towards creating healthcare solutions in the growing digital health domain. It is an IoT-based solution which incorporates a network model allowing the patient and physician facilities to be interconnected, examples include e-Health system for heart rate, ECG, diabetes, monitoring of other vital body signs based on bio-medical sensors such as for temperature, blood pressure, airflow, etc. IoHT can be classified into generic categories of ambient assisted living (AAL), remote health monitoring, wearable devices, healthcare solutions based on smartphones [12]. The new branch of IoT—the Internet of Medical Things (IoMT) denotes a collection of smart medical wearables, sensors, diagnostic and imaging devices, other gadgets, and software applications for interconnecting various remote or local healthcare software systems [13]. Besides enabling these interconnections, IoMT aims at playing a crucial role in improving the reliability, accuracy, and productivity of medical devices in the healthcare sector [11]. Using individual data-driven treatments, IoMT also promotes higher standards of health care and personalized health and wellness [13].

Figure 5.4 shows some of the IoT-enabled applications (user-centric) and services (developer-centric) for medical and healthcare field, where each service is typically general and has the potential to offer a set of health care solutions or applications, while applications developed through these services are directly used by the patients and users [6].

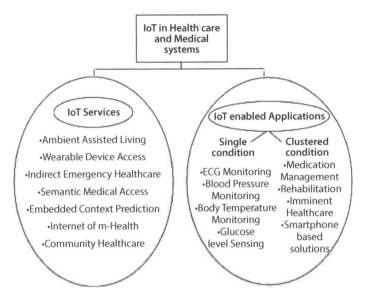

Figure 5.4 IoT healthcare services and IoT-enabled applications [6].

"IoThNet" or the IoT healthcare network forms the central element of the application of IoT in healthcare and medical sector. The IoThNet is what is responsible for providing the support for access to the IoT backbone, aids in facilitating the exchange of health data, and enables the use of healthcare-fitting communications [6].

With the aim to monitor and control objects via Internet, intelligent identification and management of data can be achieved using IoT, and the medical and healthcare field presents a promising application area for the IoT, where it has the capability to offer various applications like elderly care, remote heath monitoring, emergency handling, and personalized fitness programs [6]. State-of-the-art wireless technology-driven healthcare networks are expected to continuously monitor the patients and using different equipments and techniques for sensing, capturing, and transmitting health information, support the early diagnosis, chronic diseases, remote consultation, conformity with medication and treatment at home by healthcare professionals, and handling of medical emergencies. Health databases, medical servers, and gateways perform an important role in creating EHR and delivering health-related services to authorized stakeholders on an on-demand basis [3]. The sensors and microcontrollers are also smart and have various features such as an integrated system for precision-analog, graphical user interface, low power operation, etc., for working effectively [5].

5.2.2 Benefits of IoT in Healthcare and Medical Systems

IoT is introducing innovations in various industry segments and healthcare is one of the prompt sectors to have embraced this opportunity [12]. Due to lack of proper access to hospitals or other medical institutions and appropriate health monitoring, several people's health may suffer. But with the recent advances in technology, the progress in health of patients from all sections of the society (children, elderly, economically weaker, etc.) can be remotely monitored and diagnosed using small wireless solutions connected to IoT, eliminating the need for physically visiting the hospital. Health data can be securely captured from sensors attached to patient's body and collected using different wireless transmission technologies at the server to be analyzed by healthcare professionals in order to timely take decisions and provide remote services and affordable medical care [5, 14].

From the healthcare providers' viewpoint, through this remote supervision, the IoT offers to reduce the device downtime. It can help accurately identify the ideal time to replenish various devices' supplies for them to continue operating smoothly and also ensures best use and services by limited resources to more patients by supporting their efficient scheduling [6].

The major benefits of adopting IoT technologies in the healthcare and medical sector are the ease of access to both patients and physicians, use of cost-effective ICT for real-time solutions to providing improved medical care, i.e., involving minimal medical costs and shortest treatment time, delivering the best possible medical assistance and the most-satisfactory health services [5, 11].

Also, with the help of IoT technologies, the processes of production, anti-counterfeit, and tracking of delivery of medical equipments and services can be easily captured. Using IoT, health-related information too can be managed efficiently, including sample and medical record identification [3].

5.2.3 IoT Healthcare Challenges and Open Issues

The employment of IoT technologies in the healthcare and medical sector offers multiple benefits, but there still remain challenges that need to be tackled, such as:

- Standardization: The biggest challenge is the management of device diversity and the interoperability issues, which are raised due to the lack of any standards or rules and regulations to be adhered to for developing interfaces that are compatible across devices [13].

- The volume of health data is growing continuously. This unstructured and diverse data needs to be managed and poses scaling issues, requiring resources for real time processing and maintenance of performance such as CPU capacity, need for medical expertise, and system memory. Technical challenges also exist, such as modeling the relationship between the acquired measurements and the existing domain knowledge, hardware implementation and optimization, software implementation of schemes for performing data analytics, and introducing intelligence in health and medical care [6].
- IoT-Healthcare Platforms: The IoT-based health and medical care hardware has added severe needs in terms of the real time operating system and a customized platform for computing with run-time libraries as compared to that of the usual IoT devices. A service-oriented approach may be adopted for building the required suitable platforms, which can use application package interfaces for exploiting various services. Besides this, appropriate frameworks and libraries can be developed for the healthcare professionals to be able to make effective use of relevant data [13].
- Data Protection: Securing the personal health and medical data collected from various sensing devices poses a critical challenge. There is a need to introduce strict security policies and measures to impede any attempts at illicit access to this private information. Implementing optimal algorithms that allow sharing among authorized personnel and applications only, and a collaboration among services for data protection, breach detection and reaction for preventing the various security threats, vulnerabilities, and attacks remains an open challenge [13].

5.3   Role of SWTs in Healthcare Services

5.3.1   Scope and Benefits of Incorporating Semantics in Healthcare

The major data sources in the health and medical care industry are the clinical data from health institutions, health data with the patients and healthcare professionals, financial records from medical insurance companies, and the research and development data from pharma companies. This health-related data can answer various information needs associated with studying, monitoring, and research. The access to and reuse of this data can aid towards development in public healthcare or towards research. However, the dearth of semantic consistency and absence of standards in the healthcare systems adds to the troubles faced when trying to reuse this information [15]. The IoT-enabled medical devices used in the healthcare sector too are from different vendors and there is a lack of globally accepted standards which leads to encountering of semantic interoperability issues in heterogeneous IoT devices.

Semantics brings the capability of understanding what data is being communicated and gives structure-related details of the transferred data. In order for the heterogeneous IoT devices in any domain to interoperate without any conflicts, semantics describes the device and the information it is exchanging. This way, the meaning of data coming from a smart object is completely interpretable just the way the smart object would mean it to be. Also, semantics helps in resolving the ambiguity while adding new devices to a IoT network [16]. This introduces the concept of Semantic web of things (SWoT), which aims at associating semantically rich and easily accessible information to real-world objects, locations and events, by means of inexpensive, disposable and unobtrusive micro-devices. The dynamic SWoT environment has resource discovery as its most pivotal feature, i.e., smart wearables and medical things can be easily identified, monitored, and accessed for information [17].

SWTs offer improved capabilities which enable more effective and accurate processing of data, creating a framework that allows interoperability among healthcare and medical systems and integrates data from various IoT sources based on their semantic meaning [18]. A series of SWTs provide a promising solution for the annotation, reuse and semantic interoperability of health data—the RDF, the triple store, ontology, and SPARQL facilitate the integration and analysis of heterogeneous data. Semantic web's RDF technology is adopted to overcome the challenges of linking related data by including RDF triples for providing the missing semantics in the domain models [19]. Ontologies, which are core to the semantic web, prove to be a useful tool in representing knowledge and the semantics amid healthcare systems [18]. SPARQL queries can be further used to extract information from the RDF graphs [20].

The health data from heterogeneous devices in IoT can be annotated using RDF and this semantic annotation makes data semantically interoperable. Semantic interoperability refers to the information exchange with clear meaning and understanding. It consists self-describing tags of information which form the semantics in data [20]. The data coming from sensors or other means should be homogeneously represented and irrespective of the type of sensors and should be monitored, collected, and analyzed. The OWL technique of ontology is predominantly used for semantic representation, knowledge sharing, and promoting semantic interoperability in the web [21]. Offering complete semantics describing a data includes ontological as well as temporal and spatial information too, providing operational semantic interoperability, which refers to the complete contextual information along with the meaning of the terms, and the various possible choices, the syntactic constraints, applicable reference ranges, etc. [19]. In an example of progress towards semantic interoperability, the Dutch government, in order to realize capacity building in semantics in the field of health and medical care, started courses for introduction to SNOMED CT (Systematized Nomenclature of Medicine Clinical Terms), which is a standard medical terminology vocabulary, and highlighted the need of concept based systems and reference ontologies [22].

Using SWTs, reusability of health-related data is easily facilitated, which can prove to be beneficial in improving the knowledge of diseases, their treatments, effectiveness of treatments, various health actions, etc., along with contributions to better health surveillance and research [15]. Identifying the benefits of SWTs in healthcare, W3C formed the Semantic Web for Health Care and Life Sciences (HCLS) Interest Group with the objective to develop, support, and promote the use of SWTs in healthcare and medical[3].

5.3.2 Ontologies and Datasets for Healthcare and Medical Domain

Ontologies are the core component of the semantic web infrastructure which offer vocabularies of common technical terminology over various domains which are used for assisting in semantic annotation of data and thus forms the basis for systems' interoperability [23]. In health and medical care, ontology mainly focuses on organizing medical terminologies and is therefore the tool used for sharing the precise definitions of complex medical concepts unambiguously. Ontologies can respond to the need of communicating and reusing patient data and also provide semantic criteria for various statistical aggregations. However, no single ontology exists

---

[3] https://www.w3.org/2001/sw/hcls/.

which encompasses the complete healthcare field, and therefore, the multiple ontologies that exist must be interoperable[4].

Various ontologies developed in the healthcare and medical domain are surveyed in [23] and the list of ontologies for health and medicine is growing continuously. Among these biological and medical ontologies and terminologies providing comprehensive descriptions are: FMA (Foundational Model of Anatomy), UMLS (Unified Medical Lexicon System), SNOMED-CT, OpenEHR, and ICD (International Classification of Diseases [18]. Most of these are available and accessible via BioPortal. Similarly, OBO (Open Biological and Biomedical Ontologies) Foundry coordinates the development and interoperability of a suite of ontologies for assimilating biomedical data[4]. United Medical Language System (UMLS) [12] is another repository of various biomedical vocabularies and ontologies which are developed by the US National Library of Medicine [18]. Similar to the ontologies for healthcare domain, several existing and emerging ontologies developed for the IoT domain for the purpose of formally representing sensors' description include: W3C's SSN (Semantic Sensor Network) ontology, IoT-Lite ontology, IoT.est ontologies, SensorML (Sensor Model Language), and IOT-A information model [18, 21]. In addition to ontology, various standards and technologies like RDF have been developed by semantic web for publishing and linking data on the web. Some public health-associated datasets and repositories published using SWTs and standards are also available, like in University of California Irvine (UCI) Machine Learning Repository, Lionbridge AI training datasets, etc. Some representative repositories/datasets are surveyed in [23].

5.3.3   Challenges in the Use of SWTs in Healthcare Sector

The employment of SWTs in hospitals, clinics, or medical institutions can provide benefits of achieving the expectations of improved productivity. However, certain gaps and challenges exist, as revealed by surveys, and these issues are needed to be addressed [24, 23]:

- Heaps of data is generated on a daily basis by various health organizations. This data is generally produced in proprietary formats, which calls for a need of strong tools for mapping this local data to standard formats to be able to achieve the most relevant results [24]. Some initiatives in this direction

---

[4] https://github.com/twamarc/ScheMed/wiki/Healthcare-Ontology-and-Reusable-Clinical-Entities

have been taken up, but it remains a complex task to map the local terms to standard vocabularies' concepts. It's a resource-intensive job that requires knowledge of the specific domain and that of the vocabularies and therefore needs to be presented as an automated process for better semantic interoperability [23].

- One of the biggest challenges is the existence of multiple ontologies in the healthcare and medical sector. This poses a challenge to choose and reach a commonly agreed ontology as a standard. It requires efforts to standardize the vocabulary in the specific domain of healthcare and medicine [23, 24].

- Data is constantly updated and can be described with the use of different vocabularies, since a single ontology can't be considered sufficient enough for describing the heterogeneous healthcare data that is generated. Various tools and strategies of ontology alignment and mapping are needed for integrating these ontologies into creating a coherent view [24].

- There's a lack of interfaces that are user-friendly for the purposes of accessing, querying, navigating, and presenting in a meaningful way, the semantic data on health. Development of fewer effective interfaces is also a cause of hindrance in the wide adoption of SWTs in the healthcare and medical field [23].

- The huge flood of data in the healthcare and medical field needs to be dealt with, which requires new and improved tools and algorithms that work effectively by improving upon the traditional data mining and management techniques [23].

- Using techniques of data mining in integration with SWTs offers opportunities for discovering knowledge and hidden patterns from large datasets on healthcare and medicine [24]. The structure of the underlying semantic data generated from semantic web frameworks can affect the performance of the mining techniques, which calls for a need to develop data mining tools that work effectively on semantic data to further improve the usefulness of semantic web. The accuracy and quality of the semantic health data used for testing and training the techniques of data mining is also highly important. Further, there is a need to analyze and evaluate with care some of the results and retrieved patterns in healthcare and medicine domain, which involves using data mining techniques with high accuracy [23].

5.4 Incorporating IoT and/or SWTs in Healthcare and Medical Sector

Continuous research is going on in the field of incorporating IoT and SWTs in the health domain and the literature available can be categorized as follows.

5.4.1 Proposed Architecture or Framework or Model

An early application of semantic web or the web 3.0 was in Domotics (Domus Informatics) or IT (information technology) in homes. A framework for the representation of domotics' knowledge using semantic ontologies has been developed by Miori and Russo in [25]. The specific ontologies can automatically take into account the context information from the distributed environment, and this information modeling mechanism can serve to form the basis for implementing e-Health systems in homes, especially useful for elderly and sick people, where potential health hazards can be anticipated and prevented [25].

SemanMedical, a semantic model for medical monitoring in the sensor-based IoT healthcare system, was proposed in [26], in which all the devices' and sensors' data, structured or not, is stored in a cloud database and the structured data builds the conditions for semantic rules agreed by the patients. When the set data range is exceeded by the health indicators from patients' sensor data, the medical engine alerts the patients. Further, two algorithms for processing semantic medical rules were also designed-one with and another without external communication, and through simulations it was shown that the former works better than the latter [26].

A functional architecture resulting from requirements of providing smarter personalized healthcare services in smart home environment has been discussed in [27]. While the wearable sensors help in continuously monitoring the health of the person, sensors installed in smart homes provide for understanding of the person's environment, and thus using semantic inferencing capabilities, sensor measurements from different domains can be combined to gather actionable knowledge in cross-domain scenarios. M3 (Machine-to-Machine Measurement) framework for processing the M2M data forms the center of this proposed IoT-based healthcare system, and it implements a SWoT generator as part of its operational framework to aid developers in creating smarter solutions for health and medical care [27].

A software architecture for an IoT-based healthcare application is proposed in [21], focusing on the usage of semantic OWL for data exchanges and the principle of weak coupling. The proposed IoT architecture has the following features: the same sensor can be used in different applications, which refers to lesser connected sensors, and also the information acquired can be provided by more than one sensor, which refers to data redundancy. For this reason, semantics are used to describe sensor data and the interoperability is supported by the publish/subscribe framework. Taking the case of bedsores (or pressure ulcers), which can prove to be critical in elderly people's health, a risk detection prototype has also been designed to validate the presented architecture [21].

In the space of pervasive patient care, for providing usable and extensible services for monitoring, authors in [28] have proposed a framework for constructing healthcare systems based on sensors. The approach aims at providing anytime and anywhere monitoring of patients' health, and for that, banks on a distributed system. It can also help detect potential health complications and can alert the stakeholders accordingly. Through ontological framework-based semantic-enriched web services, automated discovery is enabled and all in all, the proposed approach facilitates scalability and interoperability. By applying this framework to a scenario of the project of Remote AAL, the usefulness of the approach has been shown [28].

Figure 5.5 shows a general healthcare system which is IoT-based, having sensors and other communication technologies, and utilizing SWTs for web services and offering scope for health data analytics.

With large health related datasets and repositories available, the scope and potential of performing health data analytics is huge. In [29], a semantics-based data analytics (SeDan) framework is proposed to explore the capabilities of implementing PR (Plausible Reasoning) using SWTs for heath data analytics. PR refers to the approach of inferencing which extracts probable assertions from incomplete yet fine-grained knowledge base and therefore extends it by leveraging information on the semantic relationship between the concepts. Using the influence of ontological knowledge, the proposed framework aims at improving the accuracy and expressiveness of PR methods for better analytics in healthcare and therefore enhanced clinical decision support system [29].

An IoT-SIM (Semantic Interoperability Model) has been proposed to annotate the communication exchanges between heterogeneous IoT devices and healthcare professionals and therefore make them semantically

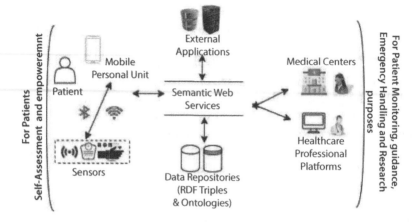

Figure 5.5 Healthcare services provision for patients and health professionals using IoT and SWTs (adapted from [28]).

interoperable [16]. This model in healthcare domain helps in communicating the information from continuous monitoring of health status of patients in a meaningful way, using RDF annotations, and also allows for SPARQL querying on that data. Similar model is also applicable in big data applications of heath, as shown by implementing on two big-datasets of details of drugs and medicines with their side effects in [20].

The current research issues and existing state-of-the-art frameworks of semantic web for health and medical care have been compared by Shah and Thakkar in [24]. A semantic framework has also been proposed by them for ubiquitous healthcare (u-healthcare) services, which is used to measure the risk level of patient's health.

5.4.2   Access Mechanisms or Approaches

The wide use of IoT-based healthcare and medical semantics, placing ontologies, and semantics on top of IoT technologies demands a semantic medical access (SMA) separate service. To deal with the heterogeneity of IoT centered data in healthcare and medical services, a ubiquitous resource-based data accessing method (UDA-IoT) using RESTful (Representational State Transfer) architecture is proposed in [14]. For describing the distributed heterogeneous IoT nodes and to facilitate their data interoperability and sharing, a unified metadata model is presented. Of the three data structure layers of value, annotation and semantic explanation, the semantic data model stresses on the self-explanation feature of data values in order to support collecting and processing of data ubiquitously and timely for improving the accessibility to IoT data resources in a mobile and cloud computing platform. To validate the support offered for flexible acquiring, integration, and interoperation among IoT data, an emergency medical service based on IoT system has also been demonstrated [14].

A flexible semantic model that can aid physicians in efficiently accessing data resources, by connecting IoT data and EHR to support true integration, interoperability is needed. Using SWTs, the IoT data collected from healthcare sensors and device can be defined and so can the complex structure and relationships among unstructured health data obtained from EHR. An ontology-based semantic middleware is proposed by Alamdri [18] which exploits ontologies in order to provide support for functional collaboration as well as semantic integration between EHR systems and IoT-based healthcare systems. The proposed semantic interoperation middleware algorithm also enables automatic inference, efficient health information retrieval and search, and hence improves patient care [18].

5.4.3   Applications or Systems

To address the issue of semantic interoperability among devices, Jin and Kim [1] proposed a system in which an ontology defined in IETF's YANG (Yet Another Next Generation) is used for modeling an e-Health system with SSN (Semantic Sensor Network) to express the sensed e-Health data in a comprehensible manner. This modeling scheme supports various data format styles and by constructing e-Health sensors' meta-models, it provides semantic interpretation of sensor data in the e-Health system, which enables querying and auto-configuration of the sensor network [1].

Recommendation Systems (RS) have been developed recently in the internet age to assist users in their day-to-day lives. In [30], a personalized travel RS—ProTrip is proposed and designed, which has the capability to suggest to travelers food items based on their health and the climatic conditions. ProTrip is thus an effective health-centered RS which takes into account the traveler's personal choice and nutrition value of food items recommended to the user, with the novel functionality of supporting them follow a strict diet in cases of long-term diseases. This is made possible because of its basis of ontological knowledge and appropriate filtering methods. The authors also demonstrate and evaluate the food RS approach for real-time healthcare system based on IoT technologies [30].

Of the various IoT-based applications in healthcare systems, in [31], using SVM (support vector machine) supervised machine learning algorithm, a method has been proposed, which while retaining an efficient and quick processing along with low cost of computation to maintain the IoT communication requirements, can deal with the problem of recognizing postures during sleep by monitoring and identifying binary patterns using minimal information of patients' binary images on the mattress. To ensure that the operation is carried out unobtrusively for both the monitored person and the monitoring party, an IoT-based communication application's remote scenario has been proposed. The satisfactory recognition results encourage further investigation in this domain [31].

Several healthcare systems integrated with IoT or ontology-based solutions have been developed for supervising health for long term care of chronically ill patients. However, it was observed that due to uncertainty of factors and high risk, these systems were not usable for acquiring precise information on patients or for extracting optimal involvement of various risk factors [32]. Owing to this poor results in case of diabetes patients, authors in [32] have presented a type-2 fuzzy ontology-based RS for effectively monitoring diabetes patients and suggesting them specific food and medicines. Wearable sensors are used for capturing precise physiological information of diabetes patients and patient's risk factors are also extracted in order to recommend prescriptions and food for a smart medicine box and refrigerator, respectively. Combination of fuzzy ontology and T2FL (Type-2 Fuzzy Logic) is used for knowledge representation and inferencing to automate the recommendation process, and DL and SPARQL for evaluation, showing that the proposed healthcare system significantly improves the prediction accuracy of health condition of patients and also the accuracy rate for diabetes-specific recommendations [32].

5.5 Healthcare Data Analytics Using Data Mining and Machine Learning

The growth in the digital health care system has generated large volumes of data from treatment plans, patient demographics, health insurance, etc. which has attracted attention from physicians and data scientists equally. The increasing population also is demanding of smart healthcare services, quality medical applications, and wearables that will help improve standard of living and lifespans [33]. This need for better healthcare facilities calls for performing analytics and data mining on health-associated data and the introduction of AI (Artificial Intelligence) and ML (Machine Learning) applications in the healthcare and medical industry.

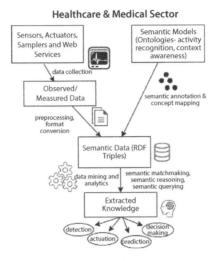

Figure 5.6 Using SWTs in IoT-enabled healthcare applications for data analytics.

Figure 5.6 shows how IoT and semantic web technologies are incorporated in healthcare and medical sector and further extended using data analytics for various applications.

Analytics refers to the techniques of efficiently using data and applying quantitative and qualitative analysis on complex and voluminous data to develop insights and extract valuable information for assisting in healthcare decision making. It can be categorized into different types which are Predictive analytics (forecasting), Descriptive analytics (business intelligence and data mining), Prescriptive analytics (optimization and simulation), and Diagnostic analytics [33]. Machine learning is the subfield of AI which evolves from exploring pattern recognition and the concept that algorithms can learn from data, become intelligent and make predictions and take decisions. With no lack of healthcare data since the rise in access to individual patient data due to high penetration rate of EHR, scope of AI and ML to be applied and their full potential to be harnessed for detecting and assessing health issues better is at the peak. Some of the prevalent machine learning applications in the healthcare and medical industry are pattern imaging analytics, personalized treatment and behavioral modification, drug discovery and manufacturing, robotics in surgery, clinical trial research, and predicting epidemic outbreaks.[5]

---

[5] https://www.upgrad.com/blog/machine-learning-applications-in-healthcare-2018/.

Extraction of hidden patterns and valuable knowledge from the large healthcare datasets is possible using data mining techniques, for applications like detection of fraud in health insurance, detection of causes of diseases, identification of medical treatment at lower cost, etc. [23]. Some of the representative techniques used for data mining in healthcare for interoperability are: K-Nearest Neighbors (KNN) Classification for applications such as diagnosing heart diseases with better accuracy, etc., Bayesian Classification which is generally used for health risks' analysis, Decision Tree Classification model helpful for diseases of the skin or for predicting breast cancer, Fuzzy KNN Classification for applications like diagnosis of thyroid disease, and Neural Network Classification that is useful for ailments like asthma, chest disease, lung cancer, etc. [23].

Several objectives that can be addressed by the application of data mining techniques on semantic web data on e-Health care system are: knowledge management for various diseases and patients' health profile, recommendation systems for patients and health providers, and real time delivery of information based on ontology for supporting decision making. In [29], a semantics-based data analytics framework (SeDan) is proposed for health data analytics, which increases the potential of employing plausible reasoning, when working with large health datasets, by using SWTs, i.e., leveraging ontological knowledge and semantic inferencing more specifically, to improve the accuracy and expressiveness of plausible reasoning methods. An example of application of machine learning in semantic e-Health data is described in [31] where SVM algorithm of ML is used for monitoring and recognizing postures remotely.

Some future research applications of integrating data analytics using data mining or machine learning along with IoT and SWTs for healthcare and medical data are: cost-effective personalized care, automation for non-experts, information loss in preprocessing, inclusion of prediction in real-time healthcare applications, and collecting healthcare data for research purposes [33].

5.6   Conclusion

Health and medical care is a huge service industry being consumed by everyone and is presently on its way to the third wave of IT adoption. All health and medical related data is being digitized and turned to strategic assets for meeting the increasing demands of improved personalized healthcare services at anytime and anyplace at cost-effective prices.

The promising role and usage of the emerging IoTs and SWTs in the healthcare and medical sector is highlighted through this chapter. The scope of e-Health, m-Health, IoT, and SWTs in health domain is explored and light is shed on their advantages, along with their applications, as discussed in literature. Also, in spite of the potential benefits, the challenges and open issues of these technologies in health domain are also reviewed. Data analytics using data mining, AI, and machine learning is influencing every possible domain, and healthcare and medical sector too, with its large datasets as its key resources, does not remain untouched with the capabilities of analytics. This significant aspect of digitized healthcare and medical field is also explored in this chapter.

5.7   Future Work

With the vision to develop improved solutions for the various healthcare stakeholders, some potential areas of future work are: enhancing quality of treatments, supporting peer-to-peer communication and collaboration, delivering information of patients' records to the point of care which assists healthcare providers to accelerate decision making, streamlining clinical operations, developing intuitive smartphone apps that facilitate easy exchanges and access to EHR, implementing advanced features like real time graphical display of data, data archiving and feedback, and enforcing strong encryption and security policies for providing only authorized access to protected health information and minimize vulnerabilities.

References

1. Jin, W. and Kim, D., Design and implementation of e-health system based on semantic sensor network using IETF YANG. *Sensors*, 18, 2, 629, 2018.
2. Vandelanotte, C., Müller, A.M., Short, C.E., Hingle, M., Nathan, N., Williams, S.L., Maher, C.A., Past, present, and future of eHealth and mHealth research to improve physical activity and dietary behaviors. *J. Nutri. Educ. Behav.*, 48, 3, 219–228, 2016.
3. Hu, F., Xie, D., Shen, S., On the application of the internet of things in the field of medical and health care, in: *2013 IEEE International Conference on Green Computing and Communications and IEEE Internet of Things and IEEE Cyber, Physical and Social Computing*, IEEE, pp. 2053–2058, 2013.
4. Kay, M., Santos, J., Takane, M., mHealth: New horizons for health through mobile technologies. *World Health Organization*, 64, 7, 66–71, 2011.

5. Ullah, K., Shah, M.A., Zhang, S., Effective ways to use Internet of Things in the field of medical and smart health care, in: *2016 International Conference on Intelligent Systems Engineering (ICISE)*, IEEE, pp. 372–379, 2016.

6. Islam, S.R., Kwak, D., Kabir, M.H., Hossain, M., Kwak, K.S., The internet of things for health care: a comprehensive survey. *IEEE Access*, 3, 678–708, 2015.

7. Yaqoob, I., Ahmed, E., Hashem, I.A.T., Ahmed, A.I.A., Gani, A., Imran, M., Guizani, M., Internet of things architecture: Recent advances, taxonomy, requirements, and open challenges. *IEEE Wireless Commun.*, 24, 3, 10–16, 2017.

8. Alesso, H.P. and Smith, C.F., *Thinking on the Web: Berners-Lee, Godel and Turing*, Wiley-Interscience, New York, 2008.

9. Berners-Lee, T., Hendler, J., Lassila, O., The semantic web. *Sci. Am.*, 284, 5, 28–37, 2001.

10. Hebeler, J., Fisher, M., Blace, R., Perez-Lopez, A., *Semantic web programming*, John Wiley & Sons, Indianapolis, Indiana, 2011.

11. Joyia, G.J., Liaqat, R.M., Farooq, A., Rehman, S., Internet of Medical Things (IOMT): Applications, benefits and future challenges in healthcare domain. *J. Commun.*, 12, 4, 240–7, 2017.

12. Rodrigues, J.J., Segundo, D.B.D.R., Junqueira, H.A., Sabino, M.H., Prince, R.M., Al-Muhtadi, J., De Albuquerque, V.H.C., Enabling technologies for the internet of health things. *IEEE Access*, 6, 13129–13141, 2018.

13. Villanueva-Miranda, I., Nazeran, H., Martinek, R., A Semantic Interoperability Approach to Heterogeneous Internet of Medical Things (IoMT) Platforms, in: *2018 IEEE 20th International Conference on e-Health Networking, Applications and Services (Healthcom)*, IEEE, pp. 1–5, 2018.

14. Xu, B., Da Xu, L., Cai, H., Xie, C., Hu, J., Bu, F., Ubiquitous data accessing method in IoT-based information system for emergency medical services. *IEEE Trans. Ind. Inf.*, 10, 2, 1578–1586, 2014.

15. Fieschi, M., *Health Data Processing: Systemic Approaches*, pp. 179–187, Elsevier, Oxford, UK, 2018.

16. Jabbar, S., Ullah, F., Khalid, S., Khan, M., Han, K., Semantic interoperability in heterogeneous IoT infrastructure for healthcare. *Wireless Commun. Mob. Comput.*, 2017, 1–10, 2017.

17. Ruta, M., Scioscia, F., Di Sciascio, E., Enabling the Semantic Web of Things: Framework and architecture, in: *2012 IEEE Sixth International Conference on Semantic Computing*, IEEE, pp. 345–347, 2012.

18. Alamri, A., Ontology Middleware for Integration of IoT Healthcare Information Systems in EHR Systems. *Computers*, 7, 4, 51, 2018.

19. Luz, M.P., de Matos Nogueira, J.R., Cavalini, L.T., Cook, T.W., Providing full semantic interoperability for the fast healthcare interoperability resources schemas with resource description framework, in: *2015 International Conference on Healthcare Informatics*, IEEE, pp. 463–466, 2015.

20. Ullah, F., Habib, M.A., Farhan, M., Khalid, S., Durrani, M.Y., Jabbar, S., Semantic interoperability for big-data in heterogeneous IoT infrastructure for healthcare. *Sustainable Cities Soc.*, 34, 90–96, 2017.

21. Zgheib, R., Conchon, E., Bastide, R., Engineering IoT healthcare applications: Towards a semantic data driven sustainable architecture, in: *eHealth 360*, pp. 407–418, Springer, Cham, 2017.

22. Lau, F., Infrastructure and Capacity Building for Semantic Interoperability in Healthcare in the Netherlands. *Buil. Capacity Health Inf. Future*, 234, 70, 2017.

23. Zenuni, X., Raufi, B., Ismaili, F., Ajdari, J., State of the art of semantic web for healthcare. *Procedia-Social Behav. Sci.*, 195, 1990–1998, 2015.

24. Shah, P. and Thakkar, A., Comparative analysis of semantic frameworks in healthcare, in: *Healthcare Data Analytics and Management*, pp. 133–154, Academic Press, UK and US, 2019.

25. Miori, V. and Russo, D., Anticipating health hazards through an ontology-based, IoT domotic environment, in: *2012 Sixth International Conference on Innovative Mobile and Internet Services in Ubiquitous Computing*, IEEE, pp. 745–750, 2012.

26. Zhang, G., Li, C., Zhang, Y., Xing, C., Yang, J., SemanMedical: A kind of semantic medical monitoring system model based on the IoT sensors, in: *2012 IEEE 14th International Conference on e-Health Networking, Applications and Services (Healthcom)*, IEEE, pp. 238–243, 2012.

27. Datta, S.K., Bonnet, C., Gyrard, A., Da Costa, R.P.F., Boudaoud, K., Applying Internet of Things for personalized healthcare in smart homes, in: *2015 24th Wireless and Optical Communication Conference (WOCC)*, IEEE, pp. 164–169, 2015.

28. Triantafyllidis, A.K., Koutkias, V.G., Chouvarda, I., Adami, I., Kouroubali, A., Maglaveras, N., Framework of sensor-based monitoring for pervasive patient care. *Healthcare Technol. Lett.*, 3, 3, 153–158, 2016.

29. Mohammadhassanzadeh, H., Abidi, S.R., Shah, M.S., Karamollahi, M., Abidi, S.S.R., SeDAn: A Plausible Reasoning Approach for Semantics-based Data Analytics in Healthcare, in: *WAIAH@ AI* IA*, pp. 50–59, 2017.

30. Subramaniyaswamy, V., Manogaran, G., Logesh, R., Vijayakumar, V., Chilamkurti, N., Malathi, D., Senthilselvan, N., An ontology-driven personalized food recommendation in IoT-based healthcare system. *J. Supercomputing*, 75, 6, 3184–3216, 2019.

31. Matar, G., Lina, J.M., Carrier, J., Riley, A., Kaddoum, G., Internet of Things in sleep monitoring: An application for posture recognition using supervised learning, in: *2016 IEEE 18th International Conference on e-Health Networking, Applications and Services (Healthcom)*, IEEE, pp. 1–6, 2016.

32. Ali, F., Islam, S.R., Kwak, D., Khan, P., Ullah, N., Yoo, S.J., Kwak, K.S., Type-2 fuzzy ontology–aided recommendation systems for IoT–based healthcare. *Comput. Commun.*, 119, 138–155, 2018.

33. Islam, M., Hasan, M., Wang, X., Germack, H., A systematic review on healthcare analytics: Application and theoretical perspective of data mining, in: *Healthcare*, vol. 6, p. 54, Multidisciplinary Digital Publishing Institute, Switzerland, 2018.

6

An Ontological Model, Design, and Implementation of CSPF for Healthcare

Pooja Mohan

*Department of IT, Goswami Ganesh Dutta Sanatan Dharma College,
Panjab University, Chandigarh, India*

Abstract

The study presents a Formal Contextual Security Privacy model for healthcare application with aim to provide services in the secure manner. The contextual information helps in improving the dynamic aspects of security and privacy as compared to existing security mechanisms which works only in static environments. Semantic web–based technique and reasoning mechanism are used for representation. Various scenarios relating to health care services as well as challenges faced by the system are presented by this study. The performance overhead of the model is evaluated by implementing simulator in Java. The system performance is studied by testing the scalability of the system and its throughput by measuring the memory usage and average inference time by varying the number of policies, size of ontology and number of instances, etc. Comparative analysis of average inference time is done for different types of reasoning engines. The response time of our proposed system is compared with the traditional model without security and privacy parameters shows significant improvements.

Keywords: Semantic web, context, security, OWL, semantic web rule language (SWRL), health, privacy

6.1 Introduction

The adoption of sensor network applications in today's life has significantly increased due to advancement of networks, sensor, and wireless

Email: pooja.mohan@ggdsd.ac.in

Vishal Jain, Ritika Wason, Jyotir Moy Chatterjee and Dac-Nhuong Le (eds.) *Ontology-Based Information Retrieval for Healthcare Systems*, (117–142) © 2020 Scrivener Publishing LLC communication technology. As nodes are deployed randomly, so their vulnerability to attack is more. For the very critical application such as healthcare where minor security breaches can result in the side effect, it's also difficult to implement security features due to scarcity of resources. It's required to understand the features of security services as well as the types of attacks encountered in the system depending upon the application for which they are designed.

Heterogeneous nature of sensor nodes, lack of physical infrastructure, and high cost of secured node due to deployment in public environments make the design of security procedures more complicated. Contextual parameters to a sensor node can be added to improve the security of the environment.

These system which uses context can sense the change in an environment and dynamically adapts their behavior without the help of any user. Using the contexts such as time, location, people, and activity, network knows which information is significant to transmit. Retrieval of information about the system can be made easily.

Network properties are commonly used contexts such as network bandwidth, error rate, connection setup time, usage costs, security requirements, contention, disconnection rate, and round-trip delay. Contextual parameters improve the security and privacy in dynamic environments.

Security is provided by using both hardware and software solutions. An encryption, authentication, intrusion detection system, and firewall come under software solutions. At the hardware level, security is ensured by using the smart card and public key cryptography. Security is also incorporated by maintaining an ACL (Access Control List) as well as by using the frame integrity. Frame integrity is implemented by appending the integrity code to the message to be transmitted. To provide secure routing in the sensor network, SPINS is introduced, consisting of both SNEP and TESLA. But these solutions seem to be an ineffective due to limitation of sensor network, i.e., energy, processor power, and the limited time span of sensor node. Security solutions along with attacks in different layers of the sensor network are described in the study [1].

These security mechanisms have not been proven to be effective in the dynamic environment, as they are not capable of adapting their security policies. The context can provide an integrated dynamic security service in ubiquitous applications to protect against all types of major attacks.

The organization of paper is as follows. Related work is presented in Section 6.2. Section 6.3 discusses the mathematical representation of CSPF model. Ontological model is represented in Section 6.4, and Section 6.5

provides design of the model. Sections 6.6 and 6.7 cover the implementation and results. Section 6.8 finally presents the conclusion and future scope.

6.2 Related Work

The context includes any parameter which is used to represent information related to physical objects, applications, and users in any application that is dynamic in the different situation according to application areas.

Context plays an important role in enhancing security in all types of computing environment for providing various services. Security types may be based on trust, access control, and identity management and reliability services, etc., as shown in Table 6.1.

The various application areas where different contextual models have been deployed to provide security services. In most of the studies [13–17], the model used is context set. Studies [11, 18] offers model based on Predicate logic. Set theory-based model is adopted by study in [19] to provide an authorization service.

Different modeling languages are *Insense* [20], to create a component-based model, *VDM* [21] (The Vienna Development Method), a specification language to describe the interpreters for languages such as PL/I., *Promela Model (PM)* [22], the modeling language used to model an Ad hoc Sensor network using Spin model checker, *SensorML* [23], XML-based language that models a sensor by the specification of Meta data such as its Id and its types, *Extended Reactive Modules (XRM)* [24], an extension language of Reactive Modules (RMs) for network issues such as communication capability, memory, and energy consumption. *Z Notation* [25] based on mathematical logic, i.e., FOPL and set theory and standardized by the ISO in 2002 as ISO/IEC, doesn't represent performance, usability, reliability, and size. The various others models are *spatial models, ER models, key-value, mark-up scheme-based, Object Oriented Models, Object Role models, and Ontology-based models* designed for specific applications. As *Spatial models* in [26–28] provides support for automated image region annotation, material detection, and navigation purpose. *ORM* is derived from *CML* (Context Modeling Language) proposed by the studies [29–31]. *Key-value models* lacked the knowledge sharing and formality and specifically used for one application only. The context oriented relationship and the complexity of constraints is not exhibited by *Mark-up scheme* models. *Ontological models* based on the semantic web offer reasoning services and

Table 6.1 Context for enhancement of security.

Author	Highlights
Mobile Ad hoc Network	
Moloney, M. *et al.* [2]	Provided trust-based security using context awareness.
Saidane, A. [3]	Presented an access control for managed resources.
Arabo, A. *et al.* [4]	Proposed a privacy framework for controlling the identity based on users' convenience.
Shankaran, R. *et al.* [5]	A Reputation-based approach used to access the trustworthiness of nodes.
Pratas, N. *et al.* [6]	Proposed a framework of identification with security and privacy mechanism for various types of scenarios.
Li, W. *et al.* [7]	Proposed a model where collected contextual information distinguishes between malicious and faulty nodes with limited overhead.
Ubiquitous Computing	
Wrona, K. *et al.* [8]	Discussed security challenges of ubiquitous systems and use of context for security configuration of services.
Lee, K. *et al.* [9]	Proposed a model to create secure context-aware applications by extending generalized RBAC model.
F. Schaub, B. *et al.* [10]	Proposed a model for a ubiquitous application with privacy reconfiguration policies with change in context.

(Continued)

Table 6.1 Context for enhancement of security. (*Continued*)

Author	Highlights
Wireless Sensor Network	
Al-Muhtadi, J. *et al.* [11]	Proposed an authentication and access control by integrating reasoning with context awareness.
Venkatesan, L. *et al.* [12]	Provided a framework to support Reliability through fault tolerance.

represent the concepts in an easiest way and also allow the standardization making the model independent of programming environment. They offer support for interoperability, heterogeneity, and representation of complex relationships and dependencies among context data. Context-oriented reasoning and the knowledge sharing among different applications systems are not represented by other models.

The study in [32–35] focused on a model based on reasoning in an ontology-based system. The model SOUPA discussed in the study [33–35] used context ontology in the pervasive computing environment while CONON [36–38] make use of extensible context ontology. It lacks the generality and the classification of context for reasoning purpose. Studies [39] present using ontology models for context representation for mobile touring and the navigation system. Some applications [40], GAIA [41], and Semantic Wallet [42] make use of hybrid technology by integrating ontology with other contextual models.

Different security models based on confidentiality and integrity are defined in the literature. The model based on confidentiality is the Bell–La Padula model [43], the Biba model [44], and the Clark-Wilson model [45], which are the integrity models. Some other models are the lattice models (Denning) [46], information flow, and the Interference models.

A number of alternate models such as Role-Based Access Control (*RBAC*) [47, 48], Discretionary (DAC), and mandatory access control (MAC). The study [49] proposed Generalized RBAC using context for accessing information by defining three types of roles subject, environment, and object roles. Context roles such as owner, provider, and broker and service provider are specified by model based on RBAC [50] for collection management and interpretation of context information. Context conditions based on securities policies are not supported by this model. The previously defined studies focused on defining the static security policies.

A model is required to update the security policies at run time as soon as some threat is detected.

According to study in [51], information usage, sensitivity of information, receiver, and disclosure of context are the factors to be considered regarding privacy in multimedia information communications. The study [52] focused on how privacy is implemented in smart office using the information spaces. The machine readable policies based on privacy is described by the model in the study [53]. The system sends the beacons to users regarding informing them about the privacy settings. Policies of authorization based on location information are specified in the study [54] to list the persons who are authorized to access their location. Context privacy in media spaces is described by the study in [55]. RFID tags are used for the localization. Monitoring is via video sensors only when some violations of policy such as some kind of suspicious movement are taking place. A toolkit Confab is developed on the basis of privacy needs of user and developer with more control of the user over information disclosure using the concept of context awareness [56]. An architecture based on virtual walls is proposed by the study in [57], to implement the digital privacy. Privacy policies about time, location and the quality of service are represented using the policy language.

The previous literature focused on either security or privacy policies. There was a need to implement a comprehensive approach for setting the dynamic security and privacy policies for wireless sensor network using context awareness. A formal Contextual Security Privacy Framework (CSPF) is designed. The framework is represented mathematically using State Machine Model.

6.3   Mathematical Representation of CSPF Model

A model is represented as a state machine model by security properties. The model of a system is composed of set of the states, the list of basic operations, initial system state, transition functions, and the set of permissions.

The model (CSPF) is represented as

$$CSPF = (C_{setofStates}, C_{listofOp}, C_{Transition}, C_{initialState}, C_{permission})$$

Where $C_{setofStates}$ is the set of various System States.

$C_{listofOp}$ is the list of operations such as testing the secure state of the sensor person or environment.
$C_{Transition}$ is the System Transition Function where transition is the sequence of actions to be performed to change a state from one to
another such as patients' health condition from normal to critical, etc.
$C_{initialState}$ is the initial input state. The initial state where there are no elements in any of the sets defined for a system.
$C_{initialState} = \{s1=\varphi, s2=\varphi, sn=\}$ $C_{permission}$ is the set of access permissions.

6.3.1 Basic Sets of CSPF Model

The various sets of the model are described in this section. The CSPF model contains the basic sets as Entities E in terms of $E_{subjects}$, $E_{objects}$, $E_{attributes}$, and $E_{contexts}$.

$$E = \{E_{subjects}, E_{objects}, E_{attributes}, E_{Contexts}\}$$

We define a Function F from set E to its set of attributes say set $E_{attributes}$
$F: E \rightarrow E_{attributes}$ such that

$$\forall e \in E \ni some \; p \; \varepsilon \; E_{attributes} \text{ such that } F(e) = p$$

A Relation $R_{attributes}$ is defined on the set of all ordered pairs, i.e., $E \; x E_{attributes}$, such that

$$R_{attributes} \subseteq E \; x \; E_{attributes}$$

6.3.2 Conditional Contextual Security and Privacy Constraints

It is the collection of constraints defined on various Entities, i.e., Subject and Objects as security and Privacy parameters. The constraints are in the form of Boolean expression which is the represented as the conjunction of conditions used to specify security.

$ContextSPC_{CSPF} = ContextSPC_{c1} \cup ContextSPC_{c2} \cup ContextSPC_{ci}\cup.........$
$\cup ContextSPC_{cn} = \cup_{i=1}^{n} ContextSPC_{ci}$
$ContextSPC_{ci} = \cap_{i=1}^{n} CCi$
$CC_i = \cap_{i=1}^{n} SubCi$
$SubC = <E_{contexts}><op><value>$
where op = $\{ =, <, >, <=, >=, \neq \}$

6.3.3 CSPF Model States $C_{setofStates}$

The representation of the system state is done by state variables representing the security and privacy related information. Security function is derived here to capture the security relevant information which is the collection of various parameters relating to security functions. This information is the combination of various policies rules for security, i.e., trusts based, context based, etc. Security functions are defined and evaluated and access is allowed or denied accordingly.

It is defined for each state that a system may be in. As the system changes its state, it's automatically computed and provides the information about the system whether it is in secure state or insecure state.

The state $s \in C_{setofStates}$ is represented as a set

$$s = (E_{contexts}, ContextSPC_{CSPP}, SEF_{context}, C_{permission})$$

6.3.4 Permission $C_{permission}$

The permission specifies the operation performed by a subject with certain attributes on an object. The access permission can be represented as

$$C_{permission} = (E_{subjects}, E_{objects}, E_{operation})$$

$E_{operation}$ is the operation to be executed by the subject on a particular object.

$$E_{operation} = \{ op1, op2, op3, ..., opn \}$$
Let $\forall s \; \varepsilon \; E_{subjects}, \forall o \; \varepsilon \; E_{objects}, \exists op \; \varepsilon \; E_{operation}$
$C_{permission} = (s, o, op)$

6.3.5 Security Evaluation Function (SEF$_{contexts}$)

The security evaluation function after evaluation if true, grants permission else permission will be denied.

$SEF_{context}: ContextSPC_{CSPF} \to \{0,1\}$

where the set ContextSPCCSPF is the set of Security Policies' constraints.

$ContextSPC_{CSPF} = \{ pol_1, pol_2, pol_3, ..., pol_n \}$

$\forall pol_i \; \varepsilon \; ContextSPC_{CSPP} \; SEF_{contexts}(pol_i) = \{0\}$, permission is denied.

$SEF_{contexts}(pol_i) = \{1\}$, permission is granted.

6.3.6   Secure State

The secure state of a system is described by defining all the basic sets and constraints relation for CSPF model. For a system to be in the secure state, all the constraints defined for the assignment of attributes to subject, object, and contexts must hold true.

Attributes assigned to a Subject, Object, and Context must follow the following constraints.

$$\forall \text{sub} \; \varepsilon \; E_{\text{subjects}}, \; \forall \text{obj} \; \varepsilon \; E_{\text{objects}}, \; \forall \; \text{contxt} \; \varepsilon \; E_{\text{contexts}} \; \exists \; E_s, E_o \; \text{and} \; E_{\text{ctxt}}$$

$$R_{\text{subAttr}}(\text{sub}) \subseteq E_s(\text{sub}, R_{\text{attributesSub}}), \; R_{\text{objAttr}}(\text{obj}) \subseteq E_o \; (\text{obj}, R_{\text{attributesObj}}), \; R_{\text{conxtAttr}} \subseteq$$

$$E_{\text{ctxt}} \; (\text{contxt}, R_{\text{attributesContext}})$$

The other constraints such as assignment of a range in which the value of the attributes assigned to a subject or an object also hold true. The state of the system also follows the domain and the range constraints.

6.3.7   CSPF Model Operations

Op_{CSPF} is the list of various operations in the system which can be performed at the administrative level or by the user. In healthcare application, operation includes the addition and deletion of a new patient, doctor, sensor, device, nurse, and visitor. A patient may be transferred from an emergency or from an operation theater to ward.

$$Op_{\text{CSPF}} = \{Op_{\text{admin}}, Op_{\text{user}}\}$$

Op_{admin} is the operation performed by the administrator such as allocation of sensors, to check the security status of various sensors, allocation of security attribute to some sensors, etc.

Op_{user} is the operation performed by the user such as request made by a user to access some resource.

6.3.7.1   Administrative Operations

AdmOperation5: To check the feasibility status of sensors
Sensors have some feasibility parameters on the basis of which it is identified whether the sensor is ready for communication or not. This operation is implemented to check the feasibility of a sensor by returning a Boolean variable Feasible as value true or false.

SensorFeasibility(p: E_{person}, Sen : E_{Sensor}, SenAttr$_i$: $E_{Senattributes}$, Feasible: Boolean)

Here a Person p is associated with sensors Sen having set of attributes SenAttr$_i$. This module checks the feasibility of sensors with Boolean value true or false.

{ $\forall$ p ε E_{person} $\exists$ some Sen ε E_{Sensor} with a relation hasSensor as hasSensor $\subseteq$ E_{person} X E_{Sensor}

$\forall$Sen ε E_{Sensor} $\exists$ some SenAttr$_i$ (i= 1 to 4) ε $E_{Senattributes}$ with a relation hasParameter as hasParameter $\subseteq$ E_{Sensor} X $E_{Senattributes}$

$\forall$ Senattributes$_i$ ε $E_{Senattributes}$ $\exists$ lb$_i$, ub$_i$ ε R [set of Real Numbers]

$\forall$Sen if (lb$_i$ <= Senattributes$_i$ <=ub$_i$) set

Feasible:=true

else Feasible: =false}

AdmOperation7: To identify the type of Attack in the sensor

This operation is basically implemented to test the type of attack if present in the sensor, it first calls the *SensorSecurity ( )* module to get the value of Boolean variable Secure. If it is false, then the constraint is further evaluated to identify the type of attack present in the variable attack.

SensorAttack(p: E_{person}, Sen: E_{Sensor}, SenAttr$_i$: $E_{Senattributes}$, attack: String)

Here a person p equipped with Sensor Sen and attack return the type of attack presents in the sensor.

{ SensorSecurity(p, Sen, SenAttri, Secure) if

(Secure = false) then

{ if (PresenceofAttacker = "implicit" AND LevelofDamage = "high"

AND　　Easeofldentity="hard") then

　　　　attack:="internal"

　　　　else attack:="external"

else if (PresenceofAttacker = "explicit" AND LevelofDamage = "high" AND Easeofldentity

　　　　= "hard") then

　　　　attack: = "active"

else attack:= "passive" end if }}

6.3.7.2   Users' Operations

Op_{user} is the operation performed by the user such as request made by a user to access some resource, i.e., the authorization privilege. Here, a person in the role of a doctor wants to access some details of a patient treated by him such as his medical history, medications, and health status, etc.

UserOp1: Authorization Privilege
The function is created to evaluate whether the Subject is authorized to perform a secure operation on an object or not by returning a Boolean value true or false.

---

authorisationPermission(sub : $E_{subjects}$, obj: $E_{objects}$, op: $E_{operation}$, permission : Boolean)

$\{ \forall sub \; \varepsilon \; E_{subjects}, \; \forall obj \; \varepsilon \; E_{objects}, \; \forall op \; \varepsilon \; E_{operation}$

if (sub, obj, op) $\varepsilon \; C_{permssion}$ then

permission = true else

permission = false

$\}$

6.4   Ontological Model

This uses an approach based on iteration to identify the various elements such as classes, subclasses, and properties relating to ontology. Ontology contains both set of classes and set of properties. The collection of individuals form a class and relationship between different individuals are represented by properties. An object property links an individual with another. An instance is linked to a literal with data property.

The Protégé tool is being used for development of ontology. After identification of the domain, the vocabulary and properties are defined.

6.4.1   Development of Class Hierarchy

The class hierarchy relating to application domain is shown in Table 6.2. The classes in the ontology with their description are as follows.

The main components of ontology are shown in Figure 6.1. The class hierarchy composed of the following concepts is as shown below.

Table 6.2 Main concepts or classes of proposed model.

Concept	Description
Person	Describes various roles such as patient, manager, and doctor
Platform	Description of hardware devices and the software used
Attack	Signifies possibilities of attacks in the system
AlarmStatus	Sends notifications to concerned person
Activity	Lists the various activities performed by a person
Location	Shows the various locations where a person may be located in
Device	Lists the devices
Role	Set of roles assigned
senParameters	Lists the parameters of sensor nodes
personalData	Lists the personal attributes
Service	Categorizes the set of services
Privacy	Privacy parameters
Security	Security parameters
sensorMeasurements	Reading measured by the sensors

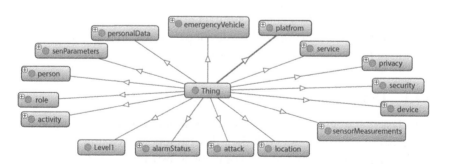

Figure 6.1 Components of ontology.

6.4.1.1   Object Properties of Sensor Class

It shows the relationship of class sensor and its subclasses with the other classes as shown in Table 6.3.

6.4.1.2   Data Properties

The data properties show the values specified for the given property. It may be in the range of integer, string, and Boolean that links the class with a value of some particular type.

Properties of a Person Class

A person class has many properties such as name, password, access permission, address, email-id, and contact details, etc., as shown in Table 6.4.

6.4.1.3   The Individuals

The individual are the instances represented in ontology. Figure 6.2 shows the individuals belonging to person, location, role, temp, pressure, heartRate, sugar, etc. It shows the range of values for the members of the class. The description of individuals of a heartRate sensor is as shown in the graph.

The instances of heartRate sensors are hs1, hs2, hs3, etc. The rules map the set of individuals to feasibleH, infesibleH, secureH, and insecureH, etc., depending upon the value of various parameters assigned to them. A possible implementation for individuals is given in Figure 6.3.

6.5   The Design of Context-Aware Security and Privacy Model for Wireless Sensor Network

This describes the basic design principle on which the layout of the model is made. The model is made up of different layers responsible for performing the different kind of tasks. The layered architecture of model CSPF is shown in Figure 6.4.

The model is divided into the number of layers. At the lowest level is the layer of sensors chosen according to an environment. The next layer is of the proposed model CSPF. This layer is further divided into sub-layers. At the lowest level, knowledge base is created by the context ontology-based model. This component is named as context ontology manager. The next

Table 6.3 Object properties of a sensor and its subclasses.

Properties	Description
Sensor	
has Attacks	It specifies the attacks in the sensor node.
SecureT	
measureTemp	It specifies the temperature measured by the temperature sensor.
SecureP	
measureSystolicPressure	It is the measurement of systolic pressure by the pressure sensor.
measureDiastolicPressure	It is the diastolic pressure measured by the pressure sensor.
Secures	
measureSugar	It signifies the sugar level measured by the sugar sensor.
SecureH	
measureHeartRate	It is the heart rate measurement from the heart sensor.
Temp	
hasTransCapacityT	It is the property of the temperature sensor which signifies the transmission capacity of the temperature sensor.
hasStorageT	It is the storage capacity of the temperature sensor.
hasSignalStrengthT	It signifies the measurement of signal strength of the temperature sensor.
hasEnergyT	It is the energy level of the temperature sensor.
Pressure	
hasTransCapacityP	It signifies the transmission capacity of the pressure sensor.

(Continued)

Table 6.3 Object properties of a sensor and its subclasses. (*Continued*)

Properties	Description
hasStorageP	It is the storage capacity of the pressure sensor.
hasSignalStrengthP	It signifies the measurement of signal strength of the temperature sensor.
hasEnergyP	It is the energy level of the pressure sensor.
HeartRate	
hasTransCapacityH	It signifies the transmission capacity of the heart sensor.
hasStorageH	It is the storage capacity of the heart sensor.
hasSignalStrengthH	It signifies the measurement of signal Strength of the temperature sensor.
hasEnergyH	It is the energy level of the heart sensor.
Sugar	
hasTransCapacity	It signifies the transmission capacity of the heart sensor.
hasEnergy	It is the energy level of the sugar sensor.
hassignalStrength	It is the storage capacity of the sugar sensor.

Table 6.4 Data properties of a class Person.

Data property	Description
hasAccessMedicaldata	Access permission of a person to read medical data
hasUserName	Specifies person's name as string
hasPassword	Signifies the person's password as string

step is to infer some higher level contexts to extract the knowledge from the knowledge base. The context is further processed by creating the policies in the reasoning layer. Some rule-based language can be used to design the policies. The main focus of a design of a model is based on improving the security services for the environment for which it is deployed. Also, the application may require the communication of information among various

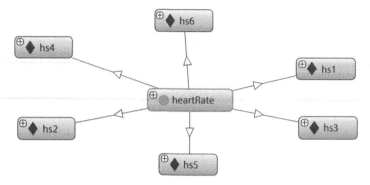

Figure 6.2 Individuals of heart rate sensor.

```
Declaration>
        <NamedIndividual IRI="#hs1"/>
    </Declaration>
    <Declaration>
        <NamedIndividual IRI="#hs2"/>
    </Declaration>
    <Declaration>
        <NamedIndividual IRI="#hs3"/>
    </Declaration>
    <Declaration>
        <NamedIndividual IRI="#hs4"/>
    </Declaration>
    <Declaration>
        <NamedIndividual IRI="#hs5"/>
    </Declaration>
    <Declaration>
        <NamedIndividual IRI="#hs6"/>

                            </Declaration>
```

Figure 6.3 Code for implementation of individuals.

modules as well as various personal involved. So, maintaining the privacy of information which is being transmitted is also equally important. The privacy manager component is responsible for implementing the privacy policies in the system.

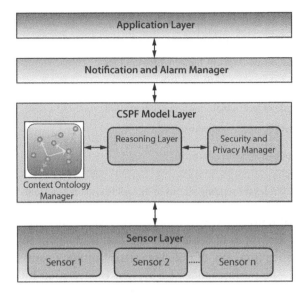

Figure 6.4 Layered architecture of CSPF framework.

Depending upon the situation the policies are executed and the notifications are forwarded to the concerned personal in case of an exceptional situation such as the occurrences of any vulnerability. The alarm manager layer is responsible for forwarding the alarms and taking quick actions in case of any emergency situation depending upon the application. The last layer is of the application layer. The software may work in any kind of application such as smart home, remote monitoring, and emergency management, etc.

6.6   Implementation

The CSPF model is implemented and analyzed by validating the designed framework. The model is simulated by varying the number of context attributes, security and privacy parameters, the size of the network, etc.

The proposed system's runtime performance is evaluated on the basis of security and privacy parameters in various types of healthcare scenarios. Various experiments have performed on the system with the Windows 10 operating system running on i5 CPU @ 2.54 GHz with 8 GB of RAM. The performance overhead of the CSPF model is quantified by conducting the experimental study. The various measures proposed for the experimental study are the number of policies versus average inference time to run the

heartRate(?x), hasEnergyH(?x, low), hasSignalStrengthH(?x,	low), hasStorageH(?x, high),
hasTransCapacityH(?x, low) -> notfeasibleH(?x)	
heartRate(?x), hasEnergyH(?x, high), hasSignalStrengthH(?x,	low), hasStorageH(?x, low),
hasTransCapacityH(?x, high) -> notfeasibleH(?x)	
heartRate(?x), hasEnergyH(?x, high), hasSignalStrengthH(?x,	low), hasStorageH(?x, low),
hasTransCapacityH(?x, low) -> notfeasibleH(?x)	
heartRate(?h), notfeasibleH(?h) -> deny)?h)	

Figure 6.5 SWRL rules for sending alarms of infeasible sensors to admin.

queries, size of ontology versus average inference time, average inference time for different types of reasoning engines, number of instance versus average inference time, no. of policies versus ontology consistence checking time, etc. The performance of a system is measured by studying the scalability of the system and its throughput.

The inference time shows the time to take request from the user, the system for required services and the desired results on the basis of security and privacy parameters to improve the services. The response time of CSPF model is also compared with the traditional model without security and privacy parameters.

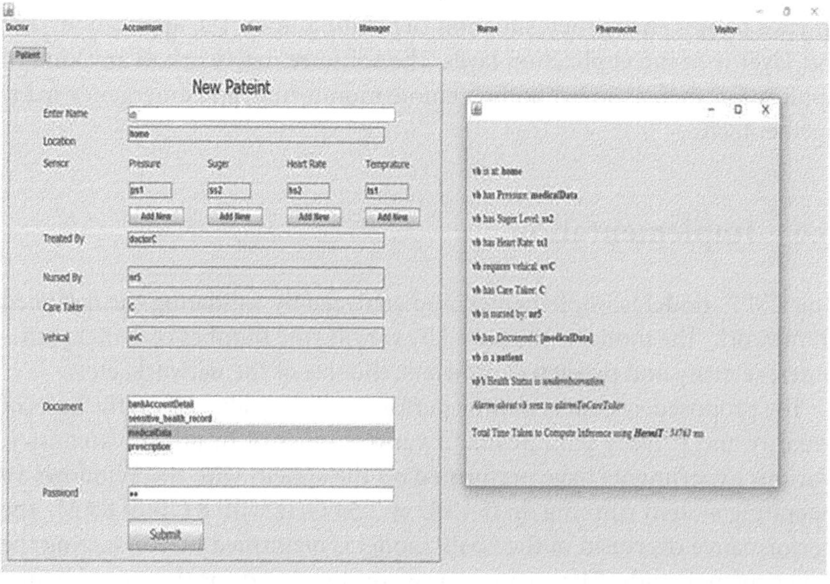

Figure 6.6 Interface for sending an alarm for health condition under observation.

The policies for forwarding an alarm to the admin in case of infeasible sensors are shown in Figure 6.5.

The sequence of activities that is taking place is represented through the interface as shown in Figure 6.6 along with the time taken to compute the inference.

6.7   Analysis and Results

The performance is computed with different parameters such as ontology size which is dependent upon the number of instances and no. of policies for designing a model.

6.7.1   Inference Time/Latency/Query Response Time vs. No. of Policies

The performance of the model is studied by measuring its latency, i.e., the time taken by the software to respond to queries. It is measured for a different set of policies. The graph of impact of response time by varying the no. of policies is shown graphically in Figure 6.7.

Performance of different Reasoners
Reasoner is used to perform the inference in the ontology. The response time for a query depends upon the time taken by the reasoner to draw

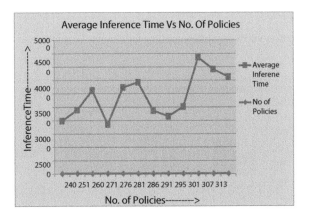

Figure 6.7 Inference time vs. no. of policies.

inference. Some reasoners are by default built into the software, while others are separately installed as plug-ins. The performance of different reasoners are compared by measuring the response time for a selected scenario for fixed number of instances. Pellet and HermiT reasoners are used here to evaluate the performance as shown in Figure 6.8.

From the graphical representation, it is obvious that HermiT is faster than the Pallet reasoner to draw inference.

6.7.2 Average Inference Time vs. Contexts

The average Inference time is computed for different conditions of policies without using context, with adding three contexts and with addition of four more contexts into it as shown in Figure 6.9. The same experiment is repeated by reducing the contextual parameters and computing the inference time.

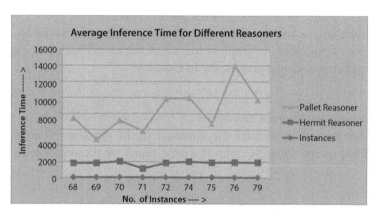

Figure 6.8 Instances vs. average inference time for different reasoners.

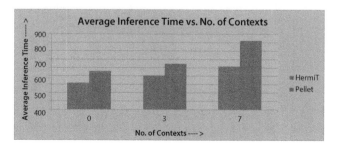

Figure 6.9 Average inference time vs. no. of contexts for different reasoners.

The result from graph shows that Pellet outperforms HerimT reasoner in terms of inference time. As the contextual parameters are adding, the enhancement of security takes place thereby increase in the inference time. But, the increase in inference time is not much enough than the benefits gained by the introduction of contextual parameters. So, the overall latency depends upon the contextual parameters, which increases with the increasing number of contexts. But, the evaluation latency or time has very little dependent upon the contexts.

6.8   Conclusion and Future Scope

The main focus of study is to improve the quality of healthcare services with improved security and privacy services. The modeling approach used here is the ontological approach for the creation of the proposed model. The rule-based approach is used to set policies relating to healthcare applications. The security and privacy components have introduced in the model. The sensors which are under attacks are not used for transmission of wrong data to the server. Instead, appropriate alarm signals are forwarded for further corrective actions. Data collected by all the secure nodes are forwarded to the hospital via base station. To implement privacy component, the user is authenticated by entering user name and password. Access is denied to a user for entering the wrong credential. Access to devices is restricted on the basis of roles assigned to them. The assumptions are specified for various scenarios and the framework is validated by simulating the scenarios using Java-based simulator. The CSPF framework is compared with the existing model without privacy and security policies shows significant improvements. The model can be extended to include the transmission of health data of a critical patient to some nearby hospital where the specialist is available to treat the patient. The context should automatically update the policies while preserving the privacy of the system. Work can be done on this to make the model more flexible without sacrificing the quality of healthcare services.

The work can be extended in the future by forwarding various alarm messages by analysis of complex policies written by studying the observation on the long-term basis. Some artificial language techniques such as based on fuzzy sets and neural network should be introduced for better decision making.

Detailed analysis of security and privacy concerns about the healthcare scenario can be done by conducting a field survey with the help of questionnaires. Detailed analysis is done to identify risks and also to suggest corresponding solutions.

Different methodologies could be analyzed to train a user about how to use a system during various emergency situations. An introduction of learning mechanism can help in reducing the processing of context every time it is encountered. Context can be accessed from existing cache history maintained as logs. This results in considerable time saving while processing contexts for evaluation of policies.

References

1. Mohan, P. and Singh, M., Security Issues in Sensor Networks: A Survey. *International Conference on Wireless Networks & Embedded Systems*, pp. 65–68, 2011, Available at: http://dspace.chitkara.edu.in/xmlui/handle/1/429.

2. Moloney, M. and Weber, S., A context-aware trust-based security system for ad hoc networks, in: *Workshop of the 1st International Conference on Security and Privacy for Emerging Areas in Communication Networks*, vol. 2005, IEEE, pp. 153–160, 2005.

3. Saidane, A., Adaptive context-aware access control policy in ad-hoc networks, in: *Third International Conference on Autonomic and Autonomous Systems (ICAS'07)*, IEEE, pp. 13–13, 2007.

4. Arabo, A., Shi, Q., Merabti, M., A framework for user-centred and context-aware identity management in mobile ad hoc networks (UCIM). *Ubiquitous Comput. Commun. J.*, 1–11, 2009.

5. Shankaran, R., Varadharajan, V., Orgun, M.A., Hitchens, M., Context-aware trust management for peer-to-peer mobile ad-hoc networks, in: *2009 33rd Annual IEEE International Computer Software and Applications Conference*, vol. 2, IEEE, pp. 188–193, 2009.

6. Pratas, N., Anggraeni, P.N., Wardana, S.A., Prasad, N.R., Rodrigues, A., Prasad, R., Context-aware trust and privacy application for mobile identification system, in: *2009 IEEE Wireless Communications and Networking Conference*, IEEE, pp. 1–6, 2009.

7. Li, W., Joshi, A., Finin, T., Cast: Context-aware security and trust framework for mobile ad-hoc networks using policies. *Ditrib. Parallel Dat.* 31, 2, 353–376, 2013.

8. Wrona, K. and Gomez, L., Context-aware security and secure context-awareness in ubiquitous computing environments, in: *Annales Universitatis Mariae Curie-Sklodowska, sectio AI– Informatica*, 4, 332–348, 2006.

9. Lee, K., Yang, S., Jun, S., Chung, M., Context-aware security service in RFID/USN environments using MAUT and extended GRBAC, in: *2007 2nd International Conference on Digital Information Management*, vol. 1, IEEE, pp. 303–308, 2007.

10. Schaub, F., Könings, B., Dietzel, S., Weber, M., Kargl, F., Privacy context model for dynamic privacy adaptation in ubiquitous computing, in: *Proceedings of*

the 2012 ACM Conference on Ubiquitous Computing, ACM, pp. 752–757, 2012.

11. Al-Muhtadi, J., Ranganathan, A., Campbell, R., Mickunas, M.D., Cerberus: A context-aware security scheme for smart spaces, in: *Proceedings of the First IEEE International Conference on Pervasive Computing and Communications, 2003. (PerCom 2003)*, IEEE, pp. 489–496, 2003.

12. Venkatesan, L., Subramaniam, C., Shanmugavel, S., Reliability Modeling of Context Aware Wireless SensorNetwork. *Int. J. Inf. Electron. Eng.*, 2, 5, 710, 2012.

13. Motta, G.H. and Furuie, S.S., A contextual role-based access control authorization model for electronic patient record. *IEEE Trans. Inf. Technol. Biomed.*, 7, 3, 202–207, 2003.

14. Zhang, G. and Parashar, M., Dynamic context-aware access control for grid applications, in: *Proceedings. First Latin American Web Congress*, IEEE, pp. 101–108, 2003.

15. Zhang, G. and Parashar, M., Context-aware dynamic access control for pervasive applications, in: *Proceedings of the Communication Networks and Distributed Systems Modeling and Simulation Conference*, pp. 21–30, 2004.

16. Liscano, R. and Wang, K., A context-based delegation access control model for pervasive computing, in: *21st International Conference on Advanced Information Networking and Applications Workshops (AINAW'07)*, vol. 2, IEEE, pp. 44–51, 2007.

17. Tang, W., Ni, J., Chen, M., Yang, X., Contextual role-based security enhancement mechanism for 2G-RFID Systems, in: *2011 IEEE Conference on Computer Communications Workshops (INFOCOM WKSHPS)*, IEEE, pp. 942–946, 2011.

18. Blount, M., Davis, J., Ebling, M., Jerome, W., Leiba, B., Liu, X., Misra, A., Privacy engine for context-aware enterprise application services, in: *2008 IEEE/IFIP International Conference on Embedded and Ubiquitous Computing*, vol. 2, IEEE, pp. 94–100, 2008.

19. Tigli, J.Y., Lavirotte, S., Rey, G., Hourdin, V., Riveill, M., Context-aware authorization in highly dynamic environments. *IJCSI Int. J. Comput. Sci. Issues*, 4, 1, 24–35, 2011.

20. Sacramento, V., Endler, M., Nascimento, F.N., A privacy service for context-aware mobile computing, in: *First International Conference on Security and Privacy for Emerging Areas in Communications Networks (SECURECOMM'05)*, IEEE, pp. 182–193, 2005.

21. Jones, C.B., *Systematic software development using VDM (Vol. 2)*, Prentice Hall, Englewood Cliffs, 1990.

22. Jacoub, J.K., Liscano, R., Bradbury, J.S., A survey of modeling techniques for wireless sensor networks, in: *Proc. of the 5th International Conference on Sensor Technologies and Applications, ser. SENSORCOMM*, vol. 2011, pp. 103–109, 2011.

23. Botts, M. and Robin, A., OpenGIS sensor model language (SensorML) implementation specification. *OpenGIS Implementation Specification OGC*,

University of Alabama in Huntsville, Sensor Model Language, V1.0 .0, 7, 000, 1–180, 2007.

24. Demaille, A., Peyronnet, S., Sigoure, B., Modeling of sensor networks using XRM, in: *Second International Symposium on Leveraging Applications of Formal Methods, Verification and Validation (isola 2006)*, IEEE, pp. 271–276, 2006.

25. Woodcock, J. and Davies, J., *Using Z: Specification, Refinement, and Proof.* Prentice Hall International., 1996.

26. Yuan, J., Li, J., Zhang, B., Exploiting spatial context constraints for automatic image region annotation, in: *Proceedings of the 15th ACM international conference on Multimedia*, ACM, pp. 595–604, 2007.

27. Heitz, G. and Koller, D., Learning spatial context: Using stuff to find things, in: *European conference on computer vision*, pp. 30–43, Springer, Berlin, Heidelberg, 2008.

28. Afyouni, I., Ray, C., Claramunt, C., Spatial models for context-aware indoor navigation systems: A survey, *J. Spat. Inf. Sci.*, 4, 85–123, 2012.

29. Henricksen, K., Indulska, J., Rakotonirainy, A., Modeling context information in pervasive computing systems, in: *International Conference on Pervasive Computing*, Springer, Berlin, Heidelberg, pp. 167–180, 2002.

30. Henricksen, K. and Indulska, J., Modelling and Using Imperfect Context Information, in: *IEEE Annual Conference on Pervasive Computing and Communications Workshops (PerCom Workshops)*, pp. 33–37, 2004.

31. Henricksen, K. and Indulska, J., Developing context-aware pervasive computing applications: Models and approach. *Pervasive Mob. Comput.*, 2, 1, 37–64, 2006.

32. Christopoulou, E., Goumopoulos, C., Kameas, A., An ontology-based context management and reasoning process for UbiComp applications, in: *Proceedings of the 2005 joint conference on Smart objects and ambient intelligence: innovative context-aware services: Usages and technologies*, ACM, pp. 265–270, 2005.

33. Chen, H., Finin, T., Joshi, A., An ontology for context-aware pervasive computing environments. *Knowl. Eng. Rev.*, 18, 3, 197–207, 2003.

34. Chen, H., Perich, F., Finin, T., Joshi, A., Soupa: Standard ontology for ubiquitous and pervasive applications, in: *The First Annual International Conference on Mobile and Ubiquitous Systems: Networking and Services, 2004. MOBIQUITOUS 2004*, IEEE, pp. 258–267, 2004.

35. Chen, H., Finin, T., Joshi, A., Semantic web in in the context broker architecture. *UMBC Faculty Collection.*, 1–10, 2004.

36. Wang, X., Zhang, D., Gu, T., Pung, H.K., Ontology Based Context Modeling and Reasoning using OWL, in: *IEEE annual conference on pervasive computing and communications workshops (Percom workshops)*, vol. 18, p. 22, 2004.

37. Zhang, D., Gu, T., Wang, X., Enabling context-aware smart home with semantic web technologies. *Int. J. Human-friendly Welfare Robotic Syst.*, 6, 4, 12–20, 2005.

38. Gu, T., Wang, X.H., Pung, H.K., Zhang, D.Q., An ontology-based context model in intelligent environments, in: *Proceedings of communication networks and distributed systems modeling and simulation conference*, vol. 2004, pp. 270–275, 2004.

39. Saeedi, S., El-Sheimy, N., Malek, M., Samani, N., An ontology based context modeling approach for mobile touring and navigation system, in: *Proceedings of the The 2010 Canadian Geomatics Conference and Symposium of Commission I, ISPRS Convergence in Geomatics–Shaping Canada's Competitive Landscape, Calgary, Canada*, pp. 15–18, 2010.

40. Bouquet, P., Giunchiglia, F., Van Harmelen, F., Serafini, L., Stuckenschmidt, H., Contextualizing ontologies. *Web Semantics: Science, Services and Agents on the World Wide Web*, 1, 4, 325–343, 2004.

41. Ranganathan, A., McGrath, R.E., Campbell, R.H., Mickunas, M.D., Use of ontologies in a pervasive computing environment. *Knowl. Eng. Rev.*, 18, 3, 209–220, 2003.

42. Gandon, F.L. and Sadeh, N.M., A semantic e-wallet to reconcile privacy and context awareness, in: *International Semantic Web Conference*, Springer, Berlin, Heidelberg, pp. 385–401, 2003.

43. Bell, D.E. and LaPadula, L.J., *Secure computer systems: Mathematical foundations*, pp. 1–29, (No. MTR-2547-VOL-1). Mitre Corp Bedford MA, 1973.

44. Biba, K.J., *Integrity considerations for secure computer systems*, pp. 1–68, (no. MTR-3153-REV-1). Mitre Corp Bedford MA, 1977.

45. Clark, D.D. and Wilson, D.R., A comparison of commercial and military computer security policies, in: *1987 IEEE Symposium on Security and Privacy*, pp. 184–184, IEEE, 1987.

46. Denning, D.E., A lattice model of secure information flow. *Commun. ACM*, 19, 5, 236–243, 1976.

47. Sandhu, R.S., Role-based access control, in: *Advances in computers*, vol. 46, pp. 237–286, Elsevier, USA, 1998.

48. Sandhu, R.S., Coyne, E.J., Feinstein, H.L., Youman, C.E., Role-based access control models. *Computer*, 29, 2, 38–47, 1996.

49. Covington, M.J., Moyer, M.J., Ahamad, M., *Generalized role-based access control for securing future applications*, Georgia Institute of Technology, 2000.

50. Hulsebosch, R.J., Salden, A.H., Bargh, M.S., Ebben, P.W., Reitsma, J., Context sensitive access control, in: *Proceedings of the tenth ACM symposium on Access control models and technologies*, ACM, pp. 111–119, 2005.

51. Adams, A., Multimedia information changes the whole privacy ballgame, in: *Proceedings of the tenth conference on Computers, freedom and privacy: challenging the assumptions*, ACM, pp. 25–32, 2000.

52. Jiang, X. and Landay, J.A., Modeling privacy control in context-aware systems. *IEEE Pervasive Comput.*, 1, 3, 59–63, 2002.

53. Langheinrich, M., A privacy awareness system for ubiquitous computing environments, in: *international conference on Ubiquitous Computing*, Springer, Berlin, Heidelberg, pp. 237–245, 2002.

54. Hengartner, U. and Steenkiste, P., Protecting access to people location information, in: *Security in pervasive computing*, pp. 25–38, Springer, Berlin, Heidelberg, 2004.

55. Wickramasuriya, J., Datt, M., Mehrotra, S., Venkatasubramanian, N., Privacy protecting data collection in media spaces, in: *Proceedings of the 12th annual ACM international conference on Multimedia*, ACM, pp. 48–55, 2004.

56. Hong, J.I. and Landay, J.A., An architecture for privacy-sensitive ubiquitous computing, in: *Proceedings of the 2nd international conference on Mobile systems, applications, and services*, ACM, pp. 177–189, 2004.

57. Kapadia, A., Henderson, T., Fielding, J.J., Kotz, D., Virtual walls: Protecting digital privacy in pervasive environments, in: *International Conference on Pervasive Computing*, Springer, Berlin, Heidelberg, pp. 162–179, 2007.

7

Ontology-Based Query Retrieval Support for E-Health Implementation

Aatif Ahmad Khan[1]* and Sanjay Kumar Malik[2]

*[1]University School of Information, Communication and Technology,
Guru Gobind Singh Indraprastha University, New Delhi, India*
*[2]University School of Information, Communication and Technology,
Guru Gobind Singh Indraprastha University, New Delhi, India*

Abstract

Digital record-keeping for health care sector has transformed the information collection and processing tasks and has provided a huge scope of using information retrieval mechanisms. But, often the vast information is non-transferable and is not easy to analyze due to underlying storage mechanisms and local terminology. E-health is an area with key objective of interoperability, secure sharing of patient health records for analysis, and informed decision making. E-health implementation requires consistent domain and process terminology across applications. Ontology, a semantic technology, could be applied here as it describes concepts in standard vocabulary for a specified domain. Further, due to consistent vocabulary, it can be utilized for querying and retrieval of concerned information from health care informatics repositories. In this chapter, scope and applications of ontology-driven retrieval for e-health implementation is explored.

Keywords: Ontology, e-health, information retrieval, health informatics, electronic health record

7.1 Introduction

Health care is a vital field with respect to human day-to-day life. In present digital era, it is being immensely benefitted by information and

Corresponding author: aatif1992@gmail.com

Vishal Jain, Ritika Wason, Jyotir Moy Chatterjee and Dac-Nhuong Le (eds.) Ontology-Based Information Retrieval for Healthcare Systems, (143–166) © 2020 Scrivener Publishing LLC

communication technologies (ICT). Health care includes clinical practices and researches conducted. By using the data available in past experiments and procedures, doctors are able to conduct successful practices. Further, availability of vital knowledge regarding medicines and procedures at centralized repositories accessible over web is helping build a global health care workforce working in cooperation. These repositories include PubMed[1], Embase[2], and MedlinePlus[3], among others.

Large amount of data is generated in health care sector in day to day basis. It includes large amount of paperwork as well as digital records. Due to huge maintenance cost of paperwork, health care is steadily shifting towards digital media instead. Health informatics include but is not limited to digital patient records, tests conducted reports, results reports, successful procedures reference, disease/allergy records, and technical terminology guides. This health informatics data is collected over patients as per-individual basis and then the collection is used for analytics over a region or over a specified population. Analytics thus generated gives a wider picture for medical practitioners to make much informed decisions regarding health care for the population in that specified region.

7.1.1   Health Care Record Management

For the purpose of digitizing medical/health care records, various standards are prescribed and are being used in the industry at present. These include but are not limited to Electronic Health Records (EHRs)/Electronic Medical Records (EMRs) for recording per patient information, Picture Archiving and Communication Systems (PACSs) for capturing imaging data, Pharmacy Systems for managing and cataloging medicines, etc.

7.1.1.1   *Electronic Health Record*

EHR refers to a standardized way of collecting patient demographics in a way it can be shared for further processing. Real time, patient-centered records are standardized for collecting and storing patient data and making it available to authorized users only. EHR often contains patient's identity, medical history along with his/her treatment, medication, and test reports. These are highly useful for making informed decisions regarding the patient.

---

[1] https://www.ncbi.nlm.nih.gov/pubmed/
[2] https://www.elsevier.com/solutions/embase-biomedical-research
[3] https://medlineplus.gov/

7.1.1.2   Electronic Medical Record

EMR is used to capture the standard medical and clinical data as available from any individual health care facility provider. EHR is essentially an extension to EMR as EHR considers the captured data across health care facility providers and hence provides a wider picture for a particular individual's health records.

7.1.1.3   Picture Archiving and Communication System

Clinical imaging data such as Magnetic Resonance Imaging (MRI), Ultrasound, and Computed Tomography (CT), etc., is recorded and stored and is used for retrieval by PACSs. These provide fully digital solutions for capturing, managing, and distributing patient imaging data to authorized channels.

7.1.1.4   Pharmacy Systems

For effectively maintaining and managing medicine catalogs, hospitals and pharmacy use certain software systems. The key features available with these software is keeping track of inbound and sold medicines, tracking expiry dates for medicines, cataloging nearby doctors information, generating reports for sales, required stock, stock nearing expiry, etc.

7.1.2   Information Retrieval

Techniques involved in fetching of concerned information as per user needs, specified by a search query are referred to as information retrieval. Efficiency of techniques involved in information retrieval is measured using standard metrics of precision and recall. Precision refers to portion of relevant results in retrieved result set and recall is the portion of relevant results retrieved from the whole corpora of results.

Information retrieval starts when user poses an input search query. Keywords contained in the query are matched with target results repository to fetch the most relevant of those results. Unfortunately, traditional retrieval approaches rely on string matching criteria to fetch results having maximum keyword matching. These do not consider context of the query, hence often yield less precise results. Incorporation of semantics in query processing and retrieval as an additional criterion increases the relevancy of results due to availability of context information. Ontology is a key technology for incorporating semantics into query retrieval techniques.

In health care sector, information retrieval support is required for generation and analysis of test reports, medical bills, medical history reports, treatment history reports, etc. Manual processing of digital records is essentially a bottleneck for effective monitoring due to bulk of information generated daily. Further, it is very difficult to get the full medical picture of a patient by manually gathering and analyzing all of his/her medical records. Hence, there is a need of a transition from this manual process, which is also error-prone due to possible human errors and unavailability of proper information, towards automation. Literature suggests solutions to this including retrieval and analysis of heterogeneous information from different sources for a particular patient [1].

Information retrieval in health care sector may further get benefitted by incorporation of semantics in its techniques. Firstly, it may improve interoperability (due to standardized vocabulary) so that the same patient's records may become interoperable between different health care facilities. Another key advantage may be knowledge integration for sharing, e.g., composition of health records of same individual from different hospitals and past medical conditions to define a more informative medical history and making informed decisions for further treatments.

7.1.3   Ontology

Ontology is an explicit specification of a specified domain, containing concept hierarchies and interrelationships of concepts for that domain. It is a semantic technology responsible for describing a domain in a machine understandable format. Its key components are concept hierarchies, individuals belonging to those concepts, relations among concepts, and some formal rules/axioms for describing restrictions. Figure 7.1 illustrates a portion of Human Disease Ontology. Due to very large number of classes available, only a few classes are depicted along with standard relation of "has subclass".

7.2   Ontology-Based Query Retrieval Support

Ontology may assist information retrieval approaches by providing knowledge about semantic relatedness among query keywords and target repository terms. Literature also suggests the notion of semantic matching along with syntactic matching to fetch better results. Some weight or scores may also be assigned to result set items and ranking may be done based on the combination of syntactic score and semantic scores [3]. Combination

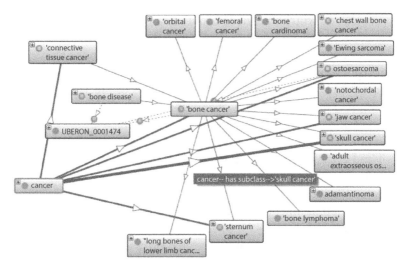

Figure 7.1 Portion of human disease ontology depicted using Protégé Tool[4] [2].

of both the scores, i.e., keyword-based (syntactic) and ontology-based (semantic) is required as using just the semantic score for retrieval may be overreliance on ontologies, which is relatively a new technology in its research stage [1].

Query retrieval process is initiated by supplying a search query to a search system or search engine. Typically, query supplied is firstly preprocessed and all its components are extracted. This stage involves breaking of query in individual tokens or logical group of tokens. Some additional syntactical processing is often applied to query after this stage such as reducing the query terms to their stem words. For example, plurals such as tomatoes or oxen may be reduced to tomato and ox. This syntactic processing stage is very crucial for information retrieval later, as plural words may have very different spellings from their singular forms but are conveying the same concept. Plural words if not processed, may lead to exclusion of some crucial results from the retrieved documents just due to discrepancies in the spelling of the two terms.

After all the syntactic processing is completed, semantic processing stage is initialized, if search system support semantics-based information retrieval. Ontology is a key technology used in this stage. Ontology consists of formal knowledge pertaining to a domain represented in a machine understandable format. It contains information about concepts and relationships of terms in that domain. Literature suggests a number

---

4 https://protege.stanford.edu/

of approaches in which knowledge contained in ontology is used to facilitate query retrieval process [4]. These include query expansion method,
keyword to concept mapping, among others. Ontology not only supports
the incorporation of semantics in syntax-based search systems but also
enhances the quality of retrieved results in terms of precision. This spike
in precision is due to capturing of additional context and intent of query
which syntax-based approaches often fail to capture.

This flow of query retrieval using ontology is depicted in Figure 7.2. In
stage 1 and 2, the user query is processed syntactically and semantically as
discussed in preceding paragraphs. Role of ontology (in semantics enabled
systems) is seen at semantic processing stage more specifically in keyword
to concept mapping and query expansion. The resultant processed query (as
shown in stage 3 of Figure 7.2), which might be expanded or having some
appended information (e.g., context related extra parameters, etc.) is then
fed to actual document retrieval system (stage 4 in Figure 7.2). Retrieval
system is responsible for matching the documents in the target information repositories based on some criteria (e.g., exact keyword matching,
fuzzy keyword matching [5], etc.). Based on the matching, some score is
assigned to each entry or document in the result set, denoting the degree
of matching with the query terms. It is implicitly assumed that higher the
matching score, more relevant is the entry or document to the query. This
assumption holds good for the semantics enabled systems but often not for
the systems based on syntactic matching only. Finally, the entries in the
result set are ranked (stage 5 in Figure 7.2) based on assigned matching

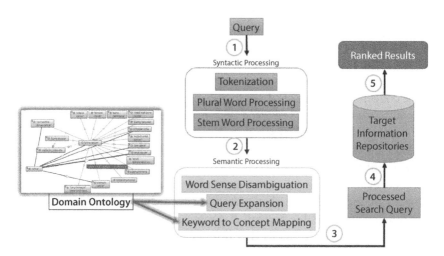

Figure 7.2 Query retrieval flow using ontology.

scores (a balanced proportion between syntactic score and semantic score derived out of empirical research) and results are presented to the end user or machine which originated the query.

Some of the techniques for semantic processing of query will be discussed next. Word Sense Disambiguation is a semantic technique to infer and assign meaningfully correct sense to a word. It is applicable for words which exhibit different meanings in different contexts or different placing order in a sentence. It works in conjunction with some Natural Language Processing (NLP) engine to infer word meaning by analyzing the rest of the sentence.

Keyword to Concept Mapping technique [6] is used for identifying concepts in participating ontologies which syntactically resembles terms present in posed query. Once the concept is found in the ontology, retrieval process advances by extracting related knowledge present in the ontology for that concept. This knowledge may include but is not limited to subclass concepts, sibling class concepts, instances of the concept (individuals), any instance of a distant class having some defined relationship with the concept, etc. These extracted terms are somehow meaningfully connected to the concept. Hence, the documents in the target information repositories containing these extra terms may also be relevant to the original query. It is the responsibility of the underlying retrieval approach to implement appropriate ranking criteria so that these extra terms should have lesser weight as compared to the weights assigned to terms originally present the input query, else precision of results may drop.

Query expansion using ontology approach works by appending additional query terms using logical disjunction (OR) operators. These additional terms are derived from knowledge contained in ontology vocabulary, considering their relatedness with the query terms. For instance, consider the following search query.

Query 1: colors in a rainbow
Now, consider an ontology pertaining to the domain of colors (e.g., Linked Open Colors Knowledge Base), from which all the instances of the concept color can be derived. After syntactic processing (as depicted in stage 1 in Figure 7.2), term "colors", which is a plural can processed to "color". Next, at the semantic processing (as depicted in stage 2 in Figure 7.2), the term "color" can be mapped to the concept "color" in the domain ontology via Keyword to Concept Mapping approach. Further, all related knowledge from the ontology can be derived which is having some relation to the concept "color" in the ontology. These relations include sub classes, instances or having some other relationship defined

in the ontology. In our case, instances of class "color" which include red, blue, yellow, green, etc., can be extracted. Once the extracted vocabulary is available, query can be expanded and reframed by placing these terms in logical disjunction with original query terms. Key point to note here is that all these newly extracted terms are having some sort of semantic relationship with the concept "color", hence, maintaining the context intact.

Query 1 (expanded): (colors OR red OR blue OR green OR violet) in a rainbow
The query 1 (expanded) is having a wider scope (retaining the context of original query) and more possibility of fetching the relevant results than the original query.

7.3   E-Health

E-health refers to a field about medical informatics and public health care, in which health services and concerned information is delivered over the internet using digital technologies. Its objective is to improve health care services, using the available networked information [7]. World Health Organization (WHO) defines e-health as the usage of ICT for health care.

A related term in this domain is m-health which is the usage of mobile communication technologies for health care. The key benefit involved with m-health is the freedom of mobility. The usage of wireless communication technologies such as Wireless Fidelity (Wi-Fi) or 4G/5G available in mobile devices along with medical sensors can help acquire required patient data without their need to visit a medical facility center physically. Although for specialized medical services, physical presence of patient is required in the facility.

7.3.1   Objectives and Scope

Key objectives of e-health are interoperability of health records and secured sharing of patient data for analysis and informed decision making. Interoperability ensures that different users across different organizations using similar systems can conclude the same thing. This requires sharing the data in compatible formats as well as preserving its meaning across systems. Thus, we need to have syntactic as well as semantic interoperability. Interoperability has to be applied at various levels such as interoperability between messages among health care applications, patient identifiers

(EHR), clinical standards, and medical business processes, etc. To achieve interoperability, the need of making standards in health care is stressed in the literature [8, 9].

Semantic Interoperability is defined as integration of resources described using different vocabularies. To achieve this, systems should communicate with data preserving its meaning and that meaning available should be understandable by underlying machine [10].

Scope of e-health includes key areas of EHR, E-prescription, Telemedicine, informed decision making, and Collaborative Health Information Network. It may also be expanded to advanced areas of robot assisted surgery, wearable devices for monitoring individual's health parameters, health care portals, etc.

7.3.2   Benefits of E-Health

E-health solutions when delivered entail benefits as tabulated in Table 7.1.

7.3.3   E-Health Implementation

Literature and government bodies suggest some field implementations of e-health. It includes nature of programs running, data collection methodologies, treatment compliances, etc. [11]. E-health initiatives in India are focused to deliver better health outcomes in terms of parameters such as quality of services, access range, affordability of facilities, lowering disease span, and effective monitoring of health care for citizens. Its scope is to ensure the availability of health care services through web and mobile technologies, messaging, and call services. Implementation is intended to cover medical consultation over web, availability of online medical records, online management of medicine supplies and Pan-India sharing of patient records. National E-Health Authority (NEHA[5]), an Indian government body, has started field programs such as Integrated Health Information Program, which is among others for this motive. Due to little digital literacy and scaling factors, e-health initiatives are slowly progressing towards implementation.

G. B. Fanta *et al.* have proposed a framework for implementing e-health focusing on the sustainability factors. The framework has identified five dimensions across which factors affecting e-health implementation are explored, which are tabulated in Table 7.2. These dimensions are Input(s), Process(es), Output(s), Impact(s), and Outcome(s) [12].

---

[5] https://www.nhp.gov.in/e-health-india_mty

Table 7.1 Key advantages of e-health.

Benefit	Description
Transparency	E-health-based solutions provide transparency in the treatment process to the patient without any biases of doctors or middlemen. Patient is able to see the progress in the procedure with all the concerned data.
Availability	Medical records of patients are ubiquitously available. Hence, the space needed for storing and the time required for finding the physical files of a patient in hospitals is saved.
Human error free	Machine automated procedures are free from human errors.
Authorized access	Access control mechanism ensures that only the concerned and authorized professionals can access records for a particular patient.
Shared records	Records of a particular patient from one medical facility can be shared with other facilities after granting required permissions without the need to transfer any physical file between facilities.
Focus on patient	E-health-based solutions focus on the data in a per patient basis. That is all the medical and clinical data of an individual patient across facilities is available on demand. Hence, any medical practitioner may get a full picture of patient's health record without any dependencies, thus focusing only on the further treatment.

J. Ross *et al.* studied the e-health implementation approaches available in state of the art in a given period from 2009 to 2014 and systematically investigated the challenges faced by them. Based on their study, they have recommended some considerations for implementation of e-health solutions [13, 14]. They stressed on considering the key factors of complexity, cost of operation, compatibility with existing approaches and adaptability to newer approaches. Other recommendations include:

- Early partnership with prospective implementation agencies
- Proper orientation and training of those involved in the implementation procedure

Table 7.2 Factors affecting e-health implementation [12].

Input(s)	Process(s)	Output(s)	Impact(s)	Outcome(s)
Technology related factors such as quality of system, services and information	E-health project management	User experience (UX)	Impact factors focusing on sustainability such as mortality rate	Decision support
Social input(s)	Data management	System usage	Life expectancy	Cost of health care services
Organizational input(s)	Communication	Information usage	Life quality	
Economic scenario	Engaging partnership(s)			

Table 7.3 Key issues concerning e-health implementation.

Issue	Description
Validity	Insights gained from a patient's health record or from a group of patient records may not be generalized for population at large.
Accuracy	Infrastructure available at different facilities may be different; hence, recordings taken at low specialty centers may not be that accurate.
Safety	Utmost care of safety procedures must be taken.
Privacy	User consent must be acquired for building e-health systems in a transparent way.
Confidentiality	All type of patient information should not be disclosed or be made sharable.
Availability	Records should be ubiquitously online when required.

- Provisioning and proper management of funding
- Early acquiring the legislative permissions
- Usage of adaptable technologies and proper measuring of improvement in acceptability
- Proper planning at organizational level
- Ongoing adaptation with changes even after implementation
- Persistent monitoring of progress.

Key issues concerned with e-health implementation are tabulated in Table 7.3.

7.4   Ontology-Driven Information Retrieval for E-Health

Using ontologies in health care may represent the knowledge contained in medical practitioner's minds into a much organized and structured manner and also make it available to wider audience for reuse [15]. Ontology-driven solutions for health care helps practitioners to automate their tasks, retaining the semantics, as knowledge contained in ontologies is machine interpretable.

7.4.1   Ontology for E-Heath Implementation

Health care is a vital field and a lot of research in this direction has yielded a number of popular ontologies (e.g., Gene Ontology [16], Human Disease Ontology [2], etc.). Nowadays, even a number of portals are also being made available for hosting and managing ontologies in the domain of health care, biology and medicine such as BioPortal[6]. Primary requirement for e-health implementation is standardization of vocabulary used in procedures for consistent sharing. In this context, SOA Health care Ontology, a standardized ontology, is developed to cater interoperability issues of e-health. It defines the service-related aspects for standardizing future e-health [17].

Ontology can assist interoperability in health care [18]. Literature suggests a lot of applications catering to different aspects of e-health implementation. A portion of Disease Ontology class hierarchy is depicted in Figure 7.3.

Ontology for integrating EHR from heterogeneous sources: H. Sun et al. proposed an approach to represent information available at a source in different representations to make it compatible with other applications [19]. The challenge is to conform with interoperability among heterogeneous clinical data sources retaining the semantics of data. In their approach, data present in sources is firstly translated to their Resource Description Framework (RDF) representations retaining the semantics in the form of database schema. Semantic conversions happen using inference and reasoning logic from N3 rules. They claim that a number of clinical applications may benefit using their approach, which is made available as a web service on demand.

Ontology for Electronic Health Care Information Exchange: J. McMurray et al. devised an ontology (HEIO Ontology) for exchange of knowledge among different EHRs [20]. Ontology contained rules that were used to derive new knowledge using ontology-based inference. With the data populated in ontology regarding the exchange in information, logical consistency among values was validated by applying inference and validation.

Ontology for Personalized Health Care: For chronically ill patients, where intervention of multiple health professionals in required, ontology may serve as a desired knowledge model for storing personalized information [21]. D. Riano et al. devised a process in which generic ontologies containing knowledge of general traits, symptoms, causes, treatments,

---

[6] https://bioportal.bioontology.org/

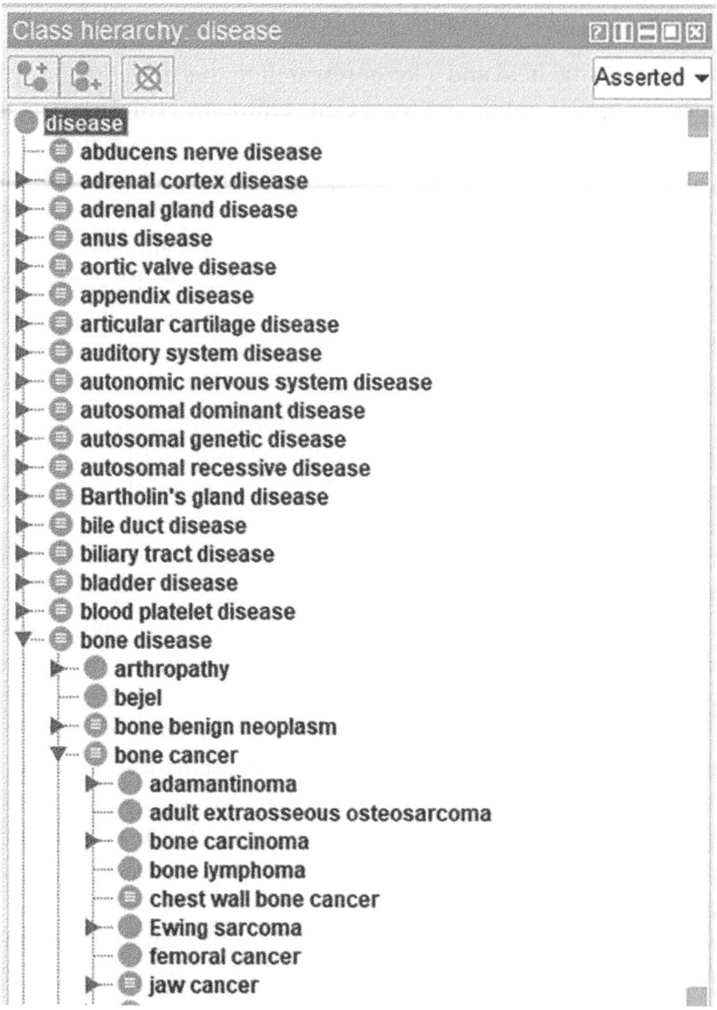

Figure 7.3 A portion of disease ontology class hierarchy [2].

etc., may be personalized for a particular patient. Personalization works by selecting a subset of classes from generic ontology that applies for the particular patient and considering the value of instances for those classes only. This results in a smaller ontology with all traits, symptoms, treatments, and interventions that are applicable to the specified patient giving a true patient personalization experience. Further, they implemented a decision-making system based on the reasoning from ontology personalization process devised for suggesting required interventions for the specified individual.

7.4.2   Frameworks for Information Retrieval Using Ontology for E-Health

State-of-the-art frameworks for information retrieval using ontology for e-health implementation are suggested in literature. An approach is to hold health care data and map into ontology concepts (for interoperability) and instances using an e-health ontology. Internet of Things (IoT) sensors may be used to collect patient data and remote monitoring [22].

Information contained in medical records dataset can be structured by feeding it to populate an ontology. However, the populating stage should be well defined with rules covering the technical validation of data. T. MuthamilSelvan *et al.* proposed a cloud-based ontology population framework for e-health [23]. Taking input from the dataset containing patient records, it can populate concepts and instances in the ontology with the help of rules defined. Their proposed framework inputs raw textual documents pertaining to health care. Then, based on rules defined in the ontology, knowledge is extracted from contents of the document. Next, the extracted knowledge is matched with existing knowledge base for all other relevant documents having similarity above some threshold. Finally, all those relevant documents are returned back to user. In conclusion, the user is getting matching documents to the query, which in this case is not explicitly obvious. That is, the search query is derived out of the input document.

S. S. El-Atawy *et al.* proposed an EHR Processing system by using the ontology as the base for information storage and retrieval [24]. For facilitating the retrieval part, they worked on optimizing the search of information contained in the ontology. For effective retrieval, they proposed a mapping approach between the vocabulary available with ontology and system components. They implemented the system in Java programming language translating the ontology classes into java classes, ontology individuals into objects of classes and ontology properties into functions. The converted constructs were then stored in relational database for stable storage. Using the new representation, users (medical practitioners in their case) were able to query the system effectively and were also able to generate reports with actual patient data efficiently.

G. Henriques *et al.* have proposed a framework for ontology-driven data collection building a repository from health care surveys which can also be shared [25]. Survey application running on iPad device was used for data collection. Their proposed framework will use ontology for primary classification of surveys by freezing the definition set of survey requirements in the ontology. Further, reasoners may be employed with the ontology knowledge for suggesting survey questions as per requirements. The populated knowledge can be shared with other applications in file formats usable for surveys (e.g., PDF) and process able by machine (e.g., XML).

H. Ajami *et al.* have proposed a framework for monitoring of patients suffering from chronic pulmonary disease in real time [26]. To keep medical practitioners updated about the severity of patient situation in real time, their proposed framework evaluates the daily activities of patients (using sensors on medical devices) along with additional parameters such as readings on environmental sensors. Role of ontology can be seen in decision making with reasoning on collected patient's data. This proposed framework is unique in the aspect that it uses a mesh of ontologies related to patient, environment sensors, location, activities of patient, disease records, etc., dealing with different aspects of data collection and knowledge processing in their system. That is, the knowledge contained in one ontology is also processed by other ontologies forming a flow of knowledge, hence requires a larger set of reasoning rules for effective decision making. This framework covers the entire flow of effective patient monitoring.

Y. Zhang *et al.* have proposed a framework for ontology automated decision support for remotely located patients suffering from chronic disorders. The automated decision making precedes collection of patient's medical records and standard criteria for assessment of disorder. They have used and modified vMR ontology that is specific to chronic disorders as a standard for capturing patient's data. If the captured values are greater than the threshold for risk, then they computed a semantic risk factor from the captured knowledge. Based on the computation, a follow up decision was made.

N. Lasierra *et al.* have proposed an ontology supported workflow for remotely monitoring patients with chronic disorders [27]. First phase of their flow collected the specifications to model an ontology for clinical purposes. Secondly, they fed in the patients' profile data who were chronically ill to make ontology adaptable to this category of clinical assessment. Finally, the automated monitoring system was developed which was responsible for keeping track of incoming patient's data for any new parameters and suggesting appropriate actions based on the knowledge. Incoming patient's data included time-based parameters such as glucose or sugar level, room and body temperatures, current pulse rate, current blood pressure, status of prescribed medication, etc.

7.4.3   Applications of Ontology-Driven Information Retrieval in Health Care

In this section, some typical applications of ontology supported information retrieval in health care domain, which are available in literature, are explored as shown in Table 7.4.

Table 7.4 Applications of ontology-driven information retrieval in e-health solutions.

Application	Description
Advisory system for health care	Patients suffering from diseases caused due to improper lifestyle may be advised by using an ontology-based system. T. Nantiruj *et al.* have developed an advisory system, which provides feedback from the knowledge of Thai herbs and considering patient's health data [28]. They have populated the knowledge in Thai herb ontology and used it along with personal health database to suggest some beneficial herb based on individual's personal data. System receives input from patient in the form of height measurement, weight measurement, and blood pressure value, etc., health parameters and sends output in the form of advised Thai herb.
Highlighting and annotating text in documents	Research scholars, particularly in the medical or biological domains, may get benefitted in their research study by an approach capable of highlighting and annotating relevant data to their search query in a paper or book they are referring. For instance, when a user or scholar tries to search for a specific disease in a research paper or text book, the system may suggest and highlight other disease names in the text which belong to the same family of diseases as the queried one. The underlying knowledge of similarity among terms is extracted by the use of domain ontologies for that field (e.g., disease ontology in this case).
Remotely diagnosing the patient with medical sensor devices	A. Rhayem *et al.* have proposed a system for monitoring of patient's health using knowledge extraction to model an ontology [29]. Their systems take input from medical sensors such as Electroencephalogram data and patient's previous health records collectively to extract knowledge. Then, this collective knowledge is modeled into an ontology, which is later used with reasoners for decision making for that specific patient. Their system is claimed to facilitate remotely diagnosing the patient and generating alerts as per condition severity.

(Continued)

Table 7.4 Applications of ontology-driven information retrieval in e-health solutions. (*Continued*)

Application	Description
Effective monitoring for patients with chronic diseases	We have discussed three frameworks focusing on monitoring, assessing, and diagnosing patients with chronic disorders in the previous section [26, 27, 30].
Rule-based validation of medical records	Medical records can be validated by rule-based reasoning and validation of ontology knowledge. A set of rules defined for ontology can check for inconsistencies in information in an automated manner and notify the concerned personnel for rectification, if required [19, 21, 26].

7.4.4   Benefits and Limitations

Upgradation to newer technologies such as semantic web technologies, which are still in their progressing phase, comes with both benefits and limitations. The benefits of a machine understandable process flow that too preserving the meanings of concepts are automation and hence the reduced cost of operation, lesser probability of human errors, and better decision support systems. But, due to lesser familiarity of technologies in this domain, it is difficult both for the patients in accepting the recent advancements and, for the medical practitioners to rely on its accuracy and correctness of knowledge. Table 7.5 highlights the key advantages of ontology supported e-health implementation.

Table 7.6 enlists some of the key limitations concerned with ontology-driven e-health implementations.

7.5   Discussion

Health care solutions are advancing towards the usage of digital solutions due to the feature and cost benefits they provide. Health care initiatives on digital platform such as e-health, m-health, etc., are being adopted by governments and other implementing organizations at large scale. Information retrieval based on query is a key process in all aspects of the digital solutions may it be capturing of patient data, sharing of individual patients records across health care providers, making decisions for a wider population, etc.

Table 7.5 Key benefits of ontology supported e-health solutions.

Benefit	Description
Semantic interoperability	The key advantage of implementing e-health solutions using ontology is the semantic interoperability among medical records. Information gathered from patient records once converted to a standard representation in ontology can be reused across different applications without losing the semantics or meaning of its contents.
Agreed upon conceptualizations	Vocabulary used to describe knowledge in ontology is formal and generic for that domain. Hence, the taxonomy used in e-health solutions using those ontologies can be implicitly assumed to be agreed upon and process able by the implemented solution.
Evidence-based practice	Availability of knowledge of patient's health and disease records may help medical practitioners to get a bigger picture of medical history and facilitate them to make better decisions. Further, applying reasoning on ontology knowledge may automate the health advice practice based on concrete evidences.
Personalized care	Literature suggests a number of ontology supported solutions for personalized health care with the use of personal health profiles [21, 28]. Thus, the system implementations will result in availability of personalized advisory to patients located remotely based on their individual data records.
Automated validation of medical records	There could be multiple issues in validation of patient medical records due to involvement of human factor which is much error prone. Ontology-driven rule-based validation with support from reasoners can help in reducing the issues due to human errors.

Traditional keyword matching-based query retrieval approaches are available at large and are used as default in health care information systems. With the increased volume and complexity of health care data, e-health solutions are suffering from the problem of interoperability. This issue is

Table 7.6 Key limitations concerned while implementing ontology-driven e-health.

Limitation	Description
Finding appropriate ontologies	As one ontology can't be applied for domain description of complete health care. Hence, for specific subdomains, we need appropriate ontologies, which may be inexistent or difficult to find.
Issues with patient acceptance	There exist limitations regarding patient acceptance of digital solutions more specifically in adapting to the recent advancements. Health care practices are difficult to advance unless patients are made comfortable towards usage and testing of new developments.
Lack of interoperability due to unavailability of proper ontologies	Lack of interoperability among e-health systems is due to varying terminology (lack of standard vocabularies). Though, there exist some well-defined ontologies that are specific to some diseases having sufficient research literature. But, for majority of health care, there is still a lack of structured information repositories.
Difficult User Experience	User experience in using e-health solutions is not good as suggested in literature, often due to complexity of tasks involved. This forces the users to keep using the traditional ways of getting treatment and health advice.
National Level Implementation (Scaling)	Another key issue pertaining to implementation of e-health is its scaling due to concerns for regulatory authorities, political factors, and digital literacy of users among others. Further, for a global stage implementation, there is a need of some regulatory authority at global stage over management of ontologies for health care, which is a vital field requiring proper regulation.
Populating ontologies with proper knowledge	Semantics-based technologies are of no use unless the knowledge stored in them is valid. Hence, utmost care should be taken while populating the ontologies with concepts, instances, and relations. There should be availability of good knowledge engineers for ontology modeling and knowledge population. There should also be a proper validation mechanism with the involvement of multiple validators.

due to lack of understanding of vocabulary available with one health care provider and the vocabulary available with the other. Terminology used in one system's implementation may be conveying same meaning or concept as the term used by other, but syntax-based retrieval approaches fail to comprehend this factor. This requires the intervention of humans (medical practitioners) and poses a gap for automating the health care data sharing process. Thus, a need arises to combine semantics-based approaches into retrieval mechanisms to capture this missing piece, the meanings, or the semantics of health care taxonomy.

Ontology, a semantic knowledge model, can help in assisting interoperability for health care sector, as it represents knowledge in a format

Table 7.7 Highlights of discussion throughout this chapter.

Highlights of discussion
Patient health profiles when appended with ontology knowledge pertaining to medical domains give medical practitioners a wider picture of patient's health profile and facilitate them to make further decisions related to treatment or medication using the concrete evidences available.
Semantic interoperability is the key benefit of ontology in health care. Information gathered from patient records once converted to a standard representation in ontology can be reused across different applications. Due to agreed vocabulary and provision for ontology mapping techniques, the meanings of medical terms are preserved among different e-health implementations.
Ontology knowledge may also be queried for validation of medical records by using the rule-based reasoning techniques. A set of validation rules needs to be supplied to ontology reasoner for consistency checks.
With the availability of large number of domain ontologies in medical and biological domain having deep concept hierarchies, a number of querying and searching applications are possible for biomedical literature and textbooks. These include applications of searching relevant concepts to a queried concept in a textbook, retrieval of relevant research papers containing research on related biological entities from the internet based on a queried biological entity.
Monitoring of patients located remotely in real time and giving them personalized advisory is possible with the use of medical sensors along with environmental parameters and ontology as a medium for knowledge storage and querying [27, 29, 30].

understandable by both humans and machines. Key application of ontology is in solving the problem of inability of medical practitioners to efficiently acquire the information of patients which is available in unstructured textual representation spanning across multiple records and often with multiple health care providers [31]. In this chapter, we discussed a number of approaches which caters to different aspects of e-health implementation process, focusing on the usage of ontology by them.

Some key insights gained by studying these frameworks are summarized in Table 7.7.

7.6   Conclusion

Health care domain is steadily advancing towards the automated use of digital solutions such as e-health, m-health, etc. This chapter highlighted the role of ontology for implementation of e-health focusing on query retrieval and analyzed the advancements in this direction. Structured knowledge present in ontology can be used for storage of medical information and retrieval of required records on demand. A number of proposed and existing frameworks for e-health domain that process ontological knowledge are also explored justifying the scope of ontology towards e-health solutions. Application areas of ontology-based knowledge flow in e-health are also highlighted.

Also, some of the recommendations for implementation of e-health utilizing ontology for knowledge storage and retrieval as extracted from the state of art are discussed. Finally, a summary of key benefits highlighted are enlisted which are interoperability, faster medical procedures, availability, secured access, focus on patient, etc. A few limitations of existing solutions in this direction are identified such as lack of proper ontologies, effort in populating ontologies with the proper knowledge, customer acceptance of fully digital solutions, scaling to national or global stage, etc.

References

1. Ibrahim, A.M., Hashi, H.A., Mohamed, A.A., Ontology-driven information retrieval for healthcare information system: A case study. *Int. J. Network Secur. Appl.*, 5, 1, 61, 2013.
2. Schriml, L.M., Mitraka, E., Munro, J., Tauber, B., Schor, M., Nickle, L., Felix, V., Jeng, L., Bearer, C., Lichenstein, R., Campion, N., Hyman, B., Kurland, D., Oates, C.P., Kibbey, S., Sreekumar, P., Le, C., Giglio, M., Greene, C., Bisordi, K., Human Disease Ontology 2018 update: Classification, content and workflow expansion. *Nucleic Acids Res.*, 47, D1, D955–D962, 2018.

3. Khan, A.A. and Malik, S.K., A semi search algorithm towards semantic search using domain ontologies. *Int. J. Auton. Comput.*, 2, 3, 191–210, 2017.
4. Khan, A.A. and Malik, S.K., Semantic Search Revisited, in: Paper presented at *2018 8th International Conference on Cloud Computing, Data Science & Engineering (Confluence)*, Noida, India, IEEE, pp. 14–15, January, 2018.
5. Remi, S. and Varghese, S.C., Domain ontology driven fuzzy semantic information retrieval. *Procedia Comput. Sci.*, 46, 676–681, 2015.
6. Mäkelä, E., Survey of semantic search research, in: *Proceedings of the seminar on knowledge management on the semantic web*, Department of Computer Science, University of Helsinki, Helsinki, 2005.
7. Eysenbach, G., What is e-health? *J. Med. Internet Res.*, 3, 2, e20, 2001.
8. Schulz, S., Stenzhorn, H., Boeker, M., Smith, B., Strengths and limitations of formal ontologies in the biomedical domain. *Revista Electronica De Comunicacao, Informacao Inovacao Em Saude: RECIIS*, 3, 1, 31, 2009.
9. Schulz, S., Stegwee, R., Chronaki, C., Standards in Healthcare Data, in: *Fundamentals of Clinical Data Science*, pp. 19–36, Springer, Cham, 2019.
10. Heflin, J. and Hendler, J., *Semantic interoperability on the web*, in: Proceedings of Extreme Markup Languages, Graphic Communications Association, Maryland University College Park, Dept. of Computer Science, pp. 11–120, 2000.
11. Jarosławski, S. and Saberwal, G., In eHealth in India today, the nature of work, the challenges and the finances: An interview-based study. *BMC Med. Inf. Decis. Making*, 14, 1, 1, 2014.
12. Fanta, G.B. and Pretorius, L., A conceptual framework for sustainable eHealth implementation in resource-constrained settings. *S. Afr. J. Ind. Eng.*, 29, 3, 132–147, 2018.
13. Ross, J., Stevenson, F., Lau, R., Murray, E., Exploring the challenges of implementing e-health: A protocol for an update of a systematic review of reviews. *BMJ Open*, 5, 4, e006773, 2015.
14. Ross, J., Stevenson, F., Lau, R., Murray, E., Factors that influence the implementation of e-health: A systematic review of systematic reviews (an update). *Implementation Science*, 11, 1, 146, 2016.
15. Moraes, E.C., Brito, K., Meira, S., OntoPHC: An Ontology Applied For Primary Health Care. Paper presented at International Conference on Computational Science (ICCS 2012). *Procedia Comput. Sci.*, 9, 1543–1552, 2012.
16. Gene Ontology Consortium, The Gene Ontology (GO) database and informatics resource. *Nucleic Acids Res.*, 32, suppl_1, D258–D261, 2004.
17. Milosevic, Z., Almeida, J.P., Nardi, J.C., Towards Better Semantics for Services in eHealth Standards: A Reference Ontology Approach, in: *2014 IEEE 18th International Enterprise Distributed Object Computing Conference Workshops and Demonstrations*, IEEE, pp. 276–285, September, 2014.
18. Garshasbi, M., Asadi, H., Asosheh, A., Application and effectiveness of ontology on e-Health, in: *7'th International Symposium on Telecommunications (IST'2014)*, IEEE, pp. 544–549, September, 2014.

19. Sun, H., Depraetere, K., De Roo, J., Mels, G., De Vloed, B., Twagirumukiza, M., Colaert, D., Semantic processing of EHR data for clinical research. *J. Biomed. Inf.*, 58, 247–259, 2015.
20. McMurray, J., Zhu, L., McKillop, I., Chen, H., Ontological modeling of electronic health information exchange. *J. Biomed. Inf.*, 56, 169–178, 2015.
21. Riaño, D., Real, F., López-Vallverdú, J.A., Campana, F., Ercolani, S., Mecocci, P., Annicchiarico, R., Caltagirone, C., An ontology-based personalization of health-care knowledge to support clinical decisions for chronically ill patients. *J. Biomed. Inf.*, 45, 3, 429–446, 2012.
22. Saad, S., Zafar, B.A., Mueen, A., Developing a Framework for E-Healthcare Applications using the Semantic Internet of Things. *Int. J. Comput. Appl.*, 182, 34, 25–33, 2018.
23. MuthamilSelvan, T. and Balamurugan, B., Cloud based automated framework for semantic rich ontology construction and similarity computation for E-health applications. *Inf. Med. Unlocked*, 8, 66–73, 2017.
24. El-Atawy, S.S. and Khalefa, M.E., Building an Ontology-Based Electronic Health Record System, in: *Proceedings of the 2nd Africa and Middle East Conference on Software Engineering (AMECSE'16)*, Cairo, Egypt, May 28–29, ACM, pp. 40–45, May, 2016.
25. Henriques, G., Lamanna, L., Kotowski, D., Hlomani, H., Stacey, D., Baker, P., Harper, S., An ontology-driven approach to mobile data collection applications for the healthcare industry. *Network Model. Anal. Health Inf. Bioinf.*, 2, 4, 213–223, 2013.
26. Ajami, H. and Mcheick, H., Ontology-Based Model to Support Ubiquitous Healthcare Systems for COPD Patients. *Electronics*, 7, 12, 371, 2018.
27. Lasierra, N., Alesanco, A., Guillén, S., García, J., A three stage ontology-driven solution to provide personalized care to chronic patients at home. *J. Biomed. Inf.*, 46, 3, 516–529, 2013.
28. Nantiruj, T., Maneerat, N., Varakulsiripunth, R., Izumi, S., Shiratori, N., Kato, T., Kato, Y., Takahashi, K., An e-health advice system with Thai herb and an ontology, in: *Proceeding of the 3rd International Symposium on Biomedical Engineering (ISBME 2008)*, pp. 315–319, 2008.
29. Rhayem, A., Mhiri, M.B., Salah, M.B., Gargouri, F., Ontology-based system for patient monitoring with connected objects. Paper presented at International Conference on Knowledge Based and Intelligent Information and Engineering Systems, KES2017, 6-8 September 2017, Marseille, France. *Procedia Comput. Sci.*, 112, 683–692, 2017.
30. Zhang, Y.F., Gou, L., Zhou, T.S., Lin, D.N., Zheng, J., Li, Y., Li, J.S., An ontology-based approach to patient follow-up assessment for continuous and personalized chronic disease management. *J. Biomed. Inf.*, 72, 45–59, 2017.
31. Gurulingappa, H., Müller, B., Hofmann-Apitius, M., Fluck, J., A Semantic Platform for Information Retrieval from E-Health Records, in: Paper presented at *Text Retrieval Conference (TREC)*, 2011.

8

Ontology-Based Case Retrieval in an E-Mental Health Intelligent Information System

Georgia Kaoura¹*, Konstantinos Kovas² and Basilis Boutsinas¹

¹Management Information Systems & Business Intelligence Lab, Department of Business Administration, University of Patras, Patras, Greece
²Department of Computer Engineering & Informatics, University of Patras, Patras, Greece

Abstract

This chapter discussed on an ontology developed for a case-based reasoning system that aims at supporting people facing autism spectrum disorders (ASD). PAVEFS is an intelligent information system designed for the personalized provision of services for the diagnosis and the care of individuals of various ages and types of autism. The objective of PAVEFS is to lead to best practices' models and to provide access to information regarding care procedures of individuals with ASD. PAVEFS is based both on scientific knowledge of autism and on practical information, acquired from experts and caregivers from various specializations, aiming at the creation of an extended basis of specialized and reliable information and at answering questions related to care procedures on children and adults facing ASD.

Keywords: E-mental health, ontology, knowledge base, case-based reasoning system

8.1 Introduction

E-mental health, as a sub-domain of e-health[1], may be defined as "the use of telecommunication and information technologies to deliver mental

---

*Corresponding author: kaourag@yahoo.com
[1] According to WHO definition e-Health is "the transfer of health resources and healthcare by electronic means".

Vishal Jain, Ritika Wason, Jyotir Moy Chatterjee and Dac-Nhuong Le (eds.) Ontology-Based Information Retrieval for Healthcare Systems, (167–192) © 2020 Scrivener Publishing LLC

health services at a distance" [12]. Respectively, the National Health Service Network (NHS) defines e-mental health as "the use of information and communication technologies to support and improve mental health, including the use of online resources, social media, and smart-phone applications".

During the last decades, the rapidly increasing use of IT and specifically Artificial Intelligence techniques influences, among other, the delivery of mental health services, i.e., the provision of information, assessment, diagnosis, counseling, and treatment. Broad definitions of e-mental health may also include delivery activities related to screening, mental health promotion and prevention, staff training, and administrative support and research [16].

Mental health care constitutes an important cost parameter to all EU countries, resulting, in many cases, in additional costs to the economy. To assist people overcoming mental disorders' challenges, an ontology-enhanced monitoring and treatment model is needed, since a well-designed ontology may contribute to a more sophisticated diagnosis and treatment. An ontology enables high scalability in searching, exporting, maintaining, and generating information. Researchers have developed context ontology for mental disorders, especially psychological, psychiatric disorders, or chronic diseases so as to serve as a basis upon which semantics and other methodologies and technologies can be developed for collecting, formalizing, and using data from patients.

This chapter describes an ontology that has been developed for a case-based reasoning (CBR) system aiming at the support of people facing Autism Spectrum Disorders (hereafter ASD). PAVEFS is an intelligent information system designed for the personalized provision of services for the diagnosis and care of individuals of various ages and types of autism. PAVEFS is a system based both on scientific knowledge of autism and on practical information, acquired from many experts and caregivers from various specializations, aiming at the creation of an extended basis of specialized and reliable information and at answering questions related to care procedures on children and adults facing ASD. It is designed to operate as a bridge interconnecting standards, predictions, and conclusions with data analysis and to provide effective and quality care procedures to individuals facing ASD. One of the main objectives of the PAVEFS system is to lead to best practices' models and to provide access to information regarding care procedures of individuals with ASD. It is considered as a critical system based on a dynamic understanding of the nature a) of individuals facing ASD and b) of their care procedures.

The system's architecture is mainly based on users (specialized/experts, analysts/investigators, and regular and advanced end users) access (information and answers' introduction) through PC, laptop, smart phones, tablets, VoiP, IVR, smart TVs, Fax, and OCR. A specially designed form facilitates experts to introduce rules/exceptions and cases to the system's knowledge base, while users submit questions (queries), also through a specially designed form. Then, taking into consideration the profile of the individual facing ASD as well as the characteristics of her/his specific behaviors described in the question, the system searches in the knowledge base for similar cases. Finally, after processing similar cases, the system returns both the similar cases and successful interventions per behavior.

The Ontology includes all the terms used for information regarding the profile, the rules, the exceptions, and the cases. The ontology is accessed each time a case/rule/exception/query is entered to the system or each time a response is returned to the user. The knowledge base is consisted of cases, rules, and exceptions represented by using terms of the Ontology. Also, the ontology terms are used to compose the end-users' questions, by allowing the users to navigate parts of the Ontology. Finally, the response of the system consists of automatically composed text based on terms of the Ontology that includes information/consultations as well as similar cases represented by using terms of the Ontology.

The core of PAVEFS is a hybrid reasoner that is based both on case based and on rule-based reasoning (RBR). It is based on experts' knowledge in order to gain an internal representation of the characteristics of individuals facing ASD to compare with the characteristics of the individual to be examined. This knowledge is continually amplified with cases and rules that are derived from the knowledge and experience of specialized experts regarding autism as well as from the international academic literature.

PAVEFS includes also an expert system of primary diagnosis, as a screening tool, contributing to the on-time detection of ASD. The system provides a primary diagnosis tool using two alternative questionnaires, one for children aged up to 4 years and another one for children aged between 49 months and 11 years old. The user answers 23 questions presented in the first case and 15 questions on the second one. After the completion of the answering to the questions, the system provides an evaluation and diagnosis and decides whether there are some indications for ASD or not and always incites the user to visit a physician.

The remaining part of the chapter is organized as follows: Section 8.2 describes the related work on the use of ontologies in e-mental health support systems. In Section 8.3, we present the problem identified, and in Section 8.4, the developed ontology, the knowledge base of the system, and the hybrid reasoning model used by the PAVEFS system are also described. Section 8.5 describes the evaluation methodology followed and the results highlighting the pros and cons of the proposed solution. Section 8.6 discusses the conclusions, and Section 8.7 provides the plans for future work.

8.2   Literature Survey

In related work, Young *et al.* incorporated an autism ontology to allow semantic data integration by annotating data with ontological concepts and enhanced searches on a database. As ASD is an inherently complex and vague phenomenon, there is difficulty in understanding its causes. The National Database for Autism Research (NDAR) has been constructed to aid in providing researchers with a meaningful data sharing and data integration [17]. NDAR has incorporated an autism ontology to allow semantic data integration while its architecture enhances queries (central and federated), on databases. The database (NDAR) allows researchers to define the phenotype through the terms of data dictionary, with the assessments and their items by also assigning accession numbers to phenotype and by associating literature citations with them. The proposed design facilitates searching and retrieval helping the researcher to relate citation with phenotypes or with phenotypes accession numbers. Additionally, the reader with the use of accession number may navigate through phenotypes and associated data.

Rodríguez-González *et al.* presented an ontology mostly targeted on evaluation and diagnosis for psychological disorders [2]. According to the authors, the ontologies created allow different forms of reasoning with the objective to support professionals of mental health in decision making by using decision support systems (DSSs). The data heterogeneity included in most mental diseases [10] has not allowed so far researchers to build a realistic ontology. The most recent and relevant approach proposes consistency between mental disease ontologies and other biomedical ontologies [6] in order to provide more reliable diagnosis and treatment. The paper presents the basic features and implementation of the ontology proposed, summarizing existing works, with the goal the ontology to become the reference point in clinical DSS in the field of PsyDis [5]. A well-designed ontology can remedy interoperability difficulties that many actual systems generate and can contribute to a more precise diagnosis and targeted treatment by practitioners.

The same stands in the works by Lin *et al.* who presented an ontology-based method, utilizing a decision tree algorithm aiming to infer psychiatric dimension's disorders. Protégé software was used for the creation of the decision tree algorithm that constructed an ontology-based meridian method, serving as an example psychiatric disorder inference and as knowledge—sharing platform. The method succeeds to detect psychiatric disorder having associated medicine with the meridian system and to build remarkable expert knowledge through the construction of domain and task ontologies [4]. The aim of the system is to eliminate the information disparity between patients and physicians while allowing experts to participate and to provide an understanding to the public. The study in general integrates an ontology-based approach with a decision-tree algorithm for the detection of psychiatric disorders.

Silva *et al.* also developed an ontology with the objective to infer psychiatric disorders upon the symptoms presented by a patient [14]. The objective is the development of an enriched ontology-based system that makes easier the diagnosis of mental disorders and especially of bipolarity and depression, illnesses which are difficult to trace. By adopting document domain knowledge of DSM-IV (Diagnostic and Statistical Manual of Mental Disorders, 4th Edition) standard, the authors create the conceptual knowledge base with the key diagnostic rules. The ontology is designed to be used as the basic reasoning which leads to a better diagnosis.

Hu *et al.* also use context ontology to regulate and accumulate patient data and an ontology-based inference engine to achieve personalization. Because of the high cost of mental health care to all EU nations, cognitive behavior therapy (hereafter CBT) is the treatment of choice for mental disorders such as depression, anxiety disorders, eating disorders, chronic insomnia, etc. The paper targets to propose a model based on an ontology in order to assist patients facing mental disorders [8]. At first, patients' data are collected and processed through the context ontology designed and at a sequent stage the proposed model is implemented on online CBT with an online statistic report also integrated into the system.

Vyas *et al.* presented an ontology-based DSS that mostly helps handling and tracking patients' records, facilitating fast and specialized health care services, taking into account the history of the patient or the specific case. Consequently, the time spent in medical institutions is reduced. The system provides fast access to accurate patient health data, reducing the documentation and formalities and increasing the usability of effective and reliable information by the medical institutions and health care specialists. The available data within the healthcare system usually don't have effective analysis tools to uncover hidden connections and patterns into them.

Ontologies allow high scalability in searching, extracting, maintaining, and generating information [15]. Additionally, with the use of e-health care systems, patients receive faster and more accurate and coordinated health services, and on the other hand, providers share information more effectively.

Diego *et al.* utilize ontologies to annotate stored data about mental health with metadata, to try to improve interoperability between information systems. Mental health managers are required to take decisions with complex data from various source, usually sharing very little standardization and integration. The interoperability between information systems is crucial for establishing the ability to exchange and reuse information for the generation of knowledge. Semantic Web technology can be used to reduce the data complexity and to assist in the data interpretation since it classifies the stored information with metadata and gives them meaning through the ontologies [7]. The proposed ontology intends to combine knowledge from databases of various context types in the RAPS, allowing the semantic annotation of the raw data and converting them into useful information and knowledge. The ontology facilitates the RAPS decision-making and the formalization of public health policies by supplying the manager with useful information derived from a variety of independent systems.

Ajami *et al.* have developed a DSS to help Chronic Obstructive Pulmonary Disease (hereafter COPD) patients, using a relevant ontology and SWRL rules. The study explored formal semantic standards used for creating an ontology knowledge repository to offer universal healthcare and medical recommendations for COPD patients to reduce harmful situations that could be prevented. The proposed approach is patient-centered monitoring and its main benefits are: the adhering of safe boundaries for the vital and signs[2], the assessment of environmental risk factors; and the monitoring and assessment of the patient's daily actions through scheduled events in order to identify and prevent risky behaviors [1]. The solution combines an interrelated set of ontologies with a knowledge base of Semantic Web Rule Language (SWRL) rules extracted by researching the medical guidelines and the opinions of independent experts (pneumologists), in order to estimate the risk of COPD exacerbation and handle all contextual situations. A DSS was developed to make safer environments for COPD patients in an ontological formal description of a health-related domain using SWRL rules. The proposed ontology includes all the relevant to COPD terms, including the individual information of patients,

---

[2] Varying on many factors.

environments, activities, symptoms, risk factors, examination results, and treatment plans.

The future steps for the researchers are the testing of the above described systems with many practical data and in different application scenarios (i.e., outdoor and indoor). Follow-up studies need to produce systems in a real-life medical practice to increase the available detection mechanisms for different mental disorders. By collecting sufficient data concerning different disorders, systems will be able to identify disorders and extract information about the valuable relationships between them, bringing added value to medical practice.

The next challenge to meet is the application of the systems on other variations of mental disorders, and the expansion of the ontology with the inference engine into a more universal mental disorder health care ontology. OWL with SWRL can be utilized for applying reasoning in complex medical applications while another issue remains the automatic generation of ontologies from the clinical databases so that the learning process of the e-health care system continues as the time goes by. The use of ontologies improves the quality of service and contributes to a better distribution of resources, bringing benefits to every community by increasing performance and effectiveness in the public health sector. Furthermore, the use of such systems, can improve a) patients' ability to engage in self-management and b) the expansion of applying the approach to other mental or chronic diseases.

8.3   Problem Identified

Autism is a serious, neuropsychiatric disorder, caused by a malfunction of the brain, characterized by qualitative differences in social interaction and relationship building, in verbal and non-verbal communication and in game-thinking-imagination. These divergences have a profound effect on the way a person perceives and experiences himself or herself and the world, the way he or she learns, behaves, adapts, and operates in daily life. They also influence the course of development, deviating from the normal with symptoms that vary depending on age and developmental stage, severity, coexistence of other medical conditions, individual temperament, and environmental factors. In Greece, there are not many specialized public services provided for children or adolescents with autism available, which are unable though to cover the full range of parents' particular needs. For adults facing ASD, specialized services are non-existent at all. In the current context, the lack of supporting services for the individuals facing ASD and their parents or caregivers has been identified and the proposed solution on mental health systems pursues to bridge this gap. Although several information systems and applications have been designed in health sector, ASD is a field that has not been covered so much. The intelligent system proposed supports and facilitates the daily life of individuals facing ASD and their caregivers by providing specialized, reliable, and professional assistance.

Since ASD is a complex and difficult to analyze field, there has not been developed a similar intelligent information system like the one proposed in the next sections, so no comparative study has been conducted.

8.4 Proposed Solution

8.4.1 The PAVEFS Ontology

The Ontology is served as a logical model providing the opportunity to represent knowledge of specific domains, describing the contexts of the domain and relations between them. For the creation of the PAVEFS' ontology, Protégé [13] has been used for facilitating the visualization, the data retrieval, the usage of inference mechanism, etc. The ontology represents in a tree format, the concepts used in cases, and rules' induction. It includes the existing ontology from Harvard [7, 8] while, with experts' intervention, it has been extended to cover all the implementation needs. More complex concepts are described with more simple concepts' definitions. Furthermore, control on the mutual validation of statements and definitions is conducted, while the depiction of the combination of the concept with the relevant definition and the proper hierarchy contribute to domain understanding. New terms have been added or renamed and the ontology has been restructured with the aim to describe the cases in a more understandable way for the user/people, not expert in the autism domain.

The ontology's structure is created so as to facilitate the user, the expert, or any other to describe an incident. The ABC (Antecedent-Behavior-Consequence) approach is followed so as to respond to system needs. From the structure, it is obvious that at first a risk factors reference is made (contribution to the appearance of the behavior, taking into account the medical record and the patient's diagnosis), then the incident (the description of the event) with the behavior and the parameters (such as frequency, tension, etc.) is described. Additional parameters are added according to the environment (natural and related to other people) before and during the event (setting events), and finally, the actions for the incident confrontment, possible dangers, and the results of the comportments (the outcome) are presented.

The Ontology is a hierarchical tree of classes (concepts relevant to autism) with the objective to cover all the necessary vocabulary for the case representation (a specific event and the way it is confronted) and the rules (conditions and conclusions). The OWL file consists of the statements of classes, hyper-classes, and their labels (rdfs: label). The schematic illustration of classes in the Protégé environment is presented in Figure 8.1.

Each class may consist of other classes and sub-classes (Figures 8.2 and 8.3) each one with a unique ID. For the definition of the label, we use the "label" property (many languages) and for the definition of a concept description the "definition" is used. The schematic illustration of classes and labels is presented in Figure 8.4.

The proposed ontology includes six basic classes (Age, Antecedents, Binaries, Description of Event, Outcome, and Profile Information). The "Age" includes seven nodes, describing the new-born, infant, school,

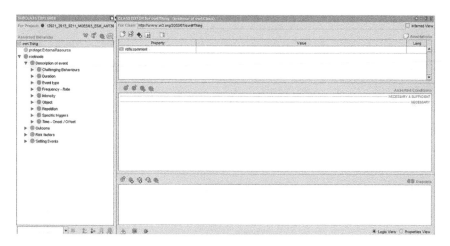

Figure 8.1 Classes in the Protégé environment.

Figure 8.2 Classes/hyper-classes.

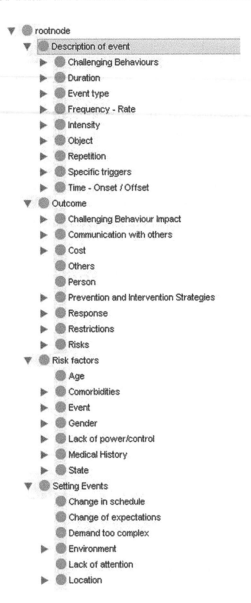

Figure 8.3 Classes and sub-classes in Protégé environment.

teenage, young-adult, adult and mature age depending on the years individuals have at the time of the event. The second class "Antecedents"
includes six other classes ("Location", "Number of the people involved",
"Physical environment", "The specific triggers", "State of the person", and
"Who was involved") that all except from the second (Number of people

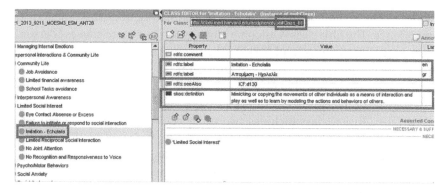

Figure 8.4 Labels and classes definitions.

involved) also include sub-classes and nodes. "Location" contains three more classes (Indoors, Outdoors, and Vehicle) and three more nodes (Other Therapeutic/training, environment/clinic, School/College, Work/Vocational Experience). The number of people involved is used to determine if the incident happens when the individual is alone, with someone else or with more people. The class of physical environment is consisted of five more classes (Change, Lighting, Noise, Temperature, and Weather) and four more nodes (Busy or Crowded environment, Environment with lots of stimuli, New environment, No structure of physical environment). The "Specific Triggers" class extends to thirteen more classes (Demand, Diversion, Event, Lack of power/control, Lack of simulation/motivation, Lighting, Location, Noise, Sensory stimuli, Temperature, Weather, The known person, Transition), and three nodes [Busy or crowded environment, Not apparent at the time of incident, Unknown person (involved)]. The classes mentioned are also extended to two or three more levels of nodes. The "State of the person" class contains four more classes (Emotional State, Health State, Mental Health State, and Physical Health State). The emotional and physical health state classes are extended to one more level (containing two more classes containing sub-classes). The "Who was involved" class contains one class (Known person)—with one sub-class (the caregiver) with two nodes (Female, Male) and a node (Unknown person).

The third class "Binaries" includes 10 other sub-classes (requiring a value YES or NO). The fourth class "Description of event" contains five more sub-classes (body part involved—28 nodes, frequency rate—high/medium/low, incident type containing eleven more sub-classes, intensity—high/medium/low/variable, location during the event). The location during the event contains three classes-indoors/outdoors/vehicle and three nodes—other therapeutic/training environment/clinic/work/vocational experience. The fifth class "Outcome" consists of four more classes (Person, Response, Restrictions, and Risks). The "Person" sub-class includes four nodes while "Response" class contains nine sub-classes and 18 nodes, referring to all the possible responses in the ASD. The "Restrictions" class includes the Environmental sub-class (with four nodes) and the Liberty node. The "Risks" class includes two other classes "To Others" with five nodes and the "To Self", the class containing six more nodes. Finally, the sixth class that is the biggest class of the ontology, "Profile Information" consists of three other classes (Diagnosis, Gender, Risk History/Factors). The Diagnosis class includes 11 sub-classes expanding from 5 to 41 nodes and five nodes. The Gender consists of three nodes while the Risk History/ Factors contains five classes and one node. The five classes expand to other classes and nodes (from two to four levels).

As an example, the graph of the class "Event" is presented in Figure 8.5.

The field ID is the unique key of each record while the field NodeID refers to the unique number of each ontology node. The field OntologyID

Figure 8.5 Graph of the sub-tree of the class «EVENT».

refers to the unique key of the ontology file to which the specific node is included. The fields LabelEN, LabelGR and DescrEN, DescrGR refer to the name and description of the node in the two languages the system supports. In ParentNode and SiblingNodes, the node-father and node-children of each node are stored, while the field FieldPrefix refers to the category the node belongs to (special trigger, behavior, etc.). All the above-mentioned fields are concluded in the OntologyNodes Table of the system.

8.4.2   Knowledge Base

PAVEFS is based on a knowledge base consisted of cases, rules, and exceptions to rules. The knowledge base is constantly updated with cases and rules, derived from the knowledge and experience of autism experts but also from international academic literature, as well as from cases submitted by end-users, after experts' evaluation.

More specifically, the PAVEFS' knowledge base includes rules, originated by the experts' team and by other scientific studies on the confrontation of autistic behaviors. Rules describe general behavior standards, reaction ways to specific stimuli and conditions, crisis cases and the procedures needed until the restoration to the previous normal condition. The knowledge base is oriented to provide information and knowledge to users, and it can update the data through review and evaluation functions.

It also includes a great number of cases that experts have introduced to the system. As the knowledge base is growing the system is becoming more efficient and accurate. The knowledge base includes general rules applying to general cases of individuals facing ASD, more specific rules (exceptions) deriving from the review of general rules that also apply to all individuals with autism and personal exceptions regarding specific cases of ASD individuals, exceptions deriving from the review of general rules applying only to specific individuals. A case record includes all the relevant information regarding an autism related incident. The fields of a case can be grouped in the following group categories: Individual's Profile and History, Environment, and involved People, Antecedents, Behaviors, Response Actions, and Risks. The case also includes temporal data of up to three sequential periods, so it is possible to represent how behaviors changed after specific response actions. The majority of the fields take as values Entities from specific branches of the Ontology.

A schematic illustration of the database implementing the knowledge base of the system is presented in Figure 8.6.

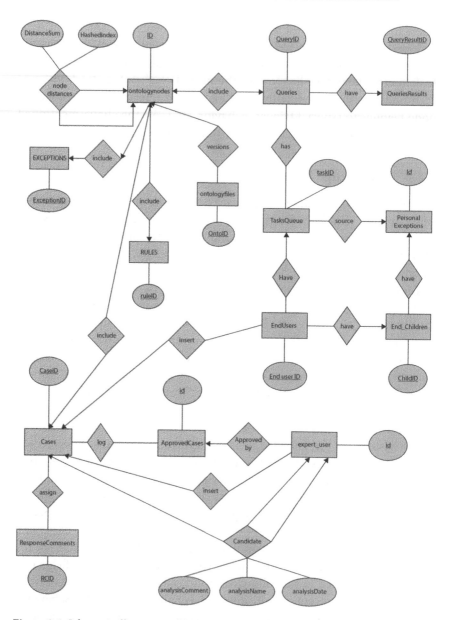

Figure 8.6 Schematic illustration of PAVEFS database.

8.4.3 Reasoning

PAVEFS has a hybrid reasoning system which is based both on CBR and RBR. RBR uses a set of rules (the rule base) that represents general knowledge about a domain. A rule usually has an "if-then" format, with a number of conditions that need to be satisfied for the rule to be activated and a set of actions or conclusions that are added in the working memory when the rule is executed. Inference takes place by introducing the input to the rule base, causing a chain of rules to be triggered and executed that eventually lead to the output. RBR is appropriate when there is a clear model of the domain or there are available experts that can represent it in the form of rules.

CBR takes advantage of stored past cases in order to deal with new similar cases. The inference is usually performed in four phases knows as the CBR cycle: retrieve, reuse, revise, and retain. Retrieval regards finding in the set of stored cases, one or more cases that appear to be the most similar to the new case. Reuse is concerned on using the retrieved, relevant cases to propose a solution for the new case. Revision regards the validation of the proposed solution, by testing if it solved the problem at hand. Retain decides if the new case is useful enough to be stored in the pool of past cases. CBR is appropriate when there are a great number of past cases available or it is easy to obtain them. It does not rely on creating a model of the domain.

RBR and CBR have been widely used together in systems in various applications and domains with quite successful results. One of the reasons for this is that they seem to have complimentary capabilities, so a system that can utilize both approaches could potentially take advantage of the positive aspects of both while minimizing the negative aspects. Furthermore, this combination of general (rules) and specific (cases) knowledge emulates the human way of thinking. Hybrid reasoning models that utilize both RBR and CBR components have been used in various domains with most notable the legal, medical, and agricultural. The way that the components are used in a hybrid system varies greatly and there have been a few attempts to categorize them. Medsker [11] has proposed a general categorization for combining intelligent techniques taking account whether and how the different integrated components interact with each other, extended later by Prentzas and Hatzilygeroudis [9] to better represent hybridizations with CBR components.

In the PAVEFS reasoning scheme, a cased-based reasoner is the main component of architecture, with the most crucial role. Also, a rule-based reasoner utilizes rules provided by experts to enhance the knowledge of the case base by populating it with additional values. Rules also include specific exceptions, provided both by the experts, and extracted from the history of stored cases.

The reasoning system of PAVEFS (along with its user interface) is based on an ontology, including all the terms used for information regarding patient profiles, rules, cases, and exceptions. The ontology is accessed each time a user inserts a query and a case/rule/exception is fetched, as a respond to this query. Thus, the key idea behind the reasoning system of PAVEFS is, given a new case of problematic behavior(s), to identify both the related rules and the most similar cases, in order to automatically adapt the corrective responses that were used in these cases and to suggest suitable actions.

Given the large amount of different features that represent a case and the fact that each case may contain multiple parallel and sequential sets of behaviors, the comparison between two different cases, to calculate a representative overall similarity measure, was one of the most challenging and complicated parts of the system and a part that required a lot of fine tuning to achieve optimal results. For each individual feature of the case, a calculation method has been determined according to the range of values. If the values of a feature are populated from a specific sub graph of the ontology, we use a specialized method that calculates the distance of the nodes of the graph [3]. Regarding the temporal data representing subsequent transitions of behaviors of an individual, we try to identify patterns of behaviors that happen concurrently or subsequently. A case may represent multiple behaviors, antecedents, and other features happening concurrently, so for each one of these features, we compare two cases using suitable similarity measures for sets of items such as the Homer metric that depends on the number of shared items between two sets. We actually applied and tested many different similarity measures for the comparison of sets to come up with the most suitable metric for each feature. Finally, there are specific weight values that have been associated with individual features or groups of features according to their significance for the calculation of the overall similarity score. Thus, the final similarity value between two cases is calculated as a weighted average of the similarities in individual features. Coming up with the suitable values for the weights (significance) of each individual feature in a case was a painstaking process that combined both the opinion of experts and trial and error methods.

8.4.4   User Interaction

The user interacting with the PAVEFS system may add an individual for whom he adds continuously information such as a code, the birth month/year, the gender, the diagnosis date, the functionality level, the education category, the insurance type, diagnosis (1st, 2nd, 3rd, 4th, 5th), and risk factors (1st, 2nd, 3rd, 4th, 5th). As soon as the individual is added, the user may add a new query for him/her by providing a name for the identification of the case. In the section that follows the user can add some general information regarding indications and/or the medical history of the person who caused the event based on a menu of available options, such as formal diagnoses and other risk factors that may have an impact on the etiology or course of challenging behaviors. At the next stage, the user describes the specific event that took place by starting with the first behavior (Behavior 1— period 1) that occurred. The description includes the selection of the specific fields representing the information of ontology's classes/sub-classes and nodes, and after completing all the forms related to the first behavior (antecedent, behavior, outcome), he continues with completing another form, given that there was another behavior happening simultaneously or close in time (see the following screenshots of the system in Figures 8.7, 8.8, and 8.9).

8.5   Pros and Cons of Solution

8.5.1   Evaluation Methodology and Results

Depending on the characteristics of the individual facing ASD, the system includes the critical examination, evaluation, and implementation of the knowledge base and the ontology of PAVEFS but also the testing of new practices for the confrontation of ASD.

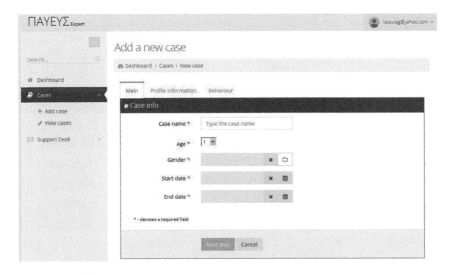

Figure 8.7 Adding a new case.

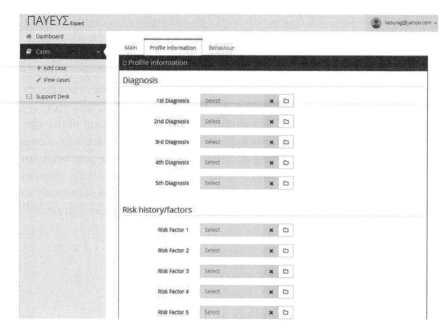

Figure 8.8 Adding diagnosis per case.

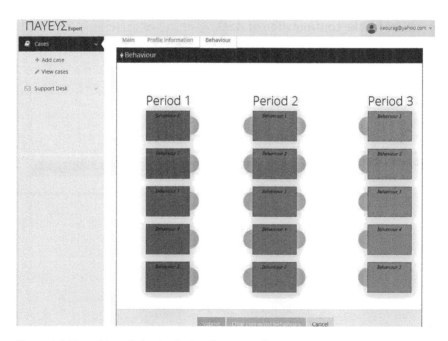

Figure 8.9 Describing a behavior during three periods.

8.5.2   Evaluation Methodology

According to Rumble [18], effectiveness concerns the output of the system, organism, software, etc., with regard to the "customers" or "final receivers" needs. Based on this approach, for evaluating the effectiveness of the software, the objectives to be achieved and the weight of each objective/evaluation criteria need to be documented. Depending on the software, the involving parts and the person conducting the evaluation, there are used different criteria and different weights for each one of them. The development of an evaluation plan for the system has been realized in line with the objectives of the program. The main evaluation parameters with regard to Technology Usage concern:

- Friendly usage: The parameter corresponds to the environment of the program for common users as well as for more experienced users.
- Efficiency: The parameter refers to system effectiveness, developed under the sight of answering all the questions submitted by users and their satisfaction from the system's answers. It refers to the quality of the information given by the system and also to the possibility of confrontation of an incident by distance (without the involvement of the professionals).
- Availability: The availability refers to the access to PAVEFS, which constitutes a closed application, since the access is not open and the user needs to make a registration for entering the system.
- Usability: The Usability has to do with the characteristics contributing to the easier access to the application.
- Reliability: The parameter ensures that the system developed (after real users have tested with use and test and trial method) promotes interaction and feedback, it is objective oriented, permits the experimenting on real situations while users understand how to navigate or at which point of the software are at any time (there are some procedure control tools available for user—queries history, individuals list, etc.) and the software's personal usage is ensured.
- Completeness: Completeness refers to the degree the application covered the needs of the families that have individuals with ASD, to the effectiveness of the proposed solutions and to the degree the application is used on a daily basis.

- Clarity: Clarity is expressed in the application with the explanation of the terms and concepts, with the explanation of ontology concepts or with the definitions' appearance either with text, image or hyperlink or video for the candidate values as for the results of the application use.
- Material quality: The parameter concerns the list of nodes that is called «Ontology» and concerns the general and more specific terms as sub-categories of the general ones. Additionally, it includes the incidents stored by the specialists/professionals tothe knowledge base, amplifying it and providing more accurate and complete information to users.
- Software quality: Users consider the software of «high quality» if it corresponds to what they want with an easiness to learn and use, by using the resources, or by using a portable device correctly and efficiently and when the experts may design, codify, control, and maintain the system easily.

8.5.2.1 Evaluation Tools

Alpha-Testing
The collaborating experts were asked to control the proposed interventions as system responses (A-testing). Control was completed with 358 queries, submitted by the experts based on real incidents with children and individuals facing ASD that differentiated upon user type. The evaluation of the queries took place in four phases:

- 1st phase: Trial users: At the first phase of the trial, 22 experts had to login to the application and insert 50 queries, each one based on real circumstances. Then, the experts evaluated the system's results, the proposed interventions and the proposed real incidents provided.
- 2nd phase: Regular Users: At the second phase of the trial, experts through a special process had become regular users and inserted 25 queries each, based on real circumstances. The users—experts as regular users had initially to register a number of persons with diagnostic and other characteristics so that they can use them to the insertion of the query followed. The fields of the ontology used were more than those of the trial user and after the insertion of the queries the users evaluated the results of the system, the proposed interventions and the proposed real incidents.

3rd phase: Advanced Users: At the third phase of the trial, experts had become though a special process the advanced users and inserted 25 queries each. As advanced users, they had the same rights with regular users (to insert and evaluate queries) and an extra opportunity to evaluate the proposed interventions in a special application tab. After, they evaluated the interventions as absolutely successful/partially successful/absolutely unsuccessful, the system stored this evaluation and created personal exceptions for each user. At a next stage, when they were asked to register the same query and evaluate the proposed solution, they were asked also a) to certify that the new interventions proposed didn't include the already negatively evaluated (on a former stage) solutions and b) to evaluate the new interventions. After the experts inserted the queries, they evaluated the system's results twice.

4th phase: Queries per period: At the fourth phase of the trial, experts as advanced users had to insert almost ten queries as followed:

- to choose third phase's queries for which at first, the intervention proposed was negatively evaluated by users.
- to register again a new query which at the first period had the same information with the one already inserted on third phase and to register all the interventions (positively and negatively evaluated) of the system at the first stage of the third phase.
- to answer positively to the question if there was a next period to the comportment and to insert the new period (the 2nd period) with the possible comportment, without answering to the question if the system corresponded to the comportment of the second period so as to receive an answer of the system and to evaluate the corresponding answer (proposed interventions and incidents).

A similar procedure was followed for the third period of the query registration and the forms with the experts' answers have been stored.

8.5.2.2   Results

The processing of the 1st and 2nd phases' results demonstrate that 61% of the proposed interventions have been absolutely accepted, 21% were partially accepted, 10% were stated as «problematic» while 8% of the queries remained without answer by the system, with no suggested intervention because there was no relevant knowledge available in the knowledge base.

Starting the evaluation, the ontology's comportments for which there were no rules or incidents in the knowledge base were searched. Then, experts amplified the knowledge base with the relevant rules and incidents and the system responded even to those cases with low acceptance by the experts' interventions. Then, the incidents to which the system responded problematically (10% of the cases) were searched. The incidents were corrected and the expertise from the correction (mainly ontology changes) was implemented to all the incidents of the knowledge base. So, the system responded problematically only to 4% of the overall cases. The reliability of the system has been also evaluated, 72% stated they absolutely accept the proposed interventions, 24% stated they partially accept the proposed interventions, and 4% considered as «problematic» the proposed interventions.

For the answers of the experts on the third phase, it is concluded that experts evaluated by 80% positively the results of the queries submitted by advanced users. They agreed with the majority of the interventions and even in cases of disagreements the reason was only the order of interventions' appearance. So, the percentage could approach 90% and 95%, respectively, if not taking into account the order of the proposed interventions' appearance. Regarding the queries that the users evaluated as «unsatisfying», only one out of four interventions did not fit. One intervention evaluated as unsuccessful in the system created a personal exception for the individual so as not to be proposed again and experts checked it in a next stage. These cases were led to the second procedure of inserting the same query repetitively, after the negative evaluation of the interventions and the system operated successfully by creating personal exceptions and proposing alternative interventions that were evaluated as more adequate (in average) by the experts.

During the 4th phase and the answers' processing: The experts followed the already-described procedure to insert queries in periods, as in the previous stage. More precisely, they chose the queries for which the system did not propose the most successful interventions at the stage of the advanced users, and they inserted them again, by proceeding with the proposed interventions in the second period. They were asked to insert 10 such queries, but experts did not reach the number because there were no such incidents in the third phase, so they inserted new queries in order to find some for which the proposed interventions were not effective. This was a time consuming process and the system had already reached the level of almost

95% acceptance. According to the evaluation, over 80% (almost 84%) of the proposed interventions were satisfying and could be effective in their use. For cases evaluated as unsuccessful, it has to be mentioned that at the majority only one didn't fit. The comments of the negatively evaluated queries usually concerned a series of proposed interventions or at least one that could be replaced by another one that would be more adequate, resulting to the overall rejection of the intervention.

Beta-Testing

The phase "Beta-testing" started just before the conduct of conferences for the presentation of the system. The methodology predicted that after the theoretical presentation of PAVEFS, the attendants of the conferences could try the system on real time, so as to test its efficiency. The attendants could submit queries, by giving some information to the system. The user could evaluate the usability and the results in real time.

It is worth mentioning that most of the attendants stated being "impressed" with the accuracy of the ontology terms and especially with the abundance and the variety of terms since they include most elements of the daily life of a child facing ASD. The attendants were also asked to use the application from the environment of their home, since users registered to the system and started their queries. The most interesting part was that during the demonstration conferences, some relevant with ASD societies were excited with the implementation of the system.

8.6   Conclusions

The application of information systems in health has achieved to overcome very important obstacles and to offer better solutions with a more accurate and reliable use of medical data. E-health covers different tools and applications based on information technology and communication, targeting to improve prevention, diagnosis, and treatment and to provide better health management leading to a better quality of life. In this perspective, the proposed system introduces a new approach for the confrontation of ASD. The fact that a user may enter the system from wherever he/she desires (either from home during his free time and for free or from any other place) is added value to the application, helping practically to the health management problem.

The possibility of on time and in-time processing of information regarding comportment, antecedents, the individual's environment, etc., provides the background for the right decision making by an individual for another one. The ontology contributes to the more accurate descriptive depiction of the clinical image of individuals facing ASD and to the presentation of the proposed interventions.

Additionally, through the primary diagnosis tool that has been developed, the possible finding of indications of ASD is innovative since it could awaken not only parents and relatives but also specialists and teachers, who may identify indications through the questions applied. So, the system has a consultative role for the individuals involved and can be a useful tool on the hands of the specialists and can also contribute to the effectiveness of their work, since it uses professional experience, based on key-user's method and provides it to the user.

8.7 Future Scope

The ambition of the researching team is to expand the ontology/system or the approach in general to other mental or chronic diseases in order to achieve better reasoning in complex medical systems and to contribute to better service quality and to increase the performance and effectiveness in the public health sector. One of the next challenges should also be the work on the testing of the proposed implementation to the conclusion of other sectors that require systematic analysis of complex data and interventions for decision making.

References

1. Ajami, H. and Mcheick, H., Ontology-Based Model to Support Ubiquitous Healthcare Systems for COPD Patients. *Electronics*, 7, 12, 371, 2018.
2. González, A.R., Rodríguez, J.M.Á., Lumbreras, C.C., Palacios, R.C., Towards an ontology for psychological disorders. *Int. J. Metadata, Semant. Ontol.*, 7, 4, 260, 2012.
3. Boutsinas, B. and Papastergiou, T., On clustering tree structured data with categorical nature. *Pattern Recognit.*, 41, 12, 3613–3623, 2008.
4. Lin, Y., Design and Implementation of an Ontology-Based Psychiatric Disorder Detection System. *WSEAS Trans. Inf. Sci. Appl.*, 7, 56–69, 2010.
5. Casado-Lumbreras, C., Rodríguez-González, A., Álvarez-Rodríguez, J.M., Colomo-Palacios, R., PsyDis: Towards a diagnosis support system for psychological disorders. *Expert Syst. Appl.*, 39, 13, 11391–11403, 2012.
6. Ceusters, W. and Smith, B., Foundations for a realist ontology of mental disease. *J. Biomed. Semant.*, 1, 1, 10, 2010.

7. Yamada, D.B., Yoshiura, V.T., Brandão Miyoshi, N.S., de Lima, I.B., Usumoto Shinoda, G.Y., Lopes Rijo, R.P.C., Domingos Alves, D., Proposal of an ontology for Mental Health Management in Brazil. *Procedia Comput. Sci.*, 138, 137–142, 2018.

8. Hu, B., Hu, B., Wan, J., Dennis, M., Chen, H.-H., Li, L., Zhou, Q., Ontology-based ubiquitous monitoring and treatment against depression. *Wireless Commun. Mobile Comput.*, 10, 10, 1303–1319, 2009.

9. Prentzas, J. and Hatzilygeroudis, I., Categorizing approaches combining rule-based and case-based reasoning. *Expert Syst.*, 24, 2, 97–122, 2007.

10. Kola, J., Harris, J., Lawrie, S., Rector, A., Goble, C., Martone, M., Towards an ontology for psychosis. *Cognit. Syst. Res.*, 11, 1, 42–52, 2010.

11. Medsker, L.R., *Hybrid Intelligent Systems*, Springer, Boston, MA, 1995.

12. Mucic, D. and Hilty, D.M., *e-Mental Health*, 1st ed. 2016, Springer International Publishing, Cham, Switzerland, 2015.

13. Musen, M.A., The protégé project. *AI Matters*, 1, 4, 4–12, 2015.

14. Silva, C., Marreiros, G., Silva, N., Development of an Ontology for Supporting Diagnosis in Psychiatry. *Adv. Intell. Syst. Comput.*, 290, 343–350, 2014.

15. Vyas, N. and R. Pal, P., E-Healthcare Decision Support System based on Ontology Learning: A Conceptual Model. *Int. J. Comput. Appl.*, 59, 9, 12–16, 2012.

16. Gaebel, W., Großimlinghaus, I., Kerst, A., Cohen, Y., Hinsche-Böckenholt, A., Johnson, B., Zielasek, J., European Psychiatric Association (EPA) guidance on the quality of eMental health interventions in the treatment of psychotic disorders. *Eur. Arch. Psychiatry Clin. Neurosci.*, 266, 2, 125–137, 2016.

17. Young, L., Tu, S.W., Tennakoon, L., Vismer, D., Astakhov, V., Gupta, A., McAuliffe, M.J., Ontology driven data integration for autism research. *2009 22nd IEEE International Symposium on Computer-Based Medical Systems*, 2009.

18. Rumble, G., *The Costs And Economics Of Open And Distance Learning*, Kogan Page, London, 1997

9

Ontology Engineering Applications in Medical Domain

Mariam Gawich[1*] **and Marco Alfonse**[2]

¹GRELITE, CRI, French University in Egypt (UFE), Cairo, Egypt
²Faculty of Computer and Information Science, Ain Shams University, Cairo, Egypt

Abstract

Ontology engineering is a subfield of artificial intelligence. It involves of a set of activities that concerns about the methodologies, tools, and languages to develop and reuse ontology. Ontology is considered as a knowledge representation technique that enables the modeling of the major types of knowledge: the simple relational knowledge, the inheritable knowledge, the inferential knowledge and the procedural knowledge. Therefore, the ontology is used in the medicine applications to provide the suitable knowledge to the users in terms of recommendations for clinical findings and treatments. This chapter presents the notion of ontology engineering that involves the major methodologies for the ontology development, the ontology languages, and the ontology tools. Furthermore, this chapter presents different ontology engineering applications applied in the medical domain.

Keywords: Ontology languages, ontology engineering, knowledge discovery, medical informatics, medical ontology-based systems

9.1 Introduction

Ontological engineering [1] is defined as a collection of activities that focus on methodologies to develop ontologies and the set of tools and languages to create them. Ontology engineering is derived from knowledge engineering which is a research area that belongs to the Artificial Intelligence (AI) domain. Several techniques such as predicate logic, rule based, semantic

*Corresponding author: mariam.gawish@ufe.edu.eg

Vishal Jain, Ritika Wason, Jyotir Moy Chatterjee and Dac-Nhuong Le (eds.) Ontology-Based Information Retrieval for Healthcare Systems, (193–232) © 2020 Scrivener Publishing LLC

network, and frames are applied in AI programs to represent the particular knowledge that will be used for problem solving. The main challenges that face the mentioned techniques are the maintenance and sharing of the represented knowledge [2]. Therefore, the ontology is proposed to handle the mentioned challenges. It is considered as the most recent knowledge representation technique.

The appearance of the semantic web creates the need to use the metadata that helps the semantic search engine to access the required webpages. The metadata is composed of attribute and value that describe the webpage. The ontology is used to present the vocabulary for metadata. In addition, a webpage can be characterized by various metadata which can be described using ontologies.

Ontology is derived from philosophy which means the science of existence. In semantic web context, ontology [3] is defined as a formal explicit specification of shared conceptualization, where "formal" means that the ontology should be understandable by the machines and "shared" implies that it is validated by a group or a community. Conceptualization means that the domain of interest is presented as a hierarchy of classes, subclasses, and relationships.

Figure 9.1 demonstrates an example of Living Things ontology which is classified to carnivore and herbivore classes. There are relationships between them, e.g., the relation "eats" associates the class "Person" to the class "Animal".

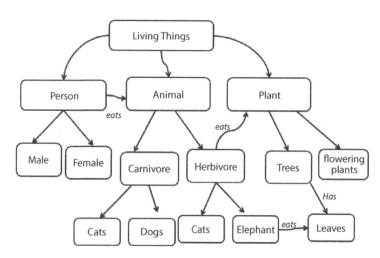

Figure 9.1 Ontology example.

Ontology is a technique for knowledge representation that enables to model all kinds of knowledge, such as simple relational knowledge, inheritable knowledge, inferential knowledge, and procedural knowledge. For the simple relational knowledge, the ontology enables the knowledge engineer to present the declarative facts as a set of relations. For the inheritable knowledge, the ontology enables the knowledge engineer to create the classes and subclasses that emulate the concepts of the domain of interest. Moreover, there are inference mechanisms that derive the property inheritance. For the inferential knowledge, the ontology enables the knowledge engineer to design inference rules as axioms. For the procedural knowledge, the ontology enables the knowledge engineer to design the procedural rules (If and Then rules).

9.2   Ontology Activities

Ontology engineering [4] involves several activities. The major activities are ontology learning, ontology matching, ontology merging, ontology validation, ontology verification, ontology alignment, ontology annotation, ontology evaluation, and ontology evolution.

9.2.1   Ontology Learning

According to Maedche and Staab [5], the ontology learning is defined as the application of knowledge acquisition techniques with machine learning techniques to generate an ontology from data sources. In the NeON glossary [6], the ontology learning is defined as the process of acquiring knowledge from data sources and transforming the acquired knowledge into conceptual structure (conceptual hierarchy).

9.2.2   Ontology Matching

According to Euzenat [7], the ontology matching is the process of finding correspondence or relations between entities "classes" expressed in different ontologies.

9.2.3   Ontology Merging (Unification)

According to the NeON glossary [6], the ontology merging is the development of a new ontology or module from two other ontologies or more that may be overlapped.

9.2.4   Ontology Validation

According to the NeON glossary [6], the validation concerns about the comparison between the developed ontology and the specification document that contains the ontology requirements and the competency questions.

9.2.5   Ontology Verification

According to Gruninger and colleagues [8], the ontology verification concerns about the comparison between the expected models and the axiomatization models performed in the ontology. The ontology verification can be applied in the decision support and semantic integration applications.

9.2.6   Ontology Alignment

According to Ehrig and Euzenat [9], the ontology alignment is the process of finding subsumption and equivalent relationships between two ontologies' entities. The entities involve classes, rules, and properties.

9.2.7   Ontology Annotation

According to the NeON glossary and Ahmed [6, 10], the ontology annotation is the process of adding metadata to an ontology. These metadata are understood by machines and facilitate the agent to find the required information. The ontology annotation is applicable in the information retrieval research area.

9.2.8   Ontology Evaluation

According to Brank and colleagues [11], the evaluation is the assessment of an ontology regard to specific criterion. Its objective is to identify the best ontologies that are suitable for a specific task.

9.2.9   Ontology Evolution

Haase and Stojanovic [12] had defined the ontology evolution as the process of adjusting and updating the ontology taking into account the ontology consistency.

9.3   Ontology Development Methodologies

There are five major methodologies used to develop ontology: TOVE methodology, Methontology methodology, Brusa methodology, Upon methodology, and Uschold and King methodology.

9.3.1   TOVE

Grüninger and Fox [13] proposed an ontology building methodology called TOVE (Toronto Virtual Enterprise) for representing the common sense enterprise. The common sense enterprise goal is to find answers to the queries provided by the ontology users. It consists of the following stages:

- Recognizing the motivating scenario; the motivation scenarios are a set of problems that the industrial partners face during their use of the applications. The motivating scenarios are designed in terms of a story problem. In addition, the motivating scenarios can involve the available solutions to the problems. The solutions are considered as a trigger to determine the initial concepts and relations that will be used in the ontology.
- Identifying ontology requirements by the use of informal competency questions; the competence questions involve a group of queries that appear during the recognition of motivating scenarios. The ontology should realize the responses of these queries. This stage is used to evaluate the new built ontology.
- Identifying ontology terminology in terms of classes, data properties, and object properties. The terminology is represented by the use of first order logic. In this stage, each competency question should be represented as concept(s), properties, and relations.
- Specifying axioms that can be modeled by the use of first order logic. In this way, the informal competence questions become formal. The axioms are used to represent the questions and its available solutions.
- Testing the ontology competency.

9.3.2 Methontology

Fernández and colleagues [14] proposed this methodology to design a chemical ontology. It provides a set of stages to build the ontology from scratch, which are:

- Specification
  Its objective is the generation of formal, informal, and semi-formal documents that can be extracted from the competence questions that focus on the purpose to build the ontology, its scope, and the user identification.
- Knowledge Acquisition
  Tacit knowledge can be acquired from the domain experts, through interviews and brainstorming. The explicit knowledge is extracted from explicit sources such as books, databases, and ontologies. The consolidations of experts help the ontology engineer to have a preliminary idea about the requirement specification document.
- Conceptualization
  In this stage, the domain of interest will be modeled in terms of concepts, instances, attributes, and rules. The methodology enables the use of a glossary of terms to facilitate the identification of ontology elements.
- Integration
  Methontology takes into account the reusability of the developed ontology by its integration with the meta ontology provided by the OntoLingua [15].
- Implementation
  Methontology methodology supposed that the ontology will be implemented by a program that enables the integration with another ontology such as the meta ontology provided by the OntoLingua.
- Evaluation
  Evaluation is implemented by the application of verification and validation. The verification focuses on the ontology correctness while the validation ensures the matching between the ontology and its documentation.

9.3.3 Brusa *et al.* Methodology

The objective of this methodology [16] is to provide a way to develop an ontology from scratch that can be used in the domain of public administration. The methodology is a hybrid approach that combines TOVE and METHONTOLOGY. It consists of the following phases:

- Specification of the ontology
  This stage is based on the ontology requirement presented by TOVE. It is executed through the domain description, ontology requirements, motivating scenarios, competency questions, determining the goal and the scope of the ontology, and estimating the costs. The domain description relies on the meetings with experts to detect the background knowledge.
- Concretization
  This stage focuses on the identification of classes, class hierarchy, rules, restriction, class relations, attributes, and individuals. The ontology elements can be graphically represented by UML that facilitates the communication between experts and ontology engineers.
- Implementation
  This stage concerns about the transformation of the ontology into formal representation that can be understood by machines. This can be established by the use of a suitable ontology language such as OWL. This stage takes into account the ontology verification and validation mentioned in METHONTOLOGY.

9.3.4 UPON Methodology

De Nicola and colleagues [17] proposed Unified Process Ontology (UPON). It is based on the use of the unified process and the UML. The methodology was applied to build an e-procurement ontology that is used in the Athena integrated project [18]. The methodology consists of the following stages:

- Requirements Workflow
  The requirements involve the domain and the scope that are determined by the experts. Moreover, it involves the business purpose (motivation to build the ontology), writing storyboards, creating the application lexicon, competency questions, and use cases identification (the use cases that reflect the business operations). The application lexicon involves the terms that are used in a

specific application which are determined by the application experts' community.

- Analysis Workflow
  This workflow concerns about getting the domain resources, constructing the domain lexicon, constructing reference lexicon, modeling application scenario by the UML, and the construction of reference glossary. The domain lexicon involves a set of terms that belongs to the domain of interest approved by the experts. The reference lexicon involves the common terms between the application lexicon and the domain lexicon. The reference lexicon is determined by the knowledge engineers, the domain experts, and the application experts. The reference glossary contains the terms that are validated by the domain experts and the application experts with the approval of the knowledge engineers.
- Design Workflow
  The inputs are reference glossary and UML diagrams. In this workflow, the concepts, concept hierarchy, and domain specific relations will be modeled using an ontology language.
- Implementation and Test Workflow
  It involves the selection of the suitable formal language for implementing the ontology. The testing relies on the consistency checking, verifying coverage, and answering the competency questions.

9.3.5 Uschold and King Methodology

Uschold and King [19] proposed a methodology that contains some guidelines in each stage to develop the ontology.

- Purpose identification
  It involves the motivation to build the ontology, the description of the intended users, the specifications of the software that will interact with the ontology, and the possibility to reuse the ontology in other applications. The competency questions are determined in this stage.
- Ontology Building
  This stage is implemented through three steps; capturing, coding, and integrating:

- Ontology capturing
  - The determination of the concepts and relations that reflect the domain.
  - The generation of the comprehensive definition of the concepts and relations.
  - The recognition of terms that denote concepts and relations.
- Ontology coding
  It refers to the selection of the formal ontology language by which the concepts and relations will be presented.
- Integrating ontology with others
  It focuses on how the created ontology can be reused to be integrated with other ontologies. The reusability should be taken into consideration during the ontology capturing and coding.
- Evaluation and documentation
  The evaluation is derived from Gomez and colleagues [20]. The ontology evaluation can be executed through its use in a system and the use of a documentation that checks whether the competency questions are considered in the ontology or not.

Table 9.1 demonstrates the comparison between the most common ontology development methodologies [21]. The comparison is based on a framework for comparative study presented in [22]. The criteria used for the comparison are the experts' intervention, application dependency, modes of development, inferences rules use, and the domain dependency.

Both of the Uschold and King methodology and the TOVE methodology did not rely on the experts' intervention during the ontology building. The usage of Uschold and King methodology doesn't require the existence of an application. Methodologies such as TOVE, METHONTOLOGY, and Brusa *et al.* rely on a system or an application to evaluate the ontology. Whereas, UPON relies on application experts to generate the application lexicon that will be matched to the domain lexicon during the ontology building.

All methodologies apply the middle out mode for ontology building through their use of competence questions with the experts or the users. The methodology of METHONTOLOGY enables the acquisition of tacit knowledge from the experts as well as the acquisition of explicit knowledge. Moreover, it concerns about the evaluation of the ontology.

Table 9.1 Comparison between the ontology development methodologies.

Criterion/ Methodology	Uschold & King (1995)	TOVE (1995)	METHONTOLOGY (1997)	Brusa et al. (2008)	UPON (2009)
Experts' intervention	X	X	√	√	√
Application dependency	X	√	√	√	√
Modes of development	Middle out	Middle out	Middle out	Middle out	Middle out
Inference rules/ axioms	X	√	√	√	X
Domain dependency	X	X	X	X	X
Evaluation	X	X	√	X	X

9.4   Ontology Languages

9.4.1   RDF-RDF Schema

RDF refers to the Resource Description Framework, a language that is designed by the WWW Consortium (W3C) [23]. It consists of triples, each of them involves an object, an attribute, and a value. The RDF [24] can be used to represent the semantic network where the node includes the object and its value, while the link includes the attribute. The RDF is based on the eXtensible Markup Language (XML) which enables to codify data identification that are provided by an internet resource. The notion of data in XML refers to anything accessed by a URL. XML enables to codify the metadata attached to an URL. Figures 9.2 and 9.3 demonstrate an example of metadata attached to a scientific article on the web [25]. The web document contains a string "Abdel-Badeeh M. Salem", the XML markup for the mentioned string will be <author>Abdel-Badeeh M. Salem</author>. With the XML, the search engine will understand that the author of the article is Abdel-Badeeh M. Salem. But with the use of the RDF language, other data can be described such as the country where this article is published, the date of publication, and the journal name. All these metadata will be attached to the URL.

The RDF language enhances the ability of the semantic search engine to find the suitable web page for the required query. The RDF-S refers to the

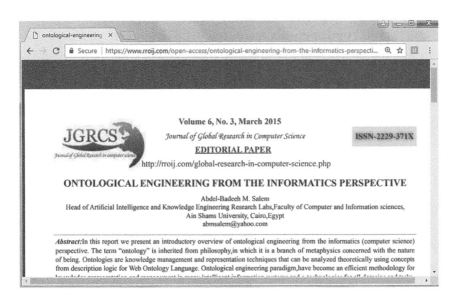

Figure 9.2 An example of a web document [25].

<rdf:Description rdf:about="https://www.rroij.com/open-access/ontological-engineering-from-the-informatics-perspective.pdf">

<author>Abdel-Badeeh M. Salem</author>

<publication_date>March 2015</publication_date>

<journal_name>Journal of Global Research in Computer Science </journal_name>

<journal_country> India </journal_country>

<mail> abmsalem@yahoo.com </mail>

</rdf:Description>

Figure 9.3 An example of RDF [24].

RDF schema language that is designed to describe the RDF tags in terms of a hierarchy of objects and relations (the relations between objects are called attributes in the RDF-S). The RDF schema language involves of predefined classes and metaclasses. The metaclasses are the classes and their relations that are created by the user. Figure 9.4 shows the RDF schema of a scientific article. This RDF schema involves the following elements:

- Classes: the main class (Class), Person, Paper, Publication, and Journal Paper.
- Attributes (Properties): Publication_Date (its domain is Journal_Paper and its range is Publication) and author (its domain is Person and its range is journal paper)
- Values: http://staff.asu.edu.eg/Badeeh-Salem, https://www.rroij.com/open-access/ontological-engineering-from-the-informatics-perspective.pdf and March 2015.

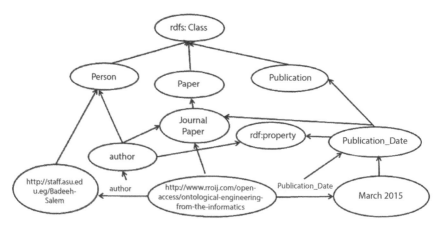

Figure 9.4 An example of RDF hierarchy [24].

9.4.2   OWL

OWL stands for Ontology Web Language; it was developed by the W3C. It can be easily interpreted by the semantic web. The OWL [26, 27] enables the communication between the ontology and other applications. It enables the reasoning on classes to discover new information. In OWL, the domain of interest can be presented through concepts (also named classes), properties, and instances (also named individuals).

There are three sublanguages that belong to OWL: OWL Lite, OWL DL, and OWL Full.

- OWL Lite
  The OWL Lite is suitable for the users who want to create a hierarchy and basic constraint characteristics. The OWL allows the user to determine constraint cardinality value between 0 and 1. The OWL Lite is also suitable to present thesauri or taxonomies.
- OWL DL
  The OWL DL is suitable for the users who desire more expressiveness of ontology elements that involves the description of classes, properties, cardinality level, and the reasoning using Description Logic (DL). The OWL DL executes the separation notion which denotes that a class label cannot be reused to define an individual or a property and vice versa. In OWL DL, the property can be a data type property or an object property. The object property represents the relation between individuals that belong to two classes. The OWL DL doesn't have full compatibility with RDF.
- OWL Full
  OWL Full enables the full combination between OWL and RDF schema. It doesn't apply the separation notion to the ontology elements. It enables the usage of the inverse functional property that can be applied to the data property.

9.4.3   OWL 2

OWL 2 [28] is the new version of OWL that is designed by the W3C. In OWL 2, some features are added to be more expressive such as enhanced annotation, capabilities, richer data types, and qualified cardinality restrictions. For the separation notion, the OWL 2 ensures that a class doesn't have the same label of a data property that belongs to this class. Moreover,

OWL 2 is created to support the huge ontologies that contain a large number of classes such as SNOMED [29], gene ontology [30], and National Cancer Institute Thesaurus (NCIt) [31].

OWL 2 involves three profiles [32]: OWL2 EL, OWL2 QL, and OWL2 RL.

- OWL2 EL
  EL refers to Extended Description Logic. OWL2 EL is suitable for users who want to create simple ontologies. It enables to use the existential quantification for a data range (DataSomeValues From), a class (ObjectSomeValues From), and an individual (Object hasValue). Furthermore, OWL2 EL enables the ontology engineer to determine axioms such as class equivalence, class disjointness, class inclusion, class assertion, object property assertion, data property assertion, etc. In addition, OWL2 EL allows the determination of domain and range restrictions for data properties and object properties.
- OWL2 QL
  QL refers to Query Language. OWL2 QL provides scalable reasoning for large datasets like thesaurus. Moreover, OWL2 QL is suitable for the users who want to integrate an ontology with a database. For this reason, the OWL2 QL imposes some syntactic restrictions on the subclass, disjoint classes, symmetric properties, range, and domain. It also supports all restriction on class axioms defined by OWL2 except disjoint union.
- OWL2 RL
  RL refers to Rule Language. OWL2 RL is suitable for users who want to use the ontology with rule extended Data Base Management System (DBMS) and the use of rule-based reasoning engines. The OWL2 RL can be used also with RDF applications. The language supports all the constructors restrictions defined in OWL2. For the axioms restrictions, the OWL2 RL imposes the axioms defined in OWL2 except the data property assertions, the disjoint union of classes and negative object assertions. In addition, the reasoner in OWL2 RL applies a function that checks the consistency of the ontology.

Table 9.2 presents the comparison between the ontology languages. This comparison is based on the following criteria:

- Semantic representation
  It refers to the ability of the language to represent the semantic relations between entities and/or the individuals. Moreover, it has the ability to represent the data property for a class and/or individual.
- Inferential adequacy
  It refers to the ability of the language to infer new knowledge from the knowledge already presented in the ontology [33].
- Interoperability with other languages
  It refers to the ability of the language to interact with other languages.

The RDFS enables the representation of classes, subclasses, and relations. All the relations between classes in the RDFS are predefined as subclassOf. The ontology engineer can't determine the label name of a relation between two entities. The data property in RDFS is represented as a slot that can be associated to a class. For the inferential adequacy, RDFS allows the ontology engineer to codify the rules following the forward chaining and the backward chaining ways. Moreover, there is a reasoner called Closed World Machine (CWM) [34] that uses the forward chaining reasoning in RDFS ontology to derive new knowledge. The RDFS is compatible with the XML language.

The OWL enables the ontology engineer to create semantic relations (object properties) between classes and between individuals. For the

Table 9.2 Comparison between the ontology languages.

Criterion/ language	Semantic representation	Inferential adequacy	Interoperability with other languages
RDFS	X	√	√
OWL	√	√	√
OWL2	√	√	√

inferential adequacy, the OWL enables the codification of inference rules using SWRL. The OWL is compatible with XML and RDF languages.

The OWL2 enables the ontology engineer to represent the semantic relations between classes and between individuals. Moreover, it involves semantic representation of the data property that can be associated to a class or to an individual. For the inferential adequacy, the reasoning can be applied on classes and individuals to derive new knowledge. The new knowledge can be a recommendation for creating a new relation between individuals based on similar individuals that have this relation. The OWL2 is compatible with the OWL.

In RDFS, the ontology is represented as a hierarchy of classes and sub-classes without the existence of semantic relations between them. The lack of the semantic representation of the relations leads to weak reasoning. Although both of OWL and OWL2 achieve the inferential adequacy, the reasoning in OWL2 is more effective because it takes into consideration the values of data properties that are asserted to the individuals. In OWL, the individual can't have its own data properties.

From the previous comparison, it is concluded that the ontology languages are evolved to represent the semantic relations between its elements in order to enhance the reasoning on the current knowledge provided by the ontology.

9.5   Ontology Tools

This section presents the current available ontology tools that enable the building as well as the manipulation and reuse of the ontology.

9.5.1   Apollo

Apollo [35, 36] was developed by the Open University in England. It is a Java-based interface that provides an easy way for knowledge modeling. Apollo didn't rely on a specific knowledge modeling language. It supports the Meta, RDF, OCM, XML, and other formats through plugins. Figure 9.5 shows the Apollo menus and panels.

In Apollo, the ontology engineer can create classes, subclasses, instances, relations, slots, axioms, and rules. Moreover, Apollo enables the ontology engineer to add a super ontology on the current opened ontology. The created ontology can be exported or saved with one of the mentioned format. Apollo is accessible through the GitHub [37].

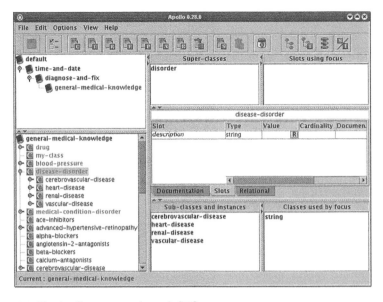

Figure 9.5 The Apollo menus and panels [35].

9.5.2   NeON

The NeON tool [38] is provided by the NeON project that concerns about the use of networked ontologies disseminated between organizations. It supports both of RDFS and OWL languages. It enables the ontology engineer to import several plugins [39] that execute different ontology activities. Examples of these plugins are:

– Alignment plugin [40] to execute the ontology matching and alignment activities.
– Text2Onto plugin [41] is used for ontology learning, it builds an ontology from text.
– General Architecture for Text Engineering (GATE) Web services plugin [42] is used for ontology annotation.

As Figure 9.6 demonstrates, NeON consists of an ontology navigation panel, entity panel, and individuals panel. Ontology navigation enables the ontology engineer to explore/create/delete the ontology classes, object properties, data properties, annotations, and datatypes. The entity panel is used to determine restrictions on ontology elements. The individual panel is used to explore the current ontology individuals and create and delete individuals.

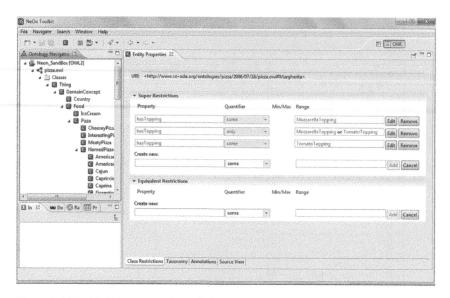

Figure 9.6 The NeON menus and panels [43].

The current version of NeON [43] supports the OWL2 language. Furthermore, it enables the ontology engineer to import a developed ontology encoded in OWL, RDF, RDFS, OWL2, and RDFS formats.

9.5.3   Protégé

Protégé [44] was created by Standford Center for Biomedical Informatics that belongs to Standford University, school of medicine. Protégé is considered as the most popular ontology tool because it provides an easy and organized interface that enables the ontology engineer to build ontology from scratch, reuse existing ontologies, compare ontologies, represent the inference rules, and merge existing ontologies. Like NeON, the protégé enables to import several plugins. Examples of these plugins are:

- The Prompt plugin [45] is used to execute the matching between ontologies.
- Reasoners plugins such as Pellet [46] and Hermit [47].
- The Ontograph plugin [48] is used to visualize the created ontology.
- The Ontop plugin [49] is used to execute the mapping between a database and an ontology. It enables the ontology engineer to execute query on a database using SPARQL [50]; the database is viewed as a virtual RDF graph.

Figure 9.7 shows the Protégé interface. It consists of several tabs. For the entities tab, it involves several panels such as class hierarchy, object property hierarchy, data property hierarchy, individuals, datatypes panel, etc. The class hierarchy panel enables the ontology engineer to explore, create, and delete classes. In object property panel, the ontology engineer can create/edit a relation between two classes by specifying the domain and the range of this relation and he/she can also specify the characteristics of this relation.

The main advantage of protégé is that it supports almost all of the ontology formats such as RDF and OWL. The current version of protégé [51] supports the OWL2 language and it enables the communication with APIs such as OWLAPI.

Table 9.3 shows the comparison between current ontology tools. This comparison is based on the languages that the tool can support, the use of plugins, and the ontology engineering activities that the tool can perform.

The Apollo supports the RDF and XML languages and other old languages such as Meta and OCM. Apollo has two plugins: the synchronization plugin and the bidirectional relation plugin. The synchronization plugin is used to compare and synchronize ontologies. The bidirectional relation plugin is used to represent bidirectional (inverse) relations between two instances. The NeON supports the RDFS, OWL, and OWL2 languages. Several plugins can be used in the NeON to execute the major

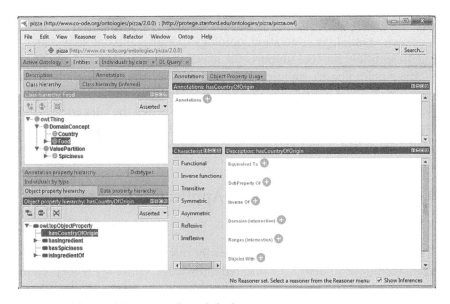

Figure 9.7 The Protégé menus and panels [51].

Table 9.3 Comparison between the ontology tools.

Criterion / tool	Supported languages	Use of plugins	Ontology engineering activities
Apollo	RDF, XML, Meta, and OCM	√	Ontology development
NeON	RDFS, OWL, and OWL2	√	Ontology development, ontology learning, ontology annotation, and ontology alignment
Protégé	RDF, RDF-XML, OWL, and OWL2, OWL-XML	√	Ontology development, ontology annotation, ontology merging, and ontology matching

ontology engineering activities such as the ontology alignment, ontology learning, and ontology annotation. Moreover, it involves other plugins to execute the reasoning on the ontology.

The current version of Protégé [51] supports RDF-XML, OWL-XML, OWL, and OWL2 languages. It also supports other formats such as the Terse RDF Triple Language (TURTLE) [52] and the Open Biomedical Ontologies (OBO) [53]. The Protégé can import several plugins that enables the ontology engineer to execute many ontology engineering activities such as ontology annotation, ontology merging, and ontology matching. In addition, the tool supports the reasoning process through plugins.

The Apollo doesn't support OWL and OWL2. The NeON enables the ontology engineer to load ontologies encoded in RDFS and RDF languages. The difference between the NeON and Protégé is that the later enables the ontology engineer to convert the current ontology to other formats such as RDF-XML, OWL, OBO, etc., which is not supported by the NeON.

9.6   Ontology Engineering Applications in Medical Domain

The huge medical datasets cannot be easily analyzed; they require an intelligent technique to detect the inferred knowledge. Ontology is adopted in the medical domain for the semantic knowledge representation that allows to the intelligent agents and the intelligent computer systems to grasp the data and discover new knowledge. This section presents an overview of the current ontology-based applications in the medical domain. These applications include Decision Support Systems (DSS), medical data integration, and knowledge management.

9.6.1 Ontology-Based Decision Support System (DSS)

Anbarasi and colleagues [54] explain the importance of the ontology in the DSS. The ontology can contain the standard medical terms. It enables the knowledge sharing and the knowledge discovering by the reasoning on the codified inference rules. Moreover, the use of ontology reasoner plugins such as Pellet [46] and Hermit [47] facilitate the decision making.

In general, the medical decision support systems are classified into disease diagnosis and patient management. The current medical DSS executes both of them.

9.6.1.1 OntoDiabetic

OntoDiabetic [55] is a Clinical Decision Support System (CDSS). It is created to recommend the suitable treatment for the patients who suffer from the diabetes. Moreover, OntoDiabetic provides clinical guidelines to control the related diseases such as hypertension and cardiovascular.

The system involves a set of ontologies that are encoded in OWL2 language. OntoDiabetic uses the OWL2 to codify the inference rules to present the suitable clinical guidelines for each patient according to his/her history.

Figure 9.8 demonstrates the OntoDiabetic architecture; it involves two principal ontologies; diabetic patient clinical analysis ontology and semantic profile ontology. The diabetic patient clinical analysis ontology involves five subontologies which are patient, adaptive questionnaire, answered questionnaire, domain, and process. The system asks the patient to answer a questionnaire on a web application. The questions are generated from the adaptive questionnaire subontology. The system will save the patient answers in the answered questionnaire subontology. The patient subontolgy contains the patient records that include the patient information acquired from the answered questionnaire subontology. The semantic profile ontology collects all the information inserted by the doctor, the patient, and the nurse. The domain and process subontologies contain the clinical guidelines as well as a set of inference rules that will be applied to the patient profile to propose the suitable treatment and determine the risk factors for the patient.

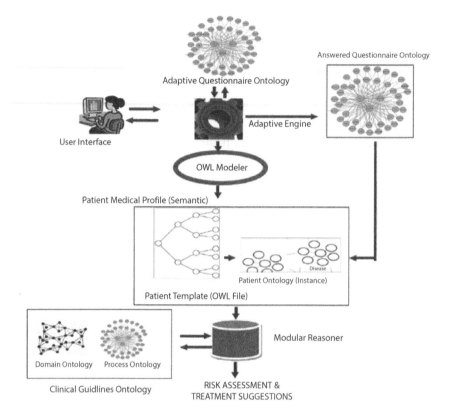

Figure 9.8 The OntoDiabetic system architecture [55].

9.6.1.2   Ontology-Based CDSS for Diabetes Diagnosis

Alharbi and colleagues [56] proposed a CDSS to diagnose the patient according to his symptoms, signs, and laboratory tests. Also, the CDSS suggests the suitable treatment plan to the patient. The CDSS uses the ontology to represent the expertise acquired from the diabetes experts. Moreover, the CDSS supports reasoning through a set of rules encoded in the Semantic Web Rule Language (SWRL) and an inference engine called Jess. As Figure 9.9 shows, CDSS involves four components: a graphical user interface, inference engine, ontologies, and knowledge base. The user interface takes the diagnosis request from the user. The Jess inference engine connects the knowledge base and the ontologies to infer the suitable diagnosis and the treatment plan. The knowledge base consists of a set of SWRL rules. While the ontologies component involves two ontologies: the domain ontology and patient ontology. The domain ontology contains the

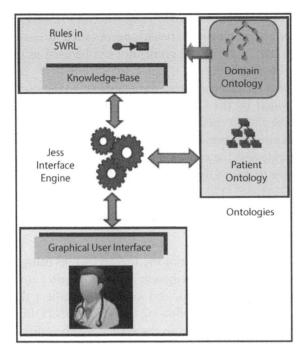

Figure 9.9 The CDSS architecture [56].

diagnosis, lab tests, and symptoms. The patient ontology contains information provided by the graphical user interface.

9.6.1.3   Ontology-Based Medical DSS within E-Care Telemonitoring Platform

Benimoune and colleagues [57] proposed a medical DSS (MDSS) that is used by E-Care home telemonitoring platform. Its objective is to improve the lifestyle of the patients who suffer from chronic diseases. The MDSS collects personalized information about the current patient life style and presents some tips and advices to improve his/her lifestyle. The MDSS involves three modules: knowledge base, data collector, and advices provider.

The knowledge base consists of four ontologies: Patient Profile Ontology (PPO), Questionnaire Ontology (QO), LifeStyle Ontology (LSO), and Guidelines Ontology (GO). The PPO includes the general information of the patient, his/her medical information, and his/her life style information. The QO involves the questions, sub-questionnaires, potential answers, and their relationships. The LSO contains the major lifestyle concepts found in Haute Autorité de Santé (HAS) [58]. The GO involves the medical guidelines that are provided by trusted sources such as European Society of Cardiology (ESC) [59]; these guidelines can be used to determine the appropriate lifestyle advices.

The data collector displays every day questions to the user. These questions are provided by the QO. The data collector adjusts the questions according to the patient medical conditions and his/her previous answers.

The advices provider presents personalized lifestyle advices according to the patient profile and the collected data. The module employs the use of inference engine to derive the appropriate advices from the GO.

9.6.2   Medical Ontology in the Dynamic Healthcare Environment

Zeshan and Mohamed [60] clarify the importance of using the ontology with the healthcare information system at the emergency time. The ontology includes concepts, relations, and axioms that reflect the emergency cases. The ontology was built following the METHONTOLOGY methodology [14]. The ontology is used in the system for the reliable knowledge representation, knowledge sharing and knowledge reusability across several heterogeneous complex health care systems and embedded devices. The ontology facilitates the communication between the software systems.

Wen and colleagues [61] proposed an ontology-based application that is used to integrate medical data collected from several regions. The regional health care application enables the transmission of the updated patient data from its location to the hospitals and healthcare institutes. The hospitals and medical institutes use different software applications with different data formats. For this reason, the ontology is employed to integrate medical data across them. The system consists of three layers: the physical layer, the semantic service layer, and the application layer. The physical layer involves different databases disseminated in various healthcare institutes. The mapping between the databases and ontologies is executed in the semantic layer. In the application layer, a web application is employed to display the required information and receives the data from the patient.

Kumar [62] proposed a health care system for emergency medical services. It relies on the Internet of Things (IoT) and an ontology. The IoT is applied in the health care system to get rapidly the required huge information. The IoT involves a network of software systems and computers. For this reason, the ontology is used to collect and integrate the information disseminated in the IoT.

9.6.3 Knowledge Management Systems

9.6.3.1 Ontology-Based System for Cancer Diseases

Alfonse and colleagues [63] proposed a system to diagnose cancer and provide guidelines for the patient. As Figure 9.10 demonstrates, the system involves three main modules. The first module is used for the diagnosis called diagnostic module. The second module is used to determine the cancer stage called staging module. The third module is adopted to recommend the appropriate treatment. The diagnostic module gets the signs and symptoms from the user and it connects to the database of cancer ontologies to determine the cancer type. Upon the result of the diagnostic module, the staging module connects to the database of cancer ontologies to determine the cancer stage. According to the cancer type and the cancer stage, the treatment module will determine the treatment protocols to the user.

All of the previous modules connect to the database trough the query module. The database involves three ontologies that belong to the cancer diseases. They are lung cancer [64], liver cancer [65], and breast cancer [66]. The role of the ontology in the system is to provide reliable knowledge to the user. The use of OWL-DL enables the representation of rules that differentiate between the various types of cancer. Moreover, the system employs the Fact++ reasoner [67] to retrieve the symptoms and signs from ontologies that correspond to the symptoms and signs inserted by the

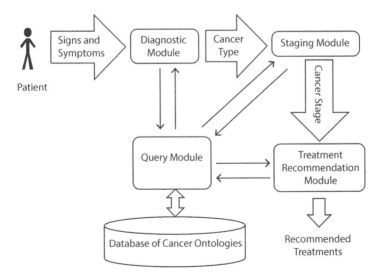

Figure 9.10 The cancer diseases ontology-based system architecture [63].

user. In addition, Fact++ reasoner is used in both of staging and treatment modules to get the appropriate cancer stage and the appropriate treatment protocol.

9.6.3.2 Personalized Care System for Chronic Patients at Home

Lasierra and colleagues [68] proposed a personalized care system used by the patients who suffer from chronic diseases and need to be monitored at home. The challenges that can face such system are the difficulty to manage a large number of patients to be monitored and the data integration between different medical devices. Therefore, the system is based on the use of the ontology to cope these challenges. As Figure 9.11 shows,

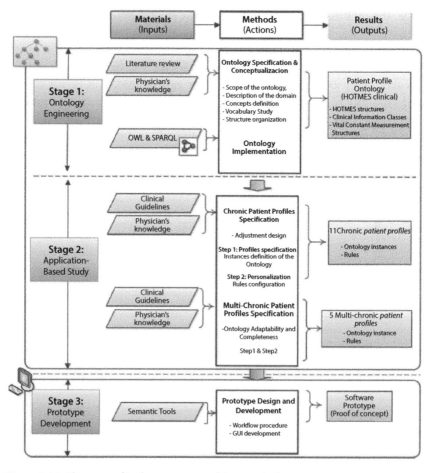

Figure 9.11 The personalized care system architecture [68].

the system consists of three stages: the ontology engineering stage, the application-based study, and the prototype development. In the ontology engineering stage, the competency questions are determined from the meetings established with the clinicians. The system takes into consideration the interoperability between the information provided by clinicians and the information provided by the medical devices. The ontology is encoded in the OWL language [27]. The output of this stage is the patient profile ontology.

The application-based study stage involves chronic patient profile specification sub-stage and multi-chronic patient profile specification sub-stage. In the chronic patient profile specification sub-stage, the ontology will be refined by the depth study of particular chronic pathologies for the patient. The multi chronic patient profile focuses on the verification of the ontology in representing new complex patient profile that has a set of chronic pathologies established in the first sub-stage. Also, the ontology is used in this stage to represent the personalized rules for each patient profile. In the prototype development stage, a software agent is developed that deals with the patient ontology to perform the tasks required by the patient.

9.7   Ontology Engineering Applications in Other Domains

9.7.1   Ontology Engineering Applications in E-Commerce

E-commerce is generally defined as the mechanism of purchasing and selling goods and services on the internet. If there are two e-commerce organizations want to make a deal, they will face a difficulty to understand each other if they don't have a homogeneous terminology provided by their ontologies. The matching between the ontologies can solve this problem.

9.7.1.1   *Automated Approach to Product Taxonomy Mapping in E-Commerce*

Nederstigt and colleagues [69] proposed this approach to match two heterogeneous taxonomies provided by two ontologies. The algorithm receives two inputs: the first input is category taxonomy and its paths of the source taxonomy (the path is a list of nodes that start from root and end to the current node), while the second input involves the categories of target taxonomy. The approach was executed following these stages:

9.7.1.1.1   Preprocessing of Category Name

The algorithm decomposes the name of a category of the source taxonomy into ampersands, comma. The result of this preprocessing is a set of multiple terms called split term set.

9.7.1.1.2   Word Sense Disambiguation

This approach is derived from Park and Kim approach [70]. Its objective is to identify the correct meaning of a term presented by a leaf node (node which doesn't have a child) in the source taxonomy. The algorithm uses the Wordnet [71] to search about the term provided by the split term set. The approach executes a comparison between the hyponyms of the term provided by the WordNet and the same term provided by the split term set provided by the source taxonomy. The result of this process is an extended term set that is composed of original term and its synonyms. In order to detect the correct closely meaning of each term, the algorithm compares the sense hierarchy (hypernym relations) of the term provided by WordNet with all ancestor nodes (upper category nodes which have children nodes) of the term provided by the current node located in the taxonomy source. The result of this comparison is a set of matched lemmas.

9.7.1.1.3   Candidate Path Identification

In this stage, the extended term set is used to determine the candidate path of the target taxonomy to be mapped with the current source category. The algorithm matches the terms provided by the extended split term set with paths provided by the target taxonomy. If one term of the extended term set is found to be a substring of the examined category of target taxonomy, the category is considered as candidate path. The candidate path identification is derived from Park and Kim algorithm [70] which compares the root node of the target path with the extended term set. The difference between the Park and Kim algorithm and proposed algorithm is that the later if it detects a term that is a substring of the actual tested category, category will be considered as candidate path and the algorithm will check the children of this category. Moreover, the proposed algorithm splits the original category name to multiple sets if it is a composite category. The algorithm compares between the multiple extended term set and the actual tested category name. This comparison requires the matching between every extended term set with its extended split term set. The result of the comparison is a Boolean value true, if a term is a substring of the actual tested category or false, if there is no term can be a substring of the actual tested category. The path of the target category will be considered as a candidate path if half of Boolean values are true.

9.7.1.1.4 Aggregated Path Similarity Score

To determine the best candidate paths of target taxonomy that can be adapted to match with source paths, an aggregated similarity score is calculated for each candidate path. Its objective is to measure the adaptation between target candidate path and the source path. The aggregated function is based on the use of Park and Kim algorithm [70] and the parent mapping similarity presented by the proposed algorithm.

9.7.1.2 *LexOnt Matching Approach*

The objective of LexOnt approach [72] is the production of frequent and significant terms provided by the corpus of Programmable Web (PW) directory [73]. Frequent and significant terms reflect the general properties of service classes provided by the PW to be automatically classified in ontology. The corpus of PW directory contains API description. The corpus is encoded as HTML format. LexOnt algorithm relies on the information provided by the HTML text which describes the APIs service and information provided by Wikipedia that describe the domain of the service. Moreover LexOnt uses the WordNet [71] to detect the synonyms of terms to produce top N list words and phrases which can be used to determine distinct features of the service. LexOnt provides a semi-automatic ontology construction.

LexOnt Approach is executed by several algorithms that are outlined in the following stages.

9.7.1.2.1 TF-IDF (Term Frequency-Inverse Document Frequency)

TF-IDF is calculated to demonstrate the importance of term appeared in the corpus. TF [74] is defined as the frequency of a term t appeared in the corpus while IDF is the inverse document frequency which can be computed using this expression: $[\log(N/(nj+1))+1]$ where N is the total number of document and nj is the document frequency of term (t).

9.7.1.2.2 Significant Phrases

A significant phrase is composed of two or more words that can be a clue that indicates the high level property of a service class. For example, in the service "Advertising" significant terms are "Mobile Advertising", "Facebook Advertising", etc. Significant phrase is detected through two steps; the first step is the determination of collocation, terms that occur together and the second step is the selection of unique collocations. The Chi Square is computed in this phase on collocated words to show the comparison between the numbers of times that words in a phrase are appeared together and the number of times that words appear alone. LexOnt uses the Wikipedia, WordNet, and constructed ontology to cover the main concepts and properties for an API service. For example, for the "Advertising" category, LexOnt algorithm will generate 20 top words provided by Wikipedia page which are (informecial, bowl, radio, placement, advertisement, marketing, promotion, advertising, semiotics, commercial, television, brand, television, billboard, product, sponsor, consumer). In addition, LexOnt applies the adoption of WordNet to find the synonyms and related terms for each term listed in top N words. Also, LexOnt applies the matching between terms which are located in the constructed ontology and the generated terms. If there exist matched terms, LexOnt algorithm will rank and label them to mark that they are already existed in the ontology.

9.7.2   Ontology Engineering Applications in Social Media Domain

Social media domain has its own informal language that encompasses particular phrases, terms, syntax, grammar, and emotions. Therefore, mining of the informal text and its analysis requires particular natural language processing as well as an ontology that provides the common slang expressions and terms. In addition, the ontology is adopted in social media to facilitate the new information acquisition through the correspondence between the slang expressions and terms provided by the social media forums and the social media ontology.

Ontology plays the role of a transitional dictionary that can be adopted to retrieve the semantic correspondence between several terms that are represented in structure or unstructured forms. The ontology can be adopted to emulate the generic terms that are used in social media platforms. The correspondence between the ontology and the social media text facilitates the organization to perceive the informal text posted by the users.

9.7.2.1   Emotive Ontology Approach

The approach is presented by Sykora and colleagues [75]. Its objective is to interpret the emotional reflections of the users towards products, services, and events. These emotional reflections are provided by the informal text circulated in the social media forums. The interpretation and the categorization of the emoticons are important to construct an emotional ontology that will be adopted to denote the most frequent human emotions. The emotive approach encompasses the correspondence between the informal text and the emotional ontology. The emotive ontology contains eight primary emotions (surprise, anger, shame, confusion, happiness, fear, disgust, and sadness). Also the emotive ontology involves intensifiers, perceived strength of individual emotions, injections, and conjunctions. The emotive ontology takes into account the slang terms as well as the relevant Part Of Speech (POS) tags. The emotion extraction from twitter text relies on the adoption of the Out of Vocabulary (OOV) to determine the slang terms, the use of Application Programming Interface (API), thesaurus.com [76], dictionary. com [77], Merriam Webster dictionary [78], and Oxford English dictionary [79]. The ontology is codified with python to enable the customization of hash tables and the wrapper objects that are interlinked with the negations, the injections, the conjunctions, and the intensifiers. Figure 9.12 shows the correspondence between the emotional ontology and the tweet texts.

As Figure 9.12 demonstrates, the twitter messages are the input of the proposed pipeline. The twitter messages are segmented into a set of phrases. The emoticons are identified by the use of a tokenizer called Potts regex [80] as well as a set of matching rules proposed by O'Connor [81]. The tokenization process takes into account the token prefixes and suffixes in order to execute the substring matching.

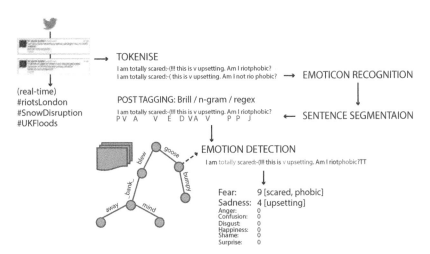

Figure 9.12 EMOTIVE's NLP pipeline [75].

The Emotive ontology is formally codified with the use of a prefix tree (Trie) and a group of hashtable. The prefix tree is adopted to store the phrases represented by the ontology. The identified token of a tweet message is verified with the use of hashtable. In case that there is no matched token, the token will be collated with the prefix tree. In case that there is a correspondent emotion, the matching process will take into account the previous conjunctions, negators, and intensifiers that are appeared before the matched emotion. Furthermore, the strength scores of each matched emotion are computed. The strength scores involve the average, sum, and the maximum score for each tweet [75]. For the assessment of the Emotive ontology, it was compared by a golden standard dataset called Emotive dataset [82]. The later involves 150 annotated tweets.

9.7.2.2   Ontology-Based Approach for Social Media Analysis

An approach for social media analysis was proposed by Alt and Wittwer [83]. The approach presents a general framework to analyze the social media text. It relies on the use of a constructed dictionary, analysis concept, social search, and ontology. The goal of this approach is to enhance the ontology development process by the knowledge acquisition provided by several enterprise systems such as Enterprise Resource Planning (ERP) and Customer Relationship Management (CRM). The framework components are shown in Figure 9.13. They are the business databases component, the ontology builder component, the text mining component, and the social media component.

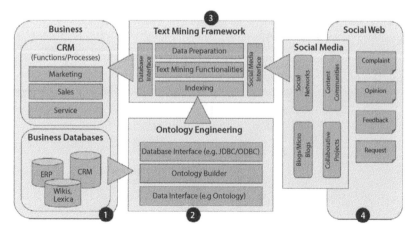

Figure 9.13 Proposed framework of an ontology-based social media analysis [83].

Business databases component reflects the important information concerning the business processes, the business structure, and its products. For the ontology builder component, it is adopted to develop the ontology; the component performs the extraction of the relevant information from structured and unstructured sources. In order to convert databases to ontology, the Open Database Connectivity (ODBC) [84] and Java Database Connectivity (JDBC) [85] are adopted in the framework. The text mining component uses the developed ontology to interpret the informal unstructured text collected from social websites and forums. The social media component adopts various APIs to extract the social media text that will be stored in ERP.

The framework assumes that the ontology is developed automatically from an ERP database. On other hand, the developed ontology will be adopted by the text mining component to match the informal text with the ontology. The text mining takes the informal text from the social media component. The role of the ontology in this framework is an intermediate dictionary that facilitates the extraction of relevant keywords for each concept as wells as its relations with other concepts. A set of algorithms can be applied for the ontology development and the mapping between database and ontology. Examples: DB2OWL [86, 87], RDB2ONT [88], and RONTO [89].

9.7.2.3   Methodological Framework for Semantic Comparison of Emotional Values

Mohammed Jabreel and colleagues proposed this framework [90]. Its goal is to interpret huge number of tweet that are gathered by a type of organization called Destination Management Organizations (DMO). DMO [91] is derived from the world tourism organization, and it is considered as harmonized management of all the factors that make up a destination (attractions, access, marketing, human resources, image, and pricing). The components of this framework are illustrated in Figure 9.14. The framework includes the definition of emotional values component, the tweet preprocessing component, and the semantic content analysis.

9.7.2.3.1   Definition of the Emotional Values

The destinations personality can be perceived from the emotional values [92, 93]. Thus, there is a classification for the emotional values that indicate the destinations personality. This classification involves various dimensions such as ruggedness, sophistication, excitement, and sincerity. Every dimension is classified into a set of categories and sub-categories.

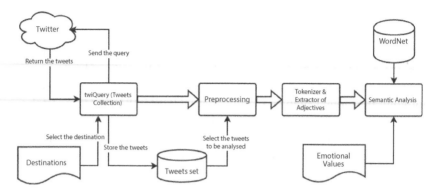

Figure 9.14 Architecture of the methodological framework of analysis [90].

9.7.2.3.2   Preprocessing of the Tweets

In this component, the WordNet is adopted to deal with the tweet messages. It is used to cope some challenges that face the tweet processing. Examples of these challenges are the spelling correction, the analysis of slang terms, the analysis of emoticons, the removal of stopwords, and the normalization.

9.7.2.3.3   Semantic Content Analysis

The objective of this component is to detect a relation between the emotional values and the tweets through the adjective analysis. The algorithms can be adopted in this component to identify semantic similarity of an adjective provided by a tweet with an emotional value. The semantic similarity can be executed by the use of the ontology and the WordNet. Example of the ontology-based semantic similarity measure is mentioned by Wu and palmer [94]. For the adjective extraction, a parser can be adopted to detect the adjectives in tweet as well as the frequency computation for each adjective.

References

1. Gomez-Perez, A., Fernández-López, M., Corcho, O., *Ontological Engineering: with examples from the areas of Knowledge Management, e-Commerce and the Semantic Web*, pp. 6–6, Springer Science & Business Media, Facultad de Informatica, Universidad Politénica de Madrid, Spain. 2006.
2. Mizoguchi, R., Tutorial on ontological engineering—Part 1: Introduction to ontological engineering. *New Gen. Comput.*, Osaka University, Japan. 21, 365–384, 2003.
3. Gruber, T.R., Toward principles for the design of ontologies used for knowledge sharing. *Int. J. Hum.Comput. Stud.*, 43, 5–6, 907–928, 1995. 1995.

4. Suárez-Figueroa, M.C., Gómez-Pérez, A., Fernández-López, M., The NeOn methodology for ontology engineering, in: *Ontology engineering in a networked world*, pp. 9–34, Springer, Berlin, Heidelberg, 2012.
5. Maedche, A. and Staab, S., Learning Ontologies for the Semantic Web. *IEEE Intell. Syst.*, 16, 2, 72–79, 2001.
6. Neon glossary of activities. (2019). Retrieved 16 August 2019, from http://kmi.open.ac.uk/events/sssw08/presentations/Gomez%20Perez-neonglossaryofactivities.pdf
7. Shvaiko, P. and Euzenat, J., *Ontology Matching*, pp. 9–9, Springer Berlin Heidelberg, Berlin, Heidelberg, 2013.
8. Grüninger, M., Hahmann, T., Hashemi, A., Ong, D., Ontology Verification with Repositories. In Proceedings of the Sixth International Conference (FOIS-2010). *Front. Artif. Intell. Appl. FOIS*, 209, 317–330, 2010.
9. Ehrig, M. and Euzenat, J., *State of the Art on Ontology Alignment. Knowledge Web Deliverable D2.2.3*, INRIA, Saint Ismier, France, 2004.
10. Ahmed, Z., 2009. Domain Specific Information Extraction for Semantic Annotation. Diploma thesis, Charles University in Prague Faculty of Mathematics and Physics and University of Nancy 2 UFR Mathematics and Informatics.
11. Brank, J., Grobelnik, M., Mladenic, D., A survey of ontology evaluation techniques, in: *In Proceedings of the conference on data mining and data warehouses (SiKDD 2005), Citeseer Ljubljana*, Slovenia, pp. 166–170, 2005, 2005.
12. Haase, P. and Stojanovic, L., Consistent evolution of OWL ontologies, in: *European Semantic Web Conference*, Springer, Berlin, Heidelberg, pp. 182–197, 2005, May 2005.
13. Grüninger, M. and Fox, M.S., Methodology for the design and evaluation of ontologies, in: *Procdings of the Workshop on Basic Ontological Issues in Knowledge Sharing (IJCAI)*, pp. 1–10, 1995.
14. Fernández-López, M., Gómez-Pérez, A., Juristo, N., Methontology: from ontological art towards ontological engineering, in: *Proceeding of the AAAI-97 Spring Symposium on Ontological Engineering*, pp. 33–40, Stanford University, USA, 1997.
15. Farquhar, A., Fikes, R., Rice, J., The ontolingua server: A tool for collaborative ontology construction. *Int. J. Hum.Comput. Stud.*, 46, 6, 707–727, 1997.
16. Brusa, G., Laura Caliusco, M., Chiotti, O., Towards ontological engineering: A process for building a domain ontology from scratch in public administration. *Expert Syst.*, 25, 5, 484–503, 2008.
17. De Nicola, A., Missikoff, M., Navigli, R., A software engineering approach to ontology building. *Inf. Syst.*, 34, 2, 258–275, 2009.
18. ATHENA - INTEROP-VLab. 2019. Retrieved 16 August 2019, from http://interop-vlab.eu/athena/
19. Uschold, M. and King, M., Towards a methodology for building ontologies. *Proceedings of Workshop on Basic Ontological Issues in Knowledge Sharing*, International Joint Conference on Artificial Intelligence, United Kingdom, pp. 1–15, 1995.

20. Gómez-Pérez, A., Juristo, N., Pazos, J., Evaluation and assessment of knowledge sharing technology, in: *Towards Very Large Knowledge Bases - Know ledge Building and Knowledge Sharing*, pp. 289–296, 1995.

21. Al-Baltah, I.A., Ghani, A.A.A., Rahman, W.N.W.A., Atan, R., Research Article A Comparative Study on Ontology Development Methodologies towards Building Semantic Conflicts Detection Ontology for Heterogeneous Web Services. *Res. J. Appl. Sci. Eng. Technol.*, 7, 13, 2674–2679, 2014. 2014.

22. Gawich, M., Badr, A., Hegazy, A., Ismail, H., A Methodology for Ontology Building. *Int. J. Comput. Appl.*, 56, 2, 39–45, 2012.

23. World Wide Web Consortium (W3C), 2019. Retrieved 16 August 2019, from https://www.w3.org/

24. Mizoguchi, R., Tutorial on ontological engineering Part 2: Ontology development, tools and languages. *New Gener. Comput.*, 22, 1, 61–96, 2004.

25. Ontological engineering from the informatics perspective. Retrieved 16 August 2019, from http://www.rroij.com/open-access/ontological-engineering-from -the-informatics-perspective.pdf

26. Roussey, C., Pinet, F., Kang, M.A., Corcho, O., An introduction to ontologies and ontology engineering, in: *Ontologies in Urban development projects*, pp. 9–38, Springer, London, 2011, 9–38.

27. OWL - Semantic Web Standards, Retrieved 16 August 2019, from https:// www.w3.org/OWL/

28. OWL 2 Web Ontology Language Primer (Second Edition), Retrieved 16 August 2019, from https://www.w3.org/TR/owl2-primer/

29. SNOMED Clinical Terms® (SNOMED CT®), Retrieved 16 August 2019, from https://www.nlm.nih.gov/research/umls/Snomed/snomed_main.html

30. Gene Ontology Resource, Retrieved 16 August 2019, from http://geneontology. org/

31. NCI Thesaurus, Retrieved 16 August 2019, from https://ncit.nci.nih.gov/ ncitbrowser/

32. OWL2 Features, Retrieved 16 August 2019, from https://www.w3.org/ TR/2012/REC-owl2-new-features-20121211/#Profiles

33. Rich, E. and Knight, K., *Artificial intelligence*, Second edition, New York: McGraw-Hill, Berlin, Germany, 1991.

34. cwm - a general purpose data processor for the semantic web. (2019). Retrieved 16 August 2019, from https://www.w3.org/2000/10/swap/doc/cwm

35. Apollo Home Page, Retrieved 16 August 2019, from http://apollo.open. ac.uk/

36. Apollo Manual, Retrieved 16 August 2019, from http://apollo.open.ac.uk/ docs/Apollo_manual.pdf

37. GMOD/Apollo, Retrieved 16 August 2019, from https://github.com/GMOD/ Apollo/releases/tag/2.0.6

38. NeOn Wiki, Retrieved 16 August 2019, from http://neon-toolkit.org/wiki/ Main_Page.html

39. Neon Plugins - NeOn Wiki, Retrieved 16 August 2019, from http://neon-tool-kit.org/wiki/Neon_Plugins.html
40. Alignment API, Retrieved 16 August 2019, from http://alignapi.gforge.inria.fr/
41. Text2onto Plugin, Retrieved 16 August 2019, from https://code.google.com/archive/p/text2onto/
42. GATE Tool, Retrieved 16 August 2019, from https://gate.ac.uk/sale/tao/splitch14.html
43. NeON Version 2.5.2, Retrieved 16 August 2019, from http://neon-toolkit.org/wiki/Download/2.5.2.html
44. Protégé Tool, Retrieved 16 August 2019, from http://protege.stanford.edu/
45. Prompt Plugin, Retrieved 16 August 2019, from https://protegewiki.stanford.edu/wiki/PROMPT
46. Pellet Reasoner, Retrieved 16 August 2019, from https://github.com/stardog-union/pellet/tree/master/protege/plugin
47. Hermit Reasoner, Retrieved 16 August 2019, from http://www.hermit-reasoner.com/
48. Ontograph Plugin, Retrieved 16 August 2019, from https://github.com/protegeproject/ontograf
49. Ontop Mapping Tool, Retrieved 16 August 2019, from http://ontop.inf.unibz.it/
50. SPARQL, Retrieved 16 August 2019, from https://www.w3.org/TR/rdf-sparql-query/
51. Protégé Version 5.0., Retrieved 16 August 2019, from http://protege.stanford.edu/download/protege/5.0/binaries/
52. Turtle Language, Retrieved 16 August 2019, from https://en.wikipedia.org/wiki/Turtle_(syntax)
53. OBO format, Retrieved 16 August 2019, from http://www.geneontology.org/faq/what-obo-file-format
54. Anbarasi, M.S., Naveen, P., Selvaganapathi, S., MOHAMED NOWSATH, A.L.I.I., Ontology based medical diagnosis decision support system. *Int. J. Eng. Res. Technol. (IJERT)*, 2, 4, 758–765, 2013.
55. Sherimon, P.C. and Krishnan, R., OntoDiabetic: an ontology-based clinical decision support system for diabetic patients. *Arabian J. Sci. Eng.*, 41, 3, 1145–1160, 2016.
56. Alharbi, R.F., Berri, J., El-Masri, S., Ontology based clinical decision support system for diabetes diagnostic, in: *Proceedings of 2015 Science and Information Conference (SAI)*, pp. 597–602, 2015.
57. Benmimoune, L., Hajjam, A., Ghodous, P., Andres, E., Talha, S., Hajjam, M., Ontology-based Medical Decision Support System to Enhance Chronic Patients' Lifestyle within E-care Telemonitoring Platform, in: *The proceedings of the International Conference on Informatics, Management and Technology in Healthcare ICIMTH*, pp. 279–282, 2015.

58. HAS, Retrieved 16 August 2019, from https://www.has-sante.fr/portail/jcms/r_1455081/Home-page
59. ESC, Retrieved 16 August 2019, from https://www.escardio.org/Guidelines
60. Zeshan, F. and Mohamad, R., Medical ontology in the dynamic healthcare environment. *Procedia Comput. Sci.*, 10, 340–348, 2012.
61. Wen, Y.X., Wang, H.Q., Zhang, Y.F., Li, J.S., Ontology-based medical data integration for regional healthcare application, in: *Frontier and Future Development of Information Technology in Medicine and Education*, vol. 269, pp. 1667–1672, Springer, Dordrecht, 2014.
62. Kumar, V., Ontology based public healthcare system in Internet of Things (IoT). *Procedia Comput. Sci.*, 50, 99–102, 2015.
63. Alfonse, M., Aref, M.M., Salem, A.B.M., An ontology-based system for cancer diseases knowledge management. *Int. J. Inf. Eng. Electronic Business*, 6, 6, 55–63, 2014. 2014.
64. Salem, A.B.M. and Alfonse, M., Building web-based lung cancer ontology. *Proceedings 1st Nat. Symp e-Health Bioeng.*, 177–182, 2007.
65. Alfonse, M., Aref, M.M., Salem, A.B.M., Ontology-based knowledge representation for liver cancer, in: *Proceedings of the International eHealth, Telemedicine and Health ICT Forum for Educational, Networking and Business*, Luxembourg, GD of Luxembourg, vol. 9334, pp. 821–825, 2012.
66. Salem, A.B.M. and Alfonse, M., Ontological engineering approach for breast cancer knowledge management, in: *the Proceedings of Med-e-Tel Med-e-Tel, the International eHealth, Telemedicine and Health ICT for Education, Networking and Business*, pp. 320–324, 2009.
67. Fact Reasoner, Retrieved 16 August 2019, from https://protegewiki.stanford.edu/wiki/Pr4_UG_rp_Reas_FaCT++
68. Lasierra, N., Alesanco, A., Guillén, S., Garcia, J., A three stage ontology-driven solution to provide personalized care to chronic patients at home. *J. Biomed. Inf.*, 46, 3, 516–529, 2013.
69. Nederstigt, L.J., Aanen, S.S., Vandić, D., Frăsincar, F., An automatic approach for mapping product taxonomies in E-commerce systems, in: *Proceedings of the 24th International Conference on Advanced Information Systems Engineering*, Springer, Berlin, Heidelberg, pp. 334–349, 2012.
70. Park, S. and Kim, W., Ontology mapping between heterogeneous product taxonomies in an electronic commerce environment. *Int. J. Electron. Commerce*, 12, 2, 69–87, 2007.
71. Miller, G.A., WordNet: a lexical database for English. *Commun. ACM*, 38, 11, 39–41, 1995.
72. Arabshian, K., Danielsen, P., Afroz, S., Lexont: A semi-automatic ontology creation tool for programmable web, in: *2012 AAAI Spring Symposium on Intelligent Web Services Meet Social Computing*, Palo Alto, CA, 2012.
73. ProgrammableWeb. (2019). Retrieved 16 August 2019, from http://www.programmableweb.com/

74. Salton, G. and McGill, M.J., *Introduction to modern information retrieval*, First edition, mcgraw-hill, New York, 1983.
75. Sykora, M.D., Jackson, T., O'Brien, A., Elayan, S., Emotive ontology: Extracting fine-grained emotions from terse, informal messages, in: *Proceedings of the IADIS International Conference Intelligent Systems and Agents*, ISA 2013, Prague, pp. 19–26, 22–26 July, 2013.
76. Thesaurus, Retrieved 16 August 2019, from http://www.thesaurus.com/
77. Dictionary, Retrieved 16 August 2019, from http://www.dictionary.com/
78. Meriam Webster, Retrieved 16 August 2019, from http://www.merriam-webster.com
79. Oxford English Dictionary, Retrieved 16 August 2019, from http://www.oed.com
80. Potts Tokenizer, Retrieved 16 August 2019, from http://sentiment.christopherpotts.net/code-data/happyfuntokenizing.py
81. O'Connor, B., Krieger, M., Ahn, D., Tweetmotif: Exploratory search and topic summarization for twitter, in: *Proceedings of the Fourth International AAAI Conference on Weblogs and Social Media*, pp. 384–385, 2010.
82. Emotive Dataset, Retrieved 16 August 2019, from http://emotive.lboro.ac.uk/resources/IJCSIS.html
83. Alt, R. and Wittwer, M., Towards an ontology-based approach for social media analysis. *Proceedings of the Twenty Second European Conference on Information Systems*, Tel Aviv, pp. 1–10, 2014.
84. ODBC, Retrieved 16 August 2019, from https://dev.mysql.com/downloads/connector/odbc/
85. JDBC Overview. (2019). Retrieved 16 August 2019, from http://www.oracle.com/technetwork/java/overview-141217.html
86. Cullot, N., Ghawi, R., Yétongnon, K., DB2OWL: A Tool for Automatic Database-to-Ontology Mapping, in: *proceedings of SEBD, pages*, pp. 491–494, 2007.
87. Barrasa Rodríguez, J., Corcho, Ó., Gómez-Pérez, A., R2O, an extensible and semantically based database-to-ontology mapping language. *Proceedings of the seventh International Workshop on the Web and Databases*, 2004.
88. Trinh, Q., Barker, K., Alhajj, R., Rdb2ont: A tool for generating owl ontologies from relational database systems. *Proceedings of the Advanced Int'l Conference on Telecommunications and Int'l Conference on Internet and Web Applications and Services (AICT-ICIW'06)*, pp. 170–170, 2006.
89. Papapanagiotou, P., Katsiouli, P., Tsetsos, V., Anagnostopoulos, C., Hadjiefthymiades, S., RONTO: Relational to ontology schema matching. *AIS Sigsemis Bulletin*, 3, 3-4, 32–36, 2006.
90. Jabreel, M., Moreno, A., Huertas, A., Semantic comparison of the emotional values communicated by destinations and tourists on social media. *J. Destination Marketing Manage.*, 6, 3, 170–183, 2017.
91. DMO, Retrieved 16 August 2019, from http://www2.unwto.org/category/technical-product-target/destination-management-organizations

92. Henderson, J.C., Selling places: the new Asia-Singapore brand. *J. Tourism Stud.*, 11, 1, 36–44, 2000.

93. Morgan, N., Pritchard, A., Piggott, R., New Zealand, 100% pure. The creation of a powerful niche destination brand. *J. Brand Manage.*, 9, 4, 335–354, 2002.

94. Wu, Z. and Palmer, M., Verbs semantics and lexical selection, in: *Proceedings of the 32nd annual meeting on Association for Computational Linguistics*, pp. 133–138, 1994.

10

Ontologies on Biomedical Informatics

Marco Alfonse[1]* and Mariam Gawich[2]

[1]Faculty of Computer and Information Science, Ain Shams University, Cairo, Egypt
[2]GRELITE, CRI, French University in Egypt (UFE), Cairo, Egypt

Abstract

Biomedical datum can be expressed in heterogeneous terms that can have the same meaning. Biologists and clinical practitioners can develop biomedical lexicons based on their own language and vocabulary. The ontology is a knowledge representation technique that describes any complex domain and it relates its data to a shared representation. Therefore, the ontology is applied in the biomedical domain to ensure the integration and the standardization between different biomedical lexicons, thesaurus, and terminologies. The biomedical ontology has two perspectives: the content oriented view and the functional view. The content view concerns about the creation of biomedical ontologies and the functional view focuses on the adoption of ontology with the biomedical systems. This chapter involves the two mentioned perspectives. It presents the major biomedical ontologies and the biomedical ontology-based systems.

Keywords: Ontology, ontology engineering, medical ontology, knowledge discovery, medical informatics

10.1 Introduction

Biomedical data are presented in different forms. The biologists and clinical researchers find a difficulty to collect and integrate the different forms into unified biomedical data. In order to overcome this difficulty, the ontology is used to depict the biomedical knowledge in terms of a hierarchy of concepts and relationships. Furthermore, the ontology enables the representation of a concept, its related terms and its synonyms. For this reason,

---

Corresponding author: marco@fcis.asu.edu.eg

Vishal Jain, Ritika Wason, Jyotir Moy Chatterjee and Dac-Nhuong Le (eds.) Ontology-Based Information Retrieval for Healthcare Systems, (233–244) © 2020 Scrivener Publishing LLC

the ontology can integrate and standardize various biomedical lexicons, thesaurus, and terminology.

The ontology [1] in the biomedicine involves two main perspectives: the content-oriented view and the functional view. The content-oriented view focuses on the development of biomedical ontologies. It also concerns about the description of the community activity and its members that supervise the development of the ontology. The functional view concerns about the users who deal with the ontology. It also concerns about the capability of the ontology to help the biomedical researchers to retrieve the necessary information as well as the interpretation of the retrieved information. The functional view will help the ontology curator and the ontology creators to discover new ideas to enhance the ontology and its applications.

The common ontological artifacts involve the terminologies or the controlled vocabularies (CVs). A CV is a list that includes the concepts, their meaning, and their equivalent lexical terms. The concepts are stored in a hierarchical form to facilitate the presentation of a set of terms to the researchers that consult the CV to index resources such as database records. The most popular type of CV is the GO which helps the biomedical researchers to find the relevant terms of biological processes, cellular components of the gene products and molecular functions.

10.2   Defining Ontology

Ontology is a Greek term that is derived from the philosophy domain. In the philosophy domain, ontology is the science of existence that copes with the reality organization and the nature. In the computer science domain, ontology is a knowledge representation technique that is used to represent the acquired knowledge in a generic form that reflects the domain of interest. The knowledge in the ontology involves the common vocabulary of the domain of interest that is represented in terms of concepts. Ontology is classified in three types according to the detail level that it covers: the general ontology, the domain ontology, and the application ontology. The general ontology describes the domain of interest as a theory; it provides concepts that reflect the primary notions of this theory as well as their related notions. This type of ontology presents a moderate detail level of the domain of interest. The domain ontology describes a specific domain of interest in terms of concepts and facts that reflect a reality about a theory. Example of this type is the medical ontology. The application ontology involves a hierarchy of concepts that is used by a particular application.

10.3   Biomedical Ontologies and Ontology-Based Systems

10.3.1   MetaMap

A program [2] developed by Alan Aronson and provided by the National Library of Medicine (NLM) [3]. It was designed to map between a biomedical text and Unified Medical Language System (UMLS) metathesaurus [4]. As Figure 10.1 demonstrates, the MetaMap relies on of the following components: the Lexical syntactic analysis component, the Variant generation component, the Candidate Identification component, the Mapping construction component and the Word Sense Disambiguation (WSD) component.

Lexical syntactic analysis involves the following modules: Tokenization, POS tagging, specialist lexicon [5] to extract nouns and Nouns phrases. Each phrase and noun that is detected by the lexical syntactic analysis will be analyzed by the following components:

- – Variant generation: it is used to detect the variant of each phrase using table lookup. The variant generation also detects the synonyms of the acronyms.

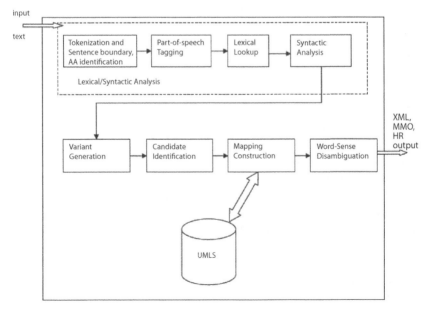

Figure 10.1 MetaMap system diagram [2].

- Candidate identification: It provides the list of metathesaurus terms that have exact or partial matching with the biomedical text. Furthermore, the component suggests the preferred name of each candidate term and its semantic type [6].
- Mapping construction: it is used to collect all candidate terms and it applies an evaluation function [7] to detect the candidate terms that have the highest matching score with the UMLS metathesaurus [4] terms.
- WSD module is applied to extract terms which are semantically suitable with the surrounding biomedical text.

10.3.2   GALEN

GALEN is a program [8] sponsored by the European Union. GALEN is the abbreviation of the "General Architecture for Languages Encyclopedias and Nomenclatures" applied in medicine. GALEN aims to provide the medical terminology which can be used by the healthcare professionals. The use of GALEN facilitates the integration between different computer health systems.

The program is based on the use of medical ontology called the Open GALEN [9]. The ontology is codified with the description logic language called "GALEN Representation And Integration Language" (GRAIL). The semantic links in the GRAIL ontology is represented in terms of part-whole relation (partonomies). In other terms, the medical concepts can be represented in hierarchical, inherited and transitive forms which enable the representation of a formal statement.

10.3.3   NIH-CDE

CDE refers to the Common Data Elements developed by the National Institutes of Health (NIH) [3]. The National Library of Medicine-Common Data Element (NIH-CDE) [10] is a web-based application that aims to integrate between the patient health record and his other clinical and biomedical information collected from various data sources. It ensures the interoperability between the clinical and biomedical data sources. The CDE glossary [11] provides controlled terms that are considered as standard terms. The Data Element (DE) is a metadata that depicts a part of data in terms of the following attributes:

Name: it is the abbreviation form or a code to indicate the DE.
Definition: it refers to the significance of the DE as well as its scope.

Query/instructions: it refers to the interpretation of DE definition. Example: the instructions concerning the way to take a
laboratory test.

Provenance: it refers to the source of the DE and its validation.
The provenance involves the citation of scientific articles and
standard terminology.

Value Set: It refers to the potential values of DE. For example,
the value set for a laboratory test is the scale of potential values and the intended units.

The CDE refers to a mutual DE that is applied in several datasets. There
are four types of CDE: universal, domain-specific, required, and core.

Universal: it refers to the CDE that can be applied in spite of
the disease. Example: the demographic data and the patient
history.

Domain-specific: it refers to the CDE that can be used in a
clinical study such as a disease study and a body system
study.

Required: it refers to the intended CDE that is used in the strategy of an institution. Example: the required CDE of the
research funder of a specific disease study.

Core: it refers to the intended CDE that can be gathered in specific studies. Example: the CDE that is used in a study for
genome wide association or the CDE that is used for a cancer disease study.

10.3.4   LOINC

LOINC [12] refers to the Logical Observation Identifier Names and codes.
LOINC aims to detect the observation in the electronic Health Level
Seven International (HL7) [13] messages which are disseminated across
Healthcare providers such as hospitals, public health department, and
health maintenance organizations. The LOINC database generates universal code for the laboratory tests. Each laboratory and any health care providers have their own particular code that is used for each test observation.
In order to integrate between the health care providers databases, there is
a need to use a universal code. The LOINC uses the RELMA program [14]
to map between the test code created by a health care provider and its universal code that is provided by LOINC.

10.3.5   Current Procedural Terminology (CPT)

CPT [15] refers to the Current Procedural Terminology was proposed by the American Medical Association (AMA). CPT is a standard terminology that is adopted to describe the medical procedures that involve the diagnosis and therapy procedures applied in surgery. Furthermore, the medical procedures contain the procedures that are used in the internal medicine. There are three categories of CPT code:

> Category I: it is a CPT code that depicts specific medical procedures used by the Qualified Healthcare Professionals (QHPs). The category I is characterized by five digits. The evolved release is published each year.
> Category II: it refers to the CPT that reflects for performance measurement. It is characterized by numeric alpha code. Example: 2029F refers to "complete physical skin exam performed". This category is published three times per year.
> Category III: it refers to the CPT code that is used to describe the new technologies that facilitate the data collection and the evaluation of the new medical services and procedures executed by the healthcare provider.

10.3.6   Medline Plus Connect

It is a web-based application developed by the National Library of Medicine (NLM) [3]. The Medline Plus Connect [16] involves information concerning the disease, medical encyclopedia, drugs, and herbs. The Medline Plus Connect enables the healthcare providers to integrate data between the patient portals and the Electronic Health Record (EHR).

The Medline Plus Connect has three types of code requests: codes for the diagnosis, codes for medication, and codes for laboratory Tests. As Figure 10.2 demonstrates, the Medline Plus Connect takes a code-based request from several users. The user can be a patient portal or an EHR or a Health IT system. The Medline Plus Connect will provide the suitable information to their users upon the type of code based request. The content of the information will be displayed on the patient portal or the clinical interface. The Medline Plus Connect uses two standard coding systems International Classification of Diseases, Ninth Revision, Clinical Modification (ICD-9-CM) [17], and the Clinical Observations Recording and Encoding (CORE) Problem List Subset of Systematized Nomenclature of Medicine (SNOMED) [18] for the manipulation of diagnosis and medication requests.

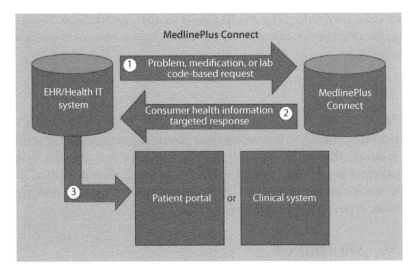

Figure 10.2 The basic structure for MedlinePlus Connect communications [16].

Medline Plus Connect interacts with other standards such as National Drug Code (NDC) [19], LOINC [20], Systemized Nomenclature of Medicine— Clinical Terms (SNOMED-CT) [21], and RxNorm [22].

10.3.7   Gene Ontology

Gene ontology (GO) [23, 24] aims to present a computerized information source for genes functions specially the proteins and the molecules and the non coding RNA. The non coding RNAs are the molecules that are generated by the gene.

The gene ontology [25, 26] describes the molecular functions, biological process, and cellular component. For the molecular function, it is an activity in biomedicine. It refers to a set of terms that reflects the disposition of the gene product. Examples of these terms are enzymes, transporter, and ligans. For the biological process, it focuses on the biological goal to the gene or the gene product. The biological process is applied through a set of molecular functions. A chemical/physical transformation can be considered as biological process. Example of biological process terms is signal transduction.

For the cellular component, it denotes the location in a cell in which the gene product is alive. Example of terms that reflect the cellular component are proteasome and ribosome.

Each concept or term in the GO is associated to various databases such as Gen-Bank [27], DDBJ [28], SwissPROT [29], EMBL [30], MIPS [31],

Pfam [32], ENZYME [33], SCOP [34], PIR [35], and YPD & WormPD [36]. The objective of this association is the rapid evolution of genes and their proteins.

10.3.8   UMLS

The UMLS [37] refers to the Unified Medical Language System. It was developed by the NLM. It involves three essential components: the semantic browser, the metathesaurus, and the specialist lexicon. The UMLS metathesaurus contains around 9,417,453 biomedical and medical concepts. Each concept in the UMLS metathesaurus is linked to one of the semantic types [6] determined by the NLM.

10.3.9   SNOMED-CT

It refers to the Systematized Nomenclature in Medicine—Clinical Terms (SNOMED-CT) [38]. It is developed by the College Of American Pathologists [39] and the United Kingdom's National Health Service [40]. SNOMED-CT can be used in three main health care applications: the clinical records, knowledge representation, and aggregation and analysis.

10.3.10   OBO Foundry

It refers to the Open Biological and Biomedical Ontology (OBO). OBO foundry [41] is a website that provides biomedical structured CVs in terms of ontologies in the domain of proteomics and genomics. The OBO foundry enables the ontology engineer to submit his ontology and the OBO foundry ensures the interoperability of ontologies in terms of its accuracy and representation.

10.3.11   Textpresso

Textpresso [42] is an information retrieval system to mine biological text. The textpresso divides the text provided from scientific articles to a set of sentences. The Textpresso marks the terms for every sentence using tags. The terms tags are classified to a set of hierarchical categories provided by an ontology. The Textpresso [43] deals with 1.5 million articles. The Textpresso interface enables the user to search for a biological term or sentence. The Textpresso will display the related copora for the required term or sentence. In addition, the Textpresso enables the user to annotate the term or sentence by selecting the category.

The Textpresso enables also the user to implement the curation process by selecting a research article. For the curation process, the Textpresso uses a converter, lexical annotation, and computational annotation. The converter tokenizes the research article into terms, phrases, and paragraphs. The lexical annotation implies the use of lexicon or dictionaries to attach each term to a category. The computational annotation implies the application of several machine learning algorithms to classify the research articles and recognize the terms.

10.3.12   National Cancer Institute Thesaurus

The National Cancer Institute Thesaurus (NCIt) [44, 45] was developed by the "National Cancer Institute". It provides a CV for cancer. It contains the terminology in the domain of bioinformatics, clinical care, administrative activities, and public information. The NCIt terminology provides unique code for each biomedical concept, preferred term for the concept, and synonyms. The NCIt repository contains around 100,000 textual definition and 400,000 links across the concepts.

The essential objectives of NCIt are:

- The representation of an evolved terminology for cancer.
- Taking an advantage of the use of the terminology by linking the concept to its related concepts. This association will enable the computer systems to implement the reasoning.
- Facilitating the evolution process [46] in terms of evolved concepts and evolved relations taking into account the user requirements.

Furthermore, the NCIt presents various services such as the searching in the NCI repository, the annotation of NCI data, as well as its compatibility with other external information sources such as SNOMED-CT [21] and Gene ontology [24].

References

1. Rubin, D.L., Shah, N.H., Noy, N.F., Biomedical ontologies: A functional perspective. *Briefings Bioinf.*, 9, 1, 75–90, 2007.
2. Aronson, A.R. and Lang, F.M., An overview of MetaMap: Historical perspective and recent advances. *J. Am. Med. Inf. Assoc.*, 17, 3, 229–236, 2010.

3. National Library of Medicine, National Institutes of Health. Retrieved 16 August 2019, from https://www.nlm.nih.gov/.

4. UMLS – Metathesaurus, Retrieved 16 August 2019, from https://www.nlm.nih.gov/research/umls/knowledge_sources/metathesaurus/.

5. The SPECIALIST LEXICON, Retrieved 16 August 2019, from https://lsg3.nlm.nih.gov/LexSysGroup/Projects/lexicon/current/web/index.html.

6. Current Semantic Types, 2019. Retrieved 16 August 2019, from https://www.nlm.nih.gov/research/umls/META3_current_semantic_types.html.

7. Stewart, S.A., Von Maltzahn, M.E., Abidi, S.S.R., Comparing Metamap to MGrep as a Tool for Mapping Free Text to Formal Medical Lexions, in: *Proceedings of the 1st International Workshop on Knowledge Extraction and Consolidation from Social-media in conjunction with the 11th International Semantic Web Conference ISWC*, pp. 63–77, 2012.

8. Sicilia, M., Handbook of metadata, semantics and ontologies, in: *Chapter III.2 Metadata and Ontologies for Health*, p. 265, World Scientific Publishing Co. Pte. Ltd, Singapour (5 Toh Tuck Link, Singapour 596224), 2014, (p. 265).

9. Haring, E., OpenGALEN Mission Statement. Retrieved 16 August 2019, from http://www.opengalen.org/.

10. National Library of Medicine-common data element, 2019. Retrieved 16 August 2019, from https://www.nlm.nih.gov/cde/.

11. Glossary, Retrieved 16 August 2019, from https://www.nlm.nih.gov/cde/glossary.html

12. McDonald, C.J., Huff, S.M., Suico, J.G., Hill, G., Leavelle, D., Aller, R., Williams, W., LOINC, a universal standard for identifying laboratory observations: A 5-year update. *Clin. Chem.*, 49, 4, 624–633, 2003.

13. International, H., Health Level Seven International - Homepage | HL7 International. Retrieved 16 August 2019, from http://www.hl7.org/.

14. RELMA — LOINC, 2019. Retrieved 16 August 2019, from https://loinc.org/relma/.

15. Dotson, P., CPT® codes: What are they, why are they necessary, and how are they developed? *Adv. Wound Care*, 2, 10, 583–587, 2013.

16. Ma, W., Dennis, S., Lanka, S., Miller, N., Potvin, J., MedlinePlus Connect: Linking health IT systems to consumer health information. *IT Prof.*, 14, 3, 22–28, 2012.

17. ICD - ICD-9-CM - International Classification of Diseases, Ninth Revision, Clinical Modification, 2019. Retrieved 16 August 2019, from https://www.cdc.gov/nchs/icd/icd9cm.htm

18. The CORE Problem List Subset of SNOMED CT, Retrieved 16 August 2019, from https://www.nlm.nih.gov/research/umls/Snomed/core_subset.html

19. National Drug Code Directory, Retrieved 16 August 2019, from https://www.fda.gov/Drugs/InformationOnDrugs/ucm142438.htm

20. LOINC — The freely available standard for identifying health measurements, observations, and documents, Retrieved 16 August 2019, from https://loinc.org/

21. SNOMED Clinical Terms® (SNOMED CT®), Retrieved 16 August 2019, from https://www.nlm.nih.gov/research/umls/Snomed/snomed_main.html
22. RxNorm Overview Retrieved 16 August 2019, from https://www.nlm.nih.gov/research/umls/rxnorm/overview.html
23. Gene Ontology Consortium, Gene ontology consortium: Going forward. *Nucleic Acids Res.*, 43, D1, D1049–D1056, 2014.
24. Gene Ontology Resource, 2019. Retrieved 16 August 2019, from http://gene-ontology.org/.
25. Shah, N. and Musen, M., Ontologies for formal representation of biological systems, in: *Handbook on ontologies*, pp. 445–461, Springer, Berlin, Heidelberg, 2009.
26. Ashburner, M., Ball, C.A., Blake, J.A., Botstein, D., Butler, H., Cherry, J.M., … Harris, M.A., Gene ontology: Tool for the unification of biology. *Nat. Genet.*, 25, 1, 25, 2000.
27. Benson, D.A., Karsch-Mizrachi, I., Lipman, D.J., Ostell, J., Wheeler, D.L., GenBank. *Nucleic Acids Res.*, 34, suppl_1, D16–D20, 2006.
28. Tateno, Y., Imanishi, T., Miyazaki, S., Fukami-Kobayashi, K., Saitou, N., Sugawara, H., Gojobori, T., DNA Data Bank of Japan (DDBJ) for genome scale research in life science. *Nucleic Acids Res.*, 30, 1, 27–30, 2002.
29. Bairoch, A. and Apweiler, R., The SWISS-PROT protein sequence database and its supplement TrEMBL in 2000. *Nucleic Acids Res.*, 28, 1, 45–48, 2000.
30. Kanz, C., Aldebert, P., Althorpe, N., Baker, W., Baldwin, A., Bates, K., Duggan, K., The EMBL nucleotide sequence database. *Nucleic Acids Res.*, 33, suppl_1, D29–D33, 2005.
31. Mewes, H.W., Frishman, D., Güldener, U., Mannhaupt, G., Mayer, K., Mokrejs, M., Weil, B., MIPS: A database for genomes and protein sequences. *Nucleic Acids Res.*, 30, 1, 31–34, 2002.
32. Bateman, A., Coin, L., Durbin, R., Finn, R.D., Hollich, V., Griffiths-Jones, S., Studholme, D.J., Yeats, C., Eddy, S.R., The Pfam protein families database. *Nucleic Acids Res.*, 32, suppl_1, D138–D141, 2004.
33. Bairoch, A., The ENZYME database in 2000. *Nucleic Acids Res.*, 28, 1, 304–305, 2000.
34. Murzin, A.G., Brenner, S.E., Hubbard, T., Chothia, C., SCOP: A structural classification of proteins database for the investigation of sequences and structures. *J. Mol. Biol.*, 247, 4, 536–540, 1995.
35. Barker, W.C., Garavelli, J.S., Huang, H., McGarvey, P.B., Orcutt, B.C., Srinivasarao, G.Y., Pfeiffer, F., Mewes, H.W., Tsugita, A., Wu, C., The protein information resource (PIR). *Nucleic Acids Res.*, 28, 1, 41–44, 2000.
36. Costanzo, M.C., Hogan, J.D., Cusick, M.E., Davis, B.P., Fancher, A.M., Hodges, P.E., Roberg-Perez, K.J., The yeast proteome database (YPD) and Caenorhabditis elegans proteome database (WormPD): Comprehensive resources for the organization and comparison of model organism protein information. *Nucleic Acids Res.*, 28, 1, 73–76, 2000.

37. RRF, M., *Metathesaurus - Rich Release Format (RRF)*, 2019, Retrieved 16 August 2019, from https://www.ncbi.nlm.nih.gov/books/NBK9685/.
38. Stearns, M.Q., Price, C., Spackman, K.A., Wang, A.Y., SNOMED clinical terms: Overview of the development process and project status, in: *Proceedings of the AMIA Symposium*, American Medical Informatics Association, p. 662, 2001.
39. College of American Pathologists, Retrieved 16 August 2019, from https://www.cap.org/.
40. NHS England, 2019. Retrieved 16 August 2019, from https://www.nhs.uk/using-the-nhs/about-the-nhs/the-nhs/.
41. WG, O., The OBO Foundry. Retrieved 16 August 2019, from http://www.obofoundry.org.
42. Müller, H.M., Van Auken, K.M., Li, Y., Sternberg, P.W., Textpresso Central: A customizable platform for searching, text mining, viewing, and curating biomedical literature. *BMC Bioinf.*, 19, 1, 94, 2018.
43. Textpresso central, Retrieved 16 August 2019, from https://textpressocentral.org/tpc
44. Ceusters, W., Smith, B., Goldberg, L., A terminological and ontological analysis of the NCI Thesaurus. *Methods Inf. Med.*, 44, 04, 498–507, 2005.
45. NCI Thesaurus, Retrieved 16 August 2019, from https://ncithesaurus-stage.nci.nih.gov/ncitbrowser
46. De Coronado, S., Haber, M.W., Sioutos, N., Tuttle, M.S., Wright, L.W., NCI Thesaurus: Using science-based terminology to integrate cancer research results, in: *Proceedings of the 11th World Congress on Medical Informatics (Medinfo)*, pp. 33–37, 20042004.

11

Machine Learning Techniques Best for Large Data Prediction: A Case Study of Breast Cancer Categorical Data: k-Nearest Neighbors

Yagyanath Rimal

School of Engineering, Pokhara University, Pokhara, Nepal

Abstract

This chapter explains machine learning prediction techniques for large data prediction using K nearest neighbor algorithm, which is the most effective tool for predicting large data having associative dependency variables like cancer disease data sets. Though there are many times miss leads the doctor's prediction for the detection of many disease identifications due to a large correlation between observed attributes. Cancer is considered as one of the deadliest diseases in the world and is responsible for around 13% of all deaths worldwide. The cancer diagnosis process also has relationships between many associative test reports for whether the patient has cancer or not. Its main purpose is to use machine learning techniques to investigate large associative data analyzes which have a wide variety of associative variables using the R package. The K-nearest neighbor machine learning algorithm is used for the accurate prediction of large categorical data sets. The output results are sufficiently explained with intermediate results and interpretation graphic to for generalization 32 dependent variables of 569 observations to predict whether a patient has cancer or not. This analytical review displays the complete procedure with an explanation for an accurate prediction of 98 percent accurate result with 95percent confidence interval, out of 114 breast cancer patient's records, only 2 records were calculated misclassification using KNN algorithm that is large enough accurate than traditional doctors' prediction in hospital diagenesis in the modern health system. Due to the model, sensitivity and specificity were largely accurate prediction from the model, accurate plot prediction demonstrates the same result after 7 iterations that matched

Email: rimal.yagya@pu.edu.np

Vishal Jain, Ritika Wason, Jyotir Moy Chatterjee and Dac-Nhuong Le (eds.) Ontology-Based Information Retrieval for Healthcare Systems, (245–256) © 2020 Scrivener Publishing LLC

the 98.25 percent accuracy prediction of breast cancer data. When data sets of largely associative relationship in modern breast cancer treatments. In many times thus, machine learning techniques have smart strengths for information analysis accurate predictions, like cancer disease using R programming.

Keywords: K-nearest neighbors, artificial intelligence, breast cancer, cancer symptoms

11.1 Introduction

Machine learning is the process of information utilizing research information and figures from past information for future purposes. As per [1], machine learning is the subset of artificial intelligence (AI) that enables the machine to gain consequently from past experience without being modified, which is like learning as a human with a progression of choices on different names of the past spare focuses. In doing as such, if there were a greater number of dependency whose expectation is more exact than a couple of information entered in the AI model. If the informational collections are in the header of the engraving, the administered learning is viewed as like the heading of the course table, almost, if the database without impossible header is viewed as free learning, the fortress learning method applies the accompanying warming and mix-up framework [2]. For example, the least demanding cat out on the town, when it is far enough away, our human personality honestly reenacts its image with the image of the pooch, in conclusion, analyzes and does not identify with the characters of different mutts, in conclusion, predicts that your catlike, due by the greater part of the votes, it depends upon the qualities of the cat. In thinking that the cat has sharp ears, the length is harmed, the shades are interested in individuals, their tones, and various features. This strategy surveys the standard minutes with relative segments with the canines and, finally, presumes that it's not a pooch, yet a catlike, whose characteristics are practically sure a cat and not a pooch. According to Stephen M. Borstelmann, MD [1] radiologist in the article does the machine beat specialist prescribed specialist doesn't do expectation for disease analysis and prediction of the solution for patients cure. Similarly, computer program beats doctors at brain tumors from radiation changes [13]. Computers beat pathologists in foreseeing lung malignant growth type, seriousness [12]. Artificial intelligence reads mammograms with 99% accuracy results than doctors' predictions. According to Li-Yu Hu, [6] that google should plan API for specialists to recommend for specialists that will send a picture and past information and, at that point, could easily anticipate forecast related for themselves. As indicated by the creator Brownlee [5], neighbor K is an administered learning calculation that groups another information point in the objective class dependent on the attributes of its contiguous information focuses. So, the KNN is a classifier dependent on the characterization of comparative components which feeds into the model of train first then prediction data occurs at last. KNN utilized both forward and feedback iteration using complex regulated program learning calculation and utilization essentially in grouping records [3]. However, Knn isn't a parametric test, which implies any of theory in various data attributes [4], in many cases, it appears on slow calculation and it doesn't store the middle of the road reference purpose of the yields for next iteration. In spite the fact that KNN broadly utilized in expectation characterization issues using, short computation time, and better accuracy of model. The knn model predicts better when the speed has broadened as the information present underneath the base and the best present in the individual instructive gatherings had a higher discerning point of confinement clearly displays the best AI model.

Min.	1st	Q. Median Mean	3rd	Q. Max.	NA's
lda	.6711	0.7532	0.7662	0.7759	0.8052
logistic	.6842	.7639	.77130	.7781	.8019
glmnet	.6842	.7557	.7662	.7773	.8019
svm	.6711	.7403	.7582	.7651	.7890
knn	.6753	.7115	.7386	.7465	.7785
nb	6316	.7305	.7597	.7569	.7869
cart	.6234	.7115	.7403	.7382	.7760
c50	.6711	.7273	.7468	.7586	.7785
bagging	.6883	.7246	.7451	.7530	.7792
rf	.6711	.7273	.7516	.7617	.7890
gbm	.6974	.7273	.7727	.7708	.8052

Source: Jason Brownlee, 2016.

This table demonstrates that knn is the best information calculation model that gives the greatest and least information interoperability. Therefore, knn application is broadly utilized by Fakebooks and google for data interpretation. The knn predicts the new approval from the reference of the past qualities with figuring the Euclidean distance between as: sqrt $(x^2-x1)^2 + (y^2-y1)^2$.

The KNN calculation performs fairs in every one of the parameters of contemplations ordinarily utilized for their straightforward understanding and decreased figuring time. The classifiers have been ordered by the conduct of their neighbors, so knn orders the new cases dependent on the similitude cases in which k and kn is a parameter that alludes to the closest numbers in the majority of the right forecasts [6]. The Knn model relies upon the comparability of features of picking the correct estimation of k is a technique called parameter change for better precision. The K is chosen in consideration of when k is equivalent to three, it is the closest triangular point when k is seven, it covers an instance of the more recognizable degree that changes most significantly than its neighbor. In this way, the factor of k is selected; k is an excess of low, and the propensity happens as a portion of the call. In like manner, if k is too much huge, it puts aside more action to process the data, along these lines, k is picked with the objective that the square establishment of the records in the database openness. For the odd number to be picked before the information is without clamor and clean. It works very well when research information is complete with harm or a generous patient. At the point when there utilize the knn calculation to break down the information in a gathering class. Another basic case of client records gets effectively unsurprising for those clients. In this manner, the knn calculation figures each separation among preparing and checks its precision with setting up test records [7] totally. What in the long run finds the briefest separation k for each record in the approval set when computing the separation, just the estimations in the x-heading of the objective expectation. The institutionalized information component is a fundamental condition for the count of the Euclidean separation that standardized the information from −1 to 1 [8]. Thus, the best k is generally taken from the square foundation of the number of perception records, while in doing as such, the blunder rate and the level of mistake approval in the informational indexes were determined. Which at last picks, the cut worth is dependent on the exhibition objective. Despite the fact that there were a few upsides and downsides, everything being equal, in any case, the hazard is risky when there is overfitting of information that requires a high count and devours a ton of time when there was a huge k [5]. As shown by [9], an assessment paper on the perspective on threatening development patients explains that numerous infection patients encountering dynamic treatment have been met to choose whether experts reason that their reports envision whether they will encounter the evil impacts of a harm disorder Ninety-eight patients have seen to have danger and 87 precisely recognized the sort of harm. Sixty-four of the 67 patients with the neighborhood or regional disorder knew this; anyway, 11 of 33 patients with metastatic disease wrongly acknowledged that the dangerous development was confined. Five of the 52 patients treated for treatment thought they were being managed palliative and 16 of the 48 patients encountering palliative treatment acknowledged that the pro's goal was to treat them. Forty of these 48 patients have in a general sense overestimated the likelihood that the treatment will haul out their life. Therefore many times doctors fails to analyze the mistakes of their patients diseases relationship. Only one of the 16 cases in which a patient, who was in treatment, acknowledged that the treatment was made a beeline for recovery, the expert saw that this misguided judgment existed. Disregarding the way that threatening development is an infirmity realized by an uncontrolled division of unpredictable cells into a bit of the body with unsafe advancement or a tumor coming about in light of an uncontrolled division of cells. As shown by [10], threatening development screening is unequivocal to explicit age social affairs and the general proficient will acknowledge which test to perform dependent upon age. People with peril factors for infection in smokers, unreasonable alcohol use, sun presentation, and innate characteristics should be extraordinarily aware of the potential signs of threatening development and be surveyed by a pro if present. The best way to deal with fight threatening developments is by shirking and early disclosure [10]. So, additionally, the uneasiness and bitterness were evaluated using the crisis center anxiety and agony scale at three in time design, 3 months in the wake of beginning treatment, and 1 year after the culmination of treatment in every one of the 18 months advancement. For example, the reviews were managed to all the assumed patients while the two patients and the examiner were unmindful concerning the last investigation [11]. Sociomeasurement and clinical data included age, guidance, matrimonial status, illness organize, and basic treatment. Repeated measure examination was performed to consider anxiety and wretchedness over the assessment time span. Determined to backslide assessment was performed to choose factors that envision apprehension and wretchedness [12]. This above methodology had failed to predict Malignant or Benign because of the gigantic data relationship of the specialist in a facility; thus, AI for desire is the best way for the new data conjecture of like chest sickness estimate and further treatment process.

11.2   R Programming

Here, we are using large data sets of breast cancer from the internet having 569 records stored data in 32 variable attributes of different laboratory's test records and various laboratory records as sample data for analysis.

```
> b=read.csv (file. Choose () , head =TRUE, sep = "," )
> attach(b)
> str (b) 'data.frame': 569 obs. of 32 components:
$ id: int 84.300.903 84.348.301 842.517 842.302 84.358.402 843 ... ..
$ fractal_dimension_worst: num 0.1189 0.089
> head (b) Identification assurance radius_mean texture_mean perimete_
mean smoothness_mean 1 842 302 M 17, 99 10.38 122.80 1001.0 M 2 842
517 20.57 17.77 132.90 1326.0 3 84300903 M 19.69 21.25 130.00 1203.0
4 84348301 M 11.42 20.38 77.58 386.1 5 84358402 M 20.29 14.34 135.10
1297.0 6 843786 M 12.45 5.70 82.57 477.1
```

The address str and head represent the properties of the information indices and the 6 initial records of the information indices.

```
> bc=b[,- 1]
> dim(bc)
[1] 569 31
> bc=as.data.frame(bc)
> bc[is.na(bc)]=0
> head(bc)
```

This determines radius_mean texture_mean perimeter_mean area_ mean smoothness_mean

1 M 17.99 10.38 122.80 1001.0 0.11840
....
6 M 12.45 15.70 82.57 477.1 0.12780

Here, the first id column is just nominal column of records whose analysis is not required, therefore, which could be eliminate from data base and if the records in 569 records na will replaced by 0 is set out to that all records in numeric type.

```
> bc$diagnosisr=factor(bc$ diagnosis,levels =c("M","B"), labels=c
("Meligant", "Benign") )
```

This command will create other attributes at last position with changing M for Malignant, i.e, occurs in cancer and B for Benign, i.e., not occurs.

```
> dim(bc)
[1] 569  32
> table(bc$diagnosisr)
Maligant  Benign
212     357
> round(prop.table(table(bc$radius_mean)) * 100, digits = 1)
To round the records, we use this command
> normalize=function(x){
+ return ((x-min(x))/(max(x)-min(x)))}
> bcc=as.data.frame(lapply(bc[2:30],normalize))
> dim(bcc)
[1] 569  29
```

The normalization is the final stage of data process which is required in many cases because records were largely varied whose percentage is reduction and lies in between −1 to 1 for data analysis whose values were apply to 2 to 30 columns in data frame. The summary command gives max, min, median first and third quartile of records, and dim command display tabular dimensions of records.

```
> summary(bcc$smoothness_mean)
Min. 1st Qu. Median   Mean 3rd Qu.   Max.
0.0000 0.3046 0.3904 0.3948 0.4755 1.0000
> dim(bcc)
[1] 569  29
> set.seed(123)
```

The set seed command is to ensure you always have same random numbers the data are partitioned with 80% for train and 20% for testing purpose and whose labels were stored in its respective labels of first records.

```
> bc_train=bcc[1:455,]# 455 records
> bc_test=bcc[456:569,] # 115 records
> bc_train_labels=bc[1:455,1]
> bc_test_labels=bc[456:569,1]
> bc_train_labels
[1] M M M M M M M M M M M M M M M M M M M M M B B B M M M M
M M M M M M M M M M M B M  .................. [452] M B B B
```

```
Levels: B M
> bc_test_labels
[1] BBBBB B M B M B M B M ..................... BBBBBBMMMMM [114]
B M
Levels: B M
```

There were 455 training data sets and 115 is testing data set of diagnosis variable categorized. The k-nearest neighbor algorithm is available in class library installed.packages("class") and attach to machine. While designing model, the train by test with k factors is set and stored in predt variable.

```
> library(class)
> dim(bc)
[1] 569 32
> predt<-knn(train=bc_train, test=bc_test,cl=bc_train_labels,k=23)
> str(b)
'data.frame':      569 obs. of 32 factors:
$ id : int 842302 842517 84300903 84348301 84358402 843
... ..
> predt
```

[1] BMBBBBBBMMMBMBB[83] B B M B Levels: B M is comparable with trial of 114 records.

```
> table(bc_test_labels)
bc_test_labels
B  M
88 26
> dim(bc)#sqrtof 569=23 k=sqrt(nrow)
[1] 569 32
Calculating k value
> NROW(bc_train_labels)
[1] 455
> NROW(bc_test_labels)
[1] 114
> table(bc_test_labels,predt)
predt
bc_test_labels  B M
B 88  0
M  2 24
```

The table command with two test labels and predict knn model display confusion matrix; there were only two records mismatched occurs.

```
> ((88+24)/114)*100
[1] 98.24561
```

From this, there is a percentage of 98.25 that accurately predicts with 95 confidence intervals whose p value is < 0.5.

```
> library(caret)
> confusionMatrix (table (predt, bc_test_labels))
```

Confusion and statistics matrix

```
bc_test_labels
predt B M
B 88 2
M 0 24
```
Accuracy: zero.9825
95% CI: (0.9381, 0.9979)
No data rate: zero.7719
Value P [Acc> NIR]: nine.116e-11
Kappa: 0.9488
Mcnemar takes a look at P-Value: zero.4795
Sensitivity: 1.0000
Specificity: zero.9231
Pos Pred. Price: zero.9778
Neg Price Pred: one.0000
Prevalence: zero.7719
Detection speed: zero.7719
Prevalence of detection: zero.7895
Balanced precision: zero.9615
'Positive' category: B

The best fit of k could determine using

```
> i=1
> k.optm=1
> for(i in 1:24){
+   predt.mod<-knn(train=bc_train, test=bc_test,cl=bc_train_labels,k=i)
```

```
+  k.optm[i]= 100* sum(bc_test_labels==predt.mod)/
NROW(bc_test_labels)
+  k=i
+  cat(k,'=',k.optm[i],'\n') }
1 = 92.10526
............
7 = 98.24561
8 = 98.24561
..........
11 = 98.24561
............
14 = 98.24561
15 = 97.36842
...............
23 = 98.24561
24 = 98.24561
```

This output displays the accurate percentage while taking different k with its accuracy.

> plot(k.optm,type="b",xlab="k_value", ylab="Accuracy")

From Figure 11.1, the k worth is most elevated at events when k is 7, 11, and 17. In this way, knn calculation of bosom malignant growth could be effectively investigated with 98.25% precision. This is prescribed that when information is in enormous numerical whose huge information could be effectively anticipated when information was in huge enough

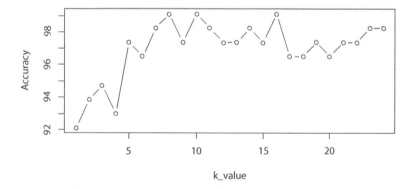

Figure 11.1 K value accuracy plot.

with dissecting different variables utilizing preparing and testing strategies of past records.

11.3   Conclusion

It is an unexpected case if a doctor purposely researches the patient records, dissecting huge ward factors of dependent associations of cancer data prediction. This could be precisely anticipated utilizing AI, forecast with assessing past coordinated records. The screening methodology and alarms were beneficiaries for patient to improve calm mental inconvenience and further treatment of specific disorders; here, the researcher uses 569 crisis center records of breast cancer dangerous development contamination gauge which unequivocally 98.25% records were accurately predicted using machine learning KNN procedure organized and new desire will be successfully foreseen from the subject to records that help prosperity structures advantage direct from the finding and treatment of prostate ailment for further treatment.

References

1. Otte, S., How does Artificial Intelligence work? https://www.innoplexus.com/blog/how-artificial-intelligence-works, 2019.
2. Wang, J., Data extraction and label assignment for web databases, 2003.
3. Weinberger, K. Q., Distance Metric Learning for Large Margin Nearest Neighbor Classification, 2009.
4. Yagyanath, R., Machine Learning Random Forest Cluster Analysis for Large Overfitting Data: Using R Programming. *2019 6th International Conference on Computing for Sustainable Global Development (INDIACom)*, 2020.
5. Brownlee, J., How to Evaluate Machine Learning Algorithms with R, 2016. https://machinelearningmastery.com/evaluate-machine-learning-algorithms-with-r/.
6. Li-Yu Hu, M.-W.H., The distance function effect on k-nearest neighbor classification for medical datasets, in: *Tenth International Symposium on Foundations of Information and Knowledge Systems*, 2018.
7. Khaleel, A., A Weighted Voting of K-Nearest Neighbor Algorithm for Diabetes Mellitus. *Int. J. Comput. Sci. Mobile Compute*, 2017.
8. Ramos, A.B., Analysis of the reliability of the fuzzy scale for assessing the students' learning styles in Mathematics. *16th World Congress of the International Fuzzy Systems Association (IFSA)*, 2015.

9. Mackillop, W.J., Stewart, W. E., Ginsburg, A. D., Stewart, S. S., Cancer patients' perceptions of their disease and its treatment, 1988. https://www.ncbi.nlm.nih.gov/pubmed.

10. Montazeri A., Milroy R., Hole D., McEwen J., Gillis, C.R., Anxiety and depression in patients with lung cancer before and after diagnosis: Findings from a population in Glasgow, Scotland, 2012. https://www.ncbi.nlm.nih.gov/pubmed,.

11. Hoshi, K., Takakura, H., Mitani, Y., Tatsumi, K., Momiyama, N., Ichikawa, Y., Togo, S., Miyagi, T., Kawai, Y., Kogo, Y., Kikuchi, T., Kato, C., Arakawa, T, Uno, S., Cizdziel, P.E., Lezhava, A., Ogawa, N., Hayashizaki, Y., Shimada, H., Rapid Detection of Epidermal Growth Factor Receptor Mutations in Lung Cancer by the SMart-Amplification Process, 2007. https://www.researchgate.net/publication/6054081_Rapid_Detection_of_Epidermal_Growth_Factor_Receptor_Mutations_in_Lung_Cancer_by_the_SMart-Amplification_Process.

12. Lei, S., Y, Noorbatcha, I.A., *Cancer recurrence prediction using machine learning*, Faculty of Engineering, IIUM, Kuala Lumpur, 2014, Malaysia, https://www.academia.edu/11222886/CANCER_RECURRENCE_PREDICTION_USING_MACHINE_LEARNING.

13. https://neurosciencenews.com/?s=computer+program+beats+doctors+at+brain+tumors+from+radiation+changes

12

Need of Ontology-Based Systems in Healthcare System

Tshepiso Larona Mokgetse

Marwadi Education Foundation's Group of Institution, Rajkot, Gujarat, India

Abstract

Originally, ontology comes from the philosophy discipline that deals with the nature and structure of reality. It was initially proposed for the representation of knowledge in a detailed way. Ontology has evolved to the computer and information science perspective. It is a designed artefact representing formally agreed semantics of computer resources.

Ontology concepts are taken and implemented in various computing systems. Health is an important aspect of life which needs attention in providing solutions to the problems at present in order to preserve life. Health is not only infirmity or absence of disease but the state of full mental and physical well-being. There is a lot of health-related information in the health environment available but practical knowledge is lacking.

In terms of healthcare system even with plenty of data, there are no effective analysis tools to discover trends and relationships hidden in the data. It has become a challenge to give affordable good quality services to patients, diagnosing and prescribing the right treatment by healthcare providers. Poor services can lead to tragic consequences, but with help of ontology-based systems, healthcare services can be greatly improved. In this chapter, we will look at the need of ontology in healthcare.

Keywords: Healthcare, ontology, systems, health, data, computer

Email: tmokgetse@gmail.com

Vishal Jain, Ritika Wason, Jyotir Moy Chatterjee and Dac-Nhuong Le (eds.) Ontology-Based Information Retrieval for Healthcare Systems, (257–274) © 2020 Scrivener Publishing LLC

12.1   Introduction

There are many studies, experiments, and research done in healthcare of the past and present diseases being discovered and treated. With all the data, there has been no method to effectively accumulate it all in a systematic and efficient way for healthcare providers to have it easily available to them to help their critical patients. Medical reports of rare diseases are written and end up in research libraries which take a lot of time and effort to find when a hospital from a different country deals with the same diseases, which may lead to death of the patient awaiting treatment. There is a solution which has been proposed to manage with the big capacity of data called ontology.

Ontology can be used as a shared knowledge that will incorporate significant domain models with their relations associated to effectively identify the patient health status [8] for the provision of an intervention that is on time. What will make the system unique is the ability to control and intelligently monitor the actively changing surrounding environment and physiological factors. This will help provide for safe ranges which are adaptive to the patient's vital signs relying of the demographic influences and their bodily movements. The patient's regular exercise, profile, and weather will show the body signs core values. Therefore, misdiagnosis can be avoided with the development of complete knowledge representation and allowing dynamic health disorder reconfiguration.

Each year, there are many diseases which kill people despite the medicine given. There are multiple diagnosis and prevention methods which healthcare providers use in the fight for the continuity of the human race, but they are still powerless to most diseases. An example is chronic diseases which have been estimated to cause 12.6 million deaths per year according to the World Health Organization [7]. With the various chronic diseases, there has been a rise in Chronic Obstructive Pulmonary Disease (COPD).

COPD is a respiratory disorder which causes obstruction in the airway causing difficulty in inhaling to empty out the lungs. In time, the airway becomes permanently blocked which then leads to a premature death of the patient. The World health statistics and Global burden of Diseases 2016 is expecting COPD by 2030 to become the third leading cause of death [11]. There are medical references which can be used to manage COPD patients, a continuous and cyclic healthcare system is needed to monitor and manage the patient. Ontology is one the best solutions which can be provided for managing and monitoring COPD.

Ontology has been implemented in many sectors of the healthcare systems. In the primary healthcare and emergency services, public healthcare specializes healthcare, chronic disease healthcare, and rehabilitation healthcare. This chapter discusses the need of ontology-based system in healthcare systems. It discusses the healthcare systems which have adopted ontology and proposed ontology healthcare systems, the system uses in healthcare specific to patient diseases, and how they have improved patient healthcare. These are some of the sectors that will be discussed in the paper showing the need of ontology in healthcare. The flow of the chapter starts with related work of other researches in regard to ontology in healthcare, brief description of what is ontology, the main section which is the need of ontology in healthcare system, and finally conclusion of the chapter.

12.2 What is Ontology?

Ontology is a term that can be defined as a philosophical term meaning the study of what exists and non-philosophical term meaning what exists specifically within determined field [13], naming parts and grouping without checking if it is real. Aristotle worked on philosophical ontology in defining it in his metaphysics as "the science of being qua being" [14] meaning the study of traits belonging to things based on their nature. It is possible, for example, to study ontology of unicorns and entities that are fictional even if their existence cannot be proven [13], the structure and nature of the entities is defined in relation of common relations and categories. In healthcare, ontology is based on the computational side defined as explicit specifications of conceptualizations.

In AI systems, it is said that what exists will be represented [14]. With computational ontology, the structure of the system is modeled according to the applicable entities and their relations based on the observed appearance useful to its purpose. In a company scenario, the system will be based on the interrelationships of the company's employees. This type of system will use significant entities to organize them to relation that will be characterized by binary and unary predicates.

The hierarchical organization of notions and their relations for the extraction of new knowledge is another way of seeing ontology [6]. Knowledge and information is explicitly provided by ontology and its core applications. Including the collection and extraction of knowledge, it is then shared and reused in a formal presentation among the systems. The information terminology managed, the terms are created, saved, then analyzed and retrieved [10]. After the retrieval, relationships among the entities are demonstrated and the system is ready to be a support system for decision making, interoperability, integrating, and information accessing.

Ontology is a planned system which will be used for the representation on knowledge in a detailed manner and be able to reuse and share the knowledge [2]. The representation is understood by humans and computers are able to process it. This type of representation is needed in healthcare because there is difficulty to easily access data fast in health, this is caused by people internalizing the information they know in their minds and not organizing or documenting it.

The retrieval of information, patient records processing, clinical trial, and management of the hospital can be done by ontology systems. There are developed classification systems to help in retrieval of knowledge that was gathered and saved from research. These systems are failing because information in medicine is more complicated than the area covered by the information systems of the big tank [13]. In the future, more ontology systems can be used because they can handle the big tank of data in medical informatics.

Ontology has different categories in healthcare which are all useful in helping patients. Activity ontology is used to identify the activity that the patient is currently doing to get more accurate data for their medical record. The past activities can also be recorded to keep record of the person who helps in diagnosing the person when they fall sick. The device ontology uses mobile devices to gather and pass data, also biomedical tools that is portable used to monitor patients vital signs. The biomedical features are sensed by blood pressure, pulse oximeter, peak flow, and body thermometer. It contains computer hardware like personal digital assistants and sensors.

Environmental ontology is one of the most important ontology types; factors in the environment play a major role in the health of our body. The most sensitive disease affected by the environment is COPD, patients with COPD are affected by pollution, air, and the weather. Another form of ontology seen as the backbone of the ontologies is the location ontology. It measures the physical parameters varying from outdoor to indoor space. In healthcare, the caregivers need to understand diseases and monitor patient status to provide efficient treatment; this is done by the disease ontology. Disease ontology includes conditions, treatment, disease stage, and features of the disease. The last sub ontology is clinical ontology which deals with patients' medical history to improve performance of healthcare systems.

12.3   Need for Ontology in Healthcare Systems

In this section of the chapter, we will be looking at the need of ontology in healthcare systems based on the different sectors of the healthcare system.

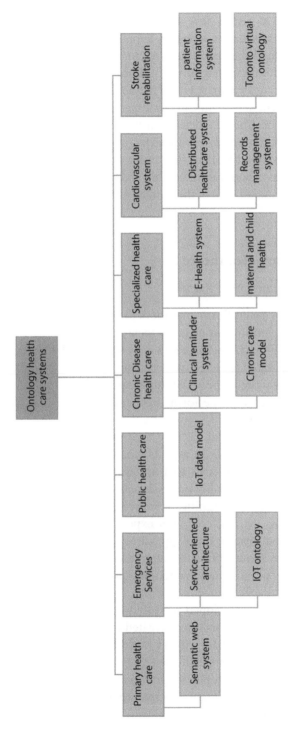

Figure 12.1 Ontology schematic diagram. Copyright 2020 by Tshepiso L. Mokgetse.

Multiple sectors of health have adopted ontology approaches and a brief detail will be discussed as to why they adopted ontology, how it is used, and how it has benefited the healthcare system.

The above schematic diagram is a summary depiction of the types of ontology healthcare system. A few of the healthcare sectors have been chosen which are primary healthcare, emergency services, public healthcare, chronic disease healthcare, specialized healthcare, cardiovascular system, and stroke rehabilitation system. In each sector, there is an ontology healthcare system developed to help healthcare provide the best treatment for patients with those conditions. In this section of the chapter, we will be looking and discussing each of the ontology healthcare system in the named healthcare sector.

12.3.1   Primary Healthcare

12.3.1.1   Semantic Web System

Each day, there is a significant amount of knowledge created by researcher; they conceive scientific expertise associated to problems in healthcare. Adequately using this knowledge is fairly a major task because it is needs to be analyzed, validated for effective detection, and then stored to be shared to help new researches. The semantic-based system ontology knowledge representation is used to perform these tasks for the Brazilian primary healthcare program [2].

The government of Brazil has invested in their primary healthcare program [2] to help its people in aspects where traditional programs could not achieve by providing costs that are low and high quality services. It was observed that for health professionals with experience in computers, ontology served as a significant source of related knowledge. For the health professions with no computer experience, they were trained using ontology with the Protégé ontology editor (http://protege.stanford.edu/), though there we some difficulties after the training. The tool is able to describe the flow of information and main processes based on the conceptual framework.

A web system was developed with Python and Django [2] after use of the Protégé ontology editor. It was created for routine support for health professionals in the Brazilian primary healthcare program; it was no effective enough. Development of the ontology representation in a semantic web system was then developed to function as a base for the health professionals as a source of information to treat their patients and in controlling their routine activities.

The system focuses more on families and not individuals, organizing it in as multidisciplinary family health teams made by the health professions like social workers, physicians, dentists, and nurses. With the evolution of computing technology, there is still a huge potential to further improve the primary care in terms of patient to doctor communication, fast access to trustworthy medical information, and sharing of information among health professions around the world and not constricted to hospitals in certain countries.

There is need for better primary healthcare data throw ontology creating a system based on ontology and not just a representation using ontology. SemanticPHC is a web system proposed to be developed with ontology OntoPHC to improve primary healthcare. OntoPHC is planned to show definitive roles, procedures, legal terms, and relationships that affect primary healthcare domain in Brazil [2].

OntoPHC ontology was created according to the bottom-up strategy suggested by Van der Vet [2]. It is an effective strategy that gives ontologies that are well-structured. The methodology uses set of terms that can specifically recognize general concepts. In return, the approach results in a broader vision of the ontology initial terms. The downside is that the ontology is developed in Portuguese to cater more for the Brazilian health professionals. It needs to be translated to English and further analyzed by other computer and ontology developers to help more people in the world.

12.3.2   Emergency Services

One of the most critical sectors of the health sector is the emergency service unit. It provides emergency medical services (EMS) and it is dedicated to providing patients with out of the hospital medical care and transportation of the patient to definitive care. They are the first correspondence of patients which have critical conditions and need fast medical help. A service-oriented architecture (SOA) can be used to help EMS respond and treat critical patients.

12.3.2.1   Service-Oriented Architecture

The creation of new and better opportunities to build applications for the provision of enterprise services for an effective, highly dynamic, and diverse environment scenario has emerged. This is because computer technology and medical care advances have expanded their parameters in terms of traditional domains in recent decades. Involvement of embedded devices and diverse professions brings about multiple factors like complex, expensive, and competitive healthcare systems that are IT based.

There have been restrictions of perfect exchange, reuse, and integration across multiple systems of information. This has been caused by information management standards, various programming languages, and platforms that have emerged [3]. Taking this into account, SOA is a methodology that is more advanced and is used for the development of distributed, cost effective, loosely coupled, and dynamic applications.

SOA works with services together with ontology handling heterogeneity and complex issues. With the aid of the domain ontology that has been developed, the healthcare system issues can be effectively handled during emergencies. There is a development process of the ontology system which is followed to carry out the processes.

The first process is the requirements analysis stage in which relationships, concepts, axioms, and attributes are being identified. After identification is the design stage where a conceptual model that is stable is defined looking a bunch of tasks for the step-by-step ontology complexity increase. When the design is verified and complete, the development has to begin. For the development stage, the ontology needs to formalize in order to do ontology updating in accordance with the domain concepts to help with the maintenance stage, an appropriate ontology language must be used. When it is successful in the testing stage, then it can be implemented and used.

Though the ontology system will be effective, it will not be able to cover all aspects of the medical services that are covers in EMS. These include patient diagnosis, assisting devices, patient care, and administrative decisions; there are many domains to be covered and it will not be possible for one ontology to cover all of them. The SOA ontology will be limited to device to actor knowledge sharing for the diagnosis process [3]. The patient condition will be studied by the actors with assistance from the device, using expertise data to help them.

This type of ontology allows a first of its kind formal knowledge representation. It is a step toward efficient communication and sharing between the actors and devices. When the SOA ontology was being developed, an interview of five paramedical staff experts [3] was conducted and some papers and manuals were reviews for information extraction.

12.3.2.2   IOT Ontology

For multiple devices to connect across the world, Internet of things (IOT) is used. This type of technology will be able to show specific security and privacy risks in devices. At the fast growing rate IOT technology, there has been predictions of new medical treatments and drugs discovered [4].

It will effectively increase the healthcare quality provided with the potential high speed, flexibility, low cost, and adaptability features.

IOT using the internet gets interconnected by multiple devices and can access information in large scales. This is why is it used is healthcare, to be able to access various information quickly from large volumes of data stored. It overcomes the problem of SOA ontology problem of not being able to store large volume of information in EMSs. The ontology-based EMS system integrates, interoperates, and collects IOT data, to allow for fast decision making in emergent situations. In IOT ontology, decision support system (DSS) is used for the decision-making process [4].

Doctors, nurses, and patient records are retrieved through ontology web ontology language (OWL) format after being saved in the IOT database in EMS. The records saved in the database are classified using meta data modeling. The model is then used for mapping input data with the output data. The meta data model works well because it is able to handle incomplete data and noise that occurs in ontology data. The model has shown to be reliable, so IOT ontology can be used as the backbone of healthcare system in sharing of information.

12.3.3   Public Healthcare

12.3.3.1   IOT Data Model

In public healthcare, delivering of information to doctors and nurses during an emergency is difficult and deadly to patients. Lack of good quality healthcare systems is the cause of this problem. With the IoT data model, there can be a major improvement in the healthcare quality. There are instances where patient health records and doctor details are stored in different databases, locations, and hospitals, making it difficult for the records to be easily collected when needed. This is why ontology was introduced in public healthcare, a resource model to locate and fetch clinical records in various hospitals information systems is used with ontology content accessing.

The process starts by collecting the patient's information and storing it in the IOT data model. Each patient's clinic record given a unique URL address defined as a resource. Another clinic with a similar patient, patient with same disease or signs and symptoms, is collected also to make a combinational resource. The information in the data model will be given access to physicians whom have been given permission.

When given permission the physician will be able to access the system through the internet at any different hospital they may be at. Information retrieval will be more convenient and faster depending on the hospitals internet connectivity. This accessibility will help doctors access patients records even from a different hospital to treat another patient with similar conditions, the doctors will also be able to add more helpful information regarding the treatment of the patient and it will be distributed so other physicians may also see it across the world. Patients can also gain an advantage from the model by checking the availability of doctors and equipment at their local hospitals. The resource model can also help patients find doctors that treat rare diseases and see their treatment plans and success rate before going to them.

With the proposed system ontology-based IoT introduced to medical science, there is hope that death rate will reduce [4]. Public healthcare services will improve. The doctor's decision-making process will be easier; once they know about the sickness, they build the ontology treatment plan shortening the treatment time. The system will also reduce time taken by doctor asking for a consultation from an expert doctor, they will be able to get the expert information from the system. Details of diseases like causes, symptoms, effects, and treatment will all be constructed in ontology format for easy access and understanding.

12.3.4 Chronic Disease Healthcare

Chronic diseases are the most critical conditions that need healthcare providers that are well informed and knowledgeable to properly take care of the patient. To improve the quality of healthcare for the patients, clinical information and DSSs have been developed in support of the chronic care ontology-based knowledge acquisition together with the modeling based on knowledge engineering approach to effectively capture specialist experts' opinions to form the clinical practice guidelines. The framework will focus on the creation of healthcare ontology and clinical reminder system to link the guideline knowledge and registries of the patient in proving evidenced-based healthcare.

12.3.4.1 Clinical Reminder System

The various technologies, lack of functionality, no reuse, and data that are redundant are some of the challenges of information systems in healthcare. The clinical environment has adopted web service architecture with ontology to implement a clinical reminder system to be used for medical knowledge services [9]. It provides a framework and implantation that will encourage data reuse, good functionality, promote integration, and interoperability to be applied in the domain of healthcare.

A use case diagram is used to depict how the clinical reminder knowledge service will work. The model has two main actors, the client system and the doctor. The client system is a representation of the various hospitals with patient database and the doctor comes from the client side. There are four use cases in the system. The register patient data use case, remind examination date use case, get recommendation use case, and the final one is alert for abnormal values use case.

Both the system can use the use cases. The client system uses register patient data after authenticating and connecting to the model, after diagnosis, treatment plan, and examinations are done of the patient, the details are then recorded in the model. The model will analyze the record and give a recommendation of the examination date and results based on the information given. Based on the results, the model will give recommendation messages for the patient and continue further analyzing the data with the information in the model [9]. At the end, the client and doctor will get alerts if there are any abnormal values in the results. The difference between the client and doctor is that the client can get results from the knowledge service and the doctor is able to make editions and updates like modify and adjust the knowledge.

12.3.4.2   Chronic Care Model

Chronic disease is a condition which usually requires constant activities of the healthcare provider and patient in their treatment. Chronic illnesses like hypertension, diabetes, cancer, and heart diseases are big problems in healthcare. They need to be given special attention and treatment to avoid fatal endings for the patients. The treatments usually need a lot of planning and management to keep the patient functioning in everyday life and alive. It is a difficult task but the Chronic Care Model (CCM) has been created [5] to help in the improvement of the patients with chronic conditions quality of life.

To achieve high quality results of chronic care, the models objective is to produce informed healthcare providers and patients with much needed knowledge. This can be done by meeting the components of improving chronic care, clinical information, and DSS. This can only be successful if the knowledge fed to model is reliable and relevant to assist the healthcare workers.

The clinical information system emphases on information management system utilization in support of the healthcare process. The healthcare process will include creating a registry for patients, reminders that are automatic to prevent mal-practice, alerts to monitor performance improvement of the care system and practice team. A diabetes healthcare knowledge management project is underway to highlight the need for the support of diabetes system process [5]. The clinical practice guidelines in place should have the knowledge taken and recorded in the model to help the decision making process of doctors and nurses.

The model can be integrated with the hospitals existing database to make the transition easy and have the already existing hospital records stored for future use. The data and model can then be used for automatic reminders about routine checkups, treatments, and examination of the patient receives based on the recommended medical guideline. The patients can monitor their health better also and improve how they take of themselves.

With the decision support component, the focus is more on implanting evidence-based procedures like the clinical practice guidelines in their daily routine clinical practice. It is reliable because it is only integrated with specialists in the chronic illnesses and based on research studies that have the carried out, proven, and produced positive results [5]. We call this evidence-based medicine.

The creators of the CCM ontology recommend the improvement of components that are related together with decision support and clinical information, namely, healthcare organization, self-management support, delivery system redesign, community resources, and clinical information system [5]. They believe that a more effective chronic management system can be achieved.

12.3.5   Specialized Healthcare

12.3.5.1   E-Health Record System

The Electronic Health Record (EHR) system will help the specialized healthcare by providing clinical data analysis in an easier manner. EHR will improve the doctor to patient time; the doctor will take less time diagnosing the patient, thus more time providing the treatment and making the patient comfortable with no rush. Physicians and specialists will form a circle of care where they share information and provide updates to the e-healthcare DSS.

The e-health DSS uses a centralized server. It is a server client type of system used in different zones [7]. It is supported in smart phones, teleconsultation, local health professions, telemedicine, non-government organization, e-medical colleges, computer literature, e-health management information system, and private sectors related to ICT healthcare.

There are multiple benefits of EHR ontology-based knowledge in healthcare. The system allows for patients to get better healthcare and medical mistakes are avoided. Patient involvement in their treatment is achieved because of the easily available information. There are fewer burdens of diseases on the society. Unfair and unlawful practices can be detected easier. Ultimately, secondary and tertiary care will be strengthened.

With diagnostics and treatment plans in place to go over and confirm drug prescription, errors will be avoided. Duplication of tests and prescriptions will not happen anymore with the system in place showing patient records. Unnecessary test will be avoided with doctors searching for the symptoms in the EHR, then carrying out the test consistent with the results of the systems. More importantly waiting time for patients will be driven way down. In the end, lives will be saved and a great deal of money will be saved.

Ontologies are for representation of things, in healthcare it is the disease and the patient. Proving what is true regardless of being known in the clinic. Definitive communication of detailed and complex medical conceptions is a major feature in the EHR information system [7]. It works by interactions between various agents taking place sharing their results. The results must be shared in clear and understandable medical terminology.

It is not easy to create these types of ontologies meeting the needs of all users involved [12]. They should be sufficient universal enough to achieve the agreement of users in the wide community. Not only that, but the ontology should be concrete enough to show huge diverse possible model concepts.

The healthcare ontology engineering is done manually with the help of medical specialist providing the reliable and useful medical knowledge. The knowledge engineers get the provided knowledge and formalize it. There are some tedious and long processes in the development phase which causes delays in launching the ontology results. This is because it is required to get an agreement translating the knowledge shared to the world model by the medical community, medical disagreements can hamper formalizing the explicit knowledge representation.

12.3.5.2 Maternal and Child Health

Users and caregivers can access health data anyway and anytime with the e-healthcare ontology system. The user can use their smart phone, smart office, smart home, and smart care for access no matter where they are. This is helpful for maternal and child healthcare. Patients will have more information about their health even when there are not at the hospital [10]. It is difficult for mothers and children to travel, especially new born babies. With this e-system they will not have to put their children in health risks of infections by going to the hospital unnecessarily.

Communication and internet technologies are used by patients to access e-healthcare DSSs [7]. They are used to help mothers manage health, deliver, account for, and arrange information in the healthcare system that can be seen and monitored by their doctor. The system aids patients to help and educate themselves in health-related matters with flexibility.

12.3.6 Cardiovascular System

12.3.6.1 Distributed Healthcare System

Distributed software system is used to manage health records of patients assuring interactive and remote medical services are accessible to those in need. The system had a problem of difficult relationships among medical concepts, like medication and symptoms, including a form of intelligence in the software an ontology-based approach was used to solve the problem [5]. The ontology-based approach used with other accepted medical standards assured transparent and interoperability exchange of data among the multiple healthcare applications mainly the cardiovascular systems.

The technology supports access with ease to medical services, diagnoses that is accurate and improved data processing of medical records. The growth of deadly and chronic diseases of the heart calls for integration of multiple medical services and its applications with no limits to regional distribution, certain medical domains, and ownership of medical records [5]. A patient suffering from a cardiovascular disease should be able to gain access to medical services transparently anywhere and anytime because their life depends on it.

Patients with heart conditions should be able to travel seamlessly with the comfort that their medical records can be accessed by medical entities such as hospital, physician, and laboratory at their destination. In the case of a health scare, the physician will be access the current treatment plan of the patient and quickly treat them, saving time of sending them back to their home country for treatment. The representation of these entities, thoughts, and events are done by the ontology-based approach together with its relations and properties as a way of knowledge representation for the world of medical healthcare system devoted to cardiovascular disease.

12.3.6.2 Records Management System

The ontology for cardiology domain implemented here motivated by the base knowledge in cardio departments to help in the management of patients with heart failure. The ontology has a role of representing

knowledge, with domain concepts and patient detailed knowledge. http://
lis.irb.hr/heartfaid/ontology/ shows a version of the heart failure ontology developed [5]. The choices and tasks which are suitable for healthcare
results and cost control are indicated as a goal of the medical plans made.
The ontology medical plans where represented theoretically with the use
of process specification language. The process specification ontology is
merged with heart failure ontology of the healthcare system.

12.3.7   Stroke Rehabilitation

Most of the stroke survivors suffer from the parts of the upper limb being
more affected. To encourage quick recovery of the upper limbs, an early
well-organized treatment plan should be implemented. Experts in stroke
rehabilitation have the duty of providing detailed assessments of the recovery process of stoke patients. Information gathered is then stored and managed in the patient information system together with an ontology-based
approach.

12.3.7.1   Patient Information System

The patient information system (PIS) is used to record information and
results of patient assessments. The PIS used presently stores the patient
data in relational databases [1]. There are disadvantages to using relational
databases mainly that a request query is made to show results and a schema
is the only representation used to show semantic database description.
These advantages brought about the use of ontologies as a relational database alternative. The performance of PIS should be improved. The same
ontology-based system is used in rehabilitation centers to help specialists
manage and assess patient records.

Before information is used in ontology, it goes through a verification
process by specialist domains. After confirmation, it can be implemented
and used by various parties accessing the system. Ontologies also help in
the PIS design with the provision of complete model of knowledge and the
processes needed in delivery of healthcare methodology in order to implement the ontology in PIS [1].

12.3.7.2   Toronto Virtual System

PIS employ enterprise ontology to create the Toronto virtual enterprise
ontology [1]. This ontology is not a large-scale ontology like most of the
systems developed; it is a small-scale to medium-scale ontology. It is good

because there is development reduction effort and time of the PIS specifications. The process of the methodology is in four stages. Each of the stages in the development of the ontology is useful for the start of the next stage. First is the requirement analysis, where the developing ontology needs are analyzed.

The next stage is ontology development using version 5.2.0 Protégé [1]. Standford center for BioMedical Informatics Research created the open source Protégé [1]. An application model using the ontology knowledge will be built from the Protégé using the ontology web language. It will make it easy and efficient to access and edit the ontology already existing. The third stage is the implementation stage where the user interface of the system will be created for testing. The developed PIS prototype system will be tested by various users.

The results expected should be users' query being sent in SPARQL form. The verification process of the system will follow to test usability and validity of the objectives from the analysis of the first stage. The PIS system is an application that is web-based developed in JavaScript and PHP programming language and the ontology information is accessed through RDF/XML format. The last stage is the evaluation and maintenance stage, the last phases of perfection of the ontology data usability with the PIS prototype is tested and perfected to be deployed.

12.4 Conclusion

Ontology is important in healthcare as proven by the systems that have already been developed and running in hospitals. That is why there are still more healthcare systems that have been proposed and developed with the adoption of ontology-based approaches. The systems will benefit both the medical entities and patients all over the world, thus improving the quality of life and reducing death rate.

References

1. Afandi, Radhi Rafiee et al., Ontology Development in Patients Information System for Stroke Rehabilitation, vol. 2137, p. paper 15, ICBO Semantic Scholar, Faculty of Science and Technology, Universiti Sains Islam Malaysia, Negeri Sembilan, Malaysia Medicine, Computer Science, 2017.
2. Moraes, Eduardo C., Brito, Kellyton, Meira, Silvio, OntoPHC: An ontology applied for primary health care, vol. 9, pp. 1543–1552, Elsevier Ltd, Instituto Federal de Alagoas IFAL - Maceió-AL Brazil, Procedia Computer Science, 2012.

3. Zeshan, Furkh and Mohamada, Radziah, *Medical Ontology in the Dynamic Healthcare Environment*, vol. 10, pp. 340–348, Elsevier Ltd, Department of Software Engineering, Faculty of Computer Science and Information Systems, Universiti Teknologi Malaysia (UTM), 81310 Skudai, Johor, Malaysia, Procedia Computer Science, 2012.

4. Vinoth, Abinaya, Kumar, Swathika, *Ontology based Public Healthcare System in Internet of Things (IoT)*, vol. 50, pp. 99–102, Elsevier Ltd, Mepco Schlenk Engineering College, Sivakasi and 626124, India, Procedia Computer Science, 2015.

5. Cenan, Calin *et al.*, *Ontology-Based Distributed Health Record Management System*, Dept. of Computer Science, Technical University of Cluj Napoca, Calin.Cenan@cs.utcluj.ro Medical Pharmacy University Cluj-Napoca, 411-4244-2577-8, 2008.

6. Meraji, Marziye *et al.*, Designing an Ontology-based Health Information System: A systematic Approach. *Life Sci. J.*, vol. 10, pp. 735–740, 2013.

7. Vyas, Nitesh and Pal, P.R., E-Healthcare Decision Support System based on Ontology Learning: A Conceptual Model. *Int. J. Comput. Appl.*, 59, 9, 12–16, December 2012. Udaipur, Rajasthan, India.

8. Poli, Roberto, Healy, Michael, Kameas, Achilles, *Theory and Applications of Ontology: Computer Applications*, Springer Science+Business Media B.V, Springer Dordrecht Heidelberg London New York, chp. 11, 2010.

9. BURANARACH, Marut *et al.*, *Design and Implementation of an Ontology-based Clinical Reminder System to Support Chronic Disease Healthcare*, vol. E85-A/B/C/D, p. 16, National Electronics and Computer Technology Center, The Institute of Electronics, Information and Communication Engineers, Thailand, May 2014.

10. Dung, Tran Quoc and Kameyama, Wataru, *Ontology-Based Information Extraction and Information Retrieval in Health Care Domain*, Springer-Verlag, Berlin Heidelberg, 2007.

11. Ajami, Hicham and Mcheick, Hamid, *Ontology-Based Model to Support Ubiquitous Healthcare Systems for COPD Patients*, vol. 2, Electronics, University of Québec at Chicoutimi; Chicoutimi, QC G7H 2B1, Canada, December 2018.

12. Abburu, Sunitha and Golla, Suresh Babu, Ontology-Driven Knowledge-Based Health-Care System an Emerging Area-Challenges and Opportunities-Indian Scenario. *Int. Arch. Photogramm. Remote Sens. Spatial Inf. Sci.*, XL-8, 239–246, 2014. Hyderabad, India.

13. Smith, Barry, Ontology and Information Systems, in: *Blackwell Guide to the Philosophy of Computing and Information*, L. Floridi (Ed.), pp. 155–166, Blackwell, Oxford, 2003.

14. Staab, Steffen, *What Is an Ontology*, Springer-Verlag, Berlin Heidelberg, 2009.

13

Exploration of Information Retrieval Approaches With Focus on Medical Information Retrieval

Mamata Rath[1*] and Jyotir Moy Chatterjee[2]

[1]School of Management (IT), Birla Global University, India
[2]Department of IT, Lord Buddha Education Foundation, Kathmandu, Nepal

Abstract

Utilization of advanced techniques regarding information retrieval in health care related applications and medicinal services incorporates emergency Hospital Management System, Electronic Medical Record (EMR), Automated Patient Record, medical finding frameworks, medical picture frameworks, etc. In spite of the fact that the elements of the frameworks referenced here are altogether different, the principle reasons for improving the proficiency and adequacy in medical practices are the equivalent. In the health check diagnosis framework, the attention is on the help of diagnosis and handling. It generally identified with the methods of computerized reasoning. Information retrieval in Health Care applications is the system of identifying relevant information and to recover it through specific procedures from stored system. These technique are used in many differentiated applications that deal with subjective intelligence. Applications based on Information retrieval generates incite identified with various issues, for example, in technology domain, the conceivably sudden size changes of the objectives as they approach the sensor. The present chapter examines and investigates the difficulties related with this new pattern of Information retrieval utilizing psychological insightful techniques with focus on medical sectors.

Keywords: Information retrieval, cognitive dynamic systems, cognitive informatics, orthogonal amplitude modulation

Corresponding author: mamata.rath200@gmail.com

Vishal Jain, Ritika Wason, Jyotir Moy Chatterjee and Dac-Nhuong Le (eds.) Ontology-Based Information Retrieval for Healthcare Systems, (275–292) © 2020 Scrivener Publishing LLC

13.1 Introduction

The improvement of technology and its related advancement has modified the whole presence of people together with, clearly, therapeutic, and restorative administrations rehearses. The utilization of information advancement in prescription and restorative administrations fuses crisis facility information system, electronic medical record (EMR), electronic patient record (EPR), therapeutic finding structures, therapeutic picture systems, and so on. Disregarding the way that the components of the systems referenced above are out and out various, the standard explanations behind improving the capability and sufficiency in restorative practices are the proportionate. In the restorative determination structure, the consideration is on the support of conclusion and management. It is by and large related to the strategies for electronic thinking, for instance, ace structure, cushy, regular lingos, and neural framework. As demonstrated by the technique of inducing, medicinal determination structures can be disengaged into regulation or closeness based. The two sorts of structures need to apply the medicinal data existed in HIS (Hospital Information System), EMR, or EPR in the time of rules or recuperation of tantamount therapeutic cases. In any case, there exist issues in the using of the present data for building therapeutic conclusion systems. In any case, restorative records are taken care of by dissimilar EMR or EPR structures controlled by different medicinal foundations and the kinds of the therapeutic accounts are one of a kind according to one association to another. Along these lines, utilization of the medicinal records asserted by different therapeutic establishments isn't straightforward.

The procedure of information recovery is normally an unending action during which inquire about issues are refined, utilizing different data stores, applying data repossession systems, and utilizing right mining administrations, and afterward, legitimate assessment methods are utilized for legitimacy of the yield. Data retrieval framework has offered ascend to imaginative thought in innovative work utilizing no-nonsense procedures just as delicate registering techniques to satisfy the necessities. The worldview of cognitive dynamic systems (CDSs) can give a system under which a consistently learning cognitive module can be structured. Specifically, CDS hypothesis portrays a fundamental jargon of parts that can be utilized as the establishing squares of a module competent to take in social standards from persistent dynamic collaborations with nature. This quality is the major to manage dynamic circumstances. A general CDS-based methodology following methodology has been arranged where a CDS-propelled configuration can prompt the self-versatility of a Bayesian tracker in melding heterogeneous item that includes defeating size change issues. The test results on infrared arrangements show how the proposed system can beat other existing far article following techniques. Typically, the unit for a positioning model in a Web IR framework is a Web page, which is, now and again, only a data section.

A bigger unit considering the linkage data might be wanted to decrease the cognitive over-burden for clients to distinguish the total data from the interconnected Web. Positioning models are wanted to quantify the significance of the entire Web website where a few delineations are made to show the thought during reenactment and give confirmations to demonstrate its adequacy. Usage of the term "cognitive" refers to the point of view toward mindfulness or learning. Regarding Cognitive Science, it gives connection between data handling, conceptualization of the assets, perceptual abilities, and points identified with the cognitive brain science. By recovering data that are dependent on cognitive ideas, procedure, and strategies, one can speak to the present client's data need, their concern state and space work, or zone of enthusiasm for the framework of structure and losses. Figure 13.1 displays information retrieval cycle. This poly-authentic methodology prompts cognitive procedure which is performing various tasks in the method for recognition, consideration, translation, comprehension, and recognition of human conduct connection. With

Figure 13.1 Information retrieval cycle.

the assistance of execution systems of pertinence criticism which approve and give unwavering quality measurements to compute client conduct utilizing learning area perception, Training structures give clients how to continue in looking and recovering data. Cognitive Informatics (CI) was acquired from the field of cognitive science and informatics. CI gives the calculated hypotheses and numerical calculations which establishes the framework for learning-based science and building like mechanical, electrical, gadgets, and PC designing. It structures computational frameworks which are proficient enough to bring together the handled data and examples that clarify the structure and association of open data. CI goal is to actualize designing arrangements like content, information mining and web, open robots, sight and sound, multimodal intelligent frameworks, and continuous or virtual condition with the end goal of conveyed community work.

13.1.1   Machine Learning-Based Medical Information System

Artificial Intelligence (AI)–based Medical Information Retrieval System (IRS) is an achievement in medicinal improvement. The same number of fields progress with the help for cognitive registering, the field for social insurance is additionally adjusting, giving numerous advantages to all clients. Be that as it may, progressions right now ruined by a few difficulties, for example, the void between client questions and the information base, inquiry jumbles, and range for area information in clients has been delineated by A. Gudivada *et al.* [12]. Existing approaches just as existing genuine applications that are utilized in the medicinal field today have been inspected by inquire about specialists right now. Inquiries investigating explicit difficulties and methods that can be utilized to beat these hindrances are explicitly identified with cognitive figuring in the medicinal area. Future data recovery (IR) models that can be customized explicitly for restoratively concentrated applications which can deal with enormous sums for information are investigated too. Uses of IR incorporate artificial resistant frameworks, transformative calculation, grid variable-based math, question handling, and set hypothesis.

13.1.2   Cognitive Information Retrieval

Cognitive Information Retrieval (CIR) is an interdisciplinary territory of concentrate that incorporates inquires from data science to cognitive science which collaborates with the human PC based on human elements. CIR is conceptualized as intricate human data related human PC connection forms that are installed inside a person's regular social and life setting. CIR is a significant piece of the human data condition and basic to the improvement of new ways to deal with the structure of Web and IR frameworks. By and by, Information Retrieval (IR) inquires begin from three separate fields: data science, software engineering, and commitments from the field of sociology. However, the three networks don't generally speak with one another and utilize various approaches. The creators inspect these various philosophies regarding needy, autonomous, and controlled for factors. As IR serves the objectives of looking for data which basically serves the objectives of the client's work undertaking (or other intrigue), and the creators propose a conceivable region of compromise in the specific circumstance or assignment for the client's data search.

13.2 Review of Literature

Z. Hu, Y *et al.* [11] present cognitive protected structure based co-evolutionary information retrieval form. The existent models for data recovery (IR) center around the connection between file terms and records. Be that as it may, the present recovery necessities request fragile control to demonstrate the client inclinations and input. Also, the accurate outcomes are underlined for data blast. Enlivened by the support capacity and mould in insusceptible framework, an original IR model is proposed dependent on cognitive intelligence framework (CIS). These create connection among terms and archives, the separation and comparability connections among terms. The question pattern, and criticism message animate the cytokine arrange that is an executable formation to for IR. Co-developmental components are additionally intended to empower the rise highlights for the sculpt enlivened by resistant framework. A cognitive control inspired approach to object tracking has been planned by Mazzu *et al.* [2]. Under a following system, the definition for the objective state is the essential advance for programmed understanding for dynamic scenes. All the more explicitly, far article following raises moves identified with the possible sudden size changes for the objectives as they approach the sensor. If not dealt with, size changes can present overwhelming issues in information affiliation and position estimation. This is the reason why flexibility and mindfulness for a following module are alluring highlights. The worldview for intellectual unique frameworks (CDSs) can give a system under which a consistently learning subjective module can be planned. Specifically, CDS hypothesis portrays an essential vocabulary for segments that can be utilized as the establishing hinders for a module able to take in conduct rules from constant dynamic collaborations with nature. This quality is the central to manage dynamic circumstances. A general CDS-based way to deal with following has been proposed. It shows such a CDS propelled configuration can prompt the self-versatility for a Bayesian tracker in melding heterogeneous article highlights, beating size modification issues. The test outputs on infrared arrangements show how the proposed system can beat other existing far article following techniques.

M. N. Ahmedabadi *et al.* [7] present information-based extraction for area expertise of alliance in learning. Utilizing each other's information and skill in realizing what we call collaboration in learning,,which is one for the major existing techniques to diminish the number for learning preliminaries, which is very urgent for genuine applications. In arranged frameworks, robots become master in various territories due to being presented to various circumstances and undertakings. As an outcome, Area for Expertise (AOE) for different specialists must be distinguished before utilizing their insight, particularly when the traded information isn't extract, and basic data trade may bring about wrong learning, which is the situation for Q learning operators. Another methodology has been presented for extraction for AOE for specialists for collaboration in getting the hang of utilizing their Q tables. The assessing robot utilizes a conduct measure to assess itself, so as to locate a set for states it is master in. That set is utilized, at that point, alongside a Q table–based component for extraction for zones for ability for different robots by methods for a classifier. Separated regions are converged in the last stage. This procedure is tried both in broad recreations and in genuine trials utilizing portable robots. The outcomes show viability for the presented methodology, both in exact extraction for zones for aptitude and expanding the quality for the consolidated information, notwithstanding when there are vulnerability and automation associating in the application and the robot. D. Zellh *et al.* (2010) introduced inductive user preference manipulation for multimedia retrieval. So as to empower clients to inquiry archives concurring their individual inclinations, another strategy of client cooperation model structures an augmentation for the outstanding importance criticism approach. The presented methodology is using in part requested sets to express quality relations between result reports, for example, the client's inclination, straightforwardly on test reports from the record set. Henceforth, the displayed framework underpins clients for faring a natural inclination definition which is known from every day life: the unconstrained quality judgment between items without more profound information for basic properties. This encourages the collaboration with the exhibited framework as no new cognitive weights are brought into the inquiry procedure. In light of these inclinations, an AI calculation finishes up a proper inquiry by means of inductive thinking so as to recover progressively pertinent reports in an iterative way. To finish up with, an underlying model is talked about.

Assistive innovation has not yet achieved an adequate level for accomplishment in tending to the requirements for the old to explore securely, easily, smoothly, and autonomously. Table 13.1 provides literature study and details of research information in a systematic order.

Figure 13.2 displays a framework proposed by Chou *et al.* [25] for health IR. Here, the area of information saver is told to gather the client's info and pertinence response.

The essential association of this exploration is the display of a strategy which is not quite the same as customary methodology in determination and recuperating support. This technique could overcome the trouble of framework usage prerequisite on the estimation of information group/information structure which normally exists as free arrangement/unstructured in the genuine earth. Another bit of leeway of this technique is that the information on determination and behavior to be applied could be stayed up with the latest. Subsequently, the anticipated technique could be one of the choices in the various endeavors attempted to finding and treatment support. F. W. Adams *et al.* [17] present a parallel system for visual discernment. The creators portray a parallel dynamical framework intended to coordinate model-based and information-driven ways to deal with picture acknowledgment in a neural system and concentrate one segment for the framework in detail. That segment is the interpretation invariant system for probabilistic cell automata (PCA), which joins finder yields and altogether performs improvement and acknowledgment capacities. Acknowledgment is a novel application for the PCA. Given a model for the objective item, conditions on the PCA loads are acquired which must be fulfilled for article upgrade and clamor dismissal to happen, and designed loads are built. For further refinement for the loads, a preparation calculation got from ideal control hypothesis is proposed. Framework activity is represented with models got from visual, infrared, and laser radar imagery.

13.3   Cognitive Methods of IR

Data Recovery Model

Y. Motomura *et al.* [20] present generative client models for versatile data recovery. For data recovery (IR) undertakings, client models are utilized to gauge client's actual goal and request. Lamentably, most client models are

Table 13.1 Research review and details.

Year	Author details	Research topic
2019	M. Hashemzadeh *et al.* [9]	Develop generalization in the subspaces for quicker model-based reinforcement education
2018	A. Gudivada *et al.* [12]	A narrative review on machine education–based medical data retrieval systems
2018	R. Wen *et al.* [19]	A model for music perceptual theory-ased on Markov chains
2018	L. Li; Q *et al.* [4]	A probabilistic model for social working memory for information retrieval in social interactions
2016	A. Mazzu *et al.* [2]	A Intelligence and cognitive based management information retrieval approach to object tracking
2016	S. B. Eryilmaz *et al.* [14]	Neuromorphic architectures with electronic synapses
2016	F. Cruz *et al.* [13]	Teaching agents with communication reinforcement erudition and contextual significance
2016	M. E. Ravinandan *et al.* [1]	Adaptive path exploration and intelligence and cognitive–based map generation using swarm intelligence
2015	L. Maatougui *et al.* [3]	Spectrum sensing applied to information retrieval system
2014	B. Mustapha *et al.* [16]	Micro-management–based information retrieval obstacle detection system for the elderly
2010	D. Zellhofer *et al.* [18]	Inductive user preference manipulation for multimedia retrieval
2008	Z. Hu; Y *et al.* [11]	Intelligence and cognitive-based resistant system-based co-evolutionary data retrieval mould

(Continued)

Table 13.1 Research review and details. (*Continued*)

Year	Author details	Research topic
2006	A. R. Mehrabian *et al.* [10]	Automatic tuning for decentralized management by swarm intelligence
2003	C. Ding *et al.* [8]	A generalized site ranking model for Web
2003	D. A. Fay *et al.* [6]	Multi-sensor and spectral image fusion and mining: from neural systems to applications
2000	Y. Motomura *et al.* [20]	Generative user models for adaptive information retrieval
1992	F. W. Adams *et al.* [17]	A parallel network for visual cognition
2007	A. H. Jamalian *et al.* [15]	Learning automata oriented algorithm to calculate mobility model

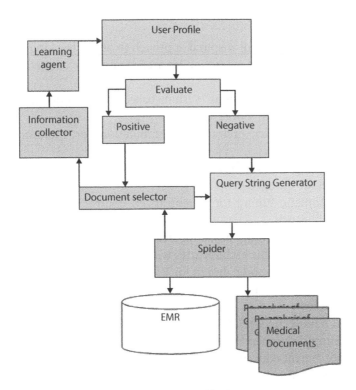

Figure 13.2 Information retrieval system proposal [25].

Social Working Memory	Cognitive Immune System	Spectrum detection in UWB
Interactive Re-enforcement		IR client model generation

Figure 13.3 Challenges in information retrieval with cognitive intelligence.

built in a particular structure that isn't connected to different frameworks or areas. This specialization makes it hard to share client models as normal assets for creating data recovery frameworks and for inquiring about cognitive qualities in different clients. So as to take care of this issue, we need a general client displaying strategy. A client model dependent on a probabilistic structure is proposed. This model is called a generative client model. The generative client model speaks to client's psychological profundity by idle (shrouded) factors. It additionally has obvious factors that mean word set and qualifier for each word as an abstract likelihood dissemination. Figure 13.3 illustrates challenges in IR with cognitive intelligence.

Proposed Research on IR

- Cognitive control-inspired approach to object tracking
- Cognitive-based extraction for area expertise of cooperation in learning
- Cognitive impervious system-based co-evolutionary in order retrieval model
- Inductive user preference manipulation for multimedia retrieval
- Micro-processor–based wireless impediment detection system for the aged people
- Automatic tuning for decentralized controllers by swarm intelligence
- Machine learning–based medical IR systems
- Neuro-morphic architectures with electronic synapses
- Site ranking model design for Web IR
- A model for music perceptual theory based on Markov chains
- A parallel network for visual cognition
- Simplification in the subspaces for earlier model-based reinforcement education
- Generative user models for adaptive IR

Orthogonal Amplitude Modulation

Spectrum detecting connected to IR UWB framework is dependent on the retrieval system. Smart vehicle framework faces difficulty in correspondence and data advancements to make existing foundations progressively powerful and increasingly dependable; it resets on capacities related with the insight (Maatougui *et al.* [3]). The utilization for the ultra wideband (UWB) shows up as an entirely reasonable innovation for this sort for applications, because of its huge data transfer capacity, its protection from the impedances with other radio frameworks and furthermore the quality for the for fered administration. Another framework committed to the area for vehicle, in view of UWB innovation is displayed. The execution for the new adjustment M-OAM (Orthogonal Amplitude Modulation), which depends on the utilization for unique scientific apparatuses called Modified Gegenbauer capacities (MGF), got from symmetrical polynomials, builds the information rate, and improves the strength guaranteed by UWB correspondence for sight and sound and transport applications. With the reason for improving the presentation for the correspondence framework and guaranteeing the self-governance for our framework, this work comprises to join the UWB and cognitive radio innovations so as to build up an adjusted and proficient beneficiary. This collector can distinguish the sign entry and recognize the coding parameters utilized in the transmission in order to be adjusted to them naturally. The beneficiary requires astute capacities with regard to perception, learning, and choice;, hence, our origination depends on range detecting for cognitive radio which is described by the capacity to distinguish the nearness for the sign.

Machine Learning Approach

In future, robots will be utilized all the more widely as aides in home situations and must almost certainly obtain mastery from mentors by learning through crossmodal connection (F. Cruz *et al.* [13]). One promising methodology is intelligent re-enforcement learning (IRL) where an outside coach prompts a disciple on activities to accelerate the learning procedure.

Cognitive Resistant System

These cognitive resistance systems are developed nowadays (Z. Hu, Y *et al.* 2008 [5]). The existent models for Information Recovery (IR) center around

Cognitive Control-Inspired Approach to Object Tracking
Knowledge-based Extraction- for Area Expertise of Cooperation in Learning
Cognitive Immune System-Based Co-Evolutionary Information Retrieval Model
Inductive User Preference Manipulation for Multimedia Retrieval
Microcontroller Based Wireless Obstacle Detection System for the Elderly
Automatic Tuning-for Decentralized Controllers by Swarm Intelligence
Neuro-morphic architectures with electronic synapses
Exploiting Generalization in the Subspaces for Fasters Model-Based Reinforcement Learning
Generative user models for adaptive information retrieval
SME: Learning Automata-Based Algorithm for Estimating the Mobility Model-for Soccer Players
Spectrum sensing applied to IR-UWB system based on M-OAM
Training Agents With Interactive Reinforcement Learning and Contextual Affordances
Cognitive Immune System-Based Co-Evolutionary Information Retrieval Model

Figure 13.4 Challenging confronts in Information Retrieval.

the connection between file terms and archives. Be that as it may, the present recovery necessities request fragile control to demonstrate the client inclinations and input. Also, the definite outcomes are underscored for data blast. Propelled by the upkeep capacity and model in resistant framework, a narrative IR model is projected dependent on compact safe framework (CIS). Expression system models the likeness connection among terms and reports the separation and comparability connections among terms. The inquiry string, client pr for ile and input message animate the cytokine organize which is a runtime structure to for IR. Co-transformative instruments are additionally intended to empower the development highlights for the model roused by resistant framework. Figure 13.4 shows challenging confronts in IR.

Predictive Model for Social Working recollection for IR in communal Interactions are used currently for IR (L. Li, Q *et al.* [4]). Social working memory (SWM) assumes a significant job in exploring social associations. Enlivened by concentrates in brain research, neuroscience, cognitive science, and AI, authors recommend a probabilistic model for SWM to copy individual social knowledge for individual data recovery (IR) in social collaborations. To start with, a semantic progression was made as shared long haul memory to determine individual data. A semantic Bayesian system as the SWM incorporates the cognitive capacities for availability and self guideline. One subgraphical model actualizes the openness capacity to get familiar with the social agreement about IR dependent on social data idea, grouping, social setting, and closeness between people.

13.4 Cognitive and Interactive IR Systems

Cognitive Intelligence–based IR examines ideas dependent on importance criticism with the assistance of client collaboration with IR framework.

Examining the cognitive conduct of the client which gives important contributions to the type of records to break down structure assess the total image of the client profile. Key ideas for conceptualizing CIR are (a) Importance, (b) Cognitive and Interactive, and (c) Poly-authentic approaches. The importance idea right now shapes the premise of rectification criticism to the IR framework, enabling the framework to reexamine its coordinating calculation with the goal that it all the more precisely coordinates the genuine rather than the at first communicated data need. The cognitive part of clients as they collaborate with and respond to natural boosts coming at them frames the IR framework. Inside a cognitive point of view, data need as a reasonable reason for the client in the cooperation is tricky. Cole, Beheshti, Leide, and Large at that point determine the terms and meanings of the client framework association they wish to inspect in detail. It looks to reconceptualize data need as the applied reason for client framework association. To this end, the cooperation is spoken to as a progression of interfacing states: the client's assignment or issue state, and the client's cognitive express, the different need states for each undertaking or issue that may emerge during the client's communication with the IR framework. Thusly, the IR framework gives the client data boosts that can possibly adjust the client's cognitive, undertaking or data need states. The framework boost message's job in the communication is to animate the client to make in a determination state. At the point when the client is in a Selection State, the client's learning structure comprehended and coordinated a data procedure.

Birger Larsen and Peter Ingwersen [22] portrayed a client and record portrayal technique that gives the IR system a fuller image of the client and the report set than current basic solicitation-based frameworks permit, in light of the rule of poly-portrayal. For the client, the poly-portrayal comprises of the client's different simultaneous data needs, enthusiastic states, assignments, hierarchical limitation, and so on—a multiprolonged portrayal of the client's cognitive space. For the record set, the poly-portrayal comprises of the reference joins, thesaurus terms, selectors (e.g., diary name, and so forth.), indexers terms and creator's headings, inscriptions, and so forth. The poly-portrayals are then spoken to in the calculation utilized by the framework to coordinate the client with the IR framework database's archive set. The outcome is a cognitive cover of the client's cognitive space and the data space of different setups of archive portrayals from different pursuit frameworks.

Clients perform various tasks on data management while the client is interfacing with an IR framework (I. Ruthven *et al.* [21]). As of now, IR frameworks expect clients to look successively and are to a great extent intended to help constrained kinds of looking through dependent on determining questions that select records or Web destinations to satisfy a solitary data task. Be that as it may, IR framework clients normally take part in performing various tasks while they are getting to data from an IR framework. The clients may start their IR framework connection with numerous subjects, or they may start with a solitary theme and after that build up extra points during the inquiry ace cess. Scientists characterize such conduct as regular and inspect potential components that empower the client to change starting with one errand then onto the next while apparently occupied with getting to data from an IR framework for one theme or undertaking. The way toward displaying performing various tasks inside a machine gear-piece native IR structure begins from Saracevic's Stratified model of client IR framework connection.

13.5   Conclusion

Electronic IR systems are popularly used for the last 50 years as the users gradually advanced from experimental frameworks to full-scale web crawlers and computerized libraries. The fields of library and data science, cognitive science, human components, and software engineering have generally been the main trains in directing exploration that tries to show human connection with IR frameworks for a wide range of data-related practices. As innovation issues have been aced, the hypothetical and connected structure for examining human cooperation with IR frameworks has developed from frameworks focused to more client focused or cognitive-focused methodologies. In any case, cognitive data recovery (CIR) inquiry about those spotlights on client connection with IR frameworks is still to a great extent under-financed and is regularly excluded at processing and frameworks configuration situated meetings. In any case, CIR-centered research proceeds, and there are signs that some IR frameworks creators in the scholarly community and the Web search business are understanding that client conduct research can give important bits of knowledge into frameworks plan and assessment. CIR research is the mix of CIR inside the more extensive human information behavior structure which makes up the human data condition. The HIB point of view for CIR looks to make an increasingly all encompassing comprehension of CIR that considers the HIB setting in which human-IR framework collaboration happens.

New directions in research ought to likewise inspect the interaction among data and non-data undertakings, just as starting to conceptualize the purported interfered with HIB practices, clients participate during inquiry session like tactful searching. Such systems ought to be dissected regarding the job these practices may play in giving organizing or exchanging instruments between individual hunt and looking for assignments when performing various tasks search session.

References

1. Ravinandan, M.E., Prasad, E.V., Kumar, M.V.V., Adaptive path exploration and cognitive map generation using swarm intelligence. *2016 International Conference on Electrical, Electronics, Communication, Computer and Optimization Techniques (ICEECCOT)*, Mysuru, pp. 318–321, 2016.
2. Mazzù, A., Morerio, P., Marcenaro, L., Regazzoni, C.S., A Cognitive Control-Inspired Approach to Object Tracking, in: *IEEE Transactions on Image Processing*, vol. 25, 6 pp. 2697–2711, 2016.
3. Maatougui, L., Ouahmane, H., Hajjaji, A., Hamidoun, K., Rivenq-Menhaj, A., Hillali, Y.E., Spectrum sensing applied to IR-UWB system based on M-OAM. *2015 Third World Conference on Complex Systems (WCCS)*, Marrakech, pp. 1–6, 2015.
4. Li, L., Xu, Q., Gan, T., Tan, C., Lim, J., A Probabilistic Model of Social Working Memory for Information Retrieval in Social Interactions, in: *IEEE Transactions on Cybernetics*, vol. 48, 5 pp. 1540–1552, May 2018.
5. Hu, Z., Ding, Y., Lua, X., Cognitive Immune System-Based Co-Evolutionary Information Retrieval Model. *2008 Second International Symposium on Intelligent Information Technology Application*, Shanghai, pp. 212–215, 2008.
6. Fay, D.A., Ivey, R.T., Bomberger, N., Waxman, A.M., Multisensor & spectral image fusion & mining: From neural systems to applications. *32nd Applied Imagery Pattern Recognition Workshop, 2003. Proceedings*, Washington, DC, USA, pp. 11–20, 2003.
7. Ahmadabadi, M.N., Imanipour, A., Araabi, B.N., Asadpour, M., Siegwart, R., Knowledge-based Extraction of Area of Expertise for Cooperation in Learning. *2006 IEEE/RSJ International Conference on Intelligent Robots and Systems*, Beijing, pp. 3700–3705, 2006.
8. Ding, C. and Chi, C., A generalized site ranking model for Web IR, in: *Proceedings IEEE/WIC International Conference on Web Intelligence (WI 2003)*, Halifax, NS, Canada, pp. 584–587, 2003.
9. Hashemzadeh, M., Hosseini, R., Ahmadabadi, M.N., Exploiting Generalization in the Subspaces for Faster Model-Based Reinforcement Learning, in: *IEEE Transactions on Neural Networks and Learning Systems*, vol. 30, 6 pp. 1635–1650, June 2019.
10. Mehrabian, A.R. and Lucas, C., Automatic Tuning of Decentralized Controllers by Swarm Intelligence. *2006 3rd International IEEE Conference Intelligent Systems*, London, pp. 350–353, 2006.

11. Hu, Z., Ding, Y., Lu, X., Cognitive Immune System-Based Co-Evolutionary Information Retrieval Model. *2008 International Symposium on Intelligent Information Technology Application Workshops*, Shanghai, pp. 1057–1060, 2008.

12. Gudivada, A. and Tabrizi, N., A Literature Review on Machine Learning Based Medical Information Retrieval Systems. *2018 IEEE Symposium Series on Computational Intelligence (SSCI)*, Bangalore, India, pp. 250–257, 2018.

13. Cruz, F., Magg, S., Weber, C., Wermter, S., Training Agents With Interactive Reinforcement Learning and Contextual Affordances, in: *IEEE Transactions on Cognitive and Developmental Systems*, vol. 8, 4 pp. 271–284, Dec. 2016.

14. Eryilmaz, S.B., Joshi, S., Neftci, E., Wan, W., Cauwenberghs, G., Wong, H.P., Neuromorphic architectures with electronic synapses. *2016 17th International Symposium on Quality Electronic Design (ISQED)*, Santa Clara, CA, pp. 118–123, 2016.

15. Jamalian, A.H., Sefidpour, A.R., Manzuri-Shalmani, M.T., Iraji, R., SME: Learning Automata-Based Algorithm for Estimating the Mobility Model of Soccer Players. *6th IEEE International Conference on Cognitive Informatics*, Lake Tahoo, CA, pp. 462–469, 2007.

16. Mustapha, B., Zayegh, A., Begg, R.K., Microcontroller Based Wireless Obstacle Detection System for the Elderly. *2014 4th International Conference on Artificial Intelligence with Applications in Engineering and Technology*, Kota Kinabalu, pp. 325–329, 2014.

17. Adams, F.W., Nguyen, H.T., Raghavan, R., Slawny, J., A parallel network for visual cognition, in: *IEEE Transactions on Neural Networks*, vol. 3, 6 pp. 906–922, Nov. 1992.

18. Zellhöfer, D., Inductive User Preference Manipulation for Multimedia Retrieval. *2010 Second International Conferences on Advances in Multimedia*, Athens, pp. 90–95, 2010.

19. Wen, R. *et al.*, A model of music perceptual theory based on Markov chains. *2018 Chinese Control And Decision Conference (CCDC)*, Shenyang, pp. 1099–1105, 2018.

20. Motomura, Y., Yoshida, K., Fujimoto, K., Generative user models for adaptive information retrieval. *Smc 2000 conference proceedings. 2000 ieee international conference on systems, man and cybernetics. 'Cybernetics evolving to systems, humans, organizations, and their complex interactions' (cat. no. 0*, Nashville, TN, vol. 1, pp. 665–670, 2000.

21. Ruthven, I., Integrating approaches to relevance, in: *New Directions in Cognitive Information Retrieval*, A. Spink and C. Cole (Eds.), pp. 61–80, Springer, Netherlands, 2005.

22. Larsen, B., Ingwersen, P., Kekäläinen, J., The polyrepresentation continuum in ir, in: *IIiX: Proceedings of the 1st international conference on Information interaction in context*, ACM, New York, NY, USA, pp. 88–96, 2006.

23. Rath, M., Security Challenges and Resolution in Cloud Computing and Cloud of Things, in: *Applying Integration Techniques and Methods in Distributed Systems and Technologies*, p. 24, 2019.
24. Rath, M., Resolution of Issues and Health Improvement Using Big Data and IoT, in: *Edge Computing and Computational Intelligence Paradigms for the IoT*, p. 22, 2019.
25. Chou, S., Chang, W., Cheng, C.-Y., Jehng, J.-C., Chang, C., An Information Retrieval System for Medical Records & Documents. *Conf. Proc. Annu. Int. Conf. IEEE Eng. Med. Biol. Soc. IEEE Eng. Med. Biol. Soc. Conf.*, vol. 2018 1474–7, 2008.

14

Ontology as a Tool to Enable Health Internet of Things Viable 5G Communication Networks

Nidhi Sharma* and R. K. Aggarwal

Department of Computer Engineering National Institute of Technology, Kurukshetra, Haryana, India

Abstract

This chapter is an attempt to review future IoT-based medicinal services frameworks to gather Medical Ontologies, which can be applied to generic frameworks. A few wearable or non-meddlesome sensors were exhibited and investigated, with a specific spotlight on those sensors which are observing indispensable signs of pulse, and blood oxygen levels. Emerging IoT technologies have revolutionized the communication system of the medical service industry. These advancements improve the perception of health by analyzing the variations of sampled data. IoT applications offer the open door for suppliers to have permeability to what occurs among patients' visits and can give a few bits of knowledge into understanding medicine adherence, action levels, and essential signs.

Keywords: Health internet of things, medical ontology, remote health monitoring, health-care automation, tele-health robotics

14.1 Introduction

Ontologies arise out of the branch of philosophy referred to as metaphysics, which deals with questions like "what exists?" and "what is that the nature of reality?" In 1980s, the Artifical Intelligence (AI) community began to use the term ontology to ask both a theory of a modeled world and a component of knowledge-based systems. David Powers introduced the word ontology

---

*Corresponding author: Sharma.sunidhi2000@gmail.com

Vishal Jain, Ritika Wason, Jyotir Moy Chatterjee and Dac-Nhuong Le (eds.) Ontology-Based Information Retrieval for Healthcare Systems, (293–312) © 2020 Scrivener Publishing LLC

to AI to ask world about robotic grounding [4]. In 1993, Tom Gruber [3] used ontology as a technical term in computing closely associated with earlier idea of semantic networks and taxonomies.

Ontology regularly manages questions about what entity or element exists or might be said to exist and how such elements might be gathered, related inside a progressive system, and subdivided by similitudes and contrasts. Brain does not alluding to an element or entity but alludes to an assortment of mental occasions experienced by an individual; society alludes to an assortment of people with some mutual qualities, and geometry alludes to an assortment of explicit sorts of scholarly exercises.

Machine perception is a research field that is still in its infancy and is confronted with many unsolved problems. In contrast, humans generally perceive their environment without problems. These facts were the motivation to develop a bionic model for human-like machine perception, which is based on neuro-scientific and neuro-psychological research findings about the structural organization and function of the perceptual system of the human brain [1]. Having systems available that are capable of a human-like perception of their environment would allow the automation of processes for which, today, human observers and their cognitive abilities are necessary [2]. The challenge to be faced is to merge and interpret large amounts of data coming from different sources. For this purpose, an information processing principle called neuro-symbolic information processing is introduced using neuro-symbols as basic information processing units [12]. Neuro-symbols are connected in a modular hierarchical fashion to a so-called neuro-symbolic network to process sensor data. The architecture of the neuro-symbolic network is derived from the structural organization of the perceptual system of the human brain. Connections and correlations between neuro-symbols can be acquired from examples in different learning phases [19]. Besides sensor data processing, memory, knowledge, and focus of attention influence perception to resolve ambiguous sensory information and to devote processing power to relevant features [5].

These technological advancements lead to the psyche in the arrangement of subjective resources including cognizance, creative mind, recognition, thinking, judgment, language, and memory, which is housed in the cerebrum including the focal sensory system. This is generally characterized as the class of an element's musings and awareness. It holds the intensity of creative mind, acknowledgment, and thankfulness and is answerable for preparing sentiments and feelings, bringing about mentalities and activities.

The introductory part of this chapter demonstrate the need of Ontology for analyzing the sampled data sent via IoT sensors used for collecting health statistics. Section 14.1 further explains the concept of ontology as a tool for comparing and contrasting the medical information for the betterment of social health issues. Section 14.2 analyzes the use IoT sensors in medical field as of now. Section 14.3 is a critical survey of technological solutions for utilizing the benefits of the Concept of Ontology as a tool for enabling Health–Internet of Things (H-IoT). This application area of H-IoT seems feasible only via the network speed of 25 Gbps and 1 ms latency. That much speed and latency are the characteristic of the upcoming 5th generation Communication system. Section 14.4 discusses the framework for the incubation of some of the IoT sensors in health Industry. Section 14.5 concludes this survey.

14.2   From Concept Representations to Medical Ontologies

Clinically significant portrayals of clinical ideas and patients are the key to health expository. In this way, there is a solid need to acquaint an information-based methodology with clinical content comprehension. From a top to bottom thought of sentence and content comprehension, refining of the essential necessities for a sufficient information portrayal system is attractive. These prerequisites are then coordinated with as of now accessible clinical ontologies (thesauri, wordings, etc.) [8]. A crucial exchange must be perceived between scope calculated inclusion from one viewpoint and formal instruments for honesty conservation and reasonable expressiveness. This will give a sufficient procedure to planning progressively advanced, adaptable clinical ontologies serving the requirements of "profound" information-based applications that are in no way, shape or form confined to clinical language preparation. The examination of the essentialness of language verbalizations has a long history in health informatics, for bookkeeping (e.g., message in clinical reports and from the biomedical composition) and sorting out information (e.g., terms from standard vocabularies utilized for clinical research, medicinal services bits of knowledge, quality assessment, and charging). The improvement of ontologies for biomedical research and the development of clinical vocabularies impel human language advancements with dynamically getting readymade data that may have changed the social insurance information science [15]. It has been proven wrong to watch the ads up change in perspective and it basically reflects changes in naming, after the normal development of philosophy research and designing exercises during the 1990s. The accessibility of incredible assets to deal with ontologies gave to specific territories of biomedicine has not brought about this huge scope which leaps forward the past advances in fundamental research [9]. New settled research zones have developed the Semantic Web, web-based social networking gathering, and web-based groundbreaking correspondence between researchers.

14.2.1   Current Medical Research Trends

Nowadays, the primary aim of having healthcare-related data has changed the dynamics of Data science. The data must be machine-readable and process capable. This has been a significant driver of the advancement of clinical data frameworks. The utilization of formal dialects, such as depiction rationales, has been a stage now. In the 1990s, "medical concept representation" was viewed as an answer by proposing a generic technique. Reasonable conceptualization of data is a restorative research practice. These endeavors were exasperated by hypothetical issues, troubles of displaying a space, and the blast of information, etc. [9]. Ontology has long been the preserve of philosophers and logicians. Recently, concepts from this field are picked up by Computer scientists as a basis for coding information and with the hope of achieving ability and intelligent system behavior. In bioinformatics, ontologies would possibly permit impossible queries and data-mining activities [10]. Scientist needs a new generation of ontologies that transcend this preoccupation with predicate logic and expand into alternative representations of information. The attempt to make computers more useful in a practical sense is forcing, biological knowledge to be used computationally. For example: the inclination of "class" over "idea" in the Semantic Web and depiction rationales network, particularly with respect to the persuasive OWL group of portrayal dialects [11].

14.2.2   Ontology as a Paradigm Shift in Health Informatics

The ubiquity of "ontology" shows another inclination wherein curiosity speaks to kinds of space substances which are all the more obviously recognized by certain scientists from antiques that depict language things. The limits among ontologies and information portrayal antiquities are less clear, albeit generally fresh criteria can be planned. Practically speaking, "ontology" is utilized by many people to allude to a wide show of assets over the semantic range, including wordings, thesaurus, arrangements, and formal ontologies [4]. Simultaneously significant territories as medicinal language handling and therapeutic phrasings, additionally metadata, semantic comment, and folksonomies have picked up significance, with the goal that they are never again subsumed under "idea portrayal". There are a technological signs that can be the focal point of research in medicinal area portrayal and semantics discussed in [7, 8]. Several 1000 years medical research practices have risen the foundation of applied ontology and the Semantic Web [13, 14] as new trains for information pathways. The focal job of the expression "idea" has been bitten by a bit relinquished, regardless of whether this truly sums to a change in outlook or a basic change in phrased inclinations. The ontology research and designing endeavors, which began around 1990, yielded significant outcomes, including the advancement of depiction rationales, devices like PROTÉGÉ, just as the notable GALEN venture [15–17].

14.3   Primer Literature Review

The development has vexed every industry including human administrations, business, cash, and others. Human administrations remain the snappiest to grasp creative changes to agitate the finding and treatment of the human body. Now, we talk about the Internet of Things (IoT), it offers an enormous number of focal points for improving the ampleness and nature of well-being organizations by passing data through IoT by means of therapeutic devices. A large number of knowledge bits reveal the usage of IoT in social protection and their impact on business [31].

1. Almost 60% of clinical administration affiliations have brought IoT contraptions to their workplaces.
2. About 73% of restorative administration's affiliations use IoT for help and watching.
3. About 87% of therapeutic administration affiliations plan to execute IoT development by 2019 which is possibly higher than the 85% of associations across various endeavors.
4. About 64% utilization of IoT in the restorative administration's industry shows limitation screens.
5. About 89% of restorative administrations' affiliations have encountered IoT-related security crack.

It has understood that associated devices are being used in such to get to data from fetal screens, blood glucose levels, and electro-cardiogram and temperature screens. A part of these instruments requires to fix up a correspondence with a therapeutic administration master. A large portion of the eminent facilities has placed assets into familiarizing innovatively splendid beds which choose if it's included or not [27]. When we talk about the IoT, there are worries also about data assurance and security. Regardless, it doesn't have any kind of effect as far as everyone is getting the right treatment, and the patients and authorities work in complete congruity. Cautions must be considered when the therapeutic administration's industry can harness the force of IoT and set up for significantly accessible, altered, and on-time social security organizations for everyone? Let's Examine it.

14.3.1 Remote Health Monitoring

The principle gain by grasping IoT in a human contributions association is cost-cutting and social protection. Remote health monitoring (RHM) office has been used to screen the patients' prosperity, whether or not the patient is at home, at his/her working environment or at any place on the planet earth. Therapeutic contributions specialists/Doctors can show the influenced individual's wellness and give directed drugs. Therefore, it could lessen the weight of well-being administrations suppliers who can't hold up the flooding of patients consistently. Likewise, the absence of the workforce at medical clinics should in no way, shape or form upset section and leave timings of patients. IoT can moreover be valuable in immature worldwide areas wherein wellness work environments are difficult to achieve.

14.3.2 Collecting and Understanding Medical Data

During a patient's remain, they are tangled in remedial contraptions including heart screens, blood siphons, respirators, and *In vitro* fertilization (IVF). The movement and recording of information from these contraptions take a lot of time and are slanted to bumbles in light of a legitimate concern for gatekeepers. Today, with the assistance of IoT, a patient's data can be gone on through Electronic Health Record systems. Along these lines, this technique helps in growing the accuracy of the data and licenses clinical chaperon to contribute more vitality sparing a thought. The authorities need to unravel data to pick the answer for patients. Due to the expanded utilization of such IoT empowered remedial contraptions, the authorities are presently ready to think about an authentic finding. To encourage this, IoT structures can be utilized to help well-being experts for gathering information from countless therapeutic devices and reviewing important data about patient's well-being, without disseminating the information.

14.3.3 Patient Monitoring

The advancement of well-being wearable contraptions like the Apple I-Watch has frightened a fundamental activity of watching an individual's health. Sooner or later these mechanical applications won't capable to give a definite difference in general restorative rigging because of equipment or programming glitches, yet the health wearable (IoT contraptions) which uniquely are intended to screen and make sense of particular health investigation, for example, circulatory strain, heartbeat, brainwaves, temperature, physical position, walks, and breathing, and so forth. With the help of information accumulated through Health-IoT devices, a specialist can share this information and give general prescriptions. Notwithstanding the way that the IoT is dynamic in the human administrations' region, there are no troubles too that ought to be recollected.

14.3.4   Tele-Health

The methodologies of telemedicine for treating patients are utilizing communicated interchanges that have decreased costs and in-office log. Remote patient monitoring (RPM) is known as residential consideration telehealth with a shrewd cellphone or brilliant casing sensor that allows a patient to play out an ordinary test and boat the persistent measurements to the health experts and master specialists. A remote observing gadget is an absolutely extraordinary approach to address and supports the patients' conditions suitably [29]. The RPM is used to help the wiped out and antique for inordinate recuperating consideration which allows the clinical specialists to deliberately show the influenced individual's sicknesses and intervene fast cure without loss of time. It is shown in the drafted arrangement of the Federal Communication Commission (FCC) that the use of RPM innovation related to computerized well-being records may expend $700 billion extra than in the last 15 to 20 years.

14.3.5   Advanced Human Services Records Frameworks

The innovative improvement of IoT has brought together the simple information gathered from the health checking systems and helpful gadgets. The digitized medicinal services insights are sent to experts, labs, orderlies, notable specialists, and others related to the influenced individual. The advanced medicinal services system is a bit by bit intends to help the clinical ventures like the centers and labs to facilitate themselves. The present systems are not organized from the perspective of IoT. What's more, the progressing data depends on understanding pushed, moderates, and from the perspective of the therapeutic contributions specialists and numerous crisis center system, since they are utilizing static insights. This strategy for holding up the influenced individual's social protection report is a vital deterrent as all the restorative administrations' records from the related devices show up inside the advanced human services systems. Henceforth, there might be a stream toward a consistent wellness system comprehensive of progressing insights abilities from the related/wearable gadgets and in IoT structure view. As showed that with the investigation of trade, the ongoing well-being structures will develop to a fundamental division for IoT in restorative contributions. As data examination will be applied to survey the static measurements for the prescient investigation to push social inclusion systems. In this way, decidedly, the service of medicinal services over the world needs to concentrate on the dynamic computerized social insurance structures.

14.3.6 Applied Autonomy and Healthcare Mechanization

Karl Capek recently utilized the expression "robot" in his play "R.U.R." (which speaks to ROSSUM'S conventional robots) that respected in 1921. Capek was given the word from the Czech word robota and used to reference mechanical humanoids worked to do humble and monotonous assignments which may be the sort of occupations the robots beat the individuals. Restorative robots don't exist essentially in Science Fiction (SCI-FI) development pixel however have recently penetrated the universe of social inclusion. Quickly from rearranging careful treatment, clinical establishment aide, old consideration, paraplegic potential outcomes, supporting chemical imbalance, automated clinical collaborator observing information basic experiences, and various such accomplices are startling the universe of restorative administrations structures [30]. By means of 2020, the cautious utilization of robots will allow the master to do the clinical procedures with exactness, control, and redesigned vision. The careful gadget DA-VINCI does this sincerely with its mechanical framework comprising of an enhanced 3D-HD vision structure [27]. The most essential piece of elbowroom these robots have over a human is that they paint constant diminishing the heaviness of agents running in night-moves and utilized for no-nonsense real artistic creations and enabling legitimate channel of the effects. In addition, there is mechanical for intuitive physical help that is used at houses for fast consideration for both moving and lifting aptitude eventually of bed into a wheelchair or makes the influenced individual plunk down, stand, and turn them in the bed for preventing sleeping cushion wounds and other restorative burdens. In the long run, medical robots are changing the restorative mind by accepting that the crucial activity is upsetting as we found in human contributions.

14.3.7   IoT Powers the Preventive Healthcare

Medicinal services' shifts to greedy IoT advancements for preventive healthcare have a lifesaving impact for appropriate medicine accommodation to cure ceaseless diseases and illnesses utilizing the prescient investigation ability of IoT for preventive attention. Since the population is increasing at an alarming rate, there may be a need or want for the social coverage industry to offer a custom designed preventive health care. The ministry of healthcare in Singapore is progressive to achieve its objective to ensure that the old, new born, and patients with regular illnesses are remotely monitored through clever connected wearable or IoT gadgets which are able in foreseeing everyday sickness or any exceptional behavior inside the patient's indispensable statistics. The machine right away sends the ongoing data of the affected person to the cloud administrations which thusly cautions the affected person's attendant or specialist for his or her proactive pastime [28]. These preventive human offerings utilizing IoT is steadily embraced in an extended manner as by analyzing the on time statistics for quick redial action. And soon, this Health internet of things (H-IoTs) will come in our day to day life practices.

14.3.8   Hospital Statistics Control System (HSCS)

IoT has upset the normal guidelines and frameworks of the scientific clinics. It has upset the short paced universe of medicine. It is an awesome venture to keep up and paints a multi-power health center and nursing houses. The HSCS framework will permit the paperless work [26]. The framework includes all the facts about the specialists, team of workers, patients, managerial subtleties, and so on. The big advantages of IoT for HSCS are decreased operational costs, progressed or exceptional effects of the treatment through digital frameworks, openness of non-stop statistics for deciding on knowledgeable picks, advanced infection that executives through RPM, reduced errors, improved management of medicinal drugs, and more desirable patient revel in. Ultimately empowering the hospitals to get proficient and address the requests of the ever-growing populace from distinctive ceaseless illnesses.

14.3.9   End-to-End Accessibility and Moderateness

IoT can robotize the work process with therapeutic administrations action and other new advancements in driving social protection workplaces. IoT engages interoperability, machine-to-machine correspondence, information exchange, and data advancement that make social security organization movement fruitful. System shows: Bluetooth LTE, Wi-Fi, Z-wave, ZigBee, and other flow shows and Social security workforce can change the way, they spot malady and ailments in patients and can improve dynamic strategies for treatment [32]. Thus, advancement has driven courses of action chop down the expense, by cleaving down pointless visits, utilizing better quality resources, and improving the parts and game plans.

14.3.10 Information Mixing and Assessment

The sizeable degree of estimations that a human regulatory machine sends in some time is conflicting to shop and administer. If the path to the cloud storage is blocked, then the IoT gadgets can get, record, and look at the estimations a few bit at a time. And hence, there is the need to store the grungy information. This all can show up that the providers basically getting consent to explicit reviews with outlines. Additionally, therapeutic commitments endeavors license foundations can get basic social assurance evaluation and experiences driven bits of understanding that animate fundamental organization and are less willing to bumbles [20].

14.3.11 Following and Alerts

The on-time alert is essential in unsafe conditions. IoT awards contraptions to aggregate information and moves that information to specialists with consistency and dropping rebukes to people about the crucial strategies for adaptable applications and other related gadgets. Reports and cautions offer a firm commitment to a patient's condition, giving little consideration to spot and time. Right now, IoT gadgets engage to pick capable choices to provide an on-time treatment. In this way, IoT to consistent licenses hands-on solutions with better precision and able for intercession by specialists and improves all outpatient records' development dependable.

14.3.12 Remote Remedial Assistance

In event of an emergency, patients can contact a specialist who is kilometers away with a keen compact application. With adaptability game plans in human administrations, the specialists can instantly check the patients and perceive the illnesses. In this manner, different social security transport fastens the checking of machines and give timely cure to patients. And infection-related data open the associated devices. IoT will improve the patient's thought in clinical facility. This will cut down expanses on human administrations.

14.4   Establishments of Health IoT

The IoT is a course of action of interrelated computing gadgets, mechanical and automated machines, articles, animals or people that are given unique identifiers (UIDs) and the ability to move data over a framework without anticipating that human-to-human or human-to-PC communication.

IoT development has pulled very late into consideration despite to its capacity to facilitate the burden on human administrative systems. Comprehensive registering ability joined with virtual framework engineering will open up the path for adaptable IoT. Progressed computerized systems will unite a framework that associates billions of gadgets and sensors propels in social insurance, training, asset the executives, transportation, farming, and different regions. It joins the cloud foundation, a visualized organize center, shrewd edge administrations, and an appropriated figuring model that gets experiences from the information produced by billions of gadgets. Associated gadgets will allow people to appreciate increasingly customized, progressively vivid and increasingly improved encounters at whatever point and any place they are. With the expenses of gadgets and sensors descending extensively, availability will be omnipresent and subtle.

As opposed to settling on a responsible choice to give a processing order, people will have frameworks that take activities dependent on the foreordained inclinations of that person [18]. A wide exhibit of organized sensors will interface machines, home security frameworks, vitality matrices, and theater setups to the web. Individuals shouldn't be home to turn a security caution on or off. They can change their indoor regulators from miles away. They can figure out what nourishment is hard to find in their fridges. Interfacing remote sensors all through their machines will transform even the smallest of gadgets into minicomputers, which will aid people with bridling the intensity of the Internet for a wide assortment of assignments. The rising device will enroll returned-give up server farms, cloud administrations, and remote file servers right into a computational behemoth. There will be "Computing at the edge," which means that calculations may be executed near the source or inside the cloud, contingent upon the prompt need. These advancements will allow packages to hastily technique content material and deliver and come upon this is extremely responsive. This may make processing steadily prudent, increasingly more powerful, and we're going to see Reserve budget on potential expenses. Simultaneously, as gadgets advance under the control of clients, server farm arrange framework and cloud administrations are developing to discuss the issues of new business. Frameworks will be improved with the goal that product can perform convoluted assignments and system capacities untethered from physical equipment [11]. This will incorporate readiness and takes into consideration fast and tweaked setups.

14.4.1   Technological Challenges

The fast velocity and insightful structure of these IoT-enabled frameworks are making new programs and devices that may possibly change the manner health is analyzed and treated. A "Mckinsey" study determined that "key adjustments to the part of healthcare devices" would be made to effective benchmarked data. The key test cases are then analyzed to get the progressive changes into the fitness factors a reality and not only an expectation. There are numerous advances that are expected to propel the imaginative and prescient medicinal services. These medical expectations are only feasible through realizing the 5G Communication system [20]. For 5G, we have to incorporate framework development, range harmonization in sufficient specialized fashions. Powerful guiding principle and adjustments may also compensate the approach to fulfill safety warranty and security of research records.

Figure 14.1 diagrammatically describe the Internet of Things (IoT) as a system of bodily items, machines, humans, and one of a kind device that

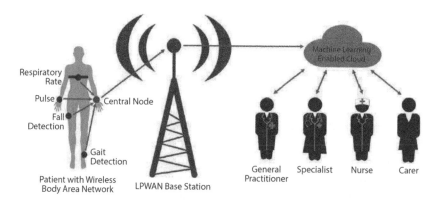

Figure 14.1 5G Network Communication System for patient's health monitoring through IoT sensors.

empowers network and interchanges the statistics for insightful packages and administrations. These gadgets consist of cell telephones, pills, patron hardware, automobiles, wearables, and sensors which can be prepared for IoT correspondences.

The need of an hour is to control the remote machine by making open doorways for direct incorporation among the bodily and superior universes bringing about stepped forward productivity, precision, and financial blessings. The important worry for administrative bodies is the security of personal fitness records, positioned away and sent through the related gadgets. While many human offerings associations ensure that the delicate statistics is put away in an included and encoded manner, they don't have authority over the health and protection of the information passageways being used to send the facts [21]. This makes a noteworthy chance that expands gradually depending on the quantity of latest devices related to the system. Remember that the maximum perfect technique to paints is through specialized obstructions, definitions, concurrence, and confirmation, through a sincere and open ideas method.

Inside the territory of human offerings, there exist these mentioned benchmarks for essential signs devices, wearables, pulse displays, movement sensors, weight displays, and circulatory pressure sleeves. This has prodded a variety of wearable gadgets and remote checking tools that empowers fitness providers to get records steadily on a scope of consumer facts. Numerous system mixes are likewise an impediment to the effective sending of IoT in social insurance [21]. These days' maximum fitness gadgets and hardware inside emergency clinics have to be associated for amassing records of the patient. As an example, if an individual is experiencing coronary infection, he/she might be experiencing hypertension too. The maximum major take a look at it is that machine, makers have not have a countless supply of conventions and hints. As unique mobile phones are related to the machine for the collection of information the difference in conventions entangle the way of collecting the facts. The absence of homogeneity among some of the medicinal gadgets doctorates the effective execution of IoT in human services. The manner towards totaling and amassing data has also joined too many complexities. Despite the consolidated statistics consequences can help in getting new ends surmised from the affected person's file. In any case, thinking of the outcomes from such a variety of statistics could be very tedious to test, without delicate investigation application and information experts. Recognizing vital and noteworthy information is fundamental to the general public. But the medicinal professionals and doctors think that it is hard to close with the development of facts [22]. The fundamental leadership is not able to manage these increasing records. Since the concerns are growing more and more with the development of related devices that constantly accumulate and create large facts.

14.4.2   Probable Solutions

There are various open doors for the IoT to have any kind of effect in patients' lives. IoT-empowered gadgets catch and screen significant patient information and let suppliers to pick up billions of bits of knowledge without patients' visits. This procedure can help improve understanding results and forestall potential complexities for the people who may be viewed as high hazard [23]. Regardless of the guarantee of what IoT can accomplish in social insurance, it keeps on confronting difficulties that could put it in danger of disappointment in the event that they are not tended to soon.

Human administrations industries over the world are changing themselves into encouraged, customer driven, and logically capable systems. This electronic change derives advance mix, inescapable and operable social protection organizations.

United access to health records and patient-related entities are interfaced to patients in their social protection viably. With this objective, the IoT will accept a fundamental activity in the redesign of passed on therapeutic administrative structures that will fulfill the patient visit update demands. IoT has prepared to disturb the Healthcare Industry with related devices, structures, and things that are used by billions of individuals from differing foundations, to utilize data and help them with the course of events and contextualize decisions [24].

The IoT will definitely speedup the development in the Healthcare section that is engaging another surge of game-changing for the life-overhauling organizations over the economy. The IoT has critical potential outcomes to convey monetary and social points of interest to the occupants, end-customers, governments, and associations through forefront improved assistance movement and personalization [25]. IoT engages the therapeutic administrations industry to get related with such an extent that has never been possible.

Disregarding the progress, IoT in the Healthcare business has prepared for certain odds to use from and troubles to be tended to. As showed by promote gauge, the IoT Healthcare Market is worth $158.07 billion with 50 billion related contraptions by 2020. IoT headway in human administrations offers the ability to respond with speed, act at a scale that impacts the system or city or a nation. Moved model for expectation and health-care statistics are prepared to screen and support an individual freed from

"Physical Constraints" thoroughly changes the manner in which how experts oversee patients [22].

14.4.3   Bit-by-Bit Action Statements

The abridgement of IoT in the Healthcare Industry has made a change in perspective and is totally changing the essence of the conventional social insurance. The Industry partners need to team up to makeup the vision of IoT in medical community into a reality, so that it will change the work culture of health industry [26]. The essential steps which should be taken care of are:

1. To create gathering persistent medicinal information that was at no other time accessible for examination and conveying care to individuals for whom care wasn't beforehand open.
2. To create IoT-driven frameworks for making it conceivable to profoundly diminish costs and improve health by expanding the accessibility and nature of care.
3. To create and make implanted innovations for use all through IoT-driven human services frameworks, including sensors that gather persistent information; Microcontrollers that procedure, break down and remotely impart the information; Microchips that empower rich graphical user interface (GUI).
4. To create healthcare-explicit passages through which sensor information is additionally dissected and sent to the cloud.
5. To execute questions that can mastermind information of tables in the structure rising ask and diving request.

14.5   Incubation of IoT in Health Industry

The ascent of IoT is energizing everyone due to its inter-disciplinary extent of use in almost every field in day-to-day life. In Health Industry also, it has a few applications [16, 18].

1. Reducing crisis room and hold uptime
2. Tracking patients, staff, and stock
3. Enhancing drug executives
4. Ensuring the accessibility of basic equipment

IoT has presented a number of wearables and gadgets which have made existence of patients agreeable. These gadgets are listed below.

14.5.1 Hearables

Hearables are new-age listening devices which have totally changed the way people who endured hearing misfortune cooperate with the world. These days, hearables are good with Bluetooth which matches up to your cell phone with it. It permits you to channel, adjust and add layered high-lights to certifiable sounds. Doppler Labs is its most appropriate case.

14.5.2 Ingestible Sensors

Ingestible sensors are truly a progressive science wonder. These are pill-sized sensors which screen the medicine in our body and caution us on the off chance that it distinguishes any inconsistencies in our bodies. These sensors can be an aid for a diabetic patient as it would help in checking manifestations and give an early admonition for illnesses. Proteus Digital Health is one such model.

14.5.3 Moodables

Moodables are state of mind upgrading gadgets which help in improving our disposition for the duration of the day. It might seem like sci-fi, yet it's not a long way from the real world. Thync and Halo Neurosciences are from now on taking a shot at it and have gained colossal ground. Moodables are head-mounted wearables that send low-force current to the mind which hoists our disposition.

14.5.4 PC Vision Innovation

PC vision innovation alongside AI has offered ascend to ramble innova-tion which plans to imitate visual recognition and later basic leadership dependent on it. Automatons like SKYDIO use PC vision innovation to recognize impediments and to explore around them. This innovation can likewise be used for outwardly disabled people to explore proficiently.

14.5.5 Social Insurance Outlining

IoT gadgets, such as AUDEMIX, decrease a lot of manual work which a specialist needs to do during quiet outlining. It is fueled by voice directions and catches the patient's information. It makes the patient's information promptly available for audit. It spares around specialists' work by 15 hours out of each week.

14.6 Concluding Remarks

In this work, we have explored a generic model for future IoT-based restorative administration structures to assemble Medical Ontologies, which can be applied to frameworks that screen explicit conditions. Then, a cautious audit of the works relating to all aspects of the reviewed model is taken. A couple of wearable and non-intrusive sensors were examined for benchmarking of medical data like fundamental signs, heartbeat, and blood oxygen levels. Short-term and long-term communication benchmarks were then investigated with respect to sensibility for therapeutic administrations applications. IoT changes the way wherein the workplaces are passed on to the therapeutic administrations industry. This technological advancement has a greater effect on health industry. Providers are cheerful that IoT will decidedly influence supporting patient thought and passing on noteworthy data. IoT applications offer the open pathway for providers to have porousness to what happens among visits and can give an analytical insight of Medical data. This rising development is undermined by the number of challenges faced by the IoT in restorative administrations. Industry and academia must have to maintain a balance among these IoT challenges, and continuous progress must be made toward settling them and allowing IoT advances to genuinely influence social protection.

References

1. Velik, R., Pratl, G., Lang, R., A Multi-sensory, Symbolic, Knowledge-based Model for Human-like Perception, in: *Proceedings of the 7th IFAC International Conference on Fieldbuses & Networks in Industrial & Embedded Systems (FeT 2007)*, pp. 273–278, 2007.
2. Bruckner, D., Zeilinger, H., Dietrich, D., Cognitive automation—Survey of novel artificial general intelligence methods for the automation of human technical environments. *IEEE Trans. Ind. Inf.*, 8, 2, 206–215, 2011.
3. Gruber, T., Toward Principles for the Design of Ontologies Used for Knowledge Sharing. *Int. J. Hum. Comput. Stud.*, 1993.
4. Powers, D.M., Characteristics and heuristics of human intelligence, in: *2013 IEEE Symposium on Computational Intelligence for Human-like Intelligence (CIHLI)*, pp. 100–107, IEEE, 2013, April.

5. Craik, F.I. and Lockhart, R.S., Levels of processing: A framework for memory research. *J. Verbal Learn. Verbal Behav.*, 11, 6, 671–684, 1972.

6. Graziano, M.S. and Kastner, S., Human consciousness and its relationship to social neuroscience: A novel hypothesis. *Cognit. Neurosci.*, 2, 2, 98–113, 2011.

7. Velik, R., A Model for Multimodal Humanlike Perception based on Modular Hierarchical Symbolic Information Processing, Knowledge Integration, and Learning, in: *Proceeding of the 2nd International Conference on Bio-Inspired Models of Network, Information, and Computing Systems*, pp. 1–8, 2007.

8. Hahn, U., Romacker, M., Schulz, S., How knowledge drives understanding—Matching medical ontologies with the needs of medical language processing. *Artif. Intell. Med.*, 15, 1, 25–51, 1999.

9. Rahmani, A.M., Gia, T.N., Negash, B., Anzanpour, A., Azimi, I., Jiang, M., Liljeberg, P., Exploiting smart e-Health gateways at the edge of healthcare Internet-of-Things: A fog computing approach. *Future Gener. Comput. Syst.*, 78, 641–658, 2018.

10. Yuehong, Y.I.N., Zeng, Y., Chen, X., Fan, Y., The internet of things in healthcare: An overview. *J. Ind. Inf. Integr.*, 1, 3–13, 2016.

11. Vermesan, O. and Friess, P. (Eds.), *Internet of things-from research and innovation to market deployment*, vol. 29, River Publishers, Aalborg, 2014.

12. Velik, R. and Bruckner, D., Neuro-symbolic networks: Introduction to a new information processing principle, in: *2008 6th IEEE International Conference on Industrial Informatics*, pp. 1042–1047, IEEE, 2008, July.

13. Gyrard, A., Bonnet, C., Boudaoud, K., Enrich machine-to-machine data with semantic web technologies for cross-domain applications, in: *2014 IEEE World Forum on Internet of Things (WF-IoT)*, pp. 559–564, IEEE, 2014, March.

14. García-Sánchez, F., Fernández-Breis, J.T., Valencia-García, R., Gómez, J.M., Martínez-Béjar, R., Combining Semantic Web technologies with Multi-Agent Systems for integrated access to biological resources. *J. Biomed. Inf.*, 41, 5, 848–859, 2008.

15. Mozzaquatro, B.A., Agostinho, C., Goncalves, D., Martins, J., Jardim-Goncalves, R., An ontology-based cybersecurity framework for the internet of things. *Sensors*, 18, 9, 3053, 2018.

16. Joyia, G.J., Liaqat, R.M., Farooq, A., Rehman, S., Internet of Medical Things (IOMT): Applications, benefits and future challenges in healthcare domain. *J. Commun.*, 12, 4, 240–7, 2017.

17. Atzori, L., Iera, A., Morabito, G., Understanding the Internet of Things: definition, potentials, and societal role of a fast evolving paradigm. *Ad. Hoc Networks*, 56, 122–140, 2017.

18. Ahmadi, H., Arji, G., Shahmoradi, L., Safdari, R., Nilashi, M., Alizadeh, M., The application of internet of things in healthcare: A systematic literature review and classification. *Universal Access Inf. Soc.*, 1–33, 2018.

19. Velik, R., Bruckner, D., Lang, R., Deutsch, T., Emulating the perceptual system of the brain for the purpose of sensor fusion, in: *Human-Computer Systems Interaction*, pp. 17–27, Springer, Berlin, Heidelberg, 2009.

20. Mavrogiorgou, A., Kiourtis, A., Touloupou, M., Kapassa, E., Kyriazis, D., Themistocleous, M., The road to the future of healthcare: Transmitting interoperable healthcare data through a 5G based communication platform, in: *European, Mediterranean, and Middle Eastern Conference on Information Systems*, pp. 383–401, Springer, Cham, 2018, October.

21. Ge, M., Bangui, H., Buhnova, B., Big data for internet of things: a survey. *Future Gener. Comput. Syst.*, 87, 601–614, 2018.

22. Jagadeeswari, V., Subramaniyaswamy, V., Logesh, R., Vijayakumar, V., A study on medical Internet of Things and Big Data in personalized healthcare system. *Health Inf. Sci. Syst.*, 6, 1, 14, 2018.

23. Dhanvijay, M.M. and Patil, S.C., Internet of Things: A survey of enabling technologies in healthcare and its applications. *Comput. Networks*, 2019.

24. Kumar, P.M., Lokesh, S., Varatharajan, R., Babu, G.C., Parthasarathy, P., Cloud and IoT based disease prediction and diagnosis system for healthcare using Fuzzy neural classifier. *Future Gener. Comput. Syst.*, 86, 527–534, 2018.

25. Kapassa, E., Kyriazis, D., Themistocleous, M., The Road to the Future of Healthcare: Transmitting Interoperable Healthcare Data Through a 5G Based Communication Platform, in: *Information Systems: 15th European, Mediterranean, and Middle Eastern Conference, EMCIS 2018, Limassol, Cyprus, October 4-5, 2018, Proceedings*, vol. 341, Springer, p. 383, 2019, January.

26. Schulz, S., Balkanyi, L., Cornet, R., Bodenreider, O., From concept representations to ontologies: A paradigm shift in health informatics? *Healthcare Inf. Res.*, 2013.

27. Rath, M., Resolution of Issues and Health Improvement Using Big Data and IoT, in: *Edge Computing and Computational Intelligence Paradigms for the IoT*, pp. 216–237, IGI Global, 2019.

28. Velik, R., A Model for Multimodal Humanlike Perception based on Modular Hierarchical Symbolic Information Processing, Knowledge Integration, and Learning, in: *Proceeding of the 2nd International Conference on Bio-Inspired Models of Network, Information, and Computing Systems*, pp. 1–8, 2007.

29. Hahn, U., Romacker, M., Schulz, S., How knowledge drives understanding—Matching medical ontologies with the needs of medical language processing. *Artif. Intell. Med.*, 15, 1, 25–51, 1999.

30. Baker, S.B., Xiang, W., Atkinson, I., Internet of things for smart healthcare: Technologies, challenges, and opportunities. *IEEE Access*, 5, 26521–26544, 2017.

31. Vippalapalli, V. and Ananthula, S., Internet of things (IoT) based smart health care system, in: *2016 International Conference on Signal Processing, Communication, Power and Embedded System (SCOPES)*, pp. 1229–1233, IEEE, 2016, October.

32. Sundaravadivel, P., Kougianos, E., Mohanty, S.P., Ganapathiraju, M.K., Everything you wanted to know about smart health care: Evaluating the different technologies and components of the Internet of Things for better health. *IEEE Consum. Electron. Mag.*, 7, 1, 18–28, 2017.

15

Tools and Techniques for Streaming Data: An Overview

K. Saranya[1], S. Chellammal[1]* and Pethuru Raj Chelliah[2]

[1]Department of Computer Science, Bharathidasan University Constituent Arts and Science College, Navalurkuttapattu, Srirangam (Tk), Tiruchirappalli, Tamilnadu, India
[2]Site Reliability Engineering (SRE) Division, Reliance Jio Infocomm. Ltd. (RJIL), Bangalore, India

Abstract

Nowadays, many organizations generate continuous flow of data. The data may arrive as rapid, multiple, continuous, time-varying data streams. Such streaming data is generated from various sources such as sensor networks, telephone networks, mobile data, satellite, healthcare, geospatial services, real time applications, etc. Processing streaming data is tedious due to its speed, heterogeneous formats of data and volume. Recent advancements in big data techniques and tools made the processing of streaming data easier. In this chapter, after a survey, the available techniques are categorized into (i) traditional streaming data techniques, (ii) data mining streaming techniques, and (iii) big data techniques for streaming data and these techniques are discussed in detail with a special emphasis to recent big data based streaming architectures.

Keywords: Streaming data, traditional techniques, reservoir sampling, histograms, sketch, clustering/classification of streaming data, big data platforms and tools for streaming data

*Corresponding author: chelsganesh@gmail.com

Vishal Jain, Ritika Wason, Jyotir Moy Chatterjee and Dac-Nhuong Le (eds.) Ontology-Based Information Retrieval for Healthcare Systems, (313–330) © 2020 Scrivener Publishing LLC

15.1 Introduction

Nowadays, in various fields of applications such as social media, sensor networks, telecommunications, geospatial services, healthcare, etc., data is recorded continuously with respect to time called data stream [1]. Data stream is a sequence of continuous and infinite data that occurs with speed. A few examples for streaming data include continuous data acquisition in weather stations during cyclone, image data collected from satellites, user's click stream data in web sites, videos uploaded in YouTube, data collected from Internet of Things (IoT) devices, etc. Stream processing is able to yield new inferences and extracts new knowledge as per the data that continuously arrives. Streaming data may be structured or unstructured [1, 2]. In structured stream, there are three models. The first model is *turnstile* model where the data can be inserted, deleted, or updated in the database. The second model is defined as *cash register model* which is used for only adding new data elements. The third model is called *time series model* where each data is considered as individual vector and processed individually. Unstructured streaming data has no schema. Examples for unstructured data that is generated by human are data available in Facebook, Twitter, LinkedIn, WhatsApp data, mobile data, data generated in chat, recorded video or audio data, etc. Similarly, machines also generate unstructured data such as satellite images, seismic imagery, cyclonic data, data from traffic, weather, oceanographic sensors, automobile related data generated at toll plazas, etc.

Time is an important factor in streaming data. Since streaming data arrives with speed as well as with growing size and heterogeneous formats, various techniques have been developed for processing it. In this work, the techniques available for streaming data processing are categorized into (i) traditional techniques, (ii) data mining techniques for streaming data, and (iii) big data–based techniques for streaming data as in Figure 15.1. Some of the traditional techniques such as random sampling, sliding window, histogram, and sketches have been discussed. Data mining techniques which facilitate streaming data processing such as clustering and classification are described. Big data streaming platforms include distributed messaging system (Apache Storm), batch processing (Apache Spark), event-driven approach (Apache Flume), and asynchronous event messaging (Apache Kafka) and Apache Flink. These techniques are discussed in detail with special emphasis to the recent big data based streaming techniques.

The chapter is organized as follows. Section 15.2 provides some review on traditional methods for processing streaming data. Section 15.3 illustrates how various data mining techniques can facilitate the processing for

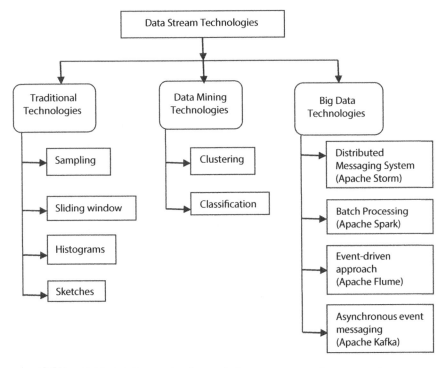

Figure 15.1 Categories of streaming data techniques.

streaming data. Section 15.4 describes different big data techniques and platforms available for streaming data. Section 15.5 concludes the chapter.

15.2   Traditional Techniques

As mentioned earlier, streaming data is of infinite length with data comes at speed, it has different challenging aspects, namely, computational storage and processing. Various research works such as [4–11] which deal with traditional techniques, namely, Random Sampling, Sliding Window, Histograms, and Sketches for streaming data. An overview of traditional techniques is presented in this section.

15.2.1   Random Sampling

In streaming data, since data is continuously arriving, the size of the data also becomes huge. Storing and processing such huge, speedy data becomes tedious. Various traditional techniques were in use. One such traditional technique is sampling. Since, it is practically infeasible to store all the continuous data, sampling technique tries to collect only a sample data which would be representative of all the data. For example, in a simple sampling data, data may be sampled at regular intervals of time [4]. When data consists of different subsets, reservoir sampling may be useful. In reservoir sampling [5], the data is divided into different subgroups and sample is drawn from each group and from the collected samples, further processing will be carried out. Further, reservoir sampling algorithms are used for both handling both dynamic datasets as well as large static datasets [6].

15.2.2   Histograms

In general performing queries on continuously arriving and huge data is complex, histogram techniques were used which gives the frequency distribution of various data elements in terms of small functions [5]. In histogram, a set of intervals is defined over the range of variables. It provides collective information such as frequency count for each interval. Histograms may be static or dynamic. In general, histograms are used to process large sized time series datasets [7]. Construction of static histograms requires the complete data set, and hence, it cannot include the newly arriving data instances whereas dynamic histograms [8] are capable of including the newly arriving data instances for the construction of histograms.

15.2.3   Sliding Window

As streaming data contains infinite length of continuous data, it becomes practically infeasible to store the data due to the constraints with storage and processor requirements. In addition, in many applications, inferences and decision can be drawn from the recent past data rather than the old past data. Keeping this idea in mind, the sliding window technique has been developed to facilitate the processing of streaming data. In time-based sliding window technique [5], two parameters are being specified. They are *window size* and *window interval*. For example, consider a time-based sliding window having *window size = 20 seconds* with *window interval = 10*. Assume the recording of data begins at 0. In the sliding model, the window collects records from 0 to 20 seconds and slides over the data according to interval 10 and continues the data collection from 10 seconds to 30 seconds. That is the sliding window collects and groups data records that occurred in 0–20 seconds and then from 10–30 seconds and 20–30 seconds and so on.

In count based sliding window, the specified number of data (count) from recent window will be considered for processing.

15.2.4   Sketches

There are situations where it is required to work with data sets that arrive from more than one data streams. In such situations, the sketch which consists of probabilistic data structures, data arrays, and some techniques like hash functions. Using the different components, sketch reads and stores the information related to multiple streams. Later, queries such as finding frequencies of items can be raised to sketch [4]. Sketches are extensively used to handle fast data streams due to their high insertion speed [10]. Popular sketching techniques include bloom filters and count-min sketch [11].

15.2.4.1   Bloom Filters

In situations, where it is required to check whether a particular data element is present or not in a given massive dataset, bloom filter is used. Bloom filter is a probabilistic data structure that consumes less memory and determines the presence of a data element very quickly. Typically, bloom filters are constructed with its size equal to the number of elements in dataset.

15.2.4.2   Count-Min Sketch

Similar to bloom filters, the *Count-Min sketch* is also a probabilistic data structure that is used to determine the frequency of an event in the data stream. Unlike a bloom filter which have its size equal to the number of elements in the set, count-min sketch consumes less space, and it works on single data instance at a time to finds its frequency.

15.3   Data Mining Techniques

Almost every domain and transactions of day-to-day life is emerged with new upcoming techniques. Because, there are lot of organizations generate bigger number of data at very high speed. The data produced across many organizations may keeps on changing continuously with respect to time period. The organizations are in greater need to process those speedy data which can change over time and extract useful information from them. Several procedures for extracting information from data stream are projected in data mining techniques [12–18]. Data mining is a field of computer science used to extract useful, hidden, and interesting knowledge from huge data by performing different kinds of mining tasks such as clustering, classification, pattern recognition, association rule mining, etc. In this section, a brief overview about different clustering and classification algorithms that are being used to process streaming data is highlighted.

15.3.1   Clustering

To facilitate the extraction of knowledge from massive data, clustering technique divides the massive data into clusters of similar objects [12]. That is similar objects are grouped into same cluster. Within a single cluster, the objects are similar, whereas the objects belong to different clusters are dissimilar. Similarity is computed using distance measure such as Euclidean distance or density measure such as number of neighbors of an object [13]. In general, clustering provides first level knowledge or characterization of data. When clustering needs to be performed on streaming data where infinite amount of data arrives with speed, in order to meet the memory and time constraints, clustering is typically performed in two stages. In the first stage, summary statistics of streaming data are collected using memory efficient data structures such as array and hash functions and in the second stage clustering algorithms are employed over the summary data to produce clusters. Algorithms such as STREAM, Balanced Iterative Reducing and Clustering Using Hierarchies (BIRCH), COBWEB, etc., are being used to cluster streaming data.

15.3.1.1   STREAM

The *STREAM* algorithm [14] applies a divide-and-conquer approach in order to have small space. It divides the stream into many subsets of data and it used K-Means or K-Median algorithm to each subset to create K clusters. Each cluster center is assigned with a weight which is based on the number of points in that cluster. Then, the weighted cluster centers are grouped into small number of clusters.

15.3.1.2   BRICH

BRICH performs clustering of streaming data in an incremental fashion where the algorithm considers a fixed number of data points at a given time. BRICH uses hierarchical data structure, namely, *feature tree* which helps in understanding the features of dataset in a hierarchical pattern. It is more appropriate for vast amount of datasets.

15.3.1.3 CLUSTREAM

There is another algorithm called CLUSTREAM [15] which initially clusters the streaming data into K number of micro clusters into which further incoming data points are clustered. Also, the algorithm stores the summary information about micro clusters. Then, based on summary statistics, the micro level clusters are again grouped into macro level clusters.

15.3.2 Classification

Classification is a supervised learning task which is used to classify the given data item into the predefined class label. Basically, classification algorithms work in two stages. They are learning stage and classification stage. In learning stage, the algorithm is trained with huge collection of what is called training data which is supposed to contain all possible combinations of inputs. The output of learning step is classifier or a set of classification rules (which is also called as model). The model has to be validated for its accuracy before it is used for classifying any unknown data. Once the model is found to have sufficient accuracy which is basically decided by concerned application, the model will be put in practice for prediction. As mentioned earlier, streaming data are continuous and rapid in nature, classification algorithms for streaming data have to handle the constraints on memory and processing time. Classification algorithm handles the data instances either one at a time or as a block at a time. A few examples for classification algorithms that are used for classifying streaming data include Naïve Bayesian, Hoeffding and Very Fast Decision Tree (VFDT) [16].

15.3.2.1 Naïve Bayesian

Naïve Bayes classifier [17] is a probabilistic algorithm which is based on the principle, Bayes's theorem which considers that the attributes or features which are used to classify an item are independent of one another and all the features are equal. Since, the attributes are considered as equal, same weight is given to all attributes. Naïve Bayes classifier is simple and it can handle problems having several target or class labels. One of the advantages of this algorithm is that it does not sort the data elements. In the research work [18], the author experimentally found that Naïve Bayes algorithm is fast enough to handle streaming data. But it has the limitation that it cannot handle *concept drift* which refers to the changes in the distribution of data elements with respect to time.

15.3.2.2   Hoeffding

In conventional decision tree, during learning process the tree is constructed by finding the best splitting attribute according to *information gain* or *gini index*. In order to find and construct the decision tree, the data instances have to be reused. But in streaming data, to avoid the repeated use of instances, Domingos and Hulten [19] proposed the Hoeffding Tree which is a VFDT where the instances are not reused. Rather new instances are used. This algorithm assumes that the distribution of data is not changing with respect to time. Like Naïve Bayes algorithm, this algorithm also does not support *concept drift*.

15.3.2.3   Very Fast Decision Tree

Very Fast Decision Tree [16, 19] has introduced some changes in Hoeffding tree in order to bring in effective memory and time utilization. In this algorithm, the decision tree is constructed using the recent data items of window sliding they arrived already. This means that though this algorithm is fast, it cannot include the arriving new instances for tree construction. It cannot handle *concept drift* in data streams [20].

15.3.2.4   Concept Adaptive Very Fast Decision Tree

Concept Adaptive Very Fast Decision Tree (CVFDT) [20] is extended from VFDT so that is can include the newly arriving data items for construction of tree. It can handle the changes in distribution of data what occur dynamically with respect to time. From [21], it is understood that there are empirical analysis which shows that CVFDT is fast and accurate like VFDT. In addition, it constructs smaller sized trees when compared to VFDT.

15.4   Big Data Platforms

Research works such as [22–34] describe various big data platforms such as Apache Storm, Apache Spark, Apache Flume, Apache Kafka, and Apache Flink that are available for stream data processing.

15.4.1   Apache Storm

Apache storm is a distributed real time computational system for processing data stream [22]. It is extremely fast as it processes a one million *tuples* per second per node. Storm can be easily integrated with any programming language. Storm architecture [23] is mainly designed for micro batch processing. The architecture of Apache storm is shown in Figure 15.2. Storm cluster consists of different types of nodes [24] such as *Nimbus* in *master node* which serves as job tracker which assigns jobs to *supervisor* which in turn initiates processes on *worker nodes*. As Apache storm does not have the capacity to manage its cluster state, Apache Zookeeper is used for managing the cluster state of storm and which provides the communication between job tracker and supervisors.

15.4.2   Apache Spark

Apache spark [22, 23] is a distributed platform used to process big data with a unique capability that it can keep huge data in memory. Hence, it gives higher performance than Hadoop. Spark platform consists of various components such as spark core (or) Resilient Distributed Dataset (RDD), Spark SQL like functions for structured data, Machine Learning library, Streaming Data API and Graph processing API (GraphX) as shown in Figure 15.3.

15.4.2.1   Apache Spark Core

Spark Core (i.e., RDD) is the general execution engine for parallel and distributed processing. It performs various functions, namely, in-memory

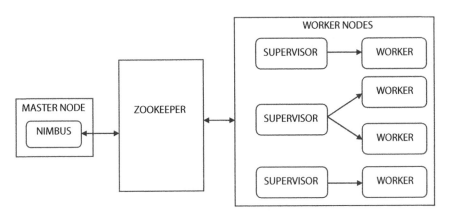

Figure 15.2 Apache Storm Architecture.

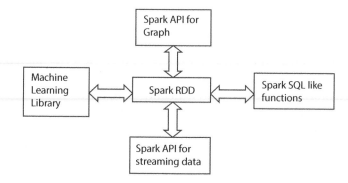

Figure 15.3 Components of Spark.

computing, scheduling, distribution and monitoring of jobs, and interactions with external storage systems.

15.4.2.2   Spark SQL

Spark includes a set of SQL like functions which help to query large sized structured data which is distributed in nature.

15.4.2.3   Machine Learning Library

The Machine learning library (*MLLib*) includes various algorithms such as Naïve Bayes, Support Vector Machine, Random Forest, Linear Regression, K-Means clustering, etc., which are used to implement various data mining tasks on massive data.

15.4.2.4   Streaming Data API

Spark Streaming API provides methods to handle streaming data. The process of streaming data has been illustrated in Figure 15.4.

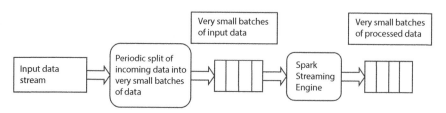

Figure 15.4 Process of Spark Streaming.

15.4.2.5   GraphX

GraphX library provides methods to handle graph data structure.

15.4.3   Apache Flume

Apache Flume [29] is a tool for gathering, aggregating, and migrating enormous amount of streaming data from several sources like log files, events, etc., from various web servers to a centralized data store. It is especially designed to transfer streaming data from various sources to Hadoop Distributed File System (HDFS). The transactions in flume are channel based where one sender and one receiver and a message are involved. Flume architecture consists of three components [30] such as *flume source, flume channel, flume sink* as shown in Figure 15.5.

As in Figure 15.5, flume data sources collects data from any web servers or log data. The data channel collects the data from data source for storage until it transfers the data to data sink. The data sink finally transfers the data to storage system such as HDFS or Hbase.

15.4.4   Apache Kafka

Apache Kafka is especially designed for distributed messaging system for gaining high throughput. When compared with other messaging systems, Kafka offers built in partitioning, replication and fault tolerance features. It is originally based on publish-subscribe model. Since it is distributed in nature, it can be scaled out easily [32]. Kafka is very fast as it performs two million writes/sec. Kafka has several components (Please see Figure 15.6),

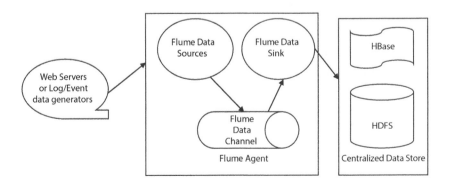

Figure 15.5 Flume Architecture.

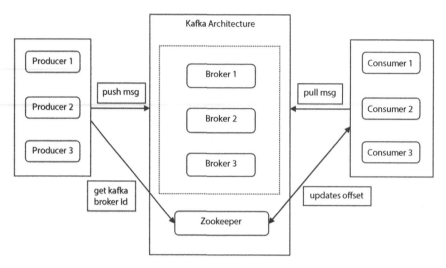

Figure 15.6 Components of Kafka Architecture.

namely, *kafka producer, kafka broker, kafka topic, kafka zookeeper, and kafka consumer* [25, 33].

(i)   *Kafka Producer:* Producer will produce or publish the messages to one or more topics. Every time, a producer sends messages to kafka broker which is then transfers the message into the concerned topic.

(ii) *Kafka Broker:* Kafka cluster consists of one or more servers called kafka broker which has the great responsibility for maintaining the published data. Kafka is mentioned as time-based retention method where the broker keeps the messages for certain amount of time.

(iii) *Kafka Topic:* Kafka topic is located within the Kafka broker. Topic is the area where the messages are stored and published. For each topic, Kafka maintains minimum of one partition. Topics may have many partitions also. Each partitioned message has a unique sequence id termed as offset.

(iv) *Kafka Zookeeper:* Zookeeper serves as the coordination interface between the kafka brokers and kafka consumers. Kafka allows zookeeper to store information about topics, brokers, consumers, and so on.

(v)   *Kafka Consumer:* Consumer consumes messages from brokers. Consumer subscribes to one or more topics and consumes published messages by pulling data from the brokers. Kafka can support a large number of consumers and retain large amount of data.

Kafka provides various APIs [34], namely, *Producer API, Consumer API, Streaming API, and Connector API* which enable the communications between various components. These APIs are shown in Figure 15.7

(i) *Producer API*: This kind of API allows an application to bring out a stream of data to one or more Kafka topics.

(ii) *Consumer API*: The Consumer API allows an application to subscribe to one or more topics and process the stream of records produced to them.

(iii) *Streaming API*: The Streams API allows an application to act as a stream processor, consuming an input stream from one or more topics and producing an output stream to one or more output topics, effectively transforming the input streams to output streams.

(iv) *Connector API*: The Connector API allows building and running reusable producers or consumers that connect Kafka topics to existing applications or data systems. For example, a connector to a relational database might capture every change to a table.

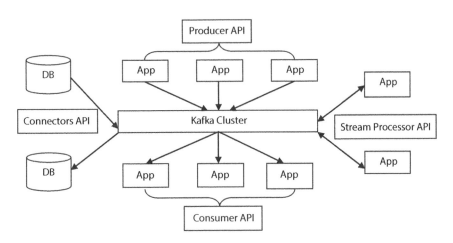

Figure 15.7 Kafka APIs.

15.4.5   Apache Flink

Apache Flink is a framework for processing streaming data in real time. It provides an open source stream processing engine for high-performance, scalable, and accurate real-time applications [35]. Flink is designed to run in all common cluster environments, performs computations at in-memory speed and at any scale. Flink is effective both as a batch and real time processing framework but it considers streaming first. Flink has methods and techniques to handle the data both in batch processing and real time processing fashions. Hence, streaming data can be processed efficiently using Flink. The components of Apache Flink [36] are shown in Figure 15.8.

(i)   *Storage*: The Read/Write operations could be performed in Apache Flink using the following basic storages such as HDFS, Local File System, MongoDB, HBase, RabbitMQ, Apache Kafka, Apache Flume, etc.

(ii)   *Deploy*: Apache Flink can be deployed using anyone of the following modes such as local mode, cluster mode, or cloud

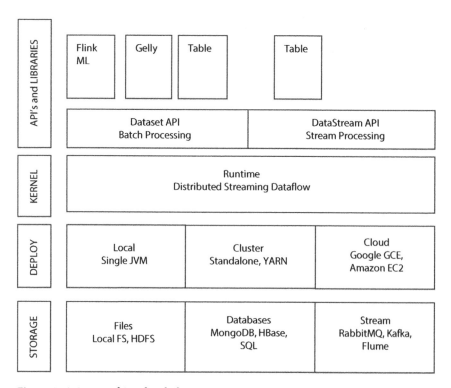

Figure 15.8 Layers of Apache Flink ecosystem.

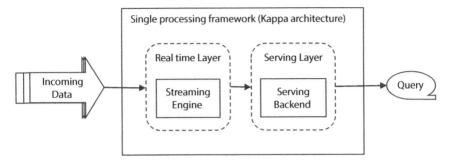

Figure 15.9 Kappa architecture.

mode. In local mode, Flink can be deployed using single JVM whereas cluster mode can be standalone, YARN, Mesos. On cloud, Flink can be deployed using Amazon EC2 and GCE.

(iii) *Kernel*: This is a runtime layer which supports distributed processing, fault tolerance, and reliability.

(iv) *API's and Libraries*: This is the top most layer of Apache Flink. It has both Dataset API and Datastream API for batch processing and stream processing, respectively. The libraries such as Flink ML for machine learning, Gelly for graph processing and Tables for SQL.

Apache Flink architecture is designed around *Kappa architecture* [37] as in Figure 15.9. The main idea behind kappa architecture is to handle both batch and real time data through a single stream processing engine as in Figure 15.9. Kappa uses only a single code path for the two layers such as real time layer and serving layer which reduces the system complexity. Since single engine handles both real time processing and batch processing, Kappa provides flexibility to developers to develop applications without thinking about the internals of the processing framework

15.5 Conclusion

Based on the review of literature related to streaming data, it is clear that the traditional techniques and data mining techniques are not sufficient to process streaming data due to its high speed, infinite, and heterogeneous formats. Most of the issues could be fixed using big data platforms since they naturally handle vast amount of data both structured and unstructured arriving at high speed.

References

1. Margara A. and Rabl. T., Definition of Data Streams. in: Encyclopedia of Big Data Technologies. S. Sakr and A. Zomaya (eds). Springer, Cham, Switzerland, 2018.

2. de Assuncao, Marcos Dias, da Silva Veith, Alexandre, Buyya, Rajkumar, Distributed data stream processing and edge computing: A survey on resource elasticity and future directions. *J. Netw. Comput Appl.*, 103, 1–17, 06 December 2017. Published by Elsevier.

3. https://www.datamation.com/big-data/structured-vs-unstructured-data. html, By Christine Taylor, Posted March 28, 2018.

4. Kholghi, Mahnoosh and Keyvanpour, Mohammadreza, An Analytical Framework for Data Stream Mining Techniques based on Challenges and Requirements. *Int. J. Eng. Technol. (IJEST)*, 3, 2507–2513, 2011.

5. Brian Babcock, Shivnath Babu,Mayur Datar, Rajeev Motwani, J. Widom, Models and issues in data stream systems PODS '02: Proceedings of the twenty-first ACM SIGMOD-SIGACT-SIGART symposium on Principles of database systems. pp. 1–16, https://doi.org/10.1145/543613.543615. 2002.

6. Bressan, Stephane and Lu, Xuesong, Sampling Data Streams: From Reservoir Sampling to Sliding Window Sampling. *The 2009 International Conference on Advanced Computer Science and Information Systems (ICACSIS)*, ResearchGate, 2009.

7. Guha, Sudipto, Koudas, Nick, Shim, Kyuseok, Data Streams and Histograms. *Proceedings of thirty-third annual ACM symposium on Theory of computing (STOC)*, 6–8 July, pp. 471–475, 2001.

8. Donjerkovic, Donko, Ioannidis, Yannis, Ramakrishnan, Raghu, Dynamic Histograms: Capturing Evolving Data Sets. *International Conference on Data Engineering (ICDE)*, pp. 1–80, 2000.

9. Badiozamany, Sobhan, Real-Time data stream clustering over sliding windows, in: *Digital Comprehensive Summaries of Uppsala Dissertations from the Faculty of Science and Technology*, pp. 1–130, 23 November 2016.

10. Yang, T., Liu, L., Yan, Y., Shahzad, M.T., Shen, Y., Li, X., Cui, B., Xie, G., SF-sketch: A Two-stage Sketch for Data Streams, in: *IEEE 33rd International Conference on Data Engineering (ICDE)*, IEEE, NY, USA, 2017.

11. Cormode, Graham, Data Sketching: The approximate approach is often faster and more efficient, in: *Article in Communications of the ACM*, vol. 15, 2 pp. 48–55, 31 May 2017.

12. Kokate, Umesh, Deshpande, Arvind, Mahalle, Parikshit, Patil, Pramod, Data Stream Clustering Techniques, Applications and Models: Comparative Analysis and Discussions. *Art. Big Data Cognit. Comput.*, 2, 32, 1–30, 17 October 2018.

13. Namiot, Dmitry, On Big Data Stream Processing. *Int. J. Open Inf. Technol.*, 3, 48–51, January 2015. Published by ResearchGate.

14. http://dsc.soic.indiana.edu/publications/survey_algorithms_streaming.pdf

15. https://ijarcce.com/wp-content/uploads/2015/12/IJARCCE-93.pdf

16. Madhu, S., Shukla, Kirit, R., Rathod, Stream Data Mining and Comparative Study of Classification Algorithms. *Int. J. Eng. Res. Appl.*, 3, 1, 163–168, January-February 2013.

17. David, Shiela, Ranjithkumar, K., Rao, Saurabh, Baradwaj, Santhosh, Sudhakar, D., Classification of Massive Data Streams using Naïve Bayes. *IAETSD J. Adv. Res. Appl. Sci.*, 5, 4, 208–215, April 2018.

18. http://iaetsdjaras.org/gallery/26-april-671.pdf

19. Domingos, Pedro and Hulten, Geoff, Mining High Speed Data Streams. *Proceedings of sixth ACM SIGKDD International Conference on Knowledge Discovery and Data Mining*, pp. 71–80, August 2000.

20. https://www.skedsoft.com/books/data-mining-data-warehousing/very-fast-decision-tree-vfdt-and-concept-adapting-very-fast-decision-tree-cvfdt-

21. Hulten, Geoff, Spencer, Laurie, Domingos, Pedro, Mining Time Changing Data Streams. *Proceedings of seventh ACM SIGKDD International Conference on Knowledge Discovery and Data Mining*, pp. 97–106, August 2001.

22. Shoro, Abdul Ghaffar and Soomro, Tariq Rahim, Big Data Analysis: Apache Spark Perspective. *Global J. Comput. Sci. Technol. C Software Eng.*, 15, 1, January 2015. Publisher Global Journals Inc. USA.

23. Ounacer, Sowmaya, Talhaoui, Mohamed Amine, Ardchir, Soufiane, Daif, Abderrahmane, Azouazi, Mohamed, A New Architecture for Real Time Data Stream Processing. *Int. J. Adv. Comput. Sci. Appl. (IJACSA)*, 8, 2017.

24. Surshanov, S., Using Apache Storm for Big Data. *12th International Scientific Conference, Technologies and Management Institute*, pp. 14–17, 10 January 2015.

25. Jain, Ashwitha and Venkatramana, Bhat P, Analysis of Bill Of Material Data using Kafka and Spark. *Int. J. Sci. Res. Publ.*, 6, 8, 44–48, 8 August 2016.

26. Bhattacharya, Abhishek and Bhatnagar, Shefali, Big Data and Apache Spark: A Review. *Int. J. Eng. Res. Sci. (IJOER)*, 2, 5, 206–210, 05 May 2016.

27. Ben Blamey, Andreas Hellander and Salman Toor, Apache Spark Streaming, Kafka and HarmonicIO: A Performance Benchmark and Architecture Comparison for Enterprise and Scientific Computing, vol.3, 12 March 2019. https://arxiv.org/abs/1807.07724v3.

28. Zaharia, Matei, Das, Tathagata, Li, Haoyuan, Hunter, Timothy, Shenker, Scott, Stoica, Ion, Discretized Streams: Fault-Tolerant Streaming Computation at Scale. *Proceedings of the Twenty-Fourth ACM Symposium on Operating Systems Principles*, 13, pp. 423–438, 2013.

29. Wang, Jun, Wang, Wenhao, Chen Renfei, Distributed Data Streams Processing based on Flume/Kafka/Spark. *3rd International Conference on Mechatronics and Industrial Informatics (ICMII)*, Atlantis Press, pp. 948–952, 2015.

30. Birjali, Marouane, Beni-Hssane, Abderrahim, Erritali, Mohammed, Analyzing Social Media Through Big Data using InfoSphere BigInsights and Apache Flume. *The 8th International Conference on Emerging Ubiquitous Systems and Pervasive Networks (EUSPN)*, Elsevier, pp. 280–285, 2017.

31. https://www.hyperlearning.ai/en/knowledgebase/blog/real-time-data-pipeline-flume-kafka-spark
32. Jay Kreps, Neha Narkhede and Jun Rao, Kafka: A Distributed Messaging System for Log Processing, in: *The proceedings of 6th International Workshop on Networking Meets DataBases (NetDB'11)*, Athens, Greece (http://notes.stephenholiday.com/Kafka.pdf). 2011.
33. https://www.cloudkarafka.com/blog/2016-11-30-part1-kafka-for-beginners-what-is-apache-kafka.html
34. https://kafka.apache.org/intro
35. Gürcan, F. and M. Berigel., Real-Time Processing of Big Data Streams: Lifecycle, Tools, Tasks, and Challenges. in: *2nd International Symposium on Multidisciplinary Studies and Innovative Technologies (ISMSIT)*, Ankara, pp. 1–6, IEEE, NY, USA, 2018.
36. Gireesh Babu, C.N., Pokhrel, Anu, Ashwini V and Thungamani, M., Real Time Big Data Analysis using Apache Flink. *Int. J. Sci. Eng. Appl. Sci. (IJSEAS)*, 3, 6, 78–83, 2017.
37. Ounacer, Soumaya, Talhaoui, Mohamed Amine, Ardchir, Soufiane, Daif, Abderrahmane, Azouazi, Mohamed, Real time Data Stream Processing Challenges and Perspectives. *Int. J. Comput. Issues (IJCSI)*, 14, 5, 6–12, 2017.

An Ontology-Based IR for Health Care

J. P. Patra*, Gurudatta Verma and Sumitra Samal

Department of Computer Science and Engineering, Shri Shankaracharya Institute of Professional Management and Technology, Raipur, India

Abstract

In the outmoded information retrieval (IR) models, although suitable retrieval function is chosen in terms of logical views, the performance of IR is always unsatisfiable because the logical views of documents and the logical views of user's information requirements cannot represent documents and user's information requirements well. In this paper, ontology-based IR model is presented for health-related data; ontology is engendered using a kind of basic description logic, which is an appropriate tradeoff between expressivity of knowledge and complexity of cognitive problems. The equivalent classes of concepts can be attained by using fuzzy logic for this kind of basic description logic; the equivalent classes of individuals can be obtained by using equivalent relations between individuals under condition that only atomic roles exist; so, the set of semantic index terms can be acquired. IR system takes input as user query, further semantics generated corresponding user's query text and passed to the IR function. Henceforth, suitable retrieval function is chosen to enhance the performance of IR system. By using a common scenario, the practicability of this model is explained in theory.

Keywords: IR, TPR, FNR, ML, NL, SVM ANN

16.1 Introduction

The IR technology research is accompanied by the arrival of the information age come and start. Every day, data collection, computer digitization, health satellite remote sensing, production and economic operations, office and management systems, etc., generate very huge volume of data. We are "submerged"

---
*Corresponding author: patra.jyotiprakash@gmail.com

Vishal Jain, Ritika Wason, Jyotir Moy Chatterjee and Dac-Nhuong Le (eds.) Ontology-Based Information Retrieval for Healthcare Systems, (331–344) © 2020 Scrivener Publishing LLC

in the ocean of data In order to do this, it is necessary to effectively retrieve information from the data set.

A document represents a unit of information, and text is a typical form, but the document can also contain other media such as images, video, and audio. Here, put text files are broadly viewed as including ordinary text documents, extended multiple forms of data, including media files and multimedia data unit.

Information retrieval (IR) [1]: From a bulky collection of document collections, find the appropriate number of document subsets related to consumer information needs.

The machine currently cannot directly use the original documents and users' information needs to achieve IR, so from the original document and starting from user information needs, establish their own suitable machine logical view (in this article, a logical view is a set of the weight of the representative index term), by calculating the logic of the document. Similarity between views and logical views of user information needs degree, you can sort the documents in the document set.

In outmoded IR models, there is no semantic, a standardized vocabulary of features, which cannot be intentionally done on the document in advance. Meaning so, the method of extracting index entries is mainly from the language from the viewpoint of law if the index term is mainly composed of nouns, adverbs, conjunctions, and adjectives that are rarely used as index entries, words (words that appear frequently in the document set), stemming, use dictionaries to expand words, etc., because they are built on words. In method analysis, the extracted index items that express semantics is always unsatisfactory, leading to document logic views cannot effectively represent the document; meanwhile, Lexical set of semantic features, logical view of user information needs the form of the picture that varied and inaccurate and cannot be effectively represented user information needs. In such IR model, IR performance is poor.

This article first establishes a universal information retrieval Model, indicating that the core task of information retrieval is to get information as per user need and the characteristics of user information needs select a good logical view to generate Function that is to select a suitable sorting function according to the characteristics of the logical view. Due to the requirement that the logical view generation function can generate valid, a logical view reflects the semantics of user information requirements and documents. Numerous literatures have shown that ontology is suitable as the basis for expressing semantics [2–6]. Based on this, this article establishes ontology-based information; the retrieval model makes IR more accurate and effective.

16.2 General Definition of Information Retrieval Model

The same document in the document set should be regarded as one document. The same user information should be treated as a user's information needs. Given the general IR model, the definition is as follows:

Definition 1 for a document set D and a set of user information for requirement Q, the logical view generation function v d of the selected document User information requirements logical view generation function vq, sort function R, the IR model can be expressed as a seven-tuple

$$F \{D, V D, v d, Q, V Q, vq, R (vq (ql), v d (dj))\}$$

Represents the cardinality of the set, the IR module Type has the following characteristics:

1. D is the set of documents, n is a positive integer, $| D | = n$, and any two documents in D are different from each other.
2. VD is a collection of logical views of the document, $n \geq | VD |$.
3. v d is a document logical view generation function that the document maps to a logical view of the document, $v d: D \rightarrow V D$, and v d It is full shot.
4. Q is the set of user information needs, and m is the positive integer Number, $| Q | = m$, and any two-user information needs in Q Different from each other.
5. V Q is a set of logical views of user information needs Together, $m \geq | V Q |$.
6. vq is a logical view of user information needs function to map user information needs to user information needs logical view, $vq: Q \rightarrow V Q$, and vq is surjective.
7. vd and vq are collectively called logical view generation functions (vd, vq).
8. $ql \in Q (l \in [1, m])$, $dj \in D (j \in [1, n])$, R (vq (ql), v d (dj)) is a sort function that returns a real number reflecting the degree of similarity between vq (ql) and vd (dj).
9. Suppose the logical view generation function (v d, vq) and sort the function R is determined and can be given according to a user's information demand ql Document set D

establishes an order relationship s l (a s lb meaning Yes: according to user information requirements ql, document a is not inferior to document b), the order relationship satisfies the condition:

It can be known from Theorem 1 that a function (v d, v q) and sort function R timing, for each user information Requirement ql (l ∈ [1, m]), a set can be established on the document set D corresponding total order relationship s l (l ∈ [1, m]). There are documents for sorting; these sorts are fully reliant on (v d, vq) and R.

That is, the core task of IR is to feature documents and user query needs select a good logical view. Generate function (v d, vq), the logical view, it generates must represents documents and user information needs effectively; logically select the appropriate sorting function R for the characteristics of the view. The logical view is a set of representative index entries. Value, logical view can be seen as points in space, distance between two points the closer, the smaller the difference between the two points, so the ranking function R take the opposite of the distance of the points in space.

16.3   Information Retrieval Model Based on Ontology

In earlier IR models, there is no semantic, a canonical vocabulary of features, without prior documentation of the document   so it can only be drawn from the perspective of grammar. Take index items, and then use a certain item weighting strategy (usually used *tf-idf* weighting strategy) [1] assign weights to index items, generate a logical view of the document, which cannot effectively reflect the text, the semantics of the document, and thus cannot effectively represent the document; Due to the lack of a standardized vocabulary with semantic features, users believe that the form of the logical view of the information demand is diverse and inaccurate. The logical view does not effectively reflect the language of the user's information needs, meaning, which cannot effectively represent the user's information needs. Here, in this kind of IR model, select the appropriate sorting function R (the sorting function R is empty). The inverse of the distance between the midpoints, because the logical view cannot be valid representation of user information needs and the document; hence, the retrieval performance is always unsatisfactory.

To effectively reflect user information needs and documentation, the semantics of the user information generated by the logical view generation function requirement logical view and document logical view can effectively represent user information requirements and documents; this article introduces ontology as expression semantics basics.

Domain ontology is a full portrayal of domain conceptualization [4]. Description, Objects, relationships, and classes are expressed by a vocabulary set, which is the domain Ontology. Using this vocabulary, a knowledge depiction can be domain knowledge. Usually, the domain ontology can also include some knowledge, then the domain ontology at this time consists of words pool and knowledge composition. There is essentially only one in this world. Ontology is a detailed description of the conceptualization of the world, but the actual in applications, people always first establish what they need in their respective fields. Domain ontology: when multiple domains need to work together, combine these. The domain ontology of each domain is integrated to form domain ontology.

Ontology construction and inference construction are based on description logic. There are many languages that can be used in the ontology. As for the method of description, description logic can accurately describe the semantics; In terms of the semi-decidability of the first-order predicate logic inference problem, description logic not only has strong knowledge expression ability, but also guarantees reasoning is determinable. As the number of constructors increases, the description logic of this book derives many suitable for different occasions. Descriptive logic form, in general, the more constructors, the knowledge table the stronger the ability to reach, but the more complicated the reasoning problem is:

Let A and B be atomic concepts, and C and D be conceptual descriptions. Atomic concepts and concept descriptions are concepts, and R and S are atomic angles and color, a and b are individuals, considering the knowledge expression ability and reasoning a trade-off of efficiency. See the following (a detailed description of these constraints can be found in [7]).

Let T be an atomic conceptual construct that appears only to the right of the definition Set BT (base symbols), the atoms that appear to the left of the definition. The concept constitutes a set NT (name symbols). The term set T is right and wrong Acyclic so that a finite number of iterations can be used. The process obtains T's expansion T ', and T and T ' have been proved to have the same BT and NT, both are equivalent, and both are ok [7]. In T ', there are only definitions, and all definitions are of the form $A \equiv C$ ', where only the symbols contained in the set BT appear in C ', No symbols included in the collection NT appear.

16.4   Literature Survey

Soeken M. *et al.* (2013) have proposed the that beginning stage is a lot of NLAs given as far as English language sentences. These statements are naturally apportioned into subsets of high deliberation level and low reflection level affirmations in the initial step. The thought is that elevated level declarations contain certain and loose data which blocks programmed interpretation and accordingly should be deciphered physically as in the ordinary stream. Subsequently, significant level declarations aren't additionally well thought-out in the rest of the stream. In the next phase the decided low-level attestations are apportioned into bunches of comparative sentences.

In 2012, Cambria E. has deliberated about Natural Language Processing (NLP). NLP inquires about as indicated by three distinct standards, specifically, the sack of words, pack of-ideas, and sack of-accounts models. Acquiring the idea of "bouncing bends" in the area of corporate management; this review paper simplifies in what way NLP investigate, has been step by step moving from lexical semantics to compositional semantic, and offers bits of knowledge on cutting edge account-based NLP innovation. This paper concluded that Web where client creates content has as of now triumph minimum amount, the requirement for sensible calculation and data collection is expanding exponentially, as showed by the "distraught surge" in the business for "enormous information specialists" and the development of another "Information Science" train.

In 2014, Bihani R. changes over the normal dialect inquiry into SQL (Structured Query Language) which is a database programming dialect. We will play out the accompanying strides for the change of question from common dialect to database inquiry (SQL) successively as recorded in the accompanying focuses. First, we will acknowledge the string in normal dialect. In the wake of tolerating the inquiry, we will check the question for incorrectly spelled words (assuming any) utilizing word match mining. After that, we will part question into tokens. In the wake of getting tokens, we play out the SQL mapping for change. This paper's conclusion is the inquiry interface that will be relevant for the online applications and gives straightforwardness to the client by diminishing their piece of reviewing complex database dialect linguistic structure. Our framework likewise redresses the spelling botches did by the clients, naturally furthermore deals with syntactic blunders. Proposed framework produces yield inquiry regardless of the database.

Cambria E. *et al.* (2013) have proposed investigation on how the high speculation execution, low computational unpredictability, and quick

S. No.	Author/year	Name of algorithm/ method	Description
1.	Mathias Soeken Proceedings ECSI 2014 [1]	High and low abstraction level	Author deliberated an approach that regulates the version of natural language statements into System Verilog Proclamations by means of NLP techniques. In place of physically translating each assertion distinctly.
2.	Ryuichiro Higashinaka Proceedings of COLING 2014 [2]	Rule-based system	This paper recommends a system for an open-domain conversational system and assesses an implemented system. The projected system is completely composed of modules based on NLP techniques.
3.	Anupriya IOSR-JCE Jan-2014 [3]	Fuzzy logic	This paper mainly explains Fuzzy Theory and the realization of Fuzzy Query on SQL Collective C #. In addition, providing a real-life application of fuzzy queries based on relational databases (patient information databases).
4.	Lei Zou SIGMOD 2014 [5]	Graph data driven approach	The author proposes a semantic query graph to model the intent of the query in a structural way in a natural language question, based on which, RDF Q/A is subtracted to minimize the matching problem. More importantly, the author resolves the ambiguity of natural language questions when questions are met. If no match is found, the cost of disbursement is saved.

(Continued)

S. No.	Author/year	Name of algorithm/ method	Description
5.	Joao P. Carvalho Processing IEEE 2012 [7]	Fuzzy Set	This paper showed that the use and applications of fuzzy sets (FS) in speech and natural language processing (SNLP) have seen a steady decline at a point where FSs are almost unknown or currently unsuitable for most researchers in the SNLP field. Attempts to discover the details behind this decline and suggests some guidelines on what can be done to reverse it and allow FS to play a relevant role in SNPP.
6.	Tareq Abed Mohammed et al. Intelligent Database Interface Techniques using Semantic Coordination/IEEE 2018 [4]	Semantic coordination	The intelligent interface uses the semantic coordinate process to transform natural language queries to Structured Query Language (SQL) based on lexicons and construction guidelines. The lexicon includes semantic sets for tables and sections.

learning rate, of outrageous learning machines can be abused toper frame a consistent thinking in a vector space model of full of feeling judgment skills information. Specifically, by empowering a quick reconfiguration of such a vector space, extraordinary learning machine colorless the extremity connected with common dialect ideas to be computed in a more dynamic and precise way and, consequently, perform better idea level supposition examination. This paper's conclusion is in a world in which a huge number of individuals express their assessments about business items and administrations wherever on the web, the siltation of learning from this gigantic measure of unstructured data is a key component for assignments, for example, web-based social networking promoting, item situating, and money-related market forecast.

We have experienced different literary works and discovered some bottleneck in normal dialect inquiry handling which are as per the following:

- Problem in query optimization to bulky distributed databases: Query optimization in large distributed databases plainly needed in numerous features of the optimization process, frequently making it imperious for the optimizer to refer fundamental data sources while doing cost-based optimization. This is not only increasing the cost of optimization, but also fluctuations the compromises intricate in the optimization process meaningfully. The foremost cost in this optimization process is the "cost of costing" that conventionally has been considered unimportant. In a large-scale distributed system, both data admittance and calculation can be carried out at numerous sites.
- POS tagger not applied to find out phrase in input query.
- Natural language query had to be in double quotes ("").
- In earlier system works on Who/How type question.
- Earlier system did not support one-word query.
- Stop/spam word removal may not present in earlier system.

16.5 Methodolgy for IR

Firstly, we take the input user query in to the web database. Our next step is to work on spell correction in sentence, then next steps in split into the tokens, then next steps in semantic analyzer in the sentence. Next steps in query builder in the database and solved the query and finally find the result. Figure 16.1 shows IR work flow.

Algorithm

---

1. Select database.

2. Input NLP Query.

3. Spell correction of Input query.

4. Stop/spam word removal from input query.

5. Divided input sentence in to tokens.

6. Apply POS tagging.

7. Semantic analyzer will analyze NLP query and NL word with RDBMS syntax.

8. Query will be generated by fuzzy approach.

9. Query passed to DBMS.

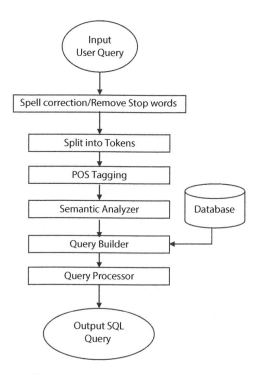

Figure 16.1 IR flow [8, 9].

For example, in a relational database of patients, to deal with a query statement such as "low age and good heartbeat or low blood sugar", SQL is difficult to construct because the query terms are fake expressions. With the intention of obtaining query results, there are two fundamental methods of research into the use of SQL Collective Fuzzy Theory in DBMS. First, one still has to build a classic relationship database is to modify or extend the SQL query only by converting the query conditions into a fuzzy scope. After that, change it to the exact SQL clause. This process is informal and reliable with common queries, but lacks flexibility. Sometimes, this leads to

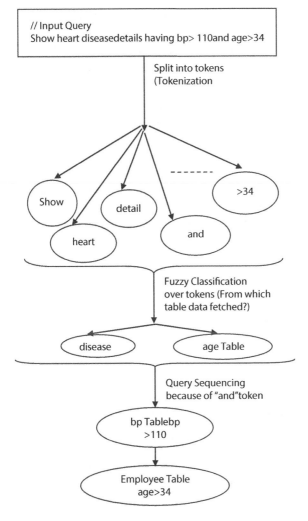

Figure 16.2 IR system.

age	sex	cp	trestbps	chol	fbs	restecg	thalach	exang	oldpeak	slope	ca	thal	num
63	1	1	145	233	1	2	150	0	2.3	3	0	6	absent
53	1	4	140	203	1	2	155	1	3.1	3	0	7	present
56	1	3	130	256	1	2	142	1	0.6	2	1	6	present
52	1	3	172	199	1	0	162	0	0.5	1	0	7	absent
58	0	1	150	283	1	2	162	0	1	1	0	3	absent
60	1	4	117	230	1	0	160	1	1.4	1	2	7	present
61	1	3	150	243	1	0	137	1	1	2	0	3	absent

Figure 16.3 Dataset snippet.

produce query mistakes. The second method is that the database is fuzzy set and fuzzy logic is used to make it easier and more humanly consistent. This is mainly done by constructing a database model based on fuzzy logic. When designing this database and modifying its data structure, several tables can be added, including values for fuzzy fields. These tables can be modified from row tables. For example, relational databases of patients have fuzzy fields such as "edge", "blood pressure", and "heartbeat". When the data is being inputted, the exact data can be transformed into fuzzy data and stored in the database. Figure 16.2 shows how SQL is generated and Figure 16.3 shows the snippet of dataset to be used for experiments.

To process a user input query, the prime rung is speech labeling (tagging) and, subsequently, word tagging. The second rung is deconstructing the tagged sentence by a grammar rule. The grammar parser examines the query sentence consistent with the tag of every word and produces the grammar trees.

Dataset having different features below table contains description of different features:

S. No.	Feature name	Description
1	age	Age
2	sex	Sex
3	cp	Chest Pain
4	trestbps	Blood Pressure
5	chol	Blood Cholesterol
6	fbs	Diabetes Present or not
7	restecg	Electro cardio Graph
8	thalach	Heart Rate

(Continued)

S. No.	Feature name	Description
9	exang	Physical Commotion
10	oldpeak	Depression induced by exercise relative to rest
11	slope	Slop (up sloping, flat, down sloping)
12	ca	Number of major vessels
13	thal	Thal (Normal, fixed defect, reversible, defect)
14	Num	Present and absent

After passing data to inference, we got decision tree as follows: in Figure 16.4 and Figure 16.5 show the snippet of confusion matrix and accuracy achieved as 85%.

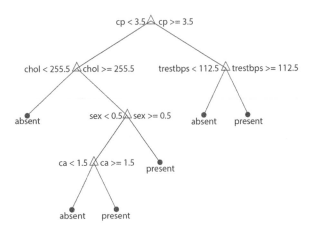

Figure 16.4 Ontology for data.

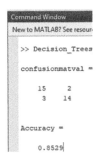

Figure 16.5 Accuracy. It's snapshot of accuracy achieved, implemented on Matlab 2019a.

References

1. Soeken, Mathias, Harris, Christopher B., Abdessaied, Nabila, Harris, Ian G., Drechsler, Rolf, *Automating the Translation of Assertions Using Natural Language Processing Techniques*, FDL Proceedings | ECSI, Munich, Germany, 2014.

2. Higashinaka1, Ryuichiro, Imamura1, Kenji, Meguro2, Toyomi, Chiaki Miyazaki Towards an open-domain conversational system fully based on natural language processing. *Proceedings of COLING 2014, the 25th International Conference on Computational Linguistics: Technical Papers*, Dublin, Ireland, August 23–29, pp. 928–939, 2014.

3. Anupriya, and Rishi, Rahul, Fuzzy Querying Based on Relational Database. *OSR J. Comput. Eng. (IOSR-JCE)*, 16, 1, 53–59, Jan. 2014.

4. Mohammed, Tareq Abed *et al.*, *Intelligent Database Interface Techniques using Semantic Coordination*, IEEE, Diyala, Iraq, 2018.

5. Zou, Lei, Huang, Ruizhe, Wang, Haixun, Natural Language Question Answering over RDF — A Graph Data Driven Approach. *SIGMOD'14*, June 22–27, 2014.

6. Termehchy, Arash, Keyword and Natural Language Query Processing for Semi-Structured Data Sources. *Proceedings of the Third SIGMOD PhD Workshop on Innovative Database Research (IDAR 2009)*, June 28, 2009.

7. Carvalho, J.P., Batista, F., Coheur, L., A critical survey on the use of Fuzzy Sets in Speech and Natural Language Processing, Brisbane, QLD, Australia IEE, 2012.

8. Satav, Akshay G., Ausekar, Archana B., Bihani, Radhika M, Shaikh, Abid, A Proposed Natural Language Query Processing System WARSE. 3, 2, March-April 2014.

9. Kaur *, Jasmeen, chauhan *, Bhawna, Korepal, Jatinder Kaur, Implementation of Query Processor Using Automata and Natural Language Processing. *Int. J. Sci. Res. Publ.*, 3, 5, May 2013.

Index